Theorising National Cinema

Theorising National Cinema

Edited by
Valentina Vitali and Paul Willemen

A BFI book published by Palgrave Macmillan

LEEDS TRINITY UNIVERSITY ᴠ.ᴧ

First published in 2006 by the
BRITISH FILM INSTITUTE
21 Stephen Street, London W1T 1LN

The British Film Institute's purpose is to champion moving image culture
in all its richness and diversity across the UK, for the benefit of as wide an
audience as possible, and to create and encourage debate.

Reprinted 2008, 2013

Cover design: Mark Swan
Cover illustration: *Goodbye Dragon Inn/ Bu San* (Tsaï Ming-Liang, 2003), Homegreen Films
Photographs courtesy of BFI Stills, Posters and Designs

Printed in China

British Library Cataloguing-in-Publication Data
A catalogue record for this book is available from the British Library

ISBN 1-84457-120-3/978–1–84457–120–8 (pbk)
ISBN 1-84457-119-x/978–1–84457–119–2 (hbk)

Contents

Notes on Contributors

John Akomfrah is a film-maker, born in Ghana and based in Britain. His films include *Handsworth Songs* (1986), *Testament* (1988), *Seven Songs to Malcolm X* (1993), *Speak Like a Child* (1998), *Riot* (1999) and many others.

Chris Berry is Professor of Film and Television Studies at Goldsmiths College, University of London. He is the author of *Postsocialist Cinema in Post-Mao China: The Cultural Revolution after the Cultural Revolution* (Routledge, 2004); the co-author, with Mary Farquhar, of *Cinema and the National: China on Screen* (forthcoming 2006), the editor of *Chinese Films in Focus: 25 New Takes* (BFI, 2003); and the co-editor, with Feii Lu, of *Island on the Edge: Taiwan New Cinema and After* (Hong Kong University Press, 2005).

Kuan-Hsing Chen is Professor of Cultural Studies at the Center for Asia-Pacific/Cultural Studies, National Tsing Hua University, Taiwan, and currently a visiting senior research fellow at the Asia Research Institute, National University of Singapore. He has published extensively, including edited volumes in English: *Stuart Hall: Critical Dialogues in Cultural Studies* (Routledge, 1996) and *Trajectories: Inter-Asia Cultural Studies* (Routledge, 1998), and in Chinese: *Cultural Studies in Taiwan* (Ju Liu, 2000) and *The Partha Chatterjee Seminar – Locating Political Society: Modernity, State Violence and Postcolonial Democracies* (2000). His own books include *Media/Cultural Criticism: A Popular-Democratic Line of Flight* (1992, in Chinese), and *The Imperialist Eye* (2003, in Korean). *Towards De-imperialization — Asia as Method* is forthcoming. He was founding president of the Cultural Studies Association, Taiwan, and a core member of *Taiwan: A Radical Quarterly in Social Studies*; he is a co-executive editor of *Inter-Asia Cultural Studies: Movements*.

David A. Cook is Founding Director of the Film Studies programme of Emory University, where he is Professor of Film in the Institute for Liberal Arts. He is the author of *A History of Narrative Film* (W. W. Norton, 1996) and *Lost Illusions: American Cinema in the Shadow of Watergate and Vienam, 1970–1979*, Vol. 9 of C. Harpole (ed.), *The History of the American Cinema* (University of California Press, 2000).

Stephen Crofts is an independent scholar and Honorary Research Associate at the Centre for Critical and Cultural Studies, University of Queensland, Australia. He has taught film and media studies at universities in Britain, Australia and New Zealand. He has published some sixty articles, book chapters and monographs in the USA, the UK and Australia, as well as the books *Identification, Gender and Genre: The Case of Shame* (Samuel French, 1998), and, with Philip Bell and Kathe Boehringer, *Programmed Politics* (Sable, 1982), on televisual constructions of politics. Forthcoming is a book comparing the Australian and New Zealand cultural formations. He has worked on the editorial boards of five film and media studies journals.

Martine Danan is Assistant Dean at the Defense Language Institute in Monterey, California. She has written extensively on the socio-political context of cinema and national identity, especially in relation to the growing competition between Hollywood and French cinema. Her essays in this area have appeared in journals ranging from *Media, Culture and Society* to *Film History* and *The Journal of Popular Film and Television*. Other recent essays appeared in *La fiction éclatée, grands et petits écrans français et francophones, Journeys of Desire: European Actors in Hollywood Cinema* (forthcoming, BFI) and *European Cinema Reader* (Routledge, 2002).

Kathe Geist is an art and film historian, she has written extensively on the films of Ozu. She lives and writes in Brookline and Charlemont, Massachusetts.

Sabry Hafez teaches Arabic and comparative literature at London University's School for Oriental and Asian Studies; he is the author of *The Genesis of Arabic Narrative Discourse* (Saqi Books, 1993) and many essays on the poetics of Arabic literatures and cinemas.

John Hill is Professor of Media at Royal Holloway, University of London. He is the author or co-editor of a number of books, including *Sex, Class and Realism: British Cinema 1956–1963* (BFI, 1986); *Cinema and Ireland* (Routledge, 1987); *The Oxford Guide to Film Studies* (Oxford University Press, 1998); *British Cinema in the 1980s* (Oxford University Press, 1999); *Cinema and Northern Ireland* (forthcoming, BFI).

Mikhail Iampolski is Associate Professor of Comparative Literature, Russian and Slavic Studies at New York University. His publications include *The Memory of Tiresias* (University of California Press, 1998), *Amnesia as a Source* (1997), *Daemon and Labyrinth* (1996), *Babel/Babel*, with A. Zholkovsky (La Carte Blanche, 1994), and *Visible World* (Kinovedcheskie Zapiski*, 1993). He is on the editorial board of *Cinema Notebooks Journal, Kinovedcheskie Zapiski* (Moscow), *New Literary Review, Novoe Literaturnoe Obozrenie* (Moscow) and of the book series *Philosophia ad Marginem* (Moscow).

Kim Soyoung lectures at the Korean National University of the Arts. Her publications include *Specters of Modernity: Fantastic Korean Cinema* (Ssiyaeul Buneun Saramdeul, 2000) and *Korean Mode of Blockbusters* (2001). Her essays have appeared in Japanese, French, Italian and

English. She recently completed the documentary *Women's History Trilogy* (available at <www.yeondvd.com>/<www.seoulselection.com>), screened at many festivals, including Yamagata, Pesaro and Seoul Women's Film Festival.

Mika Ko is a teaching fellow at the Department of East Asian Studies at the University of Leeds. She is completing her PhD at the University of Ulster on 'Otherness in Contemporary Japanese Cinema: Nationalism, Multiculturalism and the Problem of Japaneseness'.

Ana M. Lopez Until Hurricane Katrina devastated New Orleans and the Gulf Coast, Ana M. Lopez was Associate Provost at Tulane University and a member of the communication department and Latin American Studies Program. She teaches film and cultural studies and has published widely on Latin American cinema and popular culture.

Martin McLoone is Professor of Media Studies attached to the Centre for Media Research at the University of Ulster, Coleraine. He is author of *Irish Film: The Emergence of a Contemporary Cinema* (BFI, 2000) and has edited numerous collections on aspects of the media in Britain and Ireland, including *Broadcasting in a Divided Community: 70 Years of the BBC in Northern Ireland* (Institute of Irish Studies, 1996), *Big Picture, Small Screen: The Relations Between Film and Television* (University of Luton Press, 1996) and *Border Crossing: Film in Ireland, Britain and Europe* (Institute of Irish Studies/BFI, 1994).

David Morley is Professor of Communications at Goldsmiths College, London University. His most recent book is *Home Territories: Media, Mobility and Identity* (Routledge, 2000).

Kevin Robins is Professor of Sociology, City University, London, and visiting researcher at Istanbul Bilgi University. He is currently involved in an EU Framework project, Changing City Spaces: New Challenges for Cultural Policy in Europe. He is the author of *Into the Image: Culture and Politics in the Field of Vision* (Routledge, 1996) and co-editor, with David Morley, of *British Cultural Studies* (Oxford University Press, 2001).

Philip Rosen is Professor and Director of Graduate Studies in the Department of Modern Culture and Media, Brown University. His books include *Narrative, Apparatus, Ideology: A Film Theory Reader* (Columbia University Press, 1986) and *Change Mummified: Cinema, Historicity, Theory* (University of Minnesota Press, 2001).

Elia Suleiman is a Palestinian film-maker; his recent feature films include *Chronicle of a Disappearance* (1996) and *Divine Intervention* (2002).

Valentina Vitali teaches Comparative Film Studies at the Centre for Media Research, University of Ulster. Her work on cinema and historiography has appeared in the journals *Inter-Asia Cultural Studies*, *Kinema*, *Framework*, *Women: a Cultural Review*, *Journal of Asian Studies* and *Filmwaves*. Other recent essays have appeared in *Hong Kong Connections: Transnational*

Imagination in Action Cinema (Duke University Press, 2005), *Shirin Neshat: Women without Men* (Hamburger Banhof Museum, 2005) and in *The Indian Cinema Book* (forthcoming, BFI).

Paul Willemen is Professor of Film Studies at the University of Ulster. He was a member of *Screen's* editorial board in the 1970s, edited *Framework* in the 1980s and is the author of *Looks and Frictions* (BFI, 1994), co-editor, with Jim Pines, of *Questions of Third Cinema* (BFI, 1991) and, with Ashish Rajadhyaksha, of *The Encyclopaedia of Indian Cinema* (BFI, 1996).

Maria Wyke is Professor of Latin at University College London. Her research interests include the representation of ancient Rome in popular culture. She published *Projecting the Past: Ancient Rome, Cinema and History* (Routledge, 1997) and *The Roman Mistress: Ancient and Modern Representations* (Oxford University Press, 2000). With a Leverhulme Major Research Fellowship she is preparing the publication of her research into the reception of Julius Caesar in Western culture.

Mitsuhiro Yoshimoto is Associate Professor of East Asian Studies at New York University. His forthcoming books include *Possibilities of Resistance,* with Masao Miyoshi, and *Hollywood, or Empire as a Symptom.*

Introduction

Valentina Vitali and Paul Willemen

Why do we think of clusters of films as a national cinema? Why has this relationship between the nation and film become so widely and uncritically accepted? What work does such a categorisation of films perform? The economic institutions that make up an industrial sector – a film industry – were not always co-extensive with what we now call national cinemas. At the start of cinema the nationality of a cinema production company, and of the films it made, were not particularly pertinent. During the first decade of the cinema, before the practice of leasing films to distributors became established, reels of film were sold directly to exhibitors who screened them as novelty objects without paying much attention to their national provenance. The main way of differentiating product lines was provided by the name and, eventually, by the reputation of companies that produced films in different national territories. Meliès, Gaumont and Pathé, for instance, manufactured films in the United States through subsidiaries headquartered in New York, and their films were circulated as otherwise indistinguishable from local produce. Richard Abel has shown that, in important ways, 'Frenchness', or, rather, 'foreign-ness' was foisted upon those films by competitors as the latter sought to monopolise a market by defining it as a 'national' one. Along with various other measures, some fair but most of them foul, xenophobia was mobilised against certain competitors to drive them out of a geopolitically bounded market.

One implication of this is that there was a film industry in the United States well before there was such a thing as 'American cinema'. The notion of American cinema was the result of struggles, firstly to develop and unify a national market and, secondly, for some companies to achieve as close as possible to a monopoly within it. The need for regulations to achieve the rights to derive profits within a particular geographical region, in this case the United States, laid the groundwork for a complicity between the industry and the state's monopoly on legitimate violence. It is this political dimension of similar economic developments that makes a cinema 'national'. The products generated by such an economic sector are endowed with cultural 'nationality' at a later stage, partly as a competitive move and partly as a way of legitimising such a move.[1]

The particular ways in which an economic sector's productive activities and a particular set of institutional networks known collectively as the state interact to mutual benefit give us the terms in which a film industry becomes a national one. Of course, the nature of those interactions will be determined by a wide variety of factors: the nature of the ruling coalition of interest groups, the available technologies, the logistical and financial infrastructures, the need to reconcile long-term social reproduction with short-term profitability, and so on. It follows that, when considering the question of national cinema, it is necessary to distinguish between two understandings of cinema: as an industry and as a cluster of cultural strategies. As Richard Abel's historical account of Pathé's adventures in the American film market demonstrates (1999), the former undoubtedly determines the latter, but all the determinations do not go one way only.

The most common way of forestalling questions about the ways in which economic arrangements shape cultural issues and modes of thinking, while appearing to solve the problem of that interaction, has been to invoke the metaphor of the national body and its organic formation in a myth-like 'natural' past. One of the models used to narrativise the nation and its culture as a given is the *Bildungsroman* – a rhetoric that recounts the birth and maturation of some cultural practices (from literature to cinema) as if self-evidently imbued with the more intangible aspects of an assumed 'national' cultural essence. Far from being accounts of the modalities by which a national culture sought expression in that industry, the first histories of cinema – written at a time when debates as to whether cinema was an artform and, if so, what its 'language', deemed to be a universal one, might be – were, in effect, biographies of an industrial sector. Film historians, such as Georges Sadoul (1949) and Georges Charensol (1935) in France, or Paul Rotha (1949) in Britain, recounted the birth and growth of an industry that proliferated, radiating outwards from the heartlands of capital – a thrust forward, from 'advanced' societies such as Western Europe and the United States to the periphery as an exemplary trajectory of modernisation sweeping across the world. In this context, the film industry was a metonym for the industrialisation of culture and a metaphor for modernity itself, while the universal character of film language, presumed in spite of the striking diversity between different national film industries, helped to give cultural legitimacy to the economic dominance of some cinemas globally. Paul Rotha's massive effort to chronicle 'world cinema' is unwittingly explicit about this process. Entitled *The Film Till Now*, Rotha's account situates the 'now' at around World War II – an event which marked the end of a catastrophic half-century and the consolidation of industrial capitalism's political hegemony in Europe and the United States.

By casting the history of cinema in the mould of the history of an industry, the writers of these film histories admitted, if only half-heartedly, that the developmental engine of cinema is driven by industrial, rather than cultural, forces. Some intellectuals welcomed this understanding of cinema; others, most notably the intellectuals associated with the Frankfurt School, were less enthusiastic about the industrialisation of culture. Yet others, inspired by the Soviet experiment to detach Fordism from capitalism, were more concerned with identifying and promoting an alternative, but equally universal, language of cinema than with the history of the film industry. Early conceptualisations of 'the national' that aimed to rewrite the history of cinema emanated, significantly, from the two countries that competed most fiercely to globalise their industrial empires: the United States, with Lewis Jacobs' *The Rise of the American Film: A Critical History* (1939), and the Third Reich, with Oskar Kalbus' *Vom Werden Deutscher Filmkunst* (1936). Immediately after World War II, these were followed by a series of national film histories that took stock of the proliferation of the film industries over half a century in a variety of Western countries, as well as by that milestone of film historiography that is Siegfried Kracauer's *From Caligari to Hitler* (1947).

Although Kracauer's account successfully fused the industrial and the national dimensions of cinema, it was Lewis Jacobs' '*Bildungsroman*' that was adopted as a template for the writing of film histories in much of the world. Divided into six parts, entitled 'Fade In', 'Foundations', 'Development', 'Transition', 'Intensification' and 'Maturity', Jacobs' book relied on a linear notion of history that understood the nation-state as the natural, not to say organic, result of an evolutionary trajectory. Jacobs adopted this as the framework appropriate to chronicle both the cultural and the industrial dimensions of cinema. The outcome was a back-handed celebration of Hollywood films that erected a handful of film-makers as exemplary film artists for the world to emulate – even though, or perhaps because, as he saw it, the Hollywood industry was not able to give these artists the careers they deserved.[2] Since the publication of *The Rise of the American Film*, the writing of film histories in terms of some intuited national ethos that determines both the industrial arrangements and the films produced has become the norm. Only a handful of film histories to date have questioned Jabobs' template. As a rule, books on specific national cinemas acknowledge that it is impossible, or at least difficult, to write film history in terms of national cultural formations, only to proceed to do precisely that. What is swept under the carpet in this way is the question of 'the national' in the demarcation of objects of study.

Outside the field of cinema, this question was first put on the agenda in the 1960s. In Britain, it emerged most prominently through the editors and contributors of *The New Left Review* in what came to be known as the Nairn-Anderson theses on the specificity of the British formation (Anderson 1968). These debates and modes of analysis did impact on the work undertaken by journals such as *Screen*, but no major alternative paradigm of writing film histories was formulated until the 1980s. As Meghnad Desai put it, during that decade

> Capitalism in one country, with its Keynesian protective belt, was on the way out. Deregulated capital flows and flexible exchange rates put severe limits on the autonomy of national economic policy, as France discovered. Markets – now armed with fast telephone and computer links, getting faster and cheaper daily – started speculating on interest rates and exchange rates. Money began to flow in and out of countries in massive amounts.
>
> This was a new world. While the Bretton Woods era lasted, exchange rates were fixed within narrow bands, capital was not mobile, phones were slow and computers beyond the nexus of stockbrokers. In March 1973, during a currency crisis, $3 billion were traded in one day. By the late 1970s, daily turnover was $100 billion, and in the late 1980s, $650 billion. In 1960, a transatlantic cable could carry 138 conversations simultaneously. By 1995, thanks to fibre optics, this had gone up to 1.5 billion.
>
> The speed and size of these transactions unnerved many, but especially all those who had relied on using state power to control the economy. (Desai 2002: 278)

Profound changes in the telecommunications industries, the spread of computerisation driven by military requirements and the stock market, and the resulting changes in the film and television industries reposed the question of the suitability of the nation-state as a productive way of categorising clusters of films. Under the pressure of vague notions of 'globalisation', the competitive industrial logic that had informed national film historiographies came to be perceived as an obstacle to the understanding of a film's actual mode of functioning. At this point – that is, when the rise of finance capital as the driving force of American capitalism began to restructure the relations of production and consumption that had obtained in the Western world since the end of World War II – the 1920s Soviet experiments to find an alternative language for industrial cultures were rediscovered, resulting in effervescent debates about cinemas which, labelled 'independent' and 'modernist', were deemed capable of addressing the industrialisation of culture differently than mainstream films.

Out of this context, from the mid-1980s, a series of seminal essays appeared in British journals that sought to arrive at a better understanding of what it may mean to speak of cinema as a national cultural practice, while in France (Sorlin 1980; Ferro 1984; Burch 1979), Italy (Aprà and Pistangesi 1979; Micciché 1980), Australia (Moran and O'Regan 1985; Dermody and Jacka 1988; Bell, Boehringer and Crofts 1982) and Germany (Bitomsky 1972; Prokop 1970) intellectuals pursued their own attempts to reinvent the historiography of cinema in relation to intuited, but by no means conclusively identified, 'specific' national social formations. In the UK this question of *how* to circumscribe the specificity of a national formation did remain on the agenda in political and historiographic intellectual circles, but, apart from that handful of essays, it was largely ignored by writers about cinema. In the bulk of contemporary writings chronicling national cinema histories, all that remains of the national specificity question is a vague memory of a certain unease about the national film enterprise itself. This collection seeks to re-connect with those now marginalised debates and analyses that surfaced in film publications from the 1980s onwards.

Some of the essays of this period – Phil Rosen's 'History, Textuality, Nation: Kracauer, Burch, and Some Problems in the Study of National Cinema' (1984); Stephen Crofts' 'Reconceptualising National Cinema/s' (1993); John Hill's work on British Cinema (1997); and Paul Willemen's 'The National' (1994) – are reproduced here, either in part in their original version or as revisitations of arguments advanced by the authors between the mid-1980s and the 1990s. Others – including Andrew Higson's 'The Concept of National Cinema' (1993) – have reappeared in other recent anthologies (Williams 2002; Hjort and MacKenzie 2000). The template used in most of these publications to address questions of national cultural formations is Ernest Gellner's *Nations and Nationalism* (1983). Arguing that it is nationalism that constructs nations and not the other way around, Gellner explained the emergence of nationalism 'as a breakwater of differential industrialisation', emerging from the occupational mobility demanded by modern technology. The more fluid the social structure, the more unitary the culture it requires of its agents, as they shift and intermesh positions in an increasingly complex and mutable division of labour. As Perry Anderson observed in his critique of Gellner, within this analytical framework, nationalism and the nation–state are presented as 'a universal imperative of industrialism'. But, Anderson argues, the advent of industrialism

> is not only historically staggered; it hits a world already ethnically and linguistically divided. On the one hand, no single culture is as yet powerful enough to encompass the globe; on the other, the later a region comes to industrialisation, the more it risks subjugation to those which arrived earlier, and exclusion of its inhabitants from the local fruits of the process. The result is nationalism: or the spread of the drive to create states whose political frontiers roughly coincide with ethnic boundaries. (1992: 204)

For Gellner the institution that allows this diversity of cultures and temporalities to be held together under the direct political control of the state is education. From the point of view of a historically pertinent understanding of cinema as a social practice implicated in the construction of national identities, the biggest problem with Gellner's theory is not the claim that nations are an effect of nationalism and nationalism of industrialisation, but the equation of culture with education. Whereas education is a project undertaken by the state and therefore fully instrumentalised by the interest blocs of the ruling coalition, the same has never held for the cinema. For this purpose, it is worth considering the full extent of Anderson's argument:

> There is a sense in which Gellner's theory of nationalism might be described as immoderately materialist. For what it plainly neglects is the overpowering dimension of collective *meaning* that modern nationalism has always involved: that is, not its functionality for industry, but its fulfilment for identity. Here, in effect, only the rational is real: the irrational [i]s set aside – economy and psyche do not join. The result is that [G]ellner has paradoxically missed far the most important of all in the twentieth century. [He] theorized nationalism without detecting the spell. [Gellner's] liberalism has been resistant to any crossing of the division between public and private spheres. [T]he public realm is instrumental, for the management of prosperity – the more marginal its meanings (he takes monarchy as an ideal) the better. Private life, where the fruits of ease are to be enjoyed, is the proper sphere of self-expression. (1992: 205–6)

If, as Tom Nairn also put it (1997), nationalism is an *address*, then Gellner's idea of culture as education leaves no room for an understanding of how cinema as a discursive practice constructs national subjects. While stressing the importance of industrialising modernisation and the ensuing effects of the division of labour that lead to the installation and maintenance of an institutional network called the state, Gellner installs a particular separation between the public and the private spheres that, following a Romantic ideology, relegates self-expression to a private domain disconnected from the management of the extraction of profit through the exploitation of people's labour power. At the opposite end of Gellner's liberalism lay stultifying notions of ideology understood as the monolithic discourse of an all-powerful state that brainwashes individuals who, as a result, can no longer be thought of as such. These two strands have survived into university curricula to this day, not least because they are the two sides of the same humanist coin that has plagued the humanities since the nineteenth century.

Also since the nineteenth century, however, Marxian historians have worked with an understanding of individual consciousness as socially determined and, for that very reason, not reducible to an effect of state education. It is this Marx-based view of individual consciousness that, in the twentieth century, led to arguments as to *how* such a social determination may actually work, and on the functioning of culture as the cluster of determinant mechanisms. Drawing on the often-cited writings of Gramsci, this was the path taken by the *New Left Review*'s debates on national specificity. A more recent engagement with the same question by way of a clearer formulation of the relations between public and private spheres than Gellner's can be found in the work of Jürgen Habermas, who differentiates between two interconnected processes:

> Whether we think of ourselves as inhabiting a post-national, global constellation or as bound by less and less permeable frontiers, we must distinguish between two different things: on the one hand, the cognitive dissonances that lead to a hardening of national identities as different cultural forms of life come into collision; on the other, the hybrid differentiations that soften native cultures and comparatively homogeneous forms of life in the wake of assimilation into a single material world culture. (2001: 72–3)

For Habermas, the 'hardening' of identities that results from a fundamentally conflictual social formation is a centripetal procedure: that is the project of nationalism and of state education, the address and purpose of which is the construction and administration of a manageable citizenry consensually subordinate to existing coalitions of capitalist interest groups. Once again, the object of state education is to secure the social reproduction of a mode of accumulation. Habermas's alternative refers to the cluster of multidirectional movements that national cultures stage, or rather, that discursive practices *mediate* as their substance is constantly and openly re-modulated by the multiple interest groups at work within the territory controlled by the state as they operate under the pressure of assimilation and differentiation. Paul Willemen's example in the essay included here illustrates how Habermas's way of tackling the question can be made more productive in the arena of film history:

> Compared to US black films, black British films are strikingly British, and yet in no way can they be construed as nationalistic. They are part of a British specificity, but not of a British nationalism: especially not if you remember that British nationalism is in fact an imperial identification, rather than an identification with the British state. To complicate matters further, an identification with the British state is in fact English nationalism, as opposed to Welsh, Cornish or Scottish nationalisms, which relate not to a state but to nations, and are recognizable by their demand for autonomous governments, even if that autonomy may be qualified in various ways.

As this example suggests, a theoretical framework that accounts for the complex dynamics between the private and the public spheres implies that culture, like history, is not a linear, monologic process of containment, but an unstable terrain that is always contended over by the dominant and the non-dominant socio-economic forces at play in specific national formations. Which raises the question: how do the narrative strategies of any given cinema position viewers in the historical force-field that is 'the nation'? How do films address and construct 'national subjects', with the latter understood as the always unstable discursive effects of a fundamentally conflictual civil society whose constitutive relations are over-determined by, but not reducible to, the relations of production as anchored by the institutions of the state?

Both as an industry and as a discursive practice, cinema is an adjunct of capitalism – which is not to say that cinema is equivalent to (cultural) capital. Like capitalism, cinema is, and has always been, a global industry, but diverse societies and clusters of films are always inevitably positioned differently within the centrifugal expansion of capitalist modes of production, not least because any given culture encountered cinema in different circumstances. Which historical models are then most apt to grasp the dynamics that shape a cultural practice such as cinema in diverse historical constellations? Which forms has cultural industrialisation taken in these areas? Which forms does modernisation take, understood in terms of the emergence of a public sphere? And, following from these issues: how do diverse societies differentiate between identity, a function of public administration, and subjectivity? Finally: how are subjectivities – the cluster of positions put into place by discursive processes and institutional pressures – effected through historically specific cinematic narrative models?

These questions, which began to be formulated in film theory in the mid-1980s, still await answers, because, with the institutionalisation of film studies as an academic discipline, film theory and practice have become increasingly instrumentalised by the state's notion of 'education' – disciplines conceived to format unproblematic labour for the national media industries (Vitali 2005). It is too early to relegate them, still unresolved, to a bygone era, while celebrating the advent, in film studies, if not of 'globalisation', of some notion of a global or 'world' cinema. The point of departure for this collection of essays is that cinema can be thought of as pertaining to a national configuration because films, far from offering cinematic accounts of 'the nation' as seen by the coalition that sustains the forces of capital within any given nation, are clusters of historically specific cultural forms the semantic modulations of which are orchestrated and contended over by each of the forces at play in a given geographical territory. The functioning of cinema as an industry and a cultural practice in any of these territories is overdetermined by the institutions of the state – from censorship through to taxation and real estate policies – but the economic forces sustaining any given film do not necessarily mobilise the available narrative stock in the directions preferred by the state. In other words, films may and may not reflect the ideological trajectory dominant within the nation at any one time. The reason for this potential lack of a reflective fit is that the cinematic strategies on which the hegemony of a political configuration depend always also remain available to, and can be activated by, non-dominant power blocs. As the example of black British films suggests, the fact that they are very different from, for instance,

Terence Fisher's or Ken Russell's films does not mean that they are in some way less British, or that they fall outside British cinema. On the contrary, it is precisely as discursive terrains for struggle between dominant and non-dominant forces over the power to fix the meaning of the given narrative stock, that films can be seen not to 'reflect', but to 'stage' the historical conditions that constitute 'the national' and, in the process, to 'mediate' the socio-economic dynamics that shape cinematic production, along with the other production sectors governed by national industrial regulation and legislation.

The three parts of this collection have been conceived to leave room precisely to such dynamics of determination as processes which, open to constant redefinition, result in cultural configurations that may and may not take the form of 'nations'. The first part comprises three essays that address the question of national cinema as a question of historical specificity. It opens with one of the first innovative formulations of the relation between cinematic texts and history: published in 1984, Phil Rosen's essay revisits the notion of 'textuality' as it had been defined in debates on cinema since the late 1970s in order to ask the question: how does 'national specificity' manifest itself in films? Coming from a theoretical perspective that scrutinised texts as non-organic and non-unitary clusters of contradictions and gaps, Rosen observed that, against this inevitable impulse for semiotic dispersion, among the strategies at work in any given texts are also unifying mechanisms: 'The status of these coherencies is of importance; identifying them will always require sensitivity to the countervailing, dispersive forces underlying them.' By projecting onto a geo-political configuration this understanding of textuality as a push and pull towards and against unity, Rosen can read 'nationality' as 'an inter-textual *symptom*', in the process allowing for the diversity of trajectories that necessarily must be at work in any given cinema or group of films if they are to be understood as an adjunct to the longer-term construction of national subjectivities.

Paul Willemen takes this constitutive tension between cohesion and dispersal in films in a different direction. He argues that the capital intensive industrial conditions that determine film-making, along with the legal, economic and educational regulatory frameworks enacted by networks of institutions organised by or under the umbrella of the state, necessarily imprint themselves into the films. This means that film-texts cannot but register the force-field of tensions that institutions (from corporations to state departments) are there to contain while steering them in particular directions in accordance with the priorities that those institutions seek to achieve. Willemen concludes from this that one of the most important dimensions of a film is its mode of address, or, to put it another way, the direction into which texts seek to move people. A film's mode of address would then allow us to read, for instance, how a given text registers the tensions at play in the complex force-field that social scientists sometimes refer to as 'the conjuncture' and which is presided over, not always equally effectively, by the hierarchically organised combination of institutions that constitute the state. Willemen illustrates the point by arguing that texts can stress a kind of national cohesion (a nationalist mode of address) or oppose that stress, especially in the ways that meanings are 'enounced' or narrated.

Willemen's argument was first made at a conference in Australia just before the Berlin Wall came down. Stephen Crofts' essay emerges from that same Australian configuration, in which the difference between the need to address the national conjuncture and being a 'nationalist' was and remains a major cultural and political issue. Drawing from the work of Australian intellectuals (O'Regan 1985 and 1996; Dermody and Jacka 1988; Frow and Morris 1993; Langton 1993), Crofts' essay has become the *locus classicus* in relation to which current publications on national cinemas attempt to articulate their particular take on the problem of the national. Here it seemed to us to offer an ideal opening onto other accounts of individual national cinemas.

The title of the second section of this book has been chosen in order not simply to give emphasis to the specificity of the historical dynamics that must necessarily shape individual national cinemas, but above all to call attention to the notion of history – the historiographic model – that underscores the essays included here. As Chris Berry puts it in his brilliant contribution to this book, this is a framework within which 'the national is no longer confined to the form of the territorial nation-state but multiple, proliferating, contested, and overlapping'. Films are clusters of narrative strategies that position spectators within layered conceptions of the nation-state inevitably in tension with each other. Berry argues that the Taiwanese director Hou Hsiao hsien's 'Taiwan Trilogy' stages a historically grounded cosmology which 'invokes a Chineseness that is trans-"national" in the sense of the nation-state, but national in the sense of a culture'. In contrast, Kuan-Hsing Chen's essay adopts a partisan position within the Taiwanese socio-political frame to highlight the problem of cinema's relation to the state itself, especially in a context where two states claim to be the 'real' China.

Each of the essays in the 'Histories' section considers individual national cinemas as entertaining very much a similar obliqueness to the state. Maria Wyke argues that, after the unification of Italy in 1861, early Italian cinema answered the need to create 'Italians' by assimilating 'disparate peoples into a single nation'. For this very reason, even the 'invented tradition of *romanita*' – the nationalist evocation of pagan and imperial ancient Rome that was to give 'to the heterogeneous Italians a piece of common national history' – remained, in effect, available for appropriation to a variety of factions, including to 'the religious opponents of Italy's liberal government', to secular forces 'as ominous warnings of the Church's certain victory in the continuing struggle to reclaim her temporal power', and to both state and Church as a 'historical legitimation for Italy's colonial aspirations in the Mediterranean' (Wyke 1997: 18).

A non-linear model of history enables us to understand not only how 'traditions' can be reinvented for legitimation of/by the nation-state, but also how they can be appropriated by power blocs that can be both more and less modern than the nation-state. As Tom Nairn reminds us, even in the age of cultural (post)industrialisation, 'the shadow cast across history by the retreating peasantry is generally longer and deeper than most analyses have acknowledged' (1997: 92). Mikhail Iampolski's essay examines the forms that this 'pre-modern shadow' casts on Russian cinema, focusing in particular on the 'flatness' or frontality of early Russian cinema. Observing that that 'extraordinary and wonderful anomaly' that was the Soviet cinema of the 1920s 'was gradually replaced by an anti-modernist trend, the so-called Socialist Realism', Iampolski argues that, as Eisenstein's revisitation of his theory of montage in Platonic terms in the 1930s demonstrates, Russian cinema began to 'retrogressively move forward towards a pre-modern culture'. Although he acknowledges that no 'stylistic features can be unambiguously related to modern or anti-modern trends', Iampolski concludes that in Russia 'early cinema was sentenced to invent a style that was going against the grain of modernity because its underlying conception of the image was anti-modern in its core.' Martin McLoone's essay raises similar questions in relation to Irish cinema. Mapping Irish cinema through Fernando Solanas' grid of 'first', 'second' and 'third' cinemas, McLoone observes that 'the cinematic debate in Ireland is as much about the traditions of representation in the films of other countries as it is about the films produced in Ireland.' Irish cinema, he argues, is an *arrière-garde* cinema that inhabits a contradictory space between the local and the global. A younger generation of small- and medium-budget films addressing the socio-economic developments that constitute the 'Irish national' – including urbanisation and consumerism, co-exists, today, with 'first cinema' productions that continue to reinscribe the myth of romantic rural Ireland, also sold as commodity kitsch.

First published in 1997 in response to Andrew Higson's identification of a characteristic way of 'imagining the nation' as a 'knowable, organic community' in British films and of a typically 'national [film] style' (1995), John Hill similarly argues that British cinema – both as art cinema and as public service television – occupies a fundamentally different space than earlier British films, if anything for its greater dependence upon international finance and audiences for its viability. In the 1990s, the certainties concerning the nation upon which British films tended to rely until the 1960s increasingly dissolved, but British films continued to invite the individual stories of their characters to be read in terms of an 'allegory' of the 'state of the nation'. They did so not to project a unified notion of national identity and culture, but a much more fluid, hybrid and plural sense of 'Britishness' than earlier British films generally did, articulating an inclusive sense of Englishness, according recognition to the differing nationalities and identities within Britain, and thus emerging as more fully representative of national complexities than ever before. British cinema now clearly implies an English, but also a black British, a Scottish and a Welsh cinema, even if not all these films address questions of 'the nation' directly, or as questions of 'British-ness'.

The difficulties involved in establishing the difference between texts that *register* tensions operating within a national conjuncture and texts that *address* them, are raised by the two essays dealing with Japanese cinema. Kathe Geist discusses Ozu's way of registering sets of tensions within Japan over a number of decades. She demonstrates how Ozu's films, made in very different circumstances but always in studio contexts, are marked by what John Gumperz (1982: 63–8) called 'code switching': a way of conveying shared but unarticulated assumptions and aspirations by juxtaposing within the same text codes that belong to different cultural paradigms. Geist notes how Ozu switches codes between notions of (Americanised) modernity and Japaneseness, and how his films do so within and between different levels of textuality. In the process, Ozu's films can be seen to register sets of tensions which were constitutive of a particular kind of popular experience in Japan over a period of three or four decades. Mika Ko, on the other hand, argues that the films of the contemporary Japanese film-maker Miike Takashi are not shaped by an aspiration towards a kind of 'classic'-

feeling balance, but by violently centrifugal forces, as the imagined Japanese 'national body' falls apart. By constantly, even obsessively, exploding the boundaries of various kinds of bodies (of the film-as-object, of social groups and of psychologically rounded characters) Miike's films address (rather than register) the core-metaphor of Japanese nationalist exceptionalism at the same time as they stage the force-lines that constantly move into or out of Japan.

This section concludes with three essays that consider cinemas the national legitimacy of which has been radically called into question by the rise of finance capital as the dominant force of the American economy – including and beginning with American cinema itself. David Cook considers the changing strategies of risk management that have been adopted by the American film industry since its inception in New York. This perspective enables him to open a window onto a much neglected area of film history, namely Hollywood's relation to the nation-state[3] as the mechanism for orchestrating the industry's contradictory drives for profit maximisation and risk aversion. Today, Cook argues, foreign markets have emerged as an important sector to contain risk. Martine Danan examines the impact that strategy has had on French cinema in the era of the so-called 'postnational', while Kim Soyoung analyses the 'cine-mania' (cinephilia) that swept through South Korea in the 1990s. Most directly visible in a wave of film festivals and periodicals that continued beyond the IMF crisis of 1997, the craze for film turned cinema into a privileged site where the specific dynamics of Korean society can be read. Kim Soyoung extends this argument to throw light on the most recent developments in South Korean cinema: the blockbuster, export-oriented strategies and the accompanying erasure of Korean women's voices as the film industry negotiates its modernisation in the context of a suffocating variant of nationalism in tension with the pressures of American globalisation.

Section II concludes with a wonderful piece by Elia Suleiman – less a consideration of a fully fledged national cinema than a Palestinian film-maker's humorous protest against whichever national frame is foisted upon one's work. From this eminently individuated perspective, 'the national' is not containable within fixed geo-political boundaries, but should constitute a horizon that is constantly kept open to critical engagement. With this perspective in mind, in the third part of this collection the focus of attention shifts towards those cinemas which do not operate within a national frame, or rather, which operate simultaneously on national and regional scales. Ana Lopez considers the role of early cinema in creating the desire for, and suggesting the possibility of a home-grown version of, modernity in Latin America. Arguing that cinematic images of the experience of modernity 'lay bare the central characteristics of the processes through which subsequent media engaged with and contributed to the specificity of Latin American modernity', Lopez traces how cinema helped mediate 'the conflicts generated by the dilemmas of a modernity which was precariously balanced between local traditions and foreign influences, between nationalist aspirations and internationalist desires' (Lopez 2000: 158–9).

A differently configured economy of these tensions, energised by the particular historical conditions that shaped the various regions and states of the Arab world, has endowed Arabic cinema with its characteristic idioms and organisations. Focusing on the examples of   11

Egypt and Algeria, Sabry Hafez argues that the cinemas of the Egyptian-Levantine and Maghrib areas are animated by different socio-cultural dynamics. These cinematic regions do share a number of features, such as the synergy between literary and cinematic articulations of the national as well as linguistic and ethico-religious practices. Nevertheless, the socio-economic temporalities and developmental rhythms in the Egyptian-Levantine countries are marked by an autonomous experience of modernisation, even though inflected and put under pressure by invasions from the West. In the Maghrib countries, on the other hand, modernity arrived in the form of colonial domination. Hafez then connects these differing conditions of modernisation to narrative forms and to the menus of cinematic genres produced in these two regions of the Arab world.

Considering the disciplinary history and institutional politics that have contributed to the critical invention of 'Asian cinema', Mitsuhiro Yoshimoto observes that the widespread use of this new and far from self-evident category is simultaneous with the increasingly problematic status of 'national cinema' as an object of study. He situates both problematics in an economic landscape characterised by two interconnected factors: the globalisation of American capitalism and the rise of East Asia as a crucial region for the US economy and argues that, in film scholarship, the purpose of 'Asian cinema' is to sustain and reinforce the already overwhelming and still growing centrality of Hollywood cinema in the disciplinary structure of film studies.

Starting from the premise, also advanced by Yoshimoto, that the analytical framework deployed to account for the functioning of a national cinema cannot but be caught into the same pressures that shape the cinema as a global industry, Valentina Vitali observes that research on Indian films has tended to be conducted on the basis of the operational priorities of American and European films. The task at hand, she argues, is less to displace Hollywood as 'the norm'. What is needed is an understanding of history and cultural series as force-fields where multiple temporalities coexist and struggle to control the means of (cultural) production and circulation. From this theoretical perspective, Vitali proceeds to resituate the Hindi cinema within the broader economic developments that shaped modern India in its encounter with global capital. The picture that emerges is of a cinema that is 'national' precisely because, simultaneously caught in local and transnational networks, it entertains a profoundly oblique relation to the nation-state.

The tension between local networks and international dynamics that bears the imprint of colonialism is put back on the agenda in John Akomfrah's comments on African cinemas. Here, however, 'African cinema' is not a concept addressed to and for the European or any other non-African market, as is the case, for Yoshimoto, of 'Asian cinema'. Rather, for a whole generation of film-makers in sub-Saharan Africa, African cinema was that which emerged 'once it became clear that independence was going to come on the agenda, that took its cue from the renewed interest in national cultures, and ultimately something one had to work for'.

Today, even more so than in colonial Africa, African film-makers are squeezed out of the market through lack of funding and access to technology. The vestiges of colonial Europe upon which African cinemas have often depended have been transformed into a new set of policies that are responsible for a different animal: European media. What are the economic priorities that lie beneath this cultural agenda? First published in *Screen* in 1989, David Morley and Kevin Robins' essay on the reconfiguration of Europe as and through media technology and policies has been reprinted here because it seemed to us to raise questions that have become all the more urgent since. First among these is the question of how to speak of cultural 'identities' in an academic landscape that appears to have shelved as resolved debates about national specificities in the name of vague notions of 'globalisation'. To borrow a phrase from Morley and Robins' essay, our intention as editors of the present collection has been to encourage a mode of thinking that understands these 'identities' not 'one by one and then, subsequently (as an optional move)' think about how they relate to each other, but, rather, as always and 'only constituted in and through their relation to one another' (1995: 45). We hope that the essays reproduced here will help students of cinema and other cultural practices to go someway towards that kind of understanding. For this purpose, we have taken care to include as comprehensive *and* selective a list of bibliographic resources as the span of this collection allowed. References not given at end of essays can be found in the Bibliography.

Notes

1. In the United States, anti-trust legislation was in place by the beginning of World War I, which made it difficult for the American majors to act openly as a cartel within the domestic market. The 'nationality' of their products effectively enabled them to do just that. The 1918 Webb-Pomerene Act (WPA) allowed registered corporate associations such as the Motion Picture Export Association of America (MPEAA) to act as cartels abroad, in effect guaranteeing qualified immunity from anti-trust legislation outside their 'national' markets.
2. For the economic and historical background to Lewis Jacobs' work see Gomery (1984).
3. Aspects of that relation are explored in Guback (1986).

References

Abel, Richard (1999), *The Red Rooster Scare: Making Cinema American, 1900–1910*, Berkeley: University of California Press.

Anderson, Perry (1968), 'Components of the National Culture', *New Left Review* 50, reprinted in Anderson (1992).

Anderson, Perry (1992), 'Max Weber and Ernest Gellner: Science, Politics, Enchantment', in *A Zone of Engagement*, London and New York: Verso: 182–206.

Bell, Philip, Boehringer, Kathe and Crofts, Stephen (1982), *Programmed Politics: A Study of Australian Television*, Sydney: Sable Publishing.

Bitomsky, Hartmut (1972), *Die Röte des Rots von Technicolor: Kinorealität und Produktionswirklichkeit*, Neuwied, Darmstadt: Luchterhand.

Charensol, Georges (1935), *40 ans de cinéma, 1895–1935: Panorama du cinéma muet et parlant*, Paris: Editions du Sagittaire.

Crofts, Stephen (1993), 'Reconceptualising National Cinema/s', *Quarterly Review of Film and Video* 14 (3).

Desai, Meghnad (2002), *Marx's Revenge: the Resurgence of Capitalism and the Death of Statist Socialism*, London and New York: Verso.

Ferro, Marc (1984), *Film et Histoire*, Paris: Editions de l'École des Hautes Études en Sciences Sociales.

Gellner, Ernest (1983), *Nations and Nationalism*, Oxford: Blackwell.

Gomery, Douglas (1984), 'Film Culture and Industry: Recent Formulations in Economic History', *Iris* 2 (2) (1984): 17–28.

Hill, John (1997), 'British Cinema as National Cinema: Production, Audience and Representation', in Robert Murphy (1997).

Jacobs, Lewis (1968 [1939]), *The Rise of the American Film: A Critical History*, New York: Teachers College Press.

Kalbus, Oskar (1936), *Vom Werden Deutscher Filmkunst*, Berlin: Cigaretten-Bilderdienst Altona-Bahrenfeld.

Micciche', Lino (1980), *Cinema Italiano degli Anni '70*, Venice: Marsilio Editori.

Rosen, Phil (1984), 'History, Textuality, Nation: Kracauer, Burch, and Some Problems in the Study of National Cinema', *Iris* 2 (2).

Rotha, Paul (1949), *The Film Till Now*, London: Vision Press.

Sadoul, Georges (1949), *Histoire de l' art du cinéma des origines à nos jours*, Paris: Flammarion.

Vitali, Valentina (2005), 'Why Study Cinema? Serial Visions of the Culture Industry and the Future of Film Studies', *Inter-Asia Cultural Studies* 6 (2) (May).

Willemen, Paul (1994), 'The National', in Willemen (1994).

Part I Theories

1 History, Textuality, Nation

Kracauer, Burch and Some Problems in the Study of National Cinemas[1]

Philip Rosen

How might one employ recent approaches to filmic textuality in the study of film history? In addressing this question, I will limit myself to the notion of a *national cinema* as one traditionally central concept in film historiography. My examples of accounts of national cinemas will be Siegfried Kracauer's *From Caligari to Hitler: A Psychological History of the German Film* (1947) and Noël Burch's *To the Distant Observer: Form and Meaning in the Japanese Cinema* (1979), two histories by theoretically concerned writers.

Most elementally, a national cinema is a large group of films, a body of textuality. This body of textuality is usually given a certain amount of historical specificity by calling it a *national* cinema. This means that issues of national cinema revolve around an intertextuality to which one attributes a certain historical weight. What would allow a historian to attribute such a *weight* to the concept of the nation in his or her analytical construction of such large blocs of textuality?

To invoke the concept of intertextuality to describe the construction of a group of films which is thought to have a certain coherence might seem to be a somewhat contrary move. As applied to individual texts, the concept of intertextuality is most rigorously used to break down notions of organicness, unity, coherence, etc. It is well known that for well over a decade, influential kinds of criticism have been seeking gaps, contradictions, inadequacies, failures of individual texts to be self-sufficient. A theory of intertextuality treats those gaps as openings onto other texts, but those gaps can, in opposed or complementary ways, also be treated as openings onto society or history.

Now, one of the fundamental productive emphases in recent textual theory has been on a dialectic between two interpenetrating yet competing aspects of textuality. On the one hand, there is a more or less realised semiotic dispersion of meaning within and among signifiers or discourses. Over and against this textual impulse is a counter-process called containment, repression, etc. A result of this concentration has been to stress the importance of how unifying mechanisms of texts function. If this model were projected onto a national cinema as an intertextual grouping, then the coherence, or unity, of the group would not be an easy one but rather an effort or impulse of the body of textuality under investigation. Nationality as intertextual *symptom* would then become the object of analysis.

In contemporary theories of textuality which appeal to psychoanalysis, modes of discursive coherence are theorised as operations by which a text posits, addresses, appeals to a spectator. The key link between notions of discursive coherence and the study of a film's address to the spectator has been the Lacanian concept of the Imaginary Order, which grounds the postulation of an impossible desire for a sense of mastery as a sense of coherence and identity on the part of the spectator. From this perspective, the textual dialectic (semiotic dispersion vs. textual coherence) can be described as a dialectic between a potential dispersion of the ego via the drives *versus* the knotting of the drives in and as identity. That is, textual address is described as the conversion of perceptual force into an offering of identificatory force (see, for instance, Heath 1981). If this tendency in contemporary textual analysis were applied to an intertextual national grouping, then, the issue of identity – national identity? – might come to the forefront.

The question of coherence, then, becomes significant for issues of national cinema on a theoretical as well as methodological (what permits the historian to group these films together) level. But it does not end here. The discussion of a national cinema assumes not only that there is a principle or principles of coherence among a large number of films; it also involves an assumption that those principles have something to do with the production and/or reception of those films within the legal borders of (or benefiting capital controlled from within) a given nation-state. That is, the intertextual coherence is connected to a socio-political and/or socio-cultural coherence implicitly or explicitly assigned to the nation.

I am less concerned here with the old debates over 'reflection' than with the constitution of these general coherencies by the historian. Given the above considerations, I suggest that the study of a national cinema would always have to be based on three conceptualisations: (1) not just a conceptualisation of textuality, but one which describes how a large number of superficially differentiated texts can be associated in a regularised, relatively limited intertextuality in order to form a coherence, a 'national cinema'; (2) a conceptualisation of a nation as a kind of minimally coherent entity which it makes sense to analyse in conjunction with (1); (3) some conceptualisation of what is traditionally called 'history' or 'historiography'. The status of these coherences is of importance; identifying them will always require sensitivity to the countervailing, dispersive forces underlying them.

By now it is easy enough – indeed, often too easy – to agree that in most accounts of national cinemas these conceptualisations are too implicit, unthought and native. Perhaps what we need are not straw men, but rather an understanding of the avenues of historical comprehension open to us. It is therefore in search of methodologically and theoretically productive pressure points that I now turn to Kracauer and Burch.

Kracauer and Burch

The problem Kracauer defines for himself is notorious: he wishes to read psychological predispositions towards Nazism in the post-World War I German cinema. What view of textuality allows him to group together so many films as revelatory in this respect? It is true that Kracauer makes an argument for the special utility of cinema for those seeking such mass dispositions, but it will be more useful here to highlight his methodology for textual analysis. In this, his most significant argument is that generally and compulsively repeated motifs appearing throughout all levels of a nation's films – from a self consciously 'artistic' cinema to the most mass-oriented – are symptoms of a 'collective mentality', a shared 'inner life'. Such motifs consist not only in diegetic objects and actions (such as the fairground/chaotic circle form found in some films; a male protagonist placing his head on the bosom or lap of a female character, etc.), but also in components of form and style (for instance, what we recognise as expressionist *mise en scène*).

For Kracauer's project, the pertinent aspects of textuality therefore have less to do with individual films than with the vicissitudes of such motifs, in their similarities and variations, throughout the inter-war period. Thus, for example, the components of the authoritarian necromancer/sleepwalking criminal duality are clearly established by 1919 in *The Cabinet of Dr Caligari* (R. Wiene), but are found in the Mabuse film and in *M* (F. Lang, 1931) (where the necromancer is internalised into the still hapless criminal as irrational compulsion). These motifs inform individual film narratives with a historically pregnant intertextuality. In them, Kracauer can trace a great theme at the heart of the inter-war German collective mentality: that of the rejection of the multivalent, undecidable concrete real, and the resulting fascination with an authoritarianism whose alternative is figured as chaos.[2]

M (Fritz Lang, 1931)

It seems reasonable to argue that the model for Kracuer's jump from obsessively repeated motifs to a stipulated 'collective mentality' is a psychoanalytic one. This is not the same as saying that Kracauer's reading is rigorously psychoanalytic. But is not Kracauer reading the collection of motifs in their vicissitudes as a psychoanalyst reads displacements, condensations and secondary revisions in order to decode the anxieties and traumas underlying the analysand's obsessions and hysterical symptoms? In that case, Kracauer's investigation rests on something like an analogy, or the (loose) projection of an analytic framework designed to deal with *individual* human beings in terms of *collective* processes. Now, this is a kind of move which one finds in Freud himself and to which we will return. But here it is enough to notice that the necessary effect of such a move is one of massive unification. A presumably diverse national population is implicitly likened to an individual subjectivity; hence, Karacuer can link his account of the film texts to *a* nation. In order for this move to be convincing, such national coherence requires some further explanation.

On the surface, the German nation does not seem to have been the most unified socio-political entity imaginable during the period with which Kracauer is most concerned. At the beginning there was near-revolutionary discontent and upheaval; at the end, the Nazis took power at a moment when their electoral popularity was actually decreasing (contrary to what one might expect from some of Kracauer's propositions). Kracauer recognises that he is nevertheless committed to arguing for a certain basic national unity, so he introduces it as an *implicit* class phenomenon: 'In pre-Nazi Germany, middle-class penchants penetrated all strata' from the Left to the upper classes, which explains 'the nation-wide appeal of the German cinema – a cinema firmly rooted in middle-class mentality' (1947: 8–9).

It is appropriate that this claim occurs in the introduction to his study, for it is not a conclusion but an enabling premise. The existence of a culturally dominant class, or a class dominant in culture, whose social-psychological coherence can be alleged and then lent to the society as a whole, is what underlies the national coherence Kracauer requires for his reading of the films. For example, Kracauer reads the proliferation of expressionist *mise en scène* in German silent cinema of the early 1920s as a proliferation of signs of 'soul at work', that is, as signifying a film's import as an explicit meditation on difficulties of life as difficulties of interiority rather than of relations to the exterior, undecidably concrete world. He can read this as a sign of the state of mind of millions of Germans, especially in the middle classes, who 'acted as if under the influence of a terrific shock which upset normal relations between their outer and inner existence'. This was the 'shock of freedom' which resulted in a reaction against the liberties suddenly thrust upon Germans after World War I. Once he has assumed the unity of the nation around the middle classes, Kracauer can treat the films as registering a subterranean but general mental impulse to avoid directly dealing with the terrifyingly complex and unpredictable outer world and, led by that dominant class, a retreat to interiority, to reconsider the nature of the self or soul. The film image, which might otherwise seem to be so useful for recording exterior, chancy, concrete reality, is therefore utilised to deal with such spiritual agonies (1947: 58–60).[3]

As a historian of a national cinema, Kracauer is exemplary in his construction of two coherencies – a bloc of filmic (inter)textuality and the social formation of a specified period.

These are related in such a way as to enable Kracauer to investigate the kind of middle-class social-psychological patterns he treats as crucial for the appeal of Hitlerism. Once the neat logic of his enterprise is outlined, however, a number of the traditional objections to Kracauer as historian can be raised. To many readers, it has always seemed that Kracauer's approach to film history rests on simplistic reflectionist presumptions for the possibility of reading an underlying mentality from the cinema – especially the cinema – of a nation: indeed, Kracauer sometimes states these presumptions as if they had the status of a general law. However, insofar as his project rests on the attribution of a fundamental unity to the nation, it may be that Kracauer's claims are not so generalisable. In Kracauer's account there was something peculiar to Germany's social formation after World War I which permits his reading: the cultural dominance of middle-class social psychology. Against Kracauer's excessive methodological claims, then, it is also possible to read *From Caligari to Hitler* as demonstrating that the inter-war period in Germany represents an unusually fertile historical moment for treating film texts as reflecting social-psychological formations in this way. Such a view of his interpretation of German cinema would make his analysis there consistent with Kracauer's posthumous theory of history, in which he argues that there is such a thing as a specifically historical generalisation, but what makes it specifically historical is its limited range and validity in comparison with generalisations and laws in philosophy and science.[4]

Another traditional complaint about Kracauer's history is its 'teleologism', the *post hoc ergo propter hoc* logic by which everything in post-war German film texts seems to lead to the Nazis and Hitler. But to what extent is there any indication that this is a general tenet of historiography for Kracauer? Still keeping in mind Kracauer's late theory of history, such teleologism might be not a philosophy of history in the sense of universal principle, but rather a registration of the unique cataclysm of Hitlerism in German history. After all, the ultimate purpose for *From Caligari to Hitler* is not to provide *the* generally valid basis for any film history or any social readings of films (despite some inconsistent indications in the introduction). Rather Kracauer's purpose is to outline the mental preconditions which were a necessary condition for the success of National Socialism. To be sure, this means that the pertinent coherences (textual and national) of the period are defined by what followed it. However, the proposition that the rise and defeat of Hitler marks out the parameters of one of the great ruptures in German political and cultural history is certainly a defensible one, and it is hard to see how one might attempt to explain such a historical phenomenon without confronting determinant processes and factors preceding it. If we see Kracauer's teleologism not as an overarching historiographic principle, but as one possible form of understanding differentiated, local, conjunctural historical phenomena – that is, not as a philosophy of history as such, but as a method not necessarily applicable in any individual case but sometimes useful for organising historical temporality in relation to specific kinds of questions – then we may be in a better position to understand certain kinds of phenomena, despite the well-known dangers of ending up with concepts of an expressive totality, etc.[5]

Noël Burch's *To the Distant Observer* seems to be a very different approach to the study of national cinemas. Of course, Burch, like Kracauer, necessarily must claim a certain broad unity for a large group of films produced in a single nation. However, as one would expect, **21** the textual descriptions of that coherence by Burch, the materialist semiotician, differ in kind from those of Kracauer, the realist social critic. Whereas Kracauer tends to treat Hollywood as an economic force with strong but localised effects on the German film industry, Burch's claim for the textual distinctiveness of a large body of Japanese films is made in an international cinematic context dominated by the global impact of the Institutional Mode of Representation (IMR). This term of Burch's (actually developed as such elsewhere, but the concept is clearly at work in the Japanese book) denotes a set of possibilities for, and limitations on, the organisation of images and sounds in narrative feature films. This set is familiar to film theorists and important in semiotic investigations of cinema as 'the' classic Hollywood text.[6]

Thus, plot summary and characterisation, which Kracauer sometimes emphasises, are less important to Burch's textual descriptions than formal, stylistic and narrative codes which can be defined in relations of similarity and difference to this paradigmatic set. At crucial points in his accounts of major Japanese directors, Burch compares Japanese practices to patterns of editing, camerawork, narrative articulation, etc. common in dominant Western practices, the IMR. The compulsive return to such comparisons is as central to Burch's method of film-textual description as the sensitivity to intertextual vicissitudes of motifs is to Kracauer's. Indeed, a carefully chosen collection of excerpts from Burch's book on Japanese cinema could supply us with one of his fullest descriptions of the IMR.[7]

At stake in these cinematic oppositions are more general aesthetic oppositions, including such alternatives as: illusionism vs. materiality of signification; representation vs. presentation; the centred, implicated spectating subject vs. the actively reading, distanced subject; and textual homogeneity vs. textual heterogeneity. If these sound familiar, it is because Burch self-consciously draws upon a certain strain of Western theory from Brecht through Derrida and Barthes in order to explain the significance of the Japanese difference. He proposes alliances among Japanese cinema, primitive Western cinema and avant-garde Western cinema, but not an identity. The distinction he draws between Western avant-garde practices and those Japanese practices which establish a problematic relation to the IMR is crucial: 'What was a mass cultural attitude in Japan was a deeply subversive vanguard practice in the Occident.' This means that the most important Japanese film-makers are not original artists in the Western sense, but are rather 'the supreme masters of a unified cultural practice' (1979: 115, 148).

Since that unified cultural practice is a national one, Burch's account of the intertextual coherence of Japanese cinema is tied to a more generalised national-cultural coherence. Burch discusses the latter by arguing, on the basis of secondary sources, that in its development of national and cultural integration Japan is distinct from other Asian nations as well as Western nations. It is difficult to compress Burch's already compressed summary of Japanese history, but his approach to it may be indicated from his view of the nineteenth-century opening to the West and the rapid industrialisation that followed. Japan was the only major non-Western nation that was not colonised prior to industrialisation, and the only major Asian nation which had not been dominated by the 'Asiatic Mode of Production'. Thus when Japan industrialised, it was a politically unique Asian power which had maintained a relatively static feudal system internally for several centuries. On the other hand, when compared to the classic patterns of development in the West, there is also a difference. Japan modernised without undergoing a bourgeois revolution, so that the types of social classes usual to industrialisation could not emerge according to classic patterns of class stratification (1979: 27–30).

Burch argues that one of the most significant effects and reasons for the endurance of feudal socio-political structures was the existence of a truly national culture, based in part on Heian aesthetics but firmly instituted as part of the national consolidation effected by the Tokugawa shoguns. He regards the era of Tokugawa rule (1633–1867) as 'three centuries of standardization' whose impact could still be observed in the 1970s in everything from the most refined arts to the practices of everyday life:

> It is very difficult to speak of such widely shared values simply as part of the ideology of the dominant class, even though they have been confiscated in recent years by a certain bourgeois intelligentsia. [A] basic inter-class consensus on these matters had existed since time immemorial. [A] situation which contrasts sharply of course with the irreversible social segregation in all the arts which came about in capitalist society during the eighteenth and nineteenth centuries. (1979: 25,125)

Thus, the national and cultural unity imposed by the Tokugawas remained pertinent during the period which saw the development of Japan's principles of filmic representation, despite the transformative force of industrialisation and the resulting influx of Western practices and apparati, including cinema itself.

This analysis means that, with Kracauer, Burch bases his attribution of coherence to the nation on a class analysis, albeit an inverted one. For Burch, what is most significant about Japan in this respect is that the bourgeoisie manifested a socio-cultural weakness unusual among major industrialised nations. Whereas Kracauer finds a bourgeoisie that imposes its own anxieties as those of the nation, Burch argues that the socio-political structure of Japan resulted in a central contradiction of Japanese film history: a dynamic non-congruence of social and artistic practices. Members of a middle class attempting to emerge in the 1920s tended to seek 'reforms' of cinema by means of Western codes, which were seen as means of imparting increased 'realism' to films as against the 'presentationalism' so important from the feudal heritage. It was only during the years of triumph of the most reactionary social forces that an overwhelming appeal to anti-Western, nationalist values gave traditional Japanese aesthetics the strength to dominate all levels of cinematic practice. In the 1930s, as progressive class forces were politically suppressed, Japanese film-makers as a group made their most radical forays into a mass cinema which fell outside the IMR – that is, something like a materialist cinema (1979: 95, 115–6, 143–4, 148).

Thus, there is a diachronic dynamism to Burch's account of Japanese cinema, which is seen as the site of a fluid, unstable dialectic among different kinds of textual paradigms (for instance, Westernised representation vs. Japanese presentationalism). Burch does not give us a simply coherent 'Oriental cinema' whose mysterious and pure Otherness to dominant   **23**

Western modes of representation is merely founded on the geographical and cultural isolation of Japan. He insists that Japanese culture historically has been criss-crossed by foreign influences, and the Japanese tradition includes transformative integrations of many foreign practices. Representational forms have therefore often been sites of struggle, and national integration is linked in particular ways to cultural and representational processes.

The relation of Japanese cinematic practices to the IMR, then, cannot be described as a set of static oppositions; indeed, even opposition to the IMR takes on different significance for Burch during different periods. The 1920s is presented as a period of limited success for the Western, bourgeois codes, though socially progressive forces tried to use them and occasionally to deconstruct them. The 1930s are marked by the fullest development of a Japanese (that is, descended from Heian aesthetics) 'systemics'. After World War II, with the first foreign occupation ever experienced in Japan, the balance between feudal and Western values shifted once more. There was a resurgence of more 'Western' kinds of films and the traditionalist directors left their remarkable accomplishments of the 1930s behind. Younger directors of interest became those, such as Kurosawa and later Oshima, whose mastery of Western codes was turned against the latter into deconstructive operations; however, such figures, perforce, were more isolated than the important film-makers of the 1930s. Thus, there is a certain flexibility in Burch's view of filmic practice as a site of national-cultural struggle, based on shifting balances between feudal/traditional and modernising/Westernising tendencies, even among directors opposing the IMR (those whom Burch highly values). Some of Burch's 'masters' of Japanese cinema are highlighted for a 'supreme refinement and systematization of those traits which are most specifically Japanese' (such as Ozu and Mizoguchi in the 1930s and early 1940s), but others are said to have engaged in 'active "deconstruction" of the Western codes which, at certain periods of history, have tended to gain prevalence' (such as Kinugasa in the 1920s and Kurosawa in the 1950s) (Burch 1979: 16).

National Cinemas?

What avenues of approach do recent cinema semiotics provide for the study of national cinemas? Given the necessity of producing certain coherencies already discussed and the examples of Kracauer and Burch, what considerations can guide the historiography of national cinemas? To begin with the psychoanalytic impulse in recent theory, there is a temptation to investigate national identity in terms of a kind of national Imaginary readable in groups of texts. We have already encountered this kind of move in Kracauer, whose method of pulling together diverse texts into a national cinema can be likened to interpreting the discourse of a psychoanalytic patient. The diverse film texts under consideration would then originate in something like a national psyche, a national subject. Insofar as psychoanalysis remains an important basis for conceptualisations of filmic textuality, Kracauer's temptation will tend to reappear in some form. The Lacanian might see the nation as achieving and maintaining its identity against those forces threatening to disperse it by means of a network of textual mirrors which recall an original formation of identity.[8]

But what would that original experience of identity be for a nation? It probably is not fruitful to posit some kind of national mirror stage even as a heuristic fiction, despite the existence of myths of the origins of nations. The projection of individual characteristics onto a collective entity such as a nation simply cannot be made so quickly and easily. It is true that this is a kind of move not uncommon in the first half of the twentieth century, often expressed as a relation between ontogeny and phylogeny, and it can be found in Freud himself. Unfortunately, in *Group Psychology and the Analysis of the Ego*, Freud hardly discusses the nation. The works where he confronts the question of this kind of collectivity most squarely seem to be those involving his controversial anthropological 'mythology', that is, the *Totem and Taboo* narrative. In these works, individual processes are attributed to the socio-political grouping in startlingly direct ways; for example, in *Moses and Monotheism* (1939) Freud deduces an originary trauma and a return of the repressed for the Jewish people as a quasi-national entity. He is therefore forced to posit some as yet undiscovered mechanism by which such a collective entity can pass a 'group memory' on to succeeding generations.[9] It is absolutely necessary to acknowledge the difficulties of this move; however, once they are acknowledged, it may also seem difficult to dispense with it. Without the originary coherence supplied by the direct projection of individual processes onto group processes, to what extent can we reasonably expect that a psychoanalytically oriented approach is of use in historicising the study of textuality?

Putting the question like this raises the spectre of generations of controversy which have already occurred between psychology and sociology, Freud and Marx. But it would be better not to begin by submitting to some hackneyed, allegedly unbridgeable dichotomy between the individual and the social. A psychoanalytic reading of a film, for example, does not stand or fall on the explicit reaction to the film of any 'individual' spectator, and this is not just because concentrating on explicit reactions misses the nature of psychoanalytic claims. Freud once remarked, 'I do not think that much is to be gained by introducing the concept of a "collective" unconscious – the content of the unconscious is collective anyhow, a general possession of mankind' (1939: 170). There is already something shared – that is, 'collective' in a general sense – about the mechanisms explored by psychoanalytic inquiry, and there will always be a general applicability of those processes designated by the term 'unconscious' because of the very nature of the hypotheses about fundamental structures which psychoanalytic thought argues it has exposed.

In that case, the issue to be faced here is not one of discovering those aspects of unconscious processes which might fit the term 'collective'. It is rather the relation of characteristics already collectively possessed to – or their specification in – the formation and perpetuation of institutional and historical collectivities, which are organisations and regulations of human bodies and efforts in common. What would be at stake in the study of national cinemas is not the nation as a concrete and automatically unified producer/reader of films, but as an appeal to a general ego-function by means of specific configurations of textuality. If there is something particularly 'national' about a set of films, such as German films of the early 1920s or Japanese films of the 1930s, the nation would appear as a construction of that cinema's discourse, and its address.

The psychoanalytic study of cinema's address to the spectator has, of course, been one of the crucial sectors of film-semiotic investigation over the last several years. Such investigations have often centred on the conversion of perceptual and/or sexual drives more or less directly to individual spectatorial identity.[10] Perhaps what we need is a level of analysis working at more sublimated levels. Sublimation is a major, but somewhat shadowy concept in psycho-analytic thought. But we do know that from about 1923 (*The Ego and the Id*), Freud himself associated sublimation with narcissism: the ego can displace energy onto non-sexualised objects, but still at the service of uniting and binding the ego. This brings us back to the dialectic between dispersion and coherence so important in recent film theory and the great stress of its psychoanalytic tendency on, for example, narcissism. The question presenting itself is what the notion of national collectivity provides at the service of identity and subject-hood. Nationhood then becomes a sociolect (in the sense of Barthes), but a sociolect which is a component of mechanisms of textual address.[11]

Nationhood in texts, as discursively constructed ideals which are intertwined into the text's address to a spectatorial identity: this recalls Fredric Jameson's suggestion that there is always a utopian component to the figuration of collectivities in general and nationhood in particular, no matter how strong the regressive impulses of a given text. For Jameson, the construction of 'collective actants' is a facet of textual desire (1981: 80). Fantasms and wish-fulfilments are not only directly sexual; they also involve conceptions of history, in this case national history.

In this context, Kracauer and Burch are significant in that both of their accounts of national cinemas can be read as presenting a certain national unity and/or identity as an unstable, shifting variant, effective to different degrees at different points in time. For Kracauer, the fourteen years following World War I comprise a special period in the history of Germany, during which there was a special form of cultural unity which makes its cinema from that period particularly useful as evidence for understanding the underlying processes of the unity. Burch also argues for the existence of specific historical periods when the forces of Japanese cultural unification were stronger than other periods, with resulting shifts in tex-tual characteristics of Japanese films. On this reading, there is a genuine diachrony underly-ing both accounts. Kracauer and Burch, in their different ways, attempt to construct and explain certain types of intertextual coherence which they locate as being especially force-ful only during certain periods of film/national history.

If this kind of diachrony can be associated with the play of an *intertextual* dialectic between containment and dispersion, then we may be able to analyse historically specific national identities. This intertextual history would be linked in some way to another kind of dispersion/coherence dialectic – for example, on the political or national-institutional levels. The national identity of a group of films then becomes, neither the realisation of some hypo-thetical national *Geist*, nor a trivial tautology (these films were made in Germany, therefore they are part of a German national cinema), nor the catchwords of patriotic claptrap. National identity becomes an entity more or less realised precisely as a readable discursive coherence which is unstable and whose terms and/or intensity may very well shift to the point where it becomes at least theoretically possible for a historian to argue that the cine-matic output of a given nation during a given period does not embody that particular kind of intertextual address one would call a national cinema.

The latter is a limit case which may be unlikely, though film industries in colonised nations could provide objects for interesting studies in this regard. There is little doubt that the institution of the nation is basic to confronting a number of crucial historical processes of the last several centuries, and it is a reasonable assumption that its importance applies to cultural production. That is, even if one is inclined in the first instance to dispute whatever hegemonic claims to perfect or harmonious collectivity the concept of the nation includes, the historical force of the *claim* cannot be easily ignored. To investigate that force as textual aspects of films and their appeals to the spectator would be, then, one avenue of integrating the study of such appeals into socio-cultural history.

Notes

1. This essay first appeared in *Iris* 2 (2), 1984: 60–83.
2. *From Caligari to Hitler*: 6–8. For the fairground motif, see pp. 73–4 and 87. There are a large number of examples of the male with his head on the female, e.g. pp. 99, 99n, 157–8 and 171. For the necromancer/sleepwalker pair, see pp. 72–3, 81–4, 221–2.
3. Thomas Elsaesser has suggested the affiliations and distinctions between Kracauer's approach, on the one hand, and both those of certain Frankfurt School thinkers and of post-World War II American theorists of mass society (such as C. Wright Mills, Riesman, Lazarsfeld) on the other. See Elsaesser 1984: 60, 65, 67–8. Miriam Hansen (1983: 167 and 167n) would rather not separate Kracauer's realist aesthetics from his social analyses of the 1920s (Elsaesser agrees with her on the importance of the early writings). *From Caligari to Hitler* was published only thirteen years before *Theory of Film: The Redemption of Physical Reality*, New York and Oxford: Oxford University Press, 1960, and it (indeed) seems difficult to avoid the impression that the earlier book is informed by impulses formalised in the latter.
4. Kracauer's reflectionist claims are most extravagant in the introduction of *From Caligari to Hitler* (pp. 5–6). Cf. the argument concerning the *limited* nature of historical 'ideas' or generalisations in Kracauer's *History: The Last Things Before the Last*, New York and Oxford: Oxford University Press, 1969, esp. chapter 4.
5. The usual reference for the explication and critique of the expressive totality as a historical and social concept has been the work of Louis Althusser, for example the essay 'Contradiction and Overdetermination' in *For Marx* (1970), the section entitled 'The Errors of Classical Economics: Outline of a Concept of Historical Time' in *Reading Capital* (1970). In the latter, see also pp. 186–7. It is therefore startling to read in Kracauer's *History: The Last Things Before the Last* (chapter 4, esp. pp. 150–1 and 155) attacks on linear, homogeneous conceptions of historical time and the flat unification of historical periods, as well as an endorsement of conceptualising historical transitions as breaks rather than as realisations of what precedes them. While Kracauer is by no means Althusser, some limited kinship on these matters seems evident.
6. For some discussions of the concept of the Institutional Mode of Representation as opposed to other paradigms, see Burch (1979). For examples of the presence of this concept in Burch (1979), see pp. 18–23 and chapter 5.
7. For example, see the account in Burch (1979) of the account of Western shot/reverse shot during the analysis of Ozu (pp. 158–9); the account of Western use of the long take in the

chapter on Mizoguchi (pp. 224–6); the account of the functions of shot (or, more accurately, set-up) repetition in Western cinema during the discussion of Ishida's *Fallen Blossom* (*Hana Chirinu*) (pp. 204–5).

8. In social theory, the *locus classicus* of this kind of move is Louis Althusser's 'Ideology and Ideological State Apparatuses (Notes towards an Investigation)' in *Lenin and Philosophy and Other Essays* (1971: 170–82). For what might be read as working through some of the subtleties and difficulties of such an approach, see Elsaesser (1984): 59–81. A critical account of Althusser's formulations in the above essay from the viewpoint of psychoanalytic semiotics can be found in Stephen Heath's 'The Turn of the Subject' in *Cine-Tracts* 7–8 (1979).

9. See Freud (1939): Pt 3, section 1.5, esp. pp. 125–30. It sometimes seems as if Freud is giving us a wild, hazy anticipation of the discovery of DNA coding carried in the direction of an eccentric sociobiology. For some of the contradictions and difficulties he encounters, see Coward 1983: 212–18.

10. From a large body of work, two influential examples are Metz (1982) and Laura Mulvey (1975), 'Visual Pleasure and Narrative Cinema', *Screen* 16 (3).

11. See the entry under 'Sublimation' in Laplanche and Pontalis (1973). On sociolect, see Barthes 1970: 21–2, 86–8 (where it is called 'idiolect') and 'Change the Object Itself: Mythology Today', in Barthes (1977).

References

Althusser, Louis (1970), *For Marx*, translated by Ben Brewster, New York: Vintage.

Althusser, Louis (1971), *Lenin and Philosophy and Other Essays*, translated by Ben Brewster, New York: Monthly Review Press.

Althusser, Louis and Balibar, Etienne (1970), *Reading Capital*, translated by Ben Brewster, London: New Left Books.

Barthes, Roland (1970), *Elements of Semiology*, translated by A. Lavers and C. Smith, Boston: Beacon.

Barthes, Roland (1977), *Image – Music – Text*, translated and edited by Stephen Heath, New York: Hill and Wang.

Burch, Noël (1979), 'Film's Institutional Mode of Representation and the Soviet Response', *October* 11.

Coward, Rosalind (1983), *Patriarchal Precedents: Sexuality and Social Relations*, Boston: Routledge & Kegan Paul.

Elsaesser, Thomas (1984), 'Film History and Visual Pleasure', in Mellencamp, P. and Rosen, P. (eds), *Cinema Histories, Cinema Practices*, Frederick, MD: University Publications of America.

Freud, Sigmund (1939), *Moses and Monotheism*, translated by Katherine Jones, New York: Vintage.

Hansen, Miriam (1983), 'Early Silent Cinema: Whose Public Sphere?', *New German Critique* 29.

Heath, Stephen (1981), *Questions of Cinema*, London: Macmillan.

Jameson, Fredric (1981), *The Political Unconscious: Narrative as a Socially Symbolic Act*, Ithaca, NY: Cornell University Press.

Laplanche, J. and Pontalis, J. B. (1973), *The Language of Psychoanalysis*, translated by Donald Nicholson-Smith, New York: Norton.

Metz, Christian (1982), *The Imaginary Signifier: Psychoanalysis and the Cinema*, translated by Celia Britton *et al.*, Bloomington: Indiana University Press.

2   The National Revisited[1]

Paul Willemen

Notions of the national and the international are inextricably linked because they define each other. But they do not do so symmetrically, because over the last three hundred years or so, each side of that coin has become embroiled in its own history. Meanings have shifted as they entered new sets of cultural and political constellations. As Perry Anderson noted in a recent account of those shifts and changes: 'The meaning of internationalism logically depends on some prior conception of nationalism, since it only has currency as a back-construction referring to its opposite' (Anderson 2002: 5). The relation between these mutually defining opposites not only changed its class connotations.[2] Towards the end of the twentieth century it changed even more drastically: now, 'internationalism' has become equated with, as Anderson put it, a display of 'limitless loyalty to another state', that is to say, to the US's 'fervent cult of the homeland or for a missionary redemption of the world' (Anderson 2002: 15, 23–4). The often invoked international community is today simply a code word for a call to submit to the policies pursued by the American state. In the cultural realm, a similar shift has been in operation for some years: the national popular is now equated with the consumption of US cultural exports, while critiques of such export products is stigmatised as elitist. At the same time, any film that is not in English has become an example of 'world cinema', something reserved for intellectuals and other culture vultures.[3] These changes in meaning of the national and the international underscore that both terms delineate a symbolic field within which, today, an appeal to the national is located as a political ideology designed to achieve a specific goal: to delineate a bounded geographical space that a particular powerbloc, in this case a coalition that constitutes a national bourgeoisie, can reasonably expect to restructure to its own benefit on a long-term basis. In other words, national*ist* bourgeoisies sought to establish a specific 'political economy' within the limits of a bounded terrain which they could govern under conditions of relative independence and autonomy, with the range of cultural and administrative institutions needed for managing this, and an army capable of defending it (Nairn 1997:133).

The motivation for that sea-change and the supplier of the necessary energy to achieve it was what historians call 'modernisation'. Ernest Gellner put it more trenchantly in the now famous essay on nationalism in his book *Thought and Change* (1964). For Gellner, in the paraphrase provided by Tom Nairn (Nairn 1997:1), 'Modern philosophers . . . may believe that they have been ruminating upon universal standards, the Soul, God, Infinity and other capital-letter constructions. In truth, all they have been trying to do is cope with the after-effects of the steam-engine.' But Nairn then points to a key implication of Gellner's insight: not only is all modern philosophy's true subject industrialisation, but 'its immensely complex and variegated aftershock – nationalism'. While accepting Nairn's radical extension of Gellner's thesis, Anderson's examination of the conceptual pair's history re-situates better the recent wave of preoccupation with two themes characteristic of late twentieth-century film and cultural studies paradigms: multiculturalism and the (modernising, modern and even modernist) concern with 'specificity'. Briefly, I want to argue that there is a crucial difference between national*ism* and a concern with the ways a particular social formation functions . . . in order to change it.

I would like to start by making three linked suggestions. The first is that 'nationalism' is a term that should be reserved for the range of institutionalised practices seeking to define and impose a particular, reductive, politically functional identity. To oppose, criticise, subvert or otherwise challenge the kind of restrictive straitjacket which nationalism seeks to impose upon the 'subjects' of the nation-state cannot also be called nationalism, even though it plays on the very same terrain of the existing or anticipated nation-state. In such a contest, the forces seeking to define and impose a notion of identity are opposed by a concern with the complexities of that other aspect of modernisation and industrialisation: individuated subjectivity.

The second suggestion is that nationalism seeks to bind people to identities. That is to say, it mobilises cultural-political power and institutionalised weight primarily through the deployment of a broad-ranging array of modes of address organised not just rhetorically, but also embodied in the very organisation and policies of institutions. It is a mode of address carefully nurtured, reproduced and policed, ensuring that a specific cluster of assumptions is written into our social bodies from early childhood and repeated with ritualised regularity thenceforth. Nationalism is a question of address, not of origin or genes. As Tom Nairn also points out, 'nationality is not in the genes; but it is in the structure of the modern world' (Nairn 1997: 206). It is my contention that the formation, imposition, and indeed the acceptance of or consent to 'a national identity', is to be tracked in the addressing dimensions of institutions set up and maintained to select a cluster of 'differentiae', as Nairn calls them, decreed to be 'our' inheritance by those social groups or power blocs who seek to perpetuate their dominance.

The third suggestion is that there is a diametrical opposition between identity and subjectivity. The former, being what the institutionally orchestrated practices of address seek to impose, constitutes a never-quite-fitting straitjacket; the latter is an ambiguous term designating individuals as the crossroads or condensation points of multiple sets of institutionally organised discursive practices. As such, subjectivity delineates a 'space' where the plethora of grammatical subjects activated in language fold into and over each other to form what any of us might call his or her 'subjective world'. Subjectivity always exceeds identity, since identity formation consists of trying to pin 'us' to a specific, selected sub-set of the many diverse clusters of discourses we traverse in our lifetimes, and that stick to us to varying degrees. Subjectivity, then, relates to what we may think and feel to be the case regarding 'our' sexuality, kinship relations, our understanding of social-historical dynamics acquired through (self)education, work experience and so on. Some aspects of our subjectivity may be occupied or hijacked by the national identity modes of address, but there always are dimensions within our sense of 'subjective individuality' that escape and exceed any such identity straitjacket.

The rest of this essay seeks to explore the ramifications of these distinctions for the way(s) in which we conceptualise the relationships between industrialised cultural practices such as cinema and the always pre-existing, but never fixed, institutionally organised social formations we inhabit.

In each socio-cultural formation, the tensions between the national and the international as well as those between identity and subjectivity must, by definition, be played out in different ways. But the terms in which these tensions are presented will have a family resemblance. Nevertheless, the issues of the national and the international, and indeed of the colonial and the imperial, are present in film studies in specific ways that are different from those adopted, for instance, in anthropology or in comparative literature. Film and media studies have responded to the wave of massive population migrations that resulted from the accelerated circulation of Anglo-American and Japanese finance capital, by adding cross-cultural or multicultural flavours to its standard menu. But both the terms 'cross-cultural' and 'multicultural' already point to the first problem, in the sense that they suggest the existence of discrete, bounded cultural zones separated by borders which can be crossed. The term 'multicultural' also suggests that cultural zones continue to exist within a given country as small, self-contained pockets or islands, miniature replicas of an alleged community's allegedly original national culture, as repositories of some cultural authenticity to be found elsewhere in time and space. In Ukania – Tom Nairn's suggestive term for the ossified, incompletely modernised monarchical state known as the United Kingdom (Nairn 1988) – one hears references to, say, the Bangladeshi, or the Irish or indeed the Asian communities, as if a given 'ethnic' community had simply transposed a national culture from 'there' to 'here'. This transposition can then be narrativised in terms of contamination and disease, as it is in Ukania today in the light of 'foreigners' seeking to escape from economic and/or political distress, or, as it was a decade or so ago, as the development of a 'multicultural society' that is ever so 'tolerant' of 'others'. This multicultural ideology has some positive, but also some exceedingly negative consequences for a country's cultural life and policies. One very negative result is that 'ethnic' groups will be imprisoned, by arts funding bodies and local government practices, within a restrictive and fossilised notion of culture. In this way, such groups are condemned to repeat the rituals of ethnic authenticity, regardless of how uncomfortable many members of those so-called communities may feel with them. One of the political effects of such policies is that administrators and local politicians tend to recognise 'community' spokespeople who represent the more conservative and nostalgically 'traditionalist' sectors of 'the communities' in question. A further consequence is, perhaps ironically, to encourage the practice of a 'traditional' culture separated from the social conditions by and for which those cultural forms were shaped and, in so doing, to fetishise the separateness of the cultures thus called into being. In this respect, multiculturalist policies end up creating a kind of cultural apartheid. By insisting on the discreteness and the separateness of the 'other' cultures, the host culture conspires with the conservative upholders of an imagined 'ethnicity' to draw lines around those 'other' cultural practices, ghettoising them. And in that way, the host culture can reaffirm its own imaginary unity and the illusion of its own specialness and authenticity.

Although we can all agree that cultural zones are far from unified, homogeneous spaces, this should not lead us to deny or unduly relativise the existence of borders. The existence of borders is very real, and although their meaning and function are changeable, their effectiveness has not diminished in the least. At one level, it does indeed make sense to try to construct a notion of national culture by way of a spatial commutation test. The culture would then be defined in terms of the things that change in 'the whole way of life', to use Raymond Williams' phrase, when a national frontier is crossed. For instance, abortion may be legal on one side of a border and not on the other; or legal and other institutional arrangements, such as those relating to film and television finance and censorship, may be vastly different. In federal structures such as India, the United States, the former USSR or Australia, there are different inflections to this problem because of the imbrication of national and state institutions, but the problem of the nation-state's borders remains, as is demonstrated by the importance of passports for bestowing a national identity upon individuals, with the consequent legal regulation of immigration, the search for asylum under a network of governmental institutions 'elsewhere' and the whole panoply of issues implied by the notion of citizenship.

On the other hand, the construction of a cultural matrix in such a geo-structural way does not account for the sense of temporal continuity that is attributed to national cultural formations. The comparative study of, say, independent British cinema in the 1930s and in the 1970s would not be regarded as a form of cross-cultural studies. The intervention of World War II, and of a host of other socio-political and economic changes, apparently does not constitute a sufficient temporal boundary for us to be able to talk of different cultural formations.

Perhaps we should begin by becoming more aware of the complicity between periodisation in history and the drawing or the crossing of geographical boundaries. The invasion of Australia, and the declaration of a bicentenary period, is only one example of this complicity. The tendency to date England back to the invasion of 1066 is another, as is the tendency to regard World War II and its large-scale redrawing of the world map as the most significant temporal watershed of the twentieth century. It would be foolish to deny that the war is indeed a very significant marker in all kinds of respects. The point is that in other respects, such as, for instance, the periodisation of capitalism, World War II is not that significant a marker at all. The liquidation of nineteenth-century absolutist empires took over fifty years, and the consolidation of capitalism on a global scale happened sometime between the mid-1950s and the late 60s, while the triumph of finance capital over industrial capital took even longer and, although accelerating in the early 1970s, was not consolidated until the 80s. With luck, some of the gigantic financial frauds that have come to public attention around the turn of the millennium, such as the dotcom scams, the Enron scandal, the Savings and Loan frauds and the US financial assault on its East Asian competitors, may signal the imminent end of finance capital's catastrophically destructive period of hegemony. This point is worth making to show that there are temporal rhythms and periods which, although implicated in and affected by geographic changes, do not coincide with them. The synchronicity of geographical and temporal periods at work in most national histories has to be produced at some cost: the loss of perspective on the very forces that construct the vicissitudes of 'the national' in the era of international dependency.

The notion of cultural specificity that may be deployed against the universalising ethnocentricity at work in film studies operates at the level of this geo-temporal construction of the national. The question of cultural specificity can be posed on other social community levels and these may themselves be transnational, as are some constructions of gender- and class-based politics. But in film studies, the issue of specificity is primarily a national one: the boundaries of cultural specificity in cinema are established by governmental actions implemented through institutions such as the legal framework of censorship, industrial and financial measures on the economic level, the gearing of training institutions towards employment in national media structures, systems of licensing governed by aspects of corporate law, and so on. For the purposes of film culture, 'specificity' is a term derived from the vocabulary of modernism applied in the realm of political economy. Specificity thus becomes a territorial-institutional matter, and coincides with the boundaries of the nation-state, that is to say, it designates cultural practices and industries on the terrain governed by the writ of a particular state.

As a rule, the effectiveness with which national socio-cultural formations, that is to say, state-bound unities, determine particular signifying practices and regimes, is not addressed. This is a problem for a number of reasons. One result is that it encourages confusion between, on the one hand, the discourses of nationalism as objects of study or as a political project, and, on the other hand, the issue of national specificity. Compared to Afro-American films made in the US, black British films are strikingly British, and yet in no way can they be construed as nationalistic. They are part of a British specificity, but not of a British nationalism: especially not if we remember that British nationalism is in fact an imperial identification, rather than an identification with the British state. To complicate matters further, an identification with the British state is, in fact, an English nationalism, as opposed to Welsh, Cornish or Scottish nationalisms, which relate not to a state but to nations, and are recognisable by their demand for autonomous governments, even if that autonomy may be qualified in various ways.

A second area of confusion is the relation between a concern with national identity and the specificity of a cultural formation. For instance, the concern with notions of Australianness and with national identity was a temporary component of the dominant registers of Australian cultural specificity. That concern started to decline after the so-called bicentennial celebrations and resurfaced, in a different form, in the early 1990s, around notions of republicanism and, more (in)famously, around the 'One Nation' political movement which helped to set in place the Australian government's current, murderously ruthless attitude towards refugees. This simply means that the specificity of the Australian cultural formation has changed over the last decade and now generates other motifs and discourses. In that sense, the concern with socio-cultural specificity is different from identity searches and debates. The specificity of a cultural formation may be marked by the presence but also by the absence of preoccupations with national identity. Indeed, national specificity will determine which, if any, notions of identity are on the agenda.

So, the discourses of nationalism and those addressing or comprising national specificity are not identical. Similarly, the construction or the analysis of a specific cultural formation is different from preoccupations with national identity. I would go further and suggest that the construction of national specificity in fact encompasses and governs the articulation of both national identity and nationalist discourses. Nationalist discourses forever try to colonise and extend themselves to cover, by repressively homogenising, a complex but nationally specific formation. Thankfully, they are also doomed to keep falling short of that target. In that sense, nationalism is the shadow side of imperialism: it is an ideology generated by imperialism as its own counter-body, and it is in some ways even more repressively homogenising than that of the empire it seeks to undo – perhaps necessarily so.

At the same time, in art and media studies, insufficient attention is paid to the determining effects of the geographically bounded state-unity, and this encourages a kind of promiscuous or random form of alleged internationalism, which I would prefer to call an evasive cosmopolitanism masking (US) imperial aspirations. Another, more polemical way of putting this is to say that the discourse of universalist humanism is in fact an imperial and a colonising strategy in the service of US national(ist) policies. If we accept that national boundaries have a significant structuring impact on national socio-cultural formations (please note that I have written 'a significant impact' and not that these boundaries are the only determinations, nor necessarily the most important ones in all circumstances: merely that they are real and significant), this has to be accounted for in the way we approach and deal with cultural practices from 'elsewhere'. Otherwise, reading a Japanese film from within a British film studies framework may in fact be more like a cultural cross-border raid, or worse, an attempt to annex another culture in a subordinate position by requiring it to conform to the raider's cultural practices (Willemen 1994: 56–84 and Willemen 1995: 101–29).

Such practices are an acute problem in film studies for three main reasons. The first is that academic institutions are beginning to address the film cultures of non-Western countries.[4] This expansion in academia's disciplinary field creates job and departmental growth opportunities. The result is that scholars formed within the paradigm of Euro-American film theory are rushing to plant their flags on the terrain of, for instance, Chinese, Japanese or Indian film studies. In that respect, those scholars and departments are actively delaying the advent of a genuinely comparative film studies by trying to impose the paradigms of Euro-American film and aesthetic theories upon non-Euro-American cultural practices. In the process, the very questions concerning the production of specific socio-cultural formations mentioned earlier are marginalised or ignored.

The second reason for film-theoretical malpractice can be found in the assumed universality of film language. This illusion is promoted to ignore the specific knowledges that may be at work in a text, such as shorthand references to particular, historically accrued modes of making sense (often referred to as cultural traditions). As an example, we might remember the controversy generated by Antonioni's use of the close shot in his film on China (Rohdie 1990), or the different ways in which notions of realism are deployed in relation to various types of melodrama in Asia. Further examples can be found in films which engage with the connotations generated by particular landscapes or cityscapes within particular cultures, or with the differing meanings attached to, for instance, images of industrialisation. It is regarding this set of issues that notions of Third Cinema can most productively be deployed. Similarly, since the Hollywood model of character narration is accepted as the norm in Euro-American film studies, the modes of studying Hollywood narrative and its counter-cinemas have been presented as equally universal and normative, duplicating and confirming the position of the economic power enjoyed by Hollywood.

The third reason is the forced, as well as the elective, internationalism of film industries themselves. The capital intensive nature of film production, and of its necessary industrial, administrative and technological infrastructures, requires a fairly large market in which to amortise production costs, not to mention the generation of surplus for investment or profit. This means that a film industry – any film industry – must either address an international market or a very large domestic one. If the latter is available, then cinema requires large potential audience groups, with the inevitable homogenising effects that follow from this, creating an industrial logic which, if played out at a national level, will benefit from the equally homogenising project of nationalism. The economic facts of cinematic life dictate that an industrially viable cinema shall be multinational or, alternatively, that every citizen shall be made to contribute to the national film industry – mostly by way of tax and/or subsidy legislation – regardless of whether they consume its films or not.

These aspects of the film industry and of the cultural sector(s) corresponding to that industry's production processes raise two important issues, one concerning the national, one concerning cinema itself. I will return to the problem of cinema itself at the close of this essay in the form of a caveat. As to cinema's industrial nature, that means that if the question of national specificity is posed in its proper context, the issue must be addressed at the level of national and governmental institutions, since these are the only ones in a position to inflect legislation and to redistribute tax revenues. That fact has unavoidable consequences for the social power relations that govern the kind of cinema thus enabled. Consequently, a cinema which seeks to engage with the questions of national specificity from a critical, non- or counter-hegemonic position is by definition a minority and a poor cinema, dependent on the existence of a larger multinational or nationalised industrial sector (most national cinemas operate a mixed economic regime, but that does not alter the argument: it merely creates a little more breathing space for film-makers). This is a cinema that has to work 'in the interstices' of the industry, an area the dimensions of which can and do change depending on the effectiveness of cultural-political campaigns.[5] It is, of course, true that industrially made films always must *register* the pressures at work in the 'national configuration', but that is not at all the same as a cinema that seeks to address the issues that constitute and move the 'national' configuration. By the same token, and somewhat paradoxically, a cinema address-ing national specificity will be anti- or at least non-nationalistic, since the more it is com-plicit with national*ism*'s homogenising project, the less it will be able to engage critically with the complex, multidimensional and multidirectional tensions that characterise and shape a social formation's cultural configurations. The exception here is the national*ist* propaganda film, invariably sponsored by government institutions and increasingly relegated – or del-egated – to television anyway. National*ist* propaganda may well address divisions within the national formation. But it does so in order to delegitimise them and to stimulate attacks ranging from institutional to mob violence against the divisive, 'alien' or contaminating agents, thus hoping to enhance the repressive power of specific social-economic blocs within the national institutional network controlling the levers of governance.

This leads us to the ironic conclusion that a cinema positively yet critically seeking to engage with the multilayeredness of specific socio-cultural formations, is necessarily a mar-ginal and a dependent cinema: a cinema dependent for its existence on the very dominant, export and multinationally oriented cinema it seeks to criticise and displace. This too is a paradox worthy of Archibald, because this marginal and dependent cinema is simultaneously the only form of national cinema available: it is the only cinema which consciously and directly works with and addresses the materials at work within the national cultural con-stellation. The issue of national cinema is then primarily a question of address, rather than a matter of the film-makers' citizenship or even of the production finance's country of origin.

For the Soviet cultural theorist Mikhail Bakhtin, there are three kinds of interpretation which correlate with three different ways of framing relations with other socio-cultural net-works (Bakhtin 1986).

The first is a kind of projective appropriation (my term). This happens when the reader/viewer projects him or herself, his or her belief world, onto the texts. The most common example of this practice happens when a theoretical or interpretative framework elaborated for and within one cultural sphere is projected onto the signifying practices of another cultural sphere. To project early twentieth-century Western novelistic criteria of psychological verisimilitude onto 1940s commercial Indian films would be one such example. Another would be the assumption that Leavisite or Baudrillardian aesthetic ideol-ogies are universally applicable norms. Projective appropriation accompanies efforts to inter-nationalise a restrictive regime of making sense. It is concerned with conquering markets, eliminating competition and securing monopolies.

The second type is what I would call ventriloquist identification. This is the obverse of projective identification and happens when someone presents him/herself as the mouthpiece for others, as if the speaker were immersed in some ecstatic fusion with the other's voices and were speaking from within that other social or cultural space. The fantasy at play here, in the realm of film studies as well as in film-making, is that of the middle-class intellectual or entrepreneur who is so traumatised by his or her privileged education and access to expensive communications technology that s/he feels compelled to abdicate from intellectual responsibilities and to pretend to be a mere hollow vessel through which the voice of the oppressed, the voice of the people, resonates. The attitude remains the same regardless of whether those other people are defined in terms of class, gender, ethnicity, religion, nationality, community or whatever. Ventriloquism is the monopolist-imperialist's guilty conscience: it allows him or her to remain an authoritarian monopolist while parading one's crocodile tears.

The third type, predictably, avoids both these undesirable but very widespread attitudes. It does not appropriate the other's discourse, it does not subordinate itself to the other's discourse and neither does it pretend to be fused with it. With increasing frequency, this third practice is described with the Bakhtinian phrase: the dialogic mode. Unfortunately, this is a complete misunderstanding of Bakhtin's notion of dialogism, which is in fact an inherent characteristic of all language and of all communication. In other words, it is completely meaningless to try to distinguish one practice from another by calling one dialogic and the other, presumably, monologic. It is worth pointing out that Bakhtin revised his work on Dostoevsky in the light of this insight into the social nature of language itself, and tried to distinguish between the ways in which texts activated their inherently dialogic aspects.

More useful is the notion of creative understanding and the crucial concept of alterity, of otherness, which he introduces into his theories. To clarify this point, I would like to repeat the quote from Bakhtin on creative understanding, or, as Raymond Williams called it, diagnostic understanding:

> There exists a very strong, but one-sided and thus untrustworthy idea that in order better to understand a foreign culture, one must enter into it, forgetting one's own, and view the world through the eyes of this foreign culture [this is what I called ventriloquist identification]. Of course, the possibility of seeing the world through its eyes is a necessary part of the process of understanding it; but if this were the only aspect, [i]t would merely be a duplication and would not entail anything enriching. Creative understanding does not renounce itself, its own place and time, its own culture; it forgets nothing. In order to understand, it is immensely important [t]o be located outside the object of creative understanding, in time, in space, in culture. In the realm of culture, outsideness is a most powerful factor in understanding. [W]e raise new questions for a foreign culture, ones it did not raise for itself; we seek answers to our questions in it; and the foreign culture responds to us by revealing to us its new aspects and semantic depths. Without one's own questions, one cannot creatively understand anything other or foreign. Such a dialogic encounter of two cultures does not result in merging or mixing. Each retains its own unity and open totality, but they are both enriched. (Bakhtin 1986: 6–7)

My own conclusion from Bakhtin's discussion of creative understanding is that one must be 'other' oneself if anything is to be learned about the meanings of other cultures, of another culture's limits, the effectiveness of its borders, of the areas where, in another memorable phrase of Bakhtin's, 'the most intense and productive life of culture takes place'. It must be stressed that for Bakhtin, creative understanding requires a thorough knowledge of at least two cultural spheres. It is not simply a matter of engaging in a dialogue with some other culture's products, but of using one's understanding of another cultural practice to re-perceive and rethink one's own cultural constellation at the same time. If the critical study of, say, Chinese or Indian cinemas is not also aimed at modifying our Euro-American notions of cinema, then why study these cultural practices at all? Simple curiosity does not sound like a persuasive answer.

Bakhtin's three ways of relating to other cultural practices can be neatly illustrated by the way in which many film critics approach, for instance, the Hindi cinema. The first and most widespread approach is a demonstration of Bakhtin's first type of interpretation: projective identification. It deploys a scornful amusement at Indian commercial cinema, marvelling at the infantile eccentricities of an intellectually underdeveloped mass audience supplied with entertainment by a film industry that matches its quaintly simple-minded naiveté. The criteria used to justify such a discourse invariably erect a mid-twentieth-century European bourgeoisie's notions of art into a self-evident, universally applicable norm against which to test the rest of humanity's degree of civilisation. Increasingly, a variant of this approach can be found in the writings of advocates of the postmodernist persuasion, who project the modalities of finance capital's corporate cultural forms (corporate raiding and short-term investments in diversified portfolios for quick profits), operative in some large urban conurbations, onto 'the global culture' in general.

The second approach mirrors this process of projective identification, but simply operates an ethical inversion of the terms. Anglo-American notions of popular culture are projected onto the Indian cinema and, suddenly, the products of the Hindi film industry become examples of 'the people's culture' in exactly the same way that, for instance, Hollywood is said to be a site of the people's culture in the West. That is ventriloquist identification. It validates the Hindi cinema by pointing to the vast box-office takings of its more lucrative products. Something that such large numbers of people want to pay for must be popular culture. To dismiss the cultural products involved is to dismiss those who derive pleasure from them. On the other hand, to validate the products is to identify with the downtrodden people who enjoy them. An unfailing characteristic of this populist position is the constant reference to pleasure in its discourses. In fact, such a position equates units of pleasure with units of the local currency as they appear on the balance sheet of a business enterprise. It also fails to distinguish between the various types of pleasure that can be derived from cultural practices or objects: the pleasures of mastery, of submission, of repetition, of difference, of narcissism, and so on. Consequently, the populist position is also blind to the way in which particular cultural-economic practices seek to bind specific pleasures to specific types of product, while ruling other pleasures out. In discussions of popular culture in Britain and in the US, the pleasures of understanding are nearly always outlawed or stigmatised by associating them with, for instance, 'white middle-class male values', a phrase deployed as a kind of ritual curse, but which has little if any explanatory value. Indeed, in nearly all Hollywood's films, the pleasures of understanding are simply dismissed as forms of psychosis likely to turn you into a serial killer. Spot the character who reads or writes books, the one with an interest in some form of culture other than television or 'entertainment', and you will have found the psycho of the story. The odd sentimentalised hagiography of a

Iris (Richard Eyre, 2001)

canonised artist merely confirms that this is the rule (see, for instance, Richard Eyre's banal *Iris*, US/UK, 2001).

Before going on to talk about necessary outsideness, a transitional subcategory has to be taken into account. This subcategory corresponds to the traditional scholarly approach to the history of cinema in India, chronicling trends and formulating historical narratives, while avoiding, to some extent at least, legitimising or instrumentalising positions. The value of this approach depends on the quality of the historiographic skills deployed. Admittedly, these narratives are often riddled with elements of both the populist and the projectivist tendencies, which does not make life any easier for the reader who has to unravel the useful leads from a hopelessly tangled discursive web. However, this scholarly approach is still to be welcomed for its efforts to provide much-needed information, even though its narratives must be treated with extreme caution. This is a transitional moment in the process of engagement with otherness, because it still maps the familiar Western reductive paradigms onto, for instance, the development of the Indian film industry. But to the extent that the effort is genuinely scholarly, this type of historiography is also bound to register areas of difference where the object of study resists the interpretative framework projected upon it. For instance, Barnouw and Krishnaswamy's history of the *Indian Cinema* (1963; revised edn 1980) uses Lewis Jacobs' *The Rise of the American Film* (1939) as its main model. But whereas Jacobs offers a standard romantic version of the way in which the industry destroys individual genius (Chaplin, Stroheim, Welles), Barnouw and Krishnaswamy find themselves stuck for individual geniuses in the Western mould (until Satyajit Ray). Consequently, they promote powerful actors and studio bosses as the individuals of genius: genius-entrepreneurs, rather than genius-artists. In this way, they have difficulty assessing the value of Guru Dutt or of Ritwik Ghatak, since both operated in relation to India's commercial and (already industrially inflected) traditional aesthetic practices.

Bakhtin's third type of encounter is only now beginning to be attempted in the form of arguments around the mutually defining relationship between historiographic, economic and cultural analyses. One such approach was formulated in the context of debate around notions of Third Cinema in the later 1980s and early 1990s (Willemen 1994: 175–205; Shohat and Stam 1994). It is an approach which concentrates on the need to understand the dynamics of a particular cultural practice within its own social formation. However, that social formation is simultaneously taken as a historical construct, and thus as an object of transformation rather than a given essence hiding deep within the national soul. In this way, the analyst's own socio-cultural formation is brought into focus as a historical construct, equally in need of transformation. The engagement with other cultural practices can (and in my view must) thus be geared towards the unblocking, or the transformation, of aspects of the analyst's own cultural situation. In a way, we are talking here about a double outsideness: the analyst must relate to his or her own situation as an other, refusing simple identifications with pre-given, essentialised socio-cultural categories. At the same time, such identifications with group identities 'elsewhere' must be resisted as well, since the object of study is precisely the intricate, dynamic interconnections of processes which combine to form a socio-cultural constellation (a Benjaminian notion quoted in Buck-Morss 1981: 57). Some of the forces at work in such a constellation will tend towards the containment of elements likely to challenge its fragile and always provisional cohesion; others will tend towards the consolidation of unequal balances of power; still others will promote collusion with, or resistance to, the reigning balance of power. Identities, whether individuated or group ones, are riven as well as constituted by such tensions. Indeed, identities are the names we give to the more or less stable figures of condensation located at the intersection of psycho-social processes. It is, then, perfectly possible to ask questions outlawed by populist instrumentalism as well as by projectivist appropriation. In the case of Indian cinemas, it allows us to address questions regarding the mobilisation of pre-capitalist ideologies and capitalist but anti-imperialist tendencies among urban workers and underclasses; about the operative differences between central and regional capitals, and so on. Thirdly, this type of approach allows us to envisage the possibility that in some circumstances, bourgeois cultural trends may have a greater emancipatory potential than anti-capitalist ones which hark back to an idealised fantasy of pre-colonial innocence.

More importantly, the outsideness approach requires us to conceptualise texts and other practices as potentially comprising many different, even contradictory strands: some aspects of a text may pull in one direction, while others will pull in a totally different one, with yet others exerting pressure in diametrically opposed vectors. For, from a historical critical perspective, the fundamental question to ask of a film is: in which direction does this particular bundle of discourses seek to move its viewers or readers? Obviously, answers to that question will always be provisional and context-dependent, that is to say, dependent on the context within which these questions and answers are meant to achieve a degree of productivity.

Finally, two caveats may be in order. The first one is that although it is necessary for Western intellectuals to address, for instance, the cinema in India, with one eye on their own situation, their other eye must remain focused on the potential effects of their discourses within the Indian situation. This uncomfortably cross-eyed mode of operation is absolutely vital if Western intellectuals, however well-intentioned, are to avoid obstructing the work of Indian allies. The unfortunate facts of imperialism mean that the power relations between Indian and Western intellectuals are still uneven. This is clearly evident, for instance, from the fact that Indian film-makers can secure production finance at least partly on the strength of their reputation in the West. Consequently, in their efforts to draw attention to particular aspects of cultural practices in India likely to assist desirable developments in Western cultural practices, Western intellectuals must be careful not to lend inadvertent support to work which, in India, obstructs the very positions they are trying to support. Differences between, say, Ireland and Britain, or Korea and Japan, require a similar approach. If this cross-eyed dialectic is forgotten, the term 'specificity' loses any meaning and any notion of creative or diagnostic understanding. That would be unfortunate, since a position of double outsideness, that is to say, of in-between-ness, is the precondition for any useful engagement with 'the national' in film culture.

The second caveat concerns cinema itself as a so-called medium and as an industry. In many respects, the very unitarian, homogenising notions of 'the' nation and of 'the' cinema are complicit with each other: each demands its own historicising narratives, founding or originary moments, linear string of periodisations, and so on. And just as national boundaries are both a fact and a process – making the 'national' emerge in the process of addressing the compexities, failures and effectiveness of a geographically bounded network of institutions that constitutes any given 'state' – so are the boundaries of cinema itself as 'a medium', both a fact and a process. The fact of cinema is bounded by the network of industrial institutions which govern and define specific ways of producing and circulating specific objects: films. These institutions are most commonly identified as studios, production companies, distributors, exhibitors and the like. The histories of these companies may be narrated as regional sub-sets or sectors of a national industry. To ignore the effective ways in which a particular film industry is stitched into a state's institutional network amounts to depriving oneself of the means to understand the dynamics which, although rarely governing the film industry directly, at least decisively shape its options, procedures, and thus its products. At the same time, cinema is a process the boundaries of which are not reducible to those of any national industry. Different temporalities and histories of perception, rhythms of modernisation and technology, trade routes, not to mention the equally transnational dimensions of adjacent cultural industries such as publishing, theatre or music, affect the functioning of any given cinema. All of these factors are caught in the encompassing dynamics of industrialisation and in its consequent versions of cultural modernisation. Cinema itself emerges as an object in the same way that the nation becomes manifest: in the process of addressing the specific dynamics underpinning and regulating power relations between and within institutional networks. That process is never neutral; as a process, it always seeks to move in a particular direction, towards an arrangement of power-relations that is to be identified and calibrated as somewhere along the continuum between absolute democracy and absolutist authoritarianism. In the same way that 'the nation' is configured in the process of addressing the terms and consequences of a particular system of cohesion among a geographically bounded set of institutions, so is 'cinema' only an 'object' that emerges in the interactions between a loosely bounded industrial sector and that sector's complex relations to a 'national' institutional configuration.

Consequently, what may be cinema in one country may not be so in another one, a conclusion that must have some implications for film theory as well as for film history. A prominent example of such a problem is presented by the notion of cinema in Britain. Having tried to foster a 'national' cinema in the aftermath of World War II by means of quota legislation, the British government found itself being frowned upon by Washington and quickly took steps to reassure the USA of its submission. Having allowed British cinema to become a colony of Hollywood, the British government sought to regain some measure of cultural hegemony within its own territory by way of television. As the history of, and the debates around, both censorship and production in Britain demonstrate, the domestic film industry was subordinated to, and controlled via, an adjacent industry: television. One of the peculiar results of this development is that British cinema went from being a promise to being a ruin without ever having become anything much in its own right, except perhaps in the decade from the late 1930s to the late 1940s and, subsequently, only in areas that escaped television's reach – for instance, the exploitation cinema practised by Hammer or Amicus, or by the avant-garde and independent cinema sectors prior to their (voluntary) subordination to television from the early 1980s onwards. In other countries, film industries were caught within, and defined by, different kinds of institutional dynamics. In France or to some extent in the US, it would be absurd to write a history of cinematic production dominated by telefilms, whereas in Britain, it has become impossible to do otherwise. What cinema is varies according to the dynamics at work within and between industrial and governmental institutional networks. This does not entitle us to ignore cinema or to declare it dead. It merely requires us to 'think' cinema not as an immutable object, but as a historically (institutionally) delineated set of practices caught within, among others, the dynamics besetting and characterising a national configuration.

Notes

1. Parts of this essay were first given as a paper in Canberra (1989), then published as 'The National' in Willemen 1994: 206–19.

2. After 1945, internationalism migrated from the sphere of socialist and working-class politics to that of the now fully hegemonic bourgeoisies, both in Europe and in most of the decolonising independence movements, while socialist politics began to emphasise a national, even nationalist, political rhetoric.

3. In 2004, the Northern Irish representative of the UK Film Council unashamedly declared, in public, at a conference held at a university, that one needed to be mentally in top condition to

be able to deal with subtitles, and that this was not something that the UK Film Council could be expected to address since its remit was to cater for the majority of the UK's population.

4. See, for instance, the proliferation of conferences devoted to Asian film studies in 1989–90, not to mention many of the contributions published in film journals and the proliferation of 'introductory' books on non-Euro-American cinemas. This development may well be one of the main reasons why the more productive contributions to film studies are increasingly to be found in cultural studies journals such as *Positions, UTS Review, Journal of Arts and Ideas, Traces* and *Inter-Asia Cultural Studies.*

5. In this respect, the European Union constitutes a massive obstacle. Previously it was difficult but possible to create breathing spaces and a basic economic infrastructure for an independent cinema determined to address the complexities of a national socio-cultural formation by seeking to mobilise the democratic potential available in national institutions. Now the European Union's media policies have been put into place to minimise that democratic potential and to enable a few European industrialists with multinational aspirations to compete better with Hollywood's globalising project. Today in Europe, in order to bring about better opportunities for independently minded film-makers, it has been made necessary to organise a campaign for change capable of persuading a significant number of European governments to change their policies and representatives in the secretive media committees tucked away, with lavish funding, in the recesses of the European Union's labyrinthine structures.

References

Bakhtin, Mikhail M. (1986), *Speech Genres and Other Late Essays*, Emerson, Caryl and Holquist, Michael (eds), translated by Vern W. McGee, Austin: University of Texas Press.

Buck-Morss, Susan (1981), 'Walter Benjamin – Revolutionary Writer, Pt 1', *New Left Review* 128: 57.

Gellner, Ernest (1964), *Thought and Change*, London: Weidenfeld & Nicolson.

Nairn, Tom (1988), *The Enchanted Glass: Britain and its Monarchy*, London: Radius.

Rohdie, Sam (1990), *Antonioni*, London: BFI.

3 Reconceptualising National Cinema/s[1]

Stephen Crofts

Varieties of National Cinema Production

Especially in the West, national cinema production is usually defined against Hollywood. This extends to such a point that in Western discussions, Hollywood is hardly ever spoken of as a national cinema, perhaps indicating its transnational reach. That Hollywood has dominated most world film markets since as early as 1919 is well known (Thompson 1985; Guback 1976; Sklar 1975). Whereas in 1914 90 per cent of films shown worldwide were French, by 1928, 85 per cent were American (Moussinac 1967: 238). And for all the formal disinvestiture secured domestically by the 1948 Paramount Decree, transnationally Hollywood still operates effectively as a vertically integrated business organisation.

Throughout most film-viewing countries outside South and Southeast Asia, Hollywood has successfully exported and naturalised its construction of the cinema as fictional entertainment customarily requiring narrative closure and assuming a strong individual – usually male – hero as the necessary agent of that closure. In anglophone markets especially, Hollywood interests have often substantially taken control of the distribution and exhibition arms of the domestic industry. Elsaesser can thus comment: 'Hollywood can hardly be conceived [a]s totally other, since so much of any nation's film culture is implicitly "Hollywood"' (1987: 166).

In the context of such unequal cultural and economic exchange, most national cinema producers have to operate in terms of an agenda set by Hollywood – though, as indicated by the fourth variety of national cinema listed below, some Asian cinemas significantly maintain their own terrain. The political, economic and cultural regimes of different nation-states license some seven varieties of 'national cinema' sequenced in rough order of decreasing familiarity to the present readership:

1) cinemas which differ from Hollywood, but do not compete directly, by targeting a distinct, specialist market sector;
2) those which differ, do not compete directly *but* do directly *critique* Hollywood;
3) European and Third World entertainment cinemas which struggle against Hollywood with limited or no success;

4) cinemas which ignore Hollywood, an accomplishment managed by few;

5) anglophone cinemas which try to beat Hollywood at its own game;

6) cinemas which work within a wholly state-controlled and often substantially state subsidised industry; and,

7) regional or national cinemas whose culture and/or language take their distance from the nation-states which enclose them.

It should be noted at the outset that, as in most taxonomies, these categories are highly permeable. Not only do individual films cross-breed from between different groups, but a given national cinema, operating different production sectors, will often straddle these groupings. Thus French cinema operates in the first and third fields, with exceptional forays into the second, and Australian in the fifth and first with yet rarer excursions into the second, while India produces in the fourth, the first and the second. Moreover, the export of a given text may shift its category, most commonly recycling films of the second and sixth groupings as the first, as art cinema.

a) European–model Art Cinemas

This is, to most of the present readership, the best known form of national cinema. Indeed, it constitutes the limits of some accounts of national cinema which collapse national cinema into the European art film flourishing in the 1960s and 1970s (Neale 1981). This model aims to differentiate itself textually from Hollywood, to assert explicitly or implicitly an indigenous product, and to reach domestic and export markets through those specialist distribution channels and exhibition venues usually called 'arthouse'. Outside Europe, the model includes, for example, the art cinema of India exemplified by Satyajit Ray, as well as the Australian period film.

Insofar as the discourses supporting such a model of national cinema are typically bourgeois nationalist, they also subtend the European popular cinemas considered below. Those of the former are more elitist and more targeted at export markets for financial and cultural reasons. (This is not to say, of course, that popular cinemas do not seek out foreign markets.) National pride and the assertion at home and abroad of national cultural identity have been vital in arguing for art cinemas. Central, too, have been arguments about national cultural and literary traditions and quality as well as their consolidation and extension through a national cinema; hence the frequent literary sources and tendencies in this European model of national cinema (Elsaesser 1989: 108, 333).

Such arguments have issued in and maintained legislation for European cinemas of quality as well as European popular cinemas. The most meaningful legislation has been that for state subvention, directly via grants, loans, prizes and awards, or indirectly through taxation (the state in the post-World War II period replaces the private patronage which outside Russia substantially supported the art/avant-garde cinema of the 1920s). State legislation has also been used to govern quotas and tariffs on imported films. These various legislative and financial arrangements allow for the establishment of what Elsaesser calls a 'cultural mode of production' (1989: 41–3) as distinct from the industrial mode of Hollywood. Though it depends on state subsidies – increasingly via television – this production mode is successful because of a meshing, often developed over decades, between economic and cultural interests in the country concerned. Such a mesh is less common in other modes of national cinemas considered below. Significantly, as elucidated by Colin Crisp, the French cinema – that most successfully nationalist of national cinemas – became so in the post-1945 era by virtue of its cinema workers' vigorous campaign against the post-Vichy influx of Hollywood films which obliged the government to impose a quota on Hollywood imports as well as box-office taxes to subsidise indigenous feature film production (Crisp 1993). A key variant affecting the success of an art cinema is the cultural status of cinema relative to other artistic practices in the country concerned. France rates cinema more highly than West Germany, for instance, with Britain in between, and Australia, adopting a European funding model, hovers near the bottom.

Hollywood's development of its own art cinema has contributed to a blurring of boundaries between specialist and entertainment market sectors in its own market and abroad, and has weakened the assertions of independence made by other art cinemas. The generic mixing of Hollywood from, say, the early 1960s has been complicated by its interchange with European art cinema developments. Hollywood has developed its own art cinema after and alongside the spaghetti Western, *nouvelle vague hommages* to Hollywood genres and directors, Fassbinder's recasting of Hollywood melodrama and gangster genres and the adoption by such directors as Schlöndorff and Hauff of Hollywood genres and modes of character identification to deal with nationally specific West German issues. Penn, Altman, Schrader and Allen in the first wave all had their own favourite European influences, while a later star such as Lynch arrives with a more postmodernist pedigree, and Soderbergh, Hartley and Stillman have more modest projects. A principal upshot has been a blurring of national cinema differences. Coupled with the aging market demographics of the European art film – the babyboomers forsake the cinema for their families – this blurring leaves these production sectors less able to differentiate their product from Hollywood's. Such insecurity is compounded by substantial American successes at recent Cannes festivals, long the preserve of European films.

While a politicised art cinema diverges from the metaphysical orientation of the textual norms cited above, state subsidy does impose limitations. Elsaesser neatly pinpoints the contradictions ensuing from state subsidy of a cultural mode of film production: it encourages aesthetic difference from the dominant (Hollywood) product, but discourages biting the hand that feeds it (1989: 44). In the West German instance, this tension explains the adoption of political allegory as a mode of self-censorship, as variously seen in *Artists at the Top of the Big Top: Disoriented* (A. Kluge, 1967) (as regards state funding of film), *The American Friend* (W. Wenders, 1977) (American cultural influences in West Germany) and *Germany, Pale Mother* (H. Sanders Brahms, 1979) (recent German history and feminist readings of it). Left political films found their way through the liberal pluralist interstices of such cultural funding arrangements: for example, the critical realism of a Rosi or a Rossellini and the critical anti-realism of Kluge and Straub-Huillet. Godard, in the heady affluent days of turn-of-the-70s New Leftism, constituted a limit-case: on the basis of his cultural prestige as renowned art film director, he persuaded four television stations to finance ultra-leftist films, only one of which was then screened (Crofts 1972: 37). Such explicit leftism partly borrows its discourses from, and marks a border zone between, a European art cinema and the second mode of national cinema.

b) Third Cinema

1960s–1970s Third Cinema opposed the USA and Europe in its anti-imperialist insistence on national liberation, and in its insistence on the development of aesthetic models distinct from those of Hollywood and European art cinema. As Getino and Solanas proclaimed in their famous 1969 manifesto 'Towards a Third Cinema':

> While, during the early history [o]f the cinema, it was possible to speak of a German, an Italian or a Swedish cinema clearly differentiated from, and corresponding to, specific national characteristics, today such differences have disappeared. The borders were wiped out along with the expansion of US imperialism and the film model that it imposed: Hollywood movies. [T]he first alternative to this type of cinema [a]rose with the so called 'author cinema', [t]he second cinema. This alternative signified a step forward inasmuch as it demanded that the filmmaker be free to express him/herself in non-standard language. [B]ut such attempts have already reached, or are about to reach, the outer limits of what the system permits. [I]n our times it is hard to find a film within the file of commercial cinema in both the capitalist and socialist countries, that manages to avoid the models of Hollywood pictures. (1969: 20–1)

From the perspective of revolutionary, national liberation movements in Latin American, African and Asian nations, such an identification of 'first' with 'second' cinemas has an understandable basis in a critique of bourgeois individualism. For the existentialist-influenced 'universal' humanism of much 1960s art cinema (canonically Bergman, Antonioni, Resnais) shares a Western individualism with the achieving heroes of Hollywood who resolve plots within the global-capitalist terms of a US world view.

Third Cinema has proven to be one of the more elastic signifiers in the cinematic lexicon. Some writers have tried to homogenise the enormously diverse range of Third World film production under its rubric (see Burton 1985: 6-10 and Willemen 1987: 21–3 discussing Gabriel 1986), while others have sought to build on the 1960s liberationist political moment of Getino and Solanas's manifesto, a moment extending well into the 1980s in ex-Portuguese colonies in Africa. Insofar as Third Cinema distinguishes itself politically and largely aesthetically from Hollywood and European art cinema models, its history has been a fitful one. In its concern with 'a historically analytic yet culturally specific mode of cinematic discourse' (Willemen 1987: 8), its radical edge distinguished it also from the bulk of Third World production, primarily devoted to comedies, action genres, musicals and varieties of melodrama/romance/ titillation. Especially in the 1960s, such radicalism rendered Third Cinema liable to ferocious censorship. More recently, Third Cinema abuts and overlaps with art film's textual norms and, its militant underground audience lost, seeks out art cinema's international distribution-exhibition channels. Names such as those of Solanas, Mrinal Sen, **47**

Tahimik, Sembene and Cissé serve notice of the ongoing importance of Third Cinema as a cinema of political and aesthetic opposition.

It follows from its political oppositionality and Third World 'national (cultural) power-lessness' (Stam 1991: 227) that funding for such cinema is highly unreliable. In the instance of films from impoverished, black African one-party states with few cinemas and minimal film culture, film subsidy is more easily found in France, in Switzerland, or from the UK's Channel Four and BBC 2. Such production conditions give Third Cinema a more urgent intensity than the political allegories of West German cinema and raise vital questions about the cultural role played by First World financing of Third World cinemas. Rod Stoneman of Channel Four sounds an appropriate warning note on international co-productions: 'Vital though the input of hard currency from European television may be, it is important that it does not distort the direction of African cinema' (quoted in Leahy 1991: 65).

Discourses on Third Cinema undo many First World notions of national cinema, perhaps most strikingly the notion of national cultural sovereignty. As polemically adopted by the 1986 Edinburgh Film Festival Special Event on the topic, Third Cinema offered a particular reconceptualisation of national cinema. It became a means of disaggregating the congealed stolidity of a British film culture unwilling to recognise in its midst a plethora of ethnic, gender, class and regional differences (Pines and Willemen 1989). The Event extended the definition of Third Cinema to take in, for instance, black British cinema. Another conceptual

48 *Ju Dou* (Zhang Yimou, 1990)

dividend of Third Cinema is its decisive refutation of the easy Western assumption of the coincidence of ethnic background and home. Pinochet's military dictatorship in Chile, for example, produced a diasporic cinema. As Zuzana Pick notes: 'The dispersal of film-makers [m]ade problematic their identification within the Chilean national and cultural formation' (1987: 41). Similarly exiled have been such erstwhile Fifth Generation Chinese film-makers as Wu Tianming, Chen Kaige, Huang Jianxin and Zhang Yimou, whose *Ju Dou* (1990), co-produced with a Japanese company, is still banned in China, probably for its allegorical reso-nances of the 1960s–89 period as well as for the expressed concern that it is a 'foreign exposé' of a 'backward China'. And within their 'own' countries film-makers such as Paradjanov and Yilmaz Güney have been exiled and/or imprisoned. Such troublings of First World homogenising concepts of nation will be pursued later.

c) Third World and European Commercial Cinemas

Art cinema and Third Cinema, the two best-known reactions to Hollywood, do not exhaust the field. Both Europe and the Third World produce commercial cinemas which compete, with varying degrees of success, with Hollywood product in domestic markets. These cin-emas, and all those considered henceforth, are less well known than the first two because they are less exported to the European and anglophone film cultures which largely define the critical terms of national cinemas. Much Third World production, as distinct from Third Cinema, aims, like European art cinema, to compete with Hollywood in indigenous markets – or, in Africa, with Indian cinema too – but it differs from European art cinema in being populist. European commercial cinema, however, should be treated here. It targets a market sector somewhat distinct from European-model art cinema, and thus vies more directly with Hollywood for box office. Typical genres of a European commercial cinema include the thriller, comedy and, especially in the 1960s, soft-core.

Excluding the booming economies of East Asia, the dependent capitalist status of most Third World countries, with stop-go economies and vulnerability to military dictatorships with short cultural briefs, rarely provides the continuous infrastructural support which nur-tures indigenous cinemas. Economic dependency and hesitant cultural commitment typi-cally promote private over public forms of investment which further weaken indigenous film production. John King notes the common failure in Latin America to bite the bullet for import quotas:

In general the state has been more successful in stimulating production than in altering dis-tribution and exhibition circuits. The transnational and local monopolies have strongly resis-ted any measures to restrict the free entry of foreign films and have grudgingly obeyed, or even ignored, laws which purport to guarantee screen time to national products. [T]he logic of state investment was largely economic: to protect the profits of dominantly private investors. There are fewer examples of what Thomas Elsaesser calls a 'cultural mode of pro-duction'. (1990: 248–9)

Throughout the Third World, with exceptions, noted below, foreign (mainly Hollywood) films dominate local screens. Even in Turkey, where 'film production was [n]either dominated by foreign companies nor supported or tightly controlled by the state [t]he market was still dominated by the four or five hundred imported films (mostly Hollywood movies)' (Armes 1987: 195–6). Uruguay represents an extreme instance, insofar as it has a dynamic film culture and almost no local production (King 1990: 97). Yet that same film culture afforded more admissions to Solanas's *Tangos: El Exilio de Gardel* (1985) than to *Rambo: First Blood* (T. Kotcheff, 1992) (Solanas 1990: 115). Slightly differently, Tunisia has since 1966 hosted the significant Carthage Film Festival while having only some seventy film theatres, insufficient to sustain regular local production. In francophone black Africa, only recently has the French distribution duopoly been displaced, allowing the screening of more African films on African screens (Armes 1987: 212, 223).

Countries of the East Asian economic boom clearly differ. While Japan is Hollywood's largest overseas market, in 1988 domestic product retained 49.7 per cent of box office (Lent 1990: 47), specialising largely in soft-core and adolescent melodramas (Umemoto 1990: 110). And South Korea in the same year battled the MPEAA to reduce Hollywood imports to roughly five per year (Lent 1990: 122–3). As such, it broaches the category of 'Ignoring Hollywood'.

d) Ignoring Hollywood

In Paul Willemen's gloss, 'some countries (especially in Asia) have managed to prevent Hollywood from destroying their local film industry' (1987: 25). This option is open only to nation-states with large domestic markets and/or effective trade barriers, such as India and Hong Kong (there are some similarities between these countries and totalitarian cinemas considered below). In these Asian countries, culturally specific cinemas can arise and flourish. In Hong Kong, the national cinema outsells Hollywood by a factor of four to one. And in India the national cinema sells four times as many tickets per year as does Hollywood in the US. In 1988, a typical year, the Indian industry produced 773 films, 262 more than Hollywood. That Indian features are produced in some twenty languages for local consumption protects Indian films very ably from foreign competition (Lent 1990: 230–1). And in the Hollywood vein – if less expansively – Bombay exports its product to Indian communities worldwide, just as Hong Kong exports through East Asia, dominating the Taiwan market, for instance, and to Chinatowns throughout the Western world. Furthermore, Indian cinema long colonised Ceylon (now Sri Lanka). All Sinhalese films prior to 1956 were made in South India, and 'local actors were decked out as Indian heroes and heroines who mouthed Sinhalese' (Coorey and Jayatilaka 1974: 303).

e) Imitating Hollywood

Some sectors of some national cinemas have sought to beat Hollywood at its own game – and overwhelmingly failed. Such aspirations have emanated largely from anglophone countries: Britain, Canada, Australia. State investment in the countries' film industries has secured relatively stable production levels, but has not guaranteed a culturally nationalist product.

Anglophony has encouraged these nations to target the West's largest, most lucrative – and well-protected – market, that of the US. But these national cinemas have already had their indigenous cultural bases modified, if not undercut, by the substantial inroads made into domestic distribution and exhibition by Hollywood interests and product. Geoffrey Nowell-Smith's provocative remarks on British cinema are yet more pertinent to Canada and Australia: 'British cinema is in the invidious position of having to compete with an American cinema which, paradoxical as this may seem, is by now far more deeply rooted in British cultural life than is the native product' (1985: 152). Already weaker than those of major European countries, the local film cultures of these anglophone nations have been further weakened through the 1980s by the unequal economic exchanges which have locked British, Canadian and Australian film production increasingly into dependence on the US market through pre-sales and distribution guarantees. For each success story like *A Fish Called Wanda* (C. Crichton, 1988) and *Crocodile Dundee* (P. Faiman, 1986) which have drawn on some local cultural values, there have been hundreds of films made in these lesser-player countries which, in trying to second-guess the desires of the US market, have produced pallid imitations. An index of the price exacted for the American/world distribution of *Crocodile Dundee* can be seen in the re-editing required by Paramount, which quickened the narrative pace and made the film look more like a wholesome family entertainment (Crofts 1990). A fantasy of a foreign market can, then, exercise an inordinate influence over 'national' product.

The logic of such blithe bleaching-out of domestic cultural specificity can have two further consequences: the country may become an offshore production base for Hollywood – witness Britain, Canada and Australia's branch of Warner Bros' 'Hollywood on the Gold Coast' – or Hollywood may exercise its longstanding vampirism of foreign talent (Prédal 1990). In the Australian case, all the major name directors of the 1980s have now moved to Hollywood, most without returning to Australia: the two George Millers, Peter Weir, Gillian Armstrong, Fred Schepisi, Bruce Beresford, Phil Noyce, Carl Schultz, Simon Wincer. Four leading Australian actors have now made the Hollywood grade: Mel Gibson, Judy Davis, Bryan Brown, Colin Freils. Even that stalwart of Australian cultural nationalism, playwright and scriptwriter David Williamson, has been writing a script in Hollywood. Similar relations obtain between Bangladeshi and Indian cinemas.

f) Totalitarian Cinemas

Sixthly, there is the national cinema of the totalitarian state: Fascist Germany and Italy, Chinese cinema between 1949 and the mid-1980s, and, of course, the Stalinist regimes of the Soviet bloc. By far the predominant mode of the communist brand of such national cinemas has been socialist realism, which sought to convince viewers of the virtues of the existing political order (Crofts 1976). Peripheral to this core production has been the often political art cinema of Tarkovsky, Jancsó, Makaveyev, Wajda, various proponents of the Cuban and Czech New Waves, and Chinese Fifth Generation cinema. Such peripheral production has been conditional upon the liberalism or otherwise of national policies at the time, both as regards cultural production and the cultural diplomacy of products exported. A further aspect of any analysis of this mode of national cinema might seek to disentangle cultural specificities from the homogenising fictions of nationalism. As Chris Berry notes in surveying Fifth Generation departures from the Han Chinese norm, there are 'fifty six races in the People's Republic' (Berry 1992: 47). The undoubted popularity of such communist and also Fascist cinemas might need to be mapped against the discursive regimes and the range of other entertainment, within and outside the home, offered by such nation-states.

g) Regional/Ethnic Cinemas

Given the historical recentness of the disintegration of the nation-state and its forcefully homogenising discourses and political sanctions, it is not surprising that ethnic and linguistic minorities have generally lacked the funds and infrastructure to support regional cinemas or national cinemas distinct from the nation-states which enclose them. Marvin D'Lugo has written of Catalan cinema as 'something like a national cinema' (1991: 131), but perhaps the best-known regional cinema, the Québecois, has benefited from cultural and political support strong enough to propel its major name director, Denys Arcand, into international fame. Cinemas such as the Welsh have not achieved such prominence nor, within settler societies, have Aboriginal, Maori or Native American cinemas, nor indeed, within an immigrant society, has Chicano cinema, though Afro-American cinema reaches back to Oscar Micheaux and has broken into the mainstream with Spike Lee and others.

Exporting National Cinemas

Whereas Hollywood markets itself through well-established transnational networks and with relatively standardised market pitches of star, genre and production values, the export operations of (other) national cinemas are far more hit-and-miss affairs. Their three principal modes of marketing or product differentiation are by the nation of production, with different national labels serving a sub-generic function; by authorship; and for portions of art cinema, by less censored representations of sexuality, especially in the Bardot days of the 1950s and 1960s, but still now, as witness Almodóvar. All three modes of differentiation were, and remain, defined against Hollywood, promising varieties of authenticity and *frisson* which Hollywood rarely offered. As Hollywood sets the terms of national cinemas' self-marketing, so too does its market power and pervasive ideology of entertainment limit the circulation of national cinemas. In foreign, if not also in their domestic markets, national cinemas are limited to specialist exhibition circuits traditionally distinct from those of Hollywood product. These comprise arthouse cinemas – themselves recently increasingly blurred with mainstream outlets – film festivals, specialist television slots addressing middle- to high-brow viewers, and minority video and laserdisc product, not to mention other, rarer exhibition modes such as community, workplace and campus screenings.

Even for as grand a player as Hollywood, export markets can impose some limitations. Roger Ebert reports that Hollywood's persisting reluctance to figure non-white heroes is attributed within the business to the fact that export markets – despite often being less white than the domestic one – lag behind the temper of the US market (1990). So much the worse, then, for the export aspirations of culturally specific national cinema product. Few states substantially underwrite their export market operations. (The operations of, say, Sov-

ExportFilm until 1989 would repay detailed attention.) Distributor take-up of foreign film material for arthouse circulation frequently excludes the culturally specific. Thus New German Cinema is exported largely without Schroeter or Kluge, and Australian cinema almost entirely without the social-realist film. Such exclusions can enable the resultant cultural constructions of the exporting country in terms of the sun-tinted spectacles of armchair tourism. At film festivals, a major meeting point of national cinema product and potential foreign buyers, the dominant film-critical discourse is the depoliticising one of an essentialist humanism ('the human condition') complemented by a tokenist culturalism ('very French') and an aestheticising of the culturally specific ('a poetic account of local life') (Boehringer and Crofts 1980). With its emphasis on 'originality' and 'creativity', it is this discourse of art cinema which can facilitate the representation of political film in the tamer terms of art cinema (Crofts and Rose 1977: 52–4). As indicated above in 'Imitating Hollywood', national cinema producers often cautiously bank on their foreign markets' imputed disinterest in the culturally specific. Without cross-cultural contextualisation – a broadly educational project – foreign distribution of national cinemas, then, will tend to erase the culturally specific. One shrewd and successful strategy has been the combination of cultural universals (family madness, artistic ambition, rape) with specific local inflections effected by several Australian films of the last few years – *Sweetie* (J. Campion, 1987), *Shame* (S. Jodrell, 1988), *High Tide* (G. Armstrong, 1987) and *Celia* (A. Turner, 1988) – which successfully target European film and TV markets.

Conclusions

Several film-historiographical and film-theoretical conclusions can be developed from the foregoing. In general, this essay seeks to enable a consideration of national cinemas in non-First World terms. This firstly requires acknowledging a wider range of national cinemas than is regularly treated under that rubric. Film scholars' mental maps of world film production are often less than global. Even as assiduously encyclopaedic an historian as Georges Sadoul devotes more pages of his *Histoire du cinéma* to the Brighton School and the beginnings of Pathé than he does to the whole of Latin American cinema between 1900 and 1962 (1962: 43–64, 421–37). As Edward Said magisterially demonstrates with reference to Orientalism as an academic discipline and world view, so the world views of different national film cultures are substantially informed by their country's relations – military, economic, diplomatic, cultural, ethnic – with other parts of the globe (1985). Thus Sadoul, informed by French colonialism, knows more of African cinema than of Latin American, while an American scholar, informed by the US imperium and substantial Hispanic immigration, knows more of Latin American than African cinema, and a British scholar, informed by European and American cultural influences, may not see much outside that transatlantic axis. At the other end of the East–West axis, a hybrid, non-Eurocentric film culture such as the Thai – even if it does not as yet support substantial film scholarship – draws substantially on both Hong Kong and Hollywood sources as well as local production. Annette Hamilton thus remarks that 'the average viewer in Thailand or Singapore has been exposed to a much wider range of visual material in style, genre, and cultural code than is the case for any average Western viewer' (1992: 91).   **53**

Such skewed world views will demonstrably influence canon formation in the country concerned. And given that Third World production – for that is the prime excluded category – is more plentiful than European and North American by a factor of more than two to one (Sadoul 1962: 530–1), Luis Buñuel's trenchant comments on the canon of world literature could justly apply to that of world cinema:

> It seems clear to me that without the enormous influence of the canon of American culture, Steinbeck would be an unknown, as would Dos Passos and Hemingway. If they'd been born in Paraguay or Turkey, no one would ever have read them, which suggests the alarming fact that the greatness of a writer is in direct proportion to the power of his/her country. Galdós, for instance, is often as remarkable as Dostoevsky, but who outside Spain ever reads him? (1984: 222)

To pursue the question of canon formation in relation to national cinemas demands examination not only of historically changing international relations of the kinds set out above, and of the force of such institutions as SovExportFilm and the European Film Development Office in cultural diplomacy, but also of the taste-brokering functions of film festivals and film criticism.

The ongoing critical tendency to hypostatise the 'national' of national cinema must also be questioned in non-First World terms. Not only do regional and diasporic cinema production challenge notions of national cinemas as would-be autonomous cultural businesses. So, too, Hollywood's domination of world film markets renders most national cinemas profoundly unstable market entities, marginalised in most domestic and all export markets, and thus readily susceptible, inter alia, to projected appropriations of their indigenous cultural meanings. Witness the discursive (re)constructions of national cinemas in the process of their being exported. Ahead of India and Hong Kong, Hollywood remains the big(gest) other, the world's only film producer to have anything like a transnational vertical integration of its industry. Study of any national cinema should include distribution and exhibition as well as production within the nation-state.

The nation-state itself has for a while been manifestly losing its sovereignty. It has been pressured both by transnational forces – canonically American in economic and cultural spheres, and Japanese in economic, and more recently, cultural spheres – and simultaneously by the sub-national, sometimes called the local. The multiculturalism, the cultural hybridity of the nation-state has increasingly to be recognised. Recent instances of assertion of ethnicity, for instance, centre on linguistic rights and cultural protection: from the Spanish regular in public notices in American cities to people from the Iberian Peninsula who describe themselves as Basque or Catalan rather than Spanish; from the nationalism of Québecois cinema and Welsh programmes for S4C in the UK to the substantial Greek video markets throughout Australia, especially in Melbourne, the third largest Greek city in the world. Minorities or majorities defined by political dissent, class, ethnicity, gender, religion or region are the everyday stuff of many people's lives: witness the five nations, three religions, four languages and two alphabets which went to constitute the 'nation'

Yugoslavia. Recall, also, from a 1962 essay by Leroi Jones (later Amira Baraka) called 'Black is a Country': 'The Africans, Asians, and Latin Americans who are news today because of their nationalism [a]re exactly the examples the black man [sic] in this country should use in his struggle for *independence*' (1968: 84). Alongside such sub- and supra-national emphases, however, it is vital to recognise the political significance in other contexts, especially in developing countries, of rhetorics of nation and nationalism as means of fighting for independence from imperialist powers. Recall here the dominant genre of Vietnamese cinema, anti-imperialist propaganda.

Politics, in other words, is a matter of unequal distributions of power across axes of nation as well as of class, gender, ethnicity, etc. The political engagements that people do (or do not) make will vary with their social and political contexts, and their readings of those contexts. In considering national cinemas, this implies the importance of a political flexibility able, in some contexts, to challenge the fictional homogenisations of much discourse on national cinema, and in others to support them. And it would be foolhardy to underestimate the continuing power of the nation-state. To acknowledge these powers, by the same token, is not to disavow the cultural hybridity of nation-states; nor to unconditionally promote national identities over those of ethnicity, class, gender, religion, and the other axes of social division which contribute to those identities; nor, finally, to buy into originary fantasies of irrecoverable cultural roots, or into the unitary, teleological and usually masculinist fantasies in which nationalisms display themselves. That said, the struggle of many national cinemas has been one for cultural, if not also economic, self-definition against Hollywood or Indian product.

While cultural specificity, then, is by no means defined exclusively by the boundaries of that recent Western political construct, the nation-state, at certain historical moments – often moments when nationalism connects closely with genuinely populist movements, often nation-building moments (Hinde 1981) – national developments can occasion specifically national filmic manifestations which can claim a cultural authenticity or rootedness. Examples include some of the best-known cinema 'movements'. Italian Neo-Realism, Latin American Third Cinema and Fifth Generation Chinese Cinema all arose on the crest of waves of national-popular resurgence. The French *nouvelle vague* marked a national intellectual-cultural recovery in the making since the late 1940s, whereas the events of May 1968 were more nationally divisive, leaving a clear political imprint in the works of Marker, Karmitz and Godard and Gorin markedly absent from the films of Rohmer or Malle. New German Cinema drew much of its strength, as Elsaesser has shown, from a 1960–70s student audience and an allied concern to make sense of the traumas of recent German history (1989). The Australian feature film revival took off on a surge of cultural nationalism developing through the 1960s. Interestingly, such cinema 'movements' occupy a key position in conventional histories of world cinema, whose historiography is not only nationalist but also elitist in its search for the 'best' films, themselves often the product of such vital politico-cultural moments. As such, these are the films most frequently exported, and thus often occlude critical attention to films which may well be more popular.

In the context of the relations of unequal economic and cultural exchange obtaining between Hollywood and (other) national cinemas, the generation and/or survival of indigenous genres is a gauge of the strength and dynamism of a national cinema. Outstanding instances in non-Hollywood post-1945 cinema would be the Hong Kong martial arts film, the French (stylish) thriller of Chabrol, Beneix and others, and in Britain, the Gothic horror film and the Ealing comedy. Less stable indigenous genres include the *Heimat* film in West Germany and the period film and social-realist film in Australia. A vital research area concerns the intersections between given genres and the national. A range of questions present themselves. For example: under what conditions do culturally specific genres arise? How do imported (usually Hollywood) genres affect the generic range of a given national production sector? Does Chinese production even have genres?

The production category which most obviously confounds any attempts at a neat parcelling of 'national' cinemas is of course the international co-production. This is more likely than not – and regularly so at the upper end of the budget range – to encourage the culturally bland. Nowell-Smith cites *Last Tango in Paris* (B. Bertolucci, 1972) as one of 'a number of recent major films [that] have had no nationality in a meaningful sense at all' (1985: 154). And Rentschler develops a pointed comparison between *The Tin Drum's* (V. Schlöndorff, 1979) easy generalities and the more demanding cultural specificities of *The Patriot* (A. Kluge, 1979) (1984: 58–9).

Gloomy prognostications for a 'Europudding' future of European co-production may well be exaggerated. For alongside directors such as Annaud, Besson and Wenders, who, in *Variety*-speak are 'a chosen few Euro helmers able to finesse international pics' (Williams 1992: 31), there are to be reckoned the strong successes of such culturally specific product (co-produced or not) as *Toto le Heros* (J. Van Dormael, 1991) and *The Commitments* (A. Parker, 1991). While countries with smaller local markets will often use co-production agreements to recoup costs, in the lower and middle budget ranges this need not necessarily work against culturally specific interests. Co-productions are actively encouraged by the European Film Development Office's promotional support for films financed from three or more member countries, and the Office argues its respect for national cultural specificites (Schneider 1992). And international co-productions do positively facilitate the treatment of such supra-national ethnic/religious issues as are dealt with in *Europa, Europa* (A. Holland, 1990). The mesh, or conflict, between economic and culturally specific interests will vary with the interests concerned at a given point in time.

Latent in preceding sections of this essay have been some key theoretical assumptions, and this is the third respect in which cinemas need to be thought of less in First World terms. Gabriel and Stam have both critiqued the imperialist *données* of centre/periphery theories as applied to film theory (Gabriel 1986; Stam 1991) – though it has to be said that, provided multiple centres be recognised, such theories are still crucial to understanding global economic *Realpolitik*.

Underpinning First World approaches to national cinemas is the master antinomy of self/other (the linguistic sexism, as will be seen, is adopted advisedly). This essay suggests the inappropriateness, in theorising differences of nations and national cinemas, of what Homi Bhabha calls the 'exclusionary imperialist ideologies of self and other' (1989: 111). National cinematic self-definition, like *national* self-definition, likes to pride itself on its distinctiveness, on its standing apart from other(s). Such a transcendental concept of an ego repressing its other(s) urges abandonment of the self/other model as an adequate means of thinking national cinemas. For this dualist model authorises only two political stances: imperial aggression and defiant national chauvinism. It can account neither for Third Cinema's move beyond what Solanas calls its 'experimental' phase [1990], nor for the existence of such projects as those of 'Imitating Hollywood'. Still less can it make sense of the hybridity of national cultures, including those of the notionally most pristine imperial centres. Trinh T. Minh-ha well characterises the fluid, labile, hybrid nature of cultural identities:

> Difference in this context undermines opposition as well as separatism. Neither a claim for special treatment, nor a return to an authentic core (the 'unspoiled' Real Other), it acknowledges in each of its moves, the coming together and drifting apart both within and between identity/identities. What is at stake is not only the hegemony of Western cultures, but also their identities as unified cultures; in other words, the realization that there is a Third World in every First World, and vice-versa. The master is made to recognize that His Culture is not as homogeneous, not as monolithic as He once believed it to be; He discovers, often with much reluctance, that He is just an other among others. (1987: 3)

Notes

1. This essay is extracted from a fuller version published in *Quarterly Review of Film and Video* (vol. 14, no. 3: (1993), pp. 49–67) and limits itself to post-1945 feature films.

References

Armes, Roy (1987), *Third World Film Making and the West*, Berkeley: University of California Press.

Berry, Chris (1992), 'Race, Chinese Film and the Politics of Nationalism', *Cinema Journal* 31 (2).

Bhabha, Homi (1989), 'The Commitment to Theory', in Pines, Jim and Willemen, Paul (eds), *Questions of Third Cinema*, London: BFI.

Boehringer, Kathe and Crofts, Stephen (1980), 'The Triumph of Taste', *Australian Journal of Screen Theory* 8.

Bordwell, David (1979), 'Art Film as a Mode of Film Practice', *Film Criticism* 4 (1).

Borwell, David (1985), *Narration in the Fiction Film*, London: Methuen.

Buñuel, Luis (1984), *My Last Sigh*, London: Jonathan Cape.

Burton, Julianne (1985), 'Marginal Cinemas and Mainstream Critical Theory', *Screen* 26 (3–4).

Coorey, Philip and Jayatilaka, Amarnath (1974), 'Sri Lanka (Ceylon)', in Cowie Peter (ed.), *International Film Guide*, London: Tantivy Press.

Crisp, Colin (1993), *Classic French Cinema, 1930–1960*, Bloomington: Indiana University Press.

Crofts, Stephen (1972), *Jean-Luc Godard*, London: BFI.

Crofts, Stephen (1976), 'Ideology and Form: Soviet Socialist Realism and *Chapayev*', *Film Form* 1.

Crofts, Stephen (1980), '*Breaker Morant* Rethought', *Cinema Papers* 30.

Crofts, Stephen (1990), '*Crocodile Dundee* Overseas', *Cinema Papers* 77.

Crofts, Stephen (1991), 'Shifting Paradigms in the Australian Historical Film', *East-West Film Journal* 5 (2).

Crofts, Stephen and Rose, Olivia (1977), 'An Essay Towards Man with a Movie Camera', *Screen*, 18 (1): 9–57.

D'Lugo, Marvin (1991), 'Catalan Cinema: Historical Experience and Cinematic Practice', *Quarterly Review of Film and Video* 13 (1–3).

Ebert, Roger (1990), Public Lecture, University of Honolulu, Hawaii, 28 November.

Elsaesser, Thomas (1980), 'Primary Identification and the Historical Subject: Fassbinder and Germany', *Cine-Tracts* 11.

Elsaesser, Thomas (1987), 'Chronicle of a Death Foretold', *Monthly Film Bulletin* 54 (641).

Gabriel, Teshome (1986), 'Colonialism and "Law and Order" Criticism', *Screen* 27 (3–4).

Getino, Octavio and Solanas, Fernando (1969), 'Towards a Third Cinema', *Afterimage* 3.

Guback, Thomas (1976), 'Hollywood's International Market', in Balio, Tino (ed.), *The American Film Industry*, Madison: University of Wisconsin Press.

Hamilton, Annette (1992), 'The Mediascape of Modern Southeast Asia', *Screen* 33 (1).

Hinde, John (1981), *Other People's Pictures*, Sydney: Australian Broadcasting Commission.

Jones, Leroi (1968), 'Black is a Country', in *Home: Social Essays*, London: MacGibbon and Kee.

Leahy, James (1991), 'Beyond the Frontiers', *Monthly Film Bulletin* 58 (686).

Moussinac, Leon (1967), *L'Age Ingrat du Cinema*, Paris: EFR.

Neale, Steve (1981), 'Art Cinema as Institution', *Screen* 22 (1).

Nowell-Smith, Geoffrey (1985), 'But Do We Need It?', in Auty, Martin and Roddick, Nick (eds), *British Cinema Now*, London: BFI.

Pick, Zuzana (1987), 'Chilean Cinema in Exile', *Framework* 34.

Prédal, René (1990), 'Un Rassemblement mondial de talents', in Bordat, Francis (ed.), *L'amour du cinéma américain*, Paris: CinémAction 54.

Rentschler, Eric (1982), 'American Friends and the New German Cinema', *New German Critique* 24–5.

Sadoul, Georges (1962), *Histoire du cinéma*, Paris: Flammarion.

Said, Edward (1985), *Orientalism*, Harmondsworth: Penguin.

Schneider, Ute (1992), Seminar, Sydney Film Festival, 9 June.

Sklar, Robert (1975), *Movie-Made America*, New York: Random House.

Solanas, Fernando (1990), 'Amerique Latine: le point de vue d'un cinéaste', in Bordat, Francis (ed.), *L'amour du cinéma américain*, Paris: CinémAction 54.

Stam, Robert (1991), 'Eurocentrism, Afrocentrism, Polycentrism', *Quarterly Review of Film and Video* 13 (1–3).

Trinh, T. Minh-ha (1987), 'Introduction', *Discourse* 8.

Umemoto, Yoïchi (1990), 'Quelles images pour le Japon?' in Bordat, Francis (ed.), *L'amour du cinema américain*, Paris: CinémAction 54.

Willemen, Paul (1987), 'The Third Cinema Question: Notes and Reflections', *Framework* 34.

Williams, Michael (1992), 'Films without Frontiers?' *Variety*, 10 February.

Part II Histories

4 Italian Cinema and History[1]

Maria Wyke

Projecting the Past not only contributes to recent debates about definitions of classics and the classical tradition, but also provides a useful point of entry into and interaction with current debates about the nature of history and the relationship between cinema and history. Although films about Nero, for example, centre on the same historical figure and are set in the same historical time and place, they evince interesting ruptures and discontinuities in their portrayal of the emperor's persecutions and pyromania. An exploration of the changing mode of their historical reconstructions and the changing cultural force of their narratives within and between the countries of their production engages with a number of pertinent concerns about history in cinema and cinema in history.

Film is a medium that initially located itself as an extension of nineteenth-century representational forms. The new technology of the moving image could be seen as a further development of nineteenth-century technical progression through engraving, lithography and photography towards ever more refined 'realistic' representations, whether of the present or of the past. Such technological developments further abetted the nineteenth-century historical sensibility that sought to make the past live again in the present. Thus one of the most fascinating attractions which the new medium soon claimed to offer was the possibility of reconstructing the past with a precision and a vivacity superior to that of documentary sources or the nineteenth-century historical fictions of painting, theatre and the novel. In the same year as the release of *The Birth of a Nation* (1915), a monumentally successful epic film that recreated the American Civil War, its director D. W. Griffith wrote in utopian terms of the medium's newly disclosed and unique capacity to narrate history. He declared that cinema was not just a cold instrument for the recording of reality, as in documentary films, but also and above all a powerful mode of historical writing which could better transmit an historical consciousness to the public than months of study. For Griffith, cinema taught history in lightning and would soon usurp the educative value of conventional history books. A year earlier, in Italy, audiences and film reviewers had certainly responded with extraordinary enthusiasm to Giovanni Pastrone's film *Cabiria* (1914), which recreated on screen the ancient conflict between the territorial ambitions of Rome and Carthage:

An intense emotion grasped the entire audience, the emotion of the incomparable spectacle which, through a set-designer's tenacious effort, revived the people of the third century [BC] and flung them into tremendous struggles before the steep walls of a city, into the burning waves of a flaming sea, at the feet of an idol crimson with fire. [O]n their feet, on all sides of the theatre, the crowd shouted with enthusiasm and joy. A genuine, sincere, unrestrainable frenzy accompanied the majestic film from beginning to end. [C]abiria is something that will last. It will last because at that instant the vulgar art of cinema ceases and history succeeds, true history. (Martinelli 1992: 75)

For their early promoters and for many of their consumers, historical films were true histories. Cinema could supply a new mode of historiography of lasting value for the immediacy with which it reconstructed the past and for the intimacy with that past which it gave to its enthusiastic spectators. But the constant claims to truth, accuracy and the pedagogic value which have also been made for historical films throughout the twentieth century by their makers and distributors are, in a sense, a masquerade. Whatever the attention paid to accurate reconstruction in an historical film's surface texture – the antiquarian aesthetic, for example, manifest in the set designs, costumes and props of epics set in the classical world – all such films partake of fiction. Most notably, no historical film (in the terms of Stephen Heath) escapes the obligation of a narration. According to the 'classical' narrative strategies of historical epics to which films about ancient Rome largely conform, romance is the point of the historical discourse – very often pagan boy meets Christian girl. History is contained within domestic conflict and provided with the perfection of a story and an end in the rescue or the death of the loving couple (Heath 1977).

Until recently [cinema's historical fictions] were scarcely considered by professional historians and other critics as a mechanism for constructing the past that might have a legitimacy of its own. From the beginnings of cinema, many intellectuals had expressed disquiet at the public's apparently debased taste for the representation of historical romance on screen. By the time the neo-realist movement was initiated in the late 1930s, the historical films which had previously dominated Italian film production (and so excited the youthful hero of Fellini's *Roma*, 1972) were savagely castigated by Luchino Visconti as a 'cinema of corpses':

They live blissfully unaware that times have changed, in the reflection of things long extinct, in that unreal world of theirs where one could blissfully tread on false floors of coloured chalk and paper, where backdrops wobbled at the rush of air from a suddenly opened door, where tissue paper roses bloomed perpetually, where styles and epochs blended in a generous confusion, where, to drive the point home, bewigged Cleopatras, 'Liberty' style and clutching their whips, vamped morose and brawny Mark Anthonies in whalebone corsets. (*Cinema* 6.119 [1941] quoted in Fink 1974: 116–38)

Such films, according to the historian Guido Fink, produced a double masquerade in which producers adapted and distorted the Roman past to the dictates of a Fascist propaganda, which was itself inspired by the remote and rhetorical heroes of a distorted Rome. For Fink, the subsequent production of Visconti's *Ossessione* (1943) and other neo-realist works constituted a healthy and refreshing reaction against the pompous farce of the Italian historical films of earlier decades. The new neo-realist style of film production represented 'a pent-up thirst for truth, a need to discover the real Italy that the cautious and guilty artificiality of Fascist cinema had concealed for so many years' (Fink 1974: 119–20). After the United States came to dominate the international market in historical films in the 1930s and again in the 1950s, Hollywood's film histories were often similarly dismissed as garish, vulgar and sensational spectacles and derided as standardised studio products.

Projecting Ancient Rome: Invented Traditions

If historical films set in ancient Rome have now become a legitimate object of study for both classicists and historians, then what work needs to be done to write a history of such films? According to the terms recently set for cinema's own strategies for screening history, these films form part of an integrated regime of historical representation that constitutes the historical capital of twentieth-century cultures, and the reference period selected for projection ceases to be arbitrary and instead generates historical meaning through its relationship with other, extra-cinematic discourses about the past. Knowledge of those intertexts facilitates the exploration of how historical films function within a culture (Pearson and Uricchio 1990).

The two nations which have been most prolific in their manufacture of cinematic histories of ancient Rome also assiduously created a whole array of 'invented traditions' (a term taken from the historian Eric Hobsbawm) to refer to those discursive practices that, from the mid-eighteenth century, attempted to establish for a modern community a continuity with a suitable historical past. The purpose of these traditions was to cement group cohesion and legitimate action through the use of history, and the communities whose institutions, policies and social relations were being established, symbolised or legitimated historically were more often than not the newly formed nation-states. The awareness of an historical continuity, the creation of a cultural patrimony, served to enhance a sense of communal identity, legitimating the new nation and bolstering its sovereignty in the eyes of its own and other peoples. By tracing its origins back into the past, a nation could validate its claims to power, property and international prestige. And, if rooted in the remotest antiquity, a nation could make claims to the earliest precedent and the greatest dignity.

The surviving monuments and iconography of ancient Rome were frequently deployed in Italy during the course of the nineteenth century as political symbols in a struggle for power between the Papacy and the *risorgimento* revolutionaries. The Colosseum was pitted against the Roman forum, the Christian cross against the republican *fasces*. While the Church exploited archaeology as proof of the ultimate triumph of the Christian martyrs over the cruel persecutions of imperial Rome, the emerging nationalist movement sought out and paraded a precedent for a unified, secular Italy that was rooted in an earlier republican tradition of civic rather than religious virtue, of triumvirs and consuls, not tyrants. Thus when Giuseppe Garibaldi was elected to the Constituent Assembly of 1849, he declared (if some- **63** what prematurely): 'I believe profoundly that, now the papal system of government is at an end, what we need in Rome is a republic. [C]an it be that the descendants of the ancient Romans are not fit to constitute a Republic? As some people in this body evidently take offence at this word, I reiterate "Long live the republic!"' (Lovett 1982: 20; Springer 1987: 65–74, 136–57; Bondanella 1987: 158–67).

After the unification of Italy in 1861, the problem of assimilating its disparate peoples into a single nation was summarised by Massimo d'Azeglio thus: 'We have made Italy: now we must make Italians' (quoted in Hobsbawm and Ranger 1983: 267). Needing to justify itself historically, and in the face of continued opposition from the Vatican, the new secular body politic was able to find a major, and apparently self-evident, justification in the ancient civic virtues and military glories of the Roman republic and empire. The invented tradition of *romanità* gave to the heterogeneous Italians a piece of common national history, and, in an epidemic of literary production from unification into the first decade of the twentieth century, historical fictions such as Pietro Cossa's Roman tragedies or Raffaello Giovagnoli's Roman novels attempted to supply a unifying popular culture in which the grand figures of Roman history 'get off their pedestals of togaed rhetoric' and speak simply and with a quotidian *verismo* of sacrifices for or betrayals of their country (Lopez-Celly 1939: 212–16).

Until the 1910s, however, narratives of imperial Rome were often vulnerable to appropriation by religious opponents of Italy's liberal government as gruesome analogies for the state repression of Catholic organisations and as ominous warnings of the Church's certain victory in the continuing struggle to reclaim her temporal power. But by the time the fiftieth year of Italian unity was grandly celebrated in 1911, both state and Church were finding common cause in imperial Rome as historical legitimation for Italy's colonial aspirations in the Mediterranean. In a speech to open an archaeological exhibition held at the Baths of Diocletian during the Great Exhibition of 1911, the Christian archaeologist Rodolfo Lanciani expressed clearly the pressing imperial agenda that now lay behind such Italian displays of its Roman past. According to Lanciani, the *mostra archeologica* ought to form the basis of a future museum of the Roman empire 'where Italian youth may seek inspiration for all those virtues which rendered Rome, morally as well as materially, the mistress of the world'. On the eve of Italy's war against Turkey to wrest the colonies Tripolitania and Cyrenaica from the Ottoman empire, and despite the reservations of some critics, imperial Rome was everywhere invoked as the model of and reason for a new Italian empire. And, after victory in Africa, the discourse of historical continuity between ancient and modern imperialism continued to circulate widely, as a postcard reproduced in the English magazine *The Sphere* towards the end of 1911 testifies. An Italian sailor triumphantly grasps the sword of empire from the skeleton of a Roman soldier partially buried in the African sands. The caption beneath declares 'Italy brandishes the sword of ancient Rome'.

Historians of silent Italian cinema, such as Gian Piero Brunetta, have long argued that the war in Africa gave a decisive push towards the meeting of Italian cinematic production and the imperial ambitions of the nation-state. The many grand historical films set in ancient Rome which were produced in the period leading up to World War I (and which obtained enormous critical acclaim and box-office success both in Italy and abroad) held a crucial role in the formation, interrogation and dissemination of the rhetoric of *romanità*. Such films were both *about* ancient Rome and *for* modern Italy (Brunetta 1986: 67; Brunetta and Gili 1990: 64–5).

The recently established institutions of cinema changed the relationship between historical narration and its audiences. The practice of cinemagoing brought huge numbers of Italian spectators out of their homes into a shared public space and thus rendered their experience of historical reconstruction a more collective event than the private reading of a novel. The technologies of cinema spectacle could also accommodate on screen huge masses of people before whom, or even for whom, the protagonists of the narrative acted. Through these crowds of extras, mass audiences were able to visualise on screen their own collectivity and gain a stake in historical action. Historical films, therefore, became ideal vehicles for addressing the nation's sense of its own identity. In the years preceding World War I, there was a substantial increase of capital investment in the production of Italian feature-length historical films. Bound to the dictates of high finance and to the bourgeois values of its financial backers, Italian historical films began to prosper as an instrument of cultural hegemony. In the logic of their producers, they came to be regarded as a new form of popular university, capable of shaping the historical consciousness of their mass, largely illiterate audience and transmitting to them the symbols of Italy's recently constituted national identity. Historical films set in ancient Rome became a privileged means for the production and consumption of an imperial *romanità*. The projection on screen of the imperial eagles and the *fasces*, Roman military rituals and parades supplied a concentrated repertoire of glorious precedents for present combative action. Thus, soon after victory in Africa, the celebratory film *Cabiria* represented a unified Roman community under the leadership of the morally upright general Scipio triumphing over a decadent and disorganised Carthage.

Similarly, despite the relative political independence of the Italian film industry during the early years of the Fascist regime, at the time of the African campaigns of 1935–6 the Fascist government helped procure considerable capital investment for the production of the spectacular historical film *Scipione l'Africano* (Carmine Gallone, 1937), in which the hero is seen to lead a unified, rural and warlike Rome to victory in Africa. The cinematic construction of the Roman general's character rehearsed a model for the perfect Fascist citizen, and his designed analogy with Mussolini was both exploited by the *duce* himself and recognised by the film's contemporary audience. Even before the March on Rome in October 1922, Mussolini had begun to appropriate the militant rhetoric of *romanità* to establish historical legitimacy and popular support for Fascism. In a speech reproduced in his newspaper *Il Popolo d'Italia* for 21 April 1922, he declared:

We dream of a Roman Italy, that is to say wise, strong, disciplined, and imperial. Much of that which was the immortal spirit of Rome is reborn in Fascism: the Fasces are Roman; our organization of combat is Roman, our pride and our courage are Roman: *civis romanus sum*. Now, it is necessary that the history of tomorrow, the history we fervently wish to create, not represent a contrast or a parody of the history of yesterday. . . . Italy has been **65**

Roman for the first time in fifteen centuries in the War and in the Victory: now Italy must be Roman in peacetime; and this renewed and revived *romanità* bears these names: Discipline and Work. (Bondanella 1987: 176)

In the 1930s, Roman iconography, architecture and sculpture, political rhetoric and military ritual were systematically exploited to justify historically the Fascist aspiration to a colonial empire in the Mediterranean. And, under the impetus of events in Africa, with the conquest of Ethiopia and the ensuing proclamation of Empire on 9 May 1936, the production of the historical film *Scipione l'Africano* became a work of the regime, on which the Ministries of Popular Culture, Finance, Home Affairs and War collaborated (the last supplying infantry and cavalry troops as extras for the battle sequences).

Soon after shooting the film, the cinematographer Luigi Freddi (who had been appointed four years previously to run a new film directorate within the Ministry of Popular Culture) avowed that the cinematic representation of Scipio's conquest of Africa had been expressly undertaken to service Italy's renewed imperial project. Writing in *Il Popolo d'Italia* for 6 April 1937, he announced that:

> Scipione was conceived on the eve of the African undertaking and was begun soon after the victory. It was desired because no theme for translation into spectacle seemed more suited than this to symbolize the intimate union between the past grandeur of Rome and the bold accomplishment of our epoch. And it seemed also that no filmic representation was capable of showing and framing, in the august tradition of the race, before ourselves and the world, the African undertaking of today as a logical corollary of a glorious past and an ardent present's indisputable reason for living. Perhaps never, in the history of cinema, has a film initiative been so full of deep spiritual significance derived from active consideration of history. (Gili 1990: 94–7; Quartermaine 1995: 205–6)

The film was presented at the Venice Film Festival of November 1937, where it won the Mussolini Cup. Its subsequent distribution was supported by an extensive publicity campaign in the Italian press and by admiring reviews. Its political effectiveness then appeared to be confirmed by interviews with schoolchildren, whose essays on their viewing of the film were printed in a special edition of the cinema journal *Bianco e Nero* for August 1939. According to the introduction furnished by Giuseppe Bottai, the Minister for National Education: 'For the children, Scipio is not the Roman hero, it is Mussolini. Through a subconscious power of transposition, the actions of Scipio become the actions of Mussolini. The analogy becomes identity' (Cardillio 1987: 153; Gili 1990: 99; Quartermaine 1995: 205–6).

The evident meeting between liberal Italy's geopolitical ambitions and the narrative structures of *Cabiria*, the seemingly perfect propagandist match between the Fascist regime's combative discourse of *romanità* and the production, distribution and consumption of *Scipione l'Africano*, may suggest that films concerning Roman history can be read as effective instruments of ideological control which, through spectacular and engaging historical reconstructions, manipulate their audiences to assent to a celebratory model of national identity.

Yet the independently produced *Cabiria* was a huge commercial success in Italy, the (uniquely) state-supported *Scipione* a failure. Furthermore, many successful Italian films of the 1910s and 1920s resurrected ancient Rome's imperial cruelties and Christian martyrdoms rather than its republican triumphs, while Hollywood histories of Rome have appropriated Fascist constructions of *romanità* to turn them back against the regime which produced them, and have constantly exploited the ambiguities and contradictions inherent in the American national discourse of *romanitas* to address iniquities within the United States itself. Screening ancient Rome could supply equivocal history lessons for both Italians and Americans.

If film scholarship has problematised the function of historical film as a national discourse, it often seems to utilise a form of discursive slippage between film and society which requires interrogation. Ever since the psychoanalytic readings of German cinema offered by Siegfried Kracauer in his seminal book *From Caligari to Hitler: A Psychological History of German Film* (1947), where Kracauer posited a relationship between Weimar films and Fascism, many film critics have justified reading the films of a particular nation as a manifestation of that nation's psycho-social disposition, as an expression of that society's subconscious fears and desires. Against the trends of auteur theory, films are regarded as the outcome not of an individual creativity, but of a team or social group. Since film needs a public, it addresses itself and appeals to a heterogeneous mass audience whose desires it must satisfy. If filmmakers and their financial backers then seek to correspond to the beliefs and values of their audiences, films can be considered as reflections of the mentality of a nation. By means of this convenient critical shift from film to society, the historical film in particular can be viewed as a central component of the historical text that a society writes about itself, as a modern form of historiography that, if properly investigated, can disclose how a society conceives and exploits its past to construct its own present and future identities. The inadequacies of Kracauer's approach, however, are well documented. Such accounts of the relation between film and society tend to place most emphasis on the social and ideological contexts of film production and to overlook the specificities of the institution of cinema. But only a partial examination of the relation between film and society (or cinema and history) can be achieved if any sociological or psychoanalytic examination of film texts is separated from the study of the technical and economic conditions of their production, the formation and development of their representational conventions, and the process of constructing and consuming their aesthetic pleasures.

The Pleasures of the Look

The cinematic reconstructions of Roman history produced by the Italian and Hollywood film industries have always exceeded in function any imperative to make proprietorial claims on classical virtues and victories (or to question those claims). In the 1910s, for example, they were also utilised to legitimate cinema as a new artform and win international cultural prestige for their country of origin, in the 1930s to showcase commodities, and in the 1950s to combat television's assault on film industry profits. In all these respects and more, the projection of ancient Rome on screen has often worked to place its spectators on the side of decadence and tyranny.

Cabiria (Giovanne Pastrone, 1914)

In the first decades of the twentieth century, a new generation of Italian entrepreneurs began to invest heavily in the production of films (as they had in the manufacture of automobiles and aeroplanes) in order to raise Italy to the ranks of the great industrial powers and to affirm for it a position of commercial prestige on foreign markets. As a result of capital investment, industrial competition, and the economic and aesthetic need to increase the artistic status and range of motion pictures, Italian films rapidly increased in length; developed their own formal strategies of editing and camera movement, staging, set design and special effects; dealt with more ambitious themes; and often filled the screen with huge numbers of extras and expensively produced spectacles to rival and outdo theatrical shows and the narrative scale of the novel. Feature-length film narratives set in antiquity, such as *Quo Vadis?* (Enrico Guazzoni, 1913) and *Cabiria*, formed part of a strategy to win over the bourgeoisie to the new cinematic artform by bestowing on the modern medium a grandiose register and an educative justification. Such films borrowed from the whole spectrum of nineteenth-century modes of historical representation (literary, dramatic and pictorial) in pursuit of authenticity and authority for cinema as a mode of high culture, and to guarantee mass, international audiences through the reconstruction in moving images of familiar and accessible events of Roman history.

In their search for intertexts that would be familiar to bourgeois spectators, however, Italian film-makers did not confine themselves to the domestic narratives of ancient Rome available in the novels of Rafaello Giovagnoli or the tragedies of Pietro Cossa, but repeatedly adapted to screen the historical fictions of religious persecution which had permeated the popular literary imagination of nineteenth-century Europe, such as Lord Bulwer Lytton's *The Last Days of Pompeii* (1834), Cardinal Wiseman's *Fabiola* (1854) or Henryk Sienkiewicz's *Quo Vadis?* (1895), although such fictions were now at odds with the secular *romanità* being promulgated by the liberal government. The commercial and critical success of such film adaptations, therefore, cannot be explained wholly in terms of nationalistic drives. Films like *Quo Vadis?* principally won domestic and international acclaim because they were capable of demonstrating the imaginative power of the cinematic mechanism at a time of virulent attack on the new medium. Putting into the present an exhibitionist spectacle of pomp and magnificence, of grand crowds and monumental architecture, of orgies, seductions and sadistic martyrdoms, these extraordinarily costly historical reconstructions excited the voyeuristic look of their spectators and provoked the pleasure of gazing on the vividly realised vices and exoticisms of Rome's imperial villains. Even the magnificently depicted scenes in *Cabiria* of child sacrifice in the gigantic Carthaginian temple of Moloch have been described as a double conquest – over the watching Romans within the film's narrative and over the film's external spectators. According to film critic Paolo Cherchi Usai:

> Heroes and enemies – [t]hey may hesitate between the duty to defend their country and the temptation to yield to the impulses of luxury – but they are slaves to what they see: the power of the eye, in *Cabiria*, aspires to finality.
>
> The crucial theme of the film is, in this respect, the tragedy of the senses. The most fleeting of all, the look, makes palpable what cinema cannot offer to the touch: the perception of the dimensions of the royal palace's architecture, the movement of the armies beneath the gaze of the cinecamera Moloch, the sway of the figures knelt before the altar of the eternal fire. Demoniacal music accompanies the bloody scenes, the aroma of incense carries onto the film the odours of the temple. [F]or the first time cinema pretends to a total, definitive, conquest of the sensible world. (1985: 54–5)

Early Italian cinematic histories of Rome such as *Quo Vadis?* and *Cabiria* had been released in the United States to critical acclaim, obtained substantial box-office success, and achieved a significant influence over American film production in the years preceding World War I. After the war, however, Hollywood studios began to standardise both the production and the consumption of their feature-length films according to the formalised codes of a new cinematic representational system now known customarily as 'the classical Hollywood style', while nonetheless differentiating their products in accompanying publicity as both original and unique. The classical Hollywood style for representing history departed substantially from the mechanisms for the visualisation of the collective that had driven the historical narratives of Italian cinema in the 1910s. Whereas in the earlier aesthetics of Italian silent cinema its protagonists had merged visually in space with the community and its heroes had acted in a socially structured landscape, the protagonists of the classical Hollywood narrative were more frequently isolated from the collective through the use of medium, close and point-   **69** of-view shots and through their positioning in the centre of the film frame. Emphasis was now placed on individuals whose psychological motivations were seen to cause historical action. Detached from their surroundings, associated with the personae of the stars who played them, no longer located in a strongly specified historical moment or a socially structured community, they were transformed into characters endowed with traits and in search of private fulfilment. The development, in the late 1920s, of the technologies of synchronised sound also led to a preference for presentist or contemporary film narratives. The protagonists of American sound films in the late 1920s and early 1930s, whether they were housewives, gangsters, newspaper tycoons, Roman emperors or Ptolemaic queens, spoke in a dialogue that was grounded in the idioms of contemporary America.

Conclusion

The projection of ancient Rome on screen has functioned not only as mechanism for the display or interrogation of national identities but also, and often in contradiction, as a mechanism for the display of cinema itself – its technical capacities and its cultural value. One way, therefore, to interrogate films about ancient Rome is to examine their intersection with the national, political, economic and cultural identities of the communities in which they are produced while, at the same time, exploring the ways such films reformulate those identities in specifically cinematic terms, building up their own historiographic conventions of style, address and aesthetic pleasure.

Notes

1. This text is an extract from Wyke, Maria (1997), *Projecting the Past: Ancient Rome, Cinema and History*, London and New York: Routledge: 8–32. In that volume, she also considers at length Hollywood's cinematic histories of ancient Rome and compares them with those produced in Italy.

References

Bondanella, Peter (1987), *The Eternal City: Roman Images in the Modern World*, Chapel Hill and London: University of California Press.

Brunetta, Gian Piero (1986), 'L'Evocation du Passé: les Anneés d'Or du Film Historique', in Bernardini, Aldo and Gili, Jean A. (eds), *Le Cinéma Italien de la Prise de Rome (1905) à Rome Ville Ouverte (1945)*, Paris: Centre Georges Pompidou.

Brunetta, Gian Piero and Gili, Jean A. (1990), *L'Ora d'Africa del Cinema Italiano 1911–1989*, Trent: LaGrafica-Mori.

Cardillio, Massimo (1987), *Tra le Quinte del Cinematografo: Cinema, Cultura e Societá in Italia 1900–1937*, Bari: Edizioni Dedalo.

Fink, Guido (1974), 'To Be or to Have Been: Italian Cinema, Time and History', *Cultures* 1 (2): 116–38.

Gili, Jean A. (1990), 'I Film dell'Impero Fascista', in Brunetta, Gian Piero and Gili, Jean A. (eds), *L' Ora d'Africa del Cinema Italiano 1911–1989*, Trent: LaGrafica-Mori.

Heath, Stephen (1977), 'Contexts', *Edinburgh Magazine* 2: 37–43.

Lopez-Celly, Furio (1939), *Il Romanzo Storico in Italia: dai Prescottiani alle Odierne Vite Romanzate*, Bologna: Licinio-Cappelli Editori.

Lovett, Clara M. (1982), *The Democratic Movement in Italy 1830–1876*, Cambridge: Harvard University Press.

Martinelli, Vittorio (1992), 'Il Cinema Muto Italiano: 1914', *Bianco e Nero* 1–2.

Pearson, Roberta A. and Uricchio, William (1990), 'How Many Times Shall Caesar Bleed in Sport: Shakespeare and the Cultural Debate around Moving Pictures', *Screen* 31 (3): 243–61.

Quartermaine, Louisa (1995), ' "Slouching Towards Rome": Mussolini's Imperial Vision', in Cornell, T. J. and Lomas, Kathryn (eds), *Urban Society in Roman Italy*, London: University College Press.

Springer, Carolyn (1987), *The Marble Wilderness: Ruins and Representation in Italian Romanticism, 1775–1850*, Cambridge: Cambridge University Press.

Usai, Paolo Cherchi (1985), *Giovanni Pastrone*, Florence: La Nuova Italia, Il Castoro Cinema 119.

5 Russia

The Cinema of Anti-modernity and Backward Progress

Mikhail Iampolski

The specificity of Russian film culture is grounded in the ambiguous status of the image in Russian cultural tradition. For centuries, Russia was dominated by a Byzantine tradition of icon painting that rejected mimetic images as satanic delusions. As early as the seventeenth century, the orthodox iconic tradition had been contaminated by a European (mainly German) influence tending towards a more illusionist representational style, but this had been rejected by the old believers who treated it as a sign of the advent of the anti-Christ and of a general defilement of the Church. Mimetic images did arrive *en masse* in Russia at the time of the reforms under Peter the Great, but the mimetic–illusionist style of rep-resentation remained suspect for long afterwards. Its traces can be found, for instance, in the way Western art is treated in some of Gogol's stories. In a first version of a short story called 'Portret' ('The Portrait') (1835), an artist acquires a disturbingly illusionist portrait of an anti-Christ made by a former master of icons who betrayed his sacred art by seeking to emulate mimetically the 'appearances' connected with the activity of the arch counterfeiter – the anti-Christ.

Symptomatically, when cinema first makes its appearance in Russia, it is immediately perceived in Platonic terms as a pale, degraded copy of reality, a phantomatic shadow world. Maxim Gorky wrote in his famous review of one of the first film shows in Russia (1896):

> Silently the ash-gray foliage of the trees sways in the wind and the gray silhouettes of the people glide silently along the gray ground as if condemned to eternal silence and cruelly pun-ished by being deprived of all life's colours. [B]efore you a life surges, a life devoid of colours, a gray, silent, bleak and dismal life. It is terrifying to watch, but it is the movement of shadows, mere shadows. (Taylor and Christie 1988: 25)

The popular Russian writer Leonid Andreyev defined the cinematic image as 'a second life, an enigmatic existence, like that of a specter or a hallucination' (Taylor and Christie 1988: 30). He argued that cinema's function is to incarnate this pure spectral semblance of reality and thus to liberate theatre from being a spectacle of the world. He wrote:

To the question – should contemporary theatre provide a spectacle? – I shall equally decisively permit myself to answer no. This answer is merely consistent. In so far as action is visible and there is a spectacle, they should together leave the stage, leaving room for the invisible human soul and for its greatest riches that are invisible to our carnal and limited eyes. (Taylor and Christie 1988: 28)

If an image (any mimetic image) is pure semblance, it obviously requires to be *redeemed* by way of a trans-substantiation, by becoming more 'substantial'. The cinematic image can be redeemed only if it abandons the mechanical mimicking of pure appearances. This is a fundamentally Platonic attitude characteristic of a pre-modern world: it is based on the quasi-religious conviction that the world has a meaning hidden behind the empty gaudiness of the visible, so that the visible world needs to be transcended in order to reach its truth. Traces of this attitude have persisted and are active in the films of Tarkovsky. Consequently, the same Andreyev described the way 'appearance' must be replaced by the representation of an 'essence': 'Then the smartly dressed Benvenuto Cellini with his splendour and the variety of his surroundings will yield his place to Nietzsche's black frock-coat, to the immobility of the toneless and monotonous rooms, to the quiet and the dark of the bedroom and the study' (Taylor and Christie 1988: 28). Modernity in the main rejects such a Platonic attitude. The very Nietzsche invoked by Andreyev was, in fact, among the first philosophers to advocate a consideration of appearances in their own right, unrelated to any assumed underlying essences.

The demystificatory attitude towards illusion and ideology that characterises modernity summons us to take the world as it is, to deal phenomenologically with the world as it appears to our senses. In the pre-modern world of Russian culture at the start of the twentieth century, such an approach was not very popular. The milieu where cinema blossomed was a milieu of urban underclasses, of former peasants who had moved to the cities, already partly alienated from folk cultures. It is precisely in this milieu that the traditional bourgeois cult of art, regarding it as the ultimate manifestation of profound emotional and transcendental truth, degenerated to the level of melodramatic clichés. At the same time, some elements of folk culture were still very much alive. And it is this combination of degraded high art aesthetics and traditional folk culture that has defined the specificity of the Russian response to cinema. In the Russian context, cinema – the first of the completely modern cultural phenomena – was drastically aligned to a set of pre-modern imperatives. This becomes clearly evident when we look at what Yuri Tsivian called the 'Russian style' in cinema.[1] He singled out a number of features that constitute, in his view, the specificity of early Russian cinema. The most prominent among them are: a very slow pace of action, overemphatic actorial displays of emotion, so-called 'Russian endings' (tragic endings; often imported films were also given such a special 'Russian' ending) and a very accentuated 'literary' background to many films, a kind of *Film d'art* tradition adapted to the Russian market. In the first version of his essay, Tsivian explained 'Russian endings' as an imitation of tragedy, an impulse rooted in Russian cinema and popular art's tendency 'to emulate the forms of high art'.[2] In a new version of this essay the same phenomenon is explained by the presumption that 'it was influenced – in a strange, negative way – by its American counter-part',[3] that is to say, by the adoption of the happy ending as the norm for American film pro-duction. This last solution is probably partly motivated by Tsivian's refusal to interpret cinema as a 'cultural symptom', a reaction against the temptation to fall into some cultural essentialism: 'The film historian is not a geologist interested in deeper layers of culture, [t]here is no such thing as "grass-roots" cinema, American, Russian or Fregonian.'[4]

I share this cultural anti-essentialism, but I presume that the specificity of a national school of cinema is not based on a mystique of national character or folkloric peculiarities, but on a relation to the medium (image) defined by a complicated relation to *modernity* in a broad sense of this term. From such a point of view, 'Russian endings' could signify a deep mistrust of the glamour of appearances that fits all too easily with an obligatory display of superficial happiness. Many Russian melodramas (and, of course, not only Russian ones) focus on *deceptive appearances*, such as the figure of the worldly seducer who happens to be a corrupted sinner and who is exposed at the end. This final *unmasking* of the deceiving appearance and a tragic ending often go hand in glove, while happy endings tend to imply an acceptance of appearances. If this correlation is valid, we can presume that there are also connections between tragic endings and the culture of political regimes. In a recent study of ancient Greek tragedy, Nicole Loraux noted a seeming incongruity between the rhetoric of immortality in civic funerary orations and the proliferation of death in tragedies. According to Loraux, this peculiarity could be explained by the fact that the funerary oration belongs to the realm of politics, that is to say, it aims to secure the continuation of the *polis*; tragedy would then be the 'Other' of politics, a space where grief and mourning can be displayed. Loraux thus defined the tragic domain as a realm of 'women's politics' (Loraux 1999). The official sphere was given to appearances (for instance, it imposed the forgetting of conflict in order to preserve peace), while the tragic space was anti-civic, a domain of private behav-iour, excluded from public life. Without wanting to equate Russian cinema with Greek tragedy; here I simply want to suggest the possibility of a typological analogy between them in relation to separations between private and official-political domains that pre-date the sep-aration between the private and the (bourgeois) public sphere. In some respects cinema also was a kind of 'private' art of the masses in a society where private truth and officialdom's lies were separated by the walls of the imperial court. In that sense, cinema can be seen as part of the development in Russia of a public sphere still deeply marked by and aligned with the dispositions of an absolutist-hierarchical social order.

The slow pace of filmic narration is probably the most interesting stylistic feature to be identified by Tsivian. In the text quoted earlier, Andreyev welcomed the 'immobility of the toneless and monotonous rooms'. This immobility is displayed on two levels. The most evi-dent one is the level of narration. Russian cinema (excepting the 1920s films) was never expeditious; it never managed to construct speedy action in a satisfactory manner. In the early period it was much less interested in building suspense than was the American cinema. Part of the explanation could be that Russian audiences consisted mostly of the lower social strata of the urban population, many of them recent migrants from the country's rural areas. Their culture was a strange mixture of urban and rural folklore. As a 'traditional' popular culture, it was not novelty oriented. Instead, it was based on the recognition and repetition of well-known models. Many films were based on popular songs or on the most popular classical stories. In such cases, cinema was not perceived as a medium of suspense and surprise, but as a storehouse of illustrations of thoroughly familiar narratives.[5] In the USA, where a big part of the audience was made up by immigrants from different countries, the common cultural ground was lacking and narratives had to be self-sufficient. This folkloric trend conceived of images as illustrations of some original text, that is to say, as something secondary. A literary antecedent remained a main referent for the visible and was considered responsible for the meaning of an image. Cinema was, and still is, often mistaken for such an illustration. Such an aesthetics of derivativeness has produced a specific phenomenon: film recitation. This was typical not only for Russia but also for Japan, where film recitation was performed by so-called *benshi*.[6] In both cases, commentators produced a verbal text behind or in front of a screen literally turning cinematic images into *illustrations*.

However, the most striking peculiarity of narrative pace was its constant interruption with segments of narrative immobility so that actors might have an opportunity to display emotions. A famous Moscow Art Theatre actress, Olga Gzovskaya, called such interruptions 'full scenes'. Tsivian quotes I. Petrovskii's article of 1916, where this peculiarity is noted:

> A 'full' scene is one in which the actor is given the opportunity to depict in stage terms a specific spiritual experience, no matter how many metres it takes. The 'full' scene involves a complete rejection of the usual hurried tempo of the film drama. Instead of a rapidly changing kaleidoscope of images, it aspires to *rivet* the attention of the audience on to a single image. [E]ach and every one of our best film actors has his or her own *style* of mime: Moshukine has his steely hypnotized look; Gzovskaya has a gentle endlessly varying lyrical 'face'; Maximov has his nervous tension and Polonsky his refined grace.[7]

It is true that in the best of Russian films we find almost invariably such strange moments of continuous immobility. To some extent this may well have been a legacy from early photography with its super-long exposures. Such exposures were often seen as a way to mechanically synthesise an image of a person and thus to emulate the synthesising ability of a painter. Regardless of its pedigree, long periods of immobility in front of a camera were characteristic of Russian cinema. Moshukine was known to keep in such moments his mask-like face completely petrified and his eyes dilated and immobile, as for instance in *The Queen of Spades* (I. Protazanov, 1916). In *A Life for a Life* (E. Bauer, 1916), the great star Vera Kholodnaya marks the moment of tragic distress by an exaggerated breathing and turning of her eyes up without any bodily movement. This kind of acting had to convey a sense of extreme emotion.

It is impossible to claim that there was a particular national Russian style of acting. This kind of immobile acting partly stemmed from a psychological 'method' elaborated by Stanislavsky. But Stanislavsky's entire approach to expressivity was grounded in anti-modern premises. This great reformer of the stage constantly claimed the superiority of an extreme economy of acting over the physicality of bodily expressivity. For instance, he gave the following advice to actors performing a melodrama: 'They can sit without moving a muscle or making a gesture, but the spectator can see that they are seething with excitement; the great actor knows how to convey mainly through his eyes' (Stanislavsky 1961: 298). This advice is absolutely consistent with the technique of 'steely hypnotized' looks that Moshukine used in his 'full scenes'. Such an acting style reflected a particular understanding of performance that can plausibly be called Platonic. Stanislavsky believed that the content of the play had to be reduced to something he called 'the ruling idea'. This ruling idea, condensed into one single phrase, had to be internalised by every performer and thus transformed into an emotion. The performance as a whole was then conceived as a concerted externalisation of that pre-existing *idea*. A stressed bodily movement is not a good way of expressing it, because the mechanical task of such a movement (as in the circus) overpowers its purely expressive dimension. Which is why Stanislavsky welcomed relative immobility as a moment when the body mechanics are blocked by emotions, so that the purity of an ideal content may find expression. In his celebrated book *An Actor Prepares*, he describes the moment of 'tragic inaction' when an actor has to stand 'as though turned to stone'. Stanislavsky immediately rejects all conventional ways to deal with 'tragic inaction': eyes staring with horror, the 'tragic mopping of the brow', 'holding the head in both hands', 'running all five fingers through the hair', 'pressing the hand to the heart'. He disqualifies such devices as 'rubbish' and opposes to such obsolete conventions the behaviour of a 'real' woman struck by the news of her husband's death:

> The poor woman was stunned. Yet on her face there was none of that tragic expression which actors like to show on the stage. The complete absence of expression on her face, almost deathly in its extreme immobility, was what was so impressive. It was necessary to stand completely motionless beside her for more than ten minutes in order not to interrupt the process going on within her. (Stanislavsky 1948: 131–2)

When asked how to act complete immobility, because it excludes all action, Stanislavsky answered that all her activity, while unconscious, was purely internal:

> 'I think you will agree that those ten minutes of tragic inaction were full enough of activity. Just think of compressing all of your past life into ten short minutes. Isn't that action?'

> 'Of course it is', I agreed, 'But it is not physical.'

> 'Very well, [p]erhaps it is not physical. We need not think too deeply about labels or try to be too concise. In every physical act there is a psychological element and a physical one in every psychological act.' (Stanislavsky 1948: 132)

Physical activity for Stanislavsky is the sheer expression of psychological activity, governed by ideas. This is why an actor has to start with the appropriation of emotions and ideas, with the awakening of an emotional memory. Physical activity will follow as an externalisation of these ideas. The body is a visible 'copy' of an invisible psychological, ideational 'reality'. This also explains the special stress Stanislavsky puts on breathing in his 'system'. He believed that each individual body had its own vital rhythm differentiating it from all other human beings. This rhythm was supposed to find expression mainly in breathing:

> Your breathing is strictly rhythmical. And it is only when it is rhythmical that it renews all the creative functions of your organism; your heart is beating regularly and responds clearly and harmoniously to the rhythm of your breathing. But what happens to you when you are dis-tressed, cross, irritated or when you fly into a rage? All the functions of your breathing are upset. You are not only unable to control your passions, but you cannot even control the rhythm of your breathing. It has become accelerated, the intervals between the inhalations and exhalations have vanished. One wave of breathing rushes on top of another. You do not breathe through your nose but through your mouth, and that still further upsets the whole function-ing of your organism. (Stanislavsky 1961: 142)

'True' acting lies below the level of consciousness; it is a direct physiological expression of passions, emotions and ideas. The exaggerated breathing in Vera Kholodnaya's 'full scenes' can be connected to this kind of ideology. However I don't claim that her acting was a direct response to Stanislavsky's method. But I do claim that 'full scenes' of immobilisation in cinema and Stanislavky's technique are possible only in a culture that shares a common notion of aesthetics based on shared Platonic assumptions about the expression of pre-existing emotions or/and ideas. Emotions are ultimately only transformations of *ruling ideas* anyway. Bodily movements and emotions do not emerge together as a concerted reaction of an organism to a distressing stimulus. According to this aesthetics, first of all an idea pene-trates human beings and only *then* does it produces a physiological disturbance, which is its direct visible expression. This Platonic conception presumes a separation between the idea and its manifestation, and is, in my view, typical of pre-modern art and culture.

If an image (or the body) is only the layer of external signs that refer to the invisible realm of ideas, speed should be banned and contemplation has to be promoted at its expense. The grasping of an image can have two 'regimes': it can scan the surface of an object or of an image, or it can try to penetrate inside, to read the surface as a sign relegating our gaze to the depth hidden behind the surface. This last regime corresponds to a Platonic understand-ing of the image. The first reading will accentuate the plane, the flatness of a surface; the second regime will accentuate depth.

It is not surprising that the anti-modern attitude of early Russian cinema has generated a relatively developed cinematic pictorialism (so-called *Rembrandtism*) and a frequent recourse to depth of focus. Evgenii Bauer, who is now recognised as arguably the most tal-ented and innovative artist among early Russian film-makers, is the main director to develop such an aesthetic. Many of his films display very sophisticated special constructions based on camera movements, light effects and a particular structure of the sets; he even invented special devices to combat the flatness of the screen image. Bauer's assistant, Lev Kuleshov, wrote in 1917:

> One of the deficiencies of the moving photography is a lack of the three-dimensionality – a strong reduction of depth, of perspective on a colorless, flat screen; this is why it is necessary to build sets of the exaggerated depth, or to create artificially by deceit an impression of perspective and of a desirable depth of the studio floor. There are several ways of sets' setting-up. Two are basic. Cumbersome architectural constructions with the maximum of planes and of wall fractures suitable for the efficient lighting and for the creation of bigger depth and three-dimensionality (Bauer's method). (Kuleshov 1987: 58)

Bauer and Kuleshov had noticed that photography and cinema reduce the depth of the perspective associated with high art and the dominant pictorial tradition codified by the Renaissance. To remedy this loss of depth, they invented several devices (one of them described by Kuleshov in that same essay). The distribution of things in space was of primordial significance for both Bauer and Kuleshov, and the latter even declared that 'It is not important *what* is in the shot, the essential is *how* objects are distributed, how they are put together on a plane' (Kuleshov 1987: 59). Why were these artists so preoccupied with the 'correction' of photographic flatness? Several critics have now recognised in this flatness the ultimate modernity of photography. It allows the indexical aspect of photography to be treated as a direct precursor of Impressionism and of a contemporary art in general (Galassi 1981).

There are several explanations for modernism's valuation of the flatness of the picture plane. One was offered by Michael Fried, who saw in it a struggle against the kind of theatricality that was associated with the distanced spectator as implied and positioned by a representation constructed according to the system of linear perspective. According to Fried, Courbet, for instance, tried to abolish the very possibility of spectatordom, defining that condition as being assigned 'some place to stand, a position or point of view, in front of – more generally, outside – the painting' (Fried 1978: 117). From that point of view, flatness, which Fried sometimes also called *facingness*, is a repression of subjectivity (Arasse 2000: 163–8, Fried 1996: 266–72).[8] It is significant that Bauer was a very successful set designer before becoming a film director (Blumental and Tamarin 2002: 236–71). He was obviously trying to re-establish a theatrical scopic regime in his films.

Walter Benjamin offered another explanation. He related this flatness of screen images to the decay of the aura. Modernity, according to Benjamin, manifests itself in a collapse of the uniqueness of art objects, and in their mechanical reproduction it provokes the vanishing of the aura. In the theatre, the aura is attached to the living person of an actor:

> There is no facsimile of the aura. The aura surrounding Macbeth on the stage cannot be divorced from the aura which, for the living spectators, surrounds the actor who plays him. What distinguishes the shot in the film studio, however, is that the camera is substituted for the audience. As a result, the aura surrounding the actor is dispelled – and with it, the aura of the figure he portrays. (Benjamin 2003: 260)

In this context, the focal depth of the image and the restoration of the theatrical regime that surreptitiously replaced a mechanical camera by a ghost of a departed spectator, was really an attempt to rescue the aura. 'Full scenes' could also be seen as a reversal of a culture of snapshots that was gradually penetrating into photography. We know that in early photography, the need for an extremely long exposure time was responsible for the simulation of the aura. Bauer's whole method was designed to restore a vanishing aura. This is why the endless curtains and columns in Bauer's *Jugendstil* sets recall the curtains and fake columns often used as essential props in early photo studios. The same can be said about the 'intimate' lighting adopted by the cameraman, B. Zavelev, who favoured the use of 'dramatic shadows'. All this exactly corresponds to the technique Benjamin defined in his history of photography as a miming of 'aura' after 1880:

> After 1880, though, photographers made it their business to simulate the aura, which had been from the picture with the suppression of darkness through faster lenses. [T]hey saw it as their task to simulate this aura using all the arts of retouching, and especially the so-called gum print. This, especially in Jugendstil [Art Nouveau], a penumbral tone, interrupted by artificial highlights, came into vogue. Notwithstanding this fashionable twilight, however, a pose was more and more clearly in evidence, whose rigidity betrayed the impotence of that generation in the face of technical progress. (Benjamin 1999: 517)

Bauer is now recognised as the most interesting aesthetic innovator in Russian cinema. However, we have to admit that his innovations were an expression of his archaising inclination. Yuri Tynianov coined the expression 'archaist-innovator', and this is the term that fits Bauer perfectly. To some degree early Russian cinema was sentenced to invent a style that was going against the grain of modernity, because its underlying conception of the image was anti-modern in its core.

National specificity in cinema derives, I think, from the junction between two social-historical currents. The essential one is the cultural orientation of a society in relation to modernity, something that is reflected in a prevailing approach to the image, understood in a very broad sense. This orientation is manifested through sets of rather contingent elements, the appropriation of which is determined by the particularity of the cultural context of an epoch. These contingent elements constitute a second, more immediately stylistic level of national specificity, and allow us to claim that a Platonic conception of the image stands as a general characteristic of Russian anti-modernity. However, the fact that it was translated into aesthetic strategies such as a slow narrative pace and the recourse to immobility, was determined by the overall context of the evolution of acting styles in Russian theatre, as exemplified, for instance, by the particular 'psychologism' advocated by Stanislavsky. Of course, we shouldn't ignore the fact that national films are always a mixture of local cultural traditions and of foreign influences. There is no such phenomenon as a purely and exclusively 'national' film.

Some stylistic features cannot be unambiguously related to modern or anti-modern trends. Alois Riegl discovered pictorial flatness in the art of ancient Egypt and in Dutch group portraiture of the seventeenth century. Svetlana Alpers found it in Dutch landscapes and still lives, where 'They offered a geometric way to transform the world onto a working surface without the invention of viewer and picture plane, without, in other words, the invention of an Albertian picture' (Alpers 1983: 53). It could be completely inappropriate to claim that the Northern European tradition is more modern than the Italian one, or that the indiscriminate and fetishistic description of objects on a plane is more modern than their arrangement in the deep space of linear perspective (Jay 1988). I am not really convinced by the argument that makes Dutch society more advanced towards capitalism than Italian society in the seventeenth century.[9] I think that some *specific stylistic features*, which corresponded to the specific conditions in seventeenth-century Holland, are simply reused for different reasons in different times, and accordingly change their meaning. If in old Holland, as Alpers has shown, this style was inspired by the science of its time and a stress on observation which was typical for it, or by a particular mentality of Dutch craftsmen, then the recourse to the same style in more modern times does not necessarily refer us to a newly discovered uniqueness and autonomy of objects in the world, calling for an observational style, but as an expression of a 'sense of the universal equality of things' that increased to such a degree that, 'by means of reproduction, it extracts sameness even from what is unique' (Benjamin 2003: 256). It means that, roughly, the same style serves two different kinds of modernity.

Russian cinema of the 1920s (in its best films) to some degree could be defined in terms of the radical rejection of the aesthetics of Russian pre-revolutionary cinema. This reversal of a 'tradition' is astonishingly complete. The slow narrative pace is replaced by extreme speed; immobility and 'full scenes' are replaced by the athletic, quasi-mechanical movements of the actors; theatre as a model is replaced by the circus, and, most importantly, the intrinsic meaning of an image that was the main justification for contemplation, was totally denied. Montage, as a new dominant ideology, presumed the absence of any substantial meaning behind the image. An image's sense was created by an association of two or more images or by the shock of their collision.

One of the important prophets of modernity in Russia, Ossip Brik, defended photography because it was able to record multiple connections between things that produced meaning. It is not surprising that a surface was deemed to be the perfect medium for registering such connections. According to Brik, pictorialism proceeds by isolating an individual or an object from their milieu:

If a painter wanted to sketch Holy Square he would have to rebuild the houses, regroup the people, and invent some kind of connection between them besides the one that exists in reality. Only then would he be able to achieve a painterly effect – something dictated by the fact that Holly Square is not a finished, self-enclosed totality, but merely a point for the intersection of various temporal and spatial phenomena. [T]he portrait photographer always places his model so as to isolate him form the surrounding ambience. He'll take him into special studio and create an artificial photographic environment. All this in order to produce a portrait in maximum isolation, and create the maximum resemblance to a painted picture. (Brik in Phillips 1989: 230–1)

Brik criticises the isolation underpinning 'full scenes' precisely because they lack modernity. To think about a photographic object as a *totality* means to relate it to an idea that is responsible for the constitution of that totality. Montage dramatically changed that perspective. It meant that there was no pre-existing meaning, no pre-existing emotions looking for expression in an actor's deep breathing. Sense was created *a posteriori,* from the confrontation between images that already existed, from the registration of connections on a surface. This new approach constituted a radical denial of the validity of any Platonic aesthetics. With the evaporation of its intrinsic 'content', the image became pure surface. Thereafter, subjectivity lost its importance and the subject (philosophical, aesthetic or psychological) vanished. Vertov's *cine-eye* was a sign of that disappearance. It did not seek to replace the theatrical spectator with the camera's mechanical eye. Instead, it sought to eliminate subjectivity as such and to establishment of a new regime of objectivity, more radical than Germany's *Neue Sachlichkeit.* This philosophical shift was absolutely clear to the pioneers of Soviet cinema. Abram Room expressed it appropriately in terms of the opposition between theatre and cinema: 'Theatre is "seeing" whereas cinema is "being" ' (Taylor and Christie 1988: 128)

This new aesthetics was elaborated by a relatively small group of extremely gifted and dynamic young men: Eisenstein, Vertov, Kuleshov, Pudovkin, Barnet, Room, Kozintsev and

Chapayev (Sergei Vasiliev, 1934)

Trauberg, Ermler and others. But the golden age of Soviet silent cinema was short, and by the mid-1930s the avant-garde trend had been substantially reversed. Classical Soviet silent cinema now looks like an incredible outburst of utopian aspirations. The October revolution was a revolution of modernisation. Its early programme – industrialisation, universal literacy, women's equality, the overcoming of a traditional peasant culture and so on – corresponded perfectly to the ideology of modernity, and Soviet cinema emerged as a utopian realisation of this immense project of modernisation before any real achievement even took place. It is obvious that by the mid-1920s Russian industry was in an even worse condition than it had been in 1913. The relatively quick collapse of revolutionary culture was due, in my opinion, not simply to the advent of Stalin's totalitarianism, but to the fact that this culture didn't reflect reality and was mainly futurist. There was a real disagreement between the extreme modernity of this art and a Russia that was a backward, rural country. One of the usual reproaches made to avant-garde film-makers was that their films were too sophisticated for a simple folk. By the late 1920s, avant-garde artists were regularly attacked as formalists because of a formal complexity that didn't reflect, in the eyes of their detractors, Russian reality. The minister of cinema, Boris Shumiatsky, opposed the so-called 'formalist cinema' to the Vassiliev Brothers' film *Chapayev* (1934), which became the new aesthetic model. It was *Chapayev* which represented the real summit of Soviet film art. It is a film distinguished by its *exceptional* simplicity. This simplicity, which is a characteristic only of high art, is so organic to *Chapayev* that it constitutes a striking contrast to every formalist device. Its simplicity is such that on the film's release, a number of 'critics' were unable to explain the reasons for its success to their own satisfaction. 'The strength of *Chapayev* lies in the profound *vital truth* of the film' (Taylor and Christie 1988: 358).[10] Russian cinema of the 1920s was discarded as complicated and lacking in truth; the new cinema of Socialist Realism, associated with *Chapayev*, was simple and truthful because it corresponded to a certain vision of reality that was deeply anti-modern. Socialist Realism was, in fact, a double movement: from a utopian, non-mimetic, anti-Platonic modernity to a familiar and traditional, 'realist' (read: mimetic) anti-modern vision of the universe. The massacre of 'formalism' is not to be understood as the elimination of an ideologically suspicious trend (films labelled 'formalist' were, in fact, ideologically almost irreproachable), but as the destruction of a modernist vision that was perceived by the authorities, and by the masses, as alien, overcomplicated and *untrue*.

The great cinema of the 1920s was an extraordinary and wonderful anomaly that was gradually replaced by an anti-modernist trend labelled Socialist Realism. Obviously, this trend was stylistically very different from the cinema of 1910s, although it was based on a very similar attitude and relied also on literature (or on literary scripts), which played an increasing role in film production. But this literary background didn't presume any real action. The tempo of most of these films was rather slow, and the dynamic acting style of the 1920s was replaced by a 'psychological' style inspired by Stanislavsky. The pictorialism of the cinematography was eulogised[11] and, most importantly, this new Soviet style was marked by a mistrust of the self-sufficiency of images. Images were treated as allegorical or symbolic, referring to ideologies. In other words, images were regarded as 'totalities', and the general feeling was one of a return to normality after a decade of deviations.

The suggestion that the great silent revolutionary cinema was an anomaly can be supported by an example from Eisenstein, an emblematic artist of the 1920s. His artistic evolution can provide a ground for different interpretations. I will focus here on its most indisputable aspect. In 1937, the production of Eisenstein's *Bezhin Meadow* was stopped. The film was confiscated and Eisenstein became the victim of an unprecedented witch hunt. He was accused of formalism and forced publicly to admit and confess his mistakes. At the bleakest moment of this public trashing, he started to write a book on montage. This book offers a radical rethinking of Eisenstein's own earlier theory of montage and can be seen, at the same time, as an attempt to challenge the accusation of formalism routinely associated with a stress on the importance of montage. The book is not simply a self-defence. It is far too sophisticated and intense to be addressed to the authorities. Clearly, it was a dramatic attempt to find a theoretical justification for the work he had done in the 1920s by recasting it as fundamentally anti-modern. In 1935 he had already announced his new discovery that there was a fundamental law underpinning all arts: 'Art is nothing else but an artificial retrogression in the field of psychology towards the forms of earlier thought-processe.' (Eisenstein 1957: 144). Art moving forward into the future retrogressively was really a 'law' that confirmed Tynianov's intuition about the temporality of archaisising-innovation. This law later became the subject of special, book-long study, entitled *Method*.

The new investigation of montage was an attempt to show that the 'formalist' montage of the 1920s in fact moved forward retrogressively towards a pre-modern culture. Eisenstein defined this kind of movement as *dialectics*. In his Introduction, Eisenstein offered some important explanations. He claimed that he was analysing the most progressive, future-oriented kind of montage; unfortunately, 'at the present time', cinema and other arts were unable to provide him with any example of the kind he needed, and 'herein also lies the reason why, for my models and illustrative digressions, I shall be obliged to draw much more upon examples taken from the history of literature and the arts than upon contemporary sources, since the features characteristic of my subject matter have largely disappeared' (Eisenstein 1991: 5). In that same Introduction, he also elaborated on his surprisingly permanent use of Stanislavsky's theory, even though he severely criticised it in the past: 'It is, therefore, all the more interesting to observe the great degree to which the premises (and the approach) formulating the rules for my field of activity invariably, step by step, echo similar premises in Stanislavsky's "Method" approach to acting' (Eisenstein 1991: 6). And, most surprisingly, he recognises that the book is essentially not about montage at all:

> Strictly speaking, of course, this book is not about montage. Within the limits of the author's powers and abilities, it is basically attempting to show, in one particular aspect of the work of art (the method of its composition), how to disclose simultaneously the representational factor and the generalized image, and how both must form an indissoluble unity and must interpenetrate one another. (Eisenstein 1991: 5)

It is almost impossible to translate into English the kind of Byzantine terminology he used. 'Representational' here stands for *edinichno-izobrazitel'nyj* (picturing in its singularity) and the 'generalised image' stands for *obobshchionno-obraznyj* (generalising as an idea). For the Eisenstein of the 1930s, montage no longer produced meaning through the shock of two images, but by extracting an idea from the singularity of the photographs (in certain way, it was a deliberate archaicisation of his famous notion of intellectual montage). Basically, Eisenstein rethought montage in terms of a Platonist ideology, and, seen in that light, it is not surprising that he refers to Plato as interpreted by a Marxist philosopher called V. Asmus:

> Similar moments of the idealist dialectics can be found in Plato's doctrine of the beautiful. Plato defines the relation of sensual things to supersensory 'species' or 'ideas' not only in terms of polarity between eternal ideas and changeable things of the sensual world. He defines this relation equally as a relation of *participation*: changeable sensual things 'participate' in unchangeable ideas or imitate them. [T]he contemplation of the sensual beauty of things, in particular of the beauty that is revealed by *vision*, of the *visible, perceptible, observable* beauty, leads, according to Plato, from a sensual likeness of beauty to its truly existent supersensory original. (Eisenstein 2000: 60–1)[12]

It is difficult to imagine such a reference to Plato in Eisenstein's early writings, but here it is absolutely appropriate. In 1937, art, according to him, has to 'abstract from a phenomenon its generalized, essential reality, freeing it from whatever is transitory and impermanent' (Eisenstein 1991: 28).

At the start of the 1940s, Eisenstein formulated his new vision of the history of Soviet cinema. Montage emerges as a dualistic system of contrasts (in line with the attitude adopted by D. W. Griffith) that doesn't go beyond a simple juxtaposition of things. In the 1920s, in Russia, montage transcended this dualism and its stress on pure visuality, becoming a conceptual tool dealing with meaning. Montage thus evolved or moved from a 'primitive' stage of sheer visuality towards a stage of generalised, mental images and ideas that are given through the dialectics that transcends the sensual in a synthetic revelation of the supersensory. In other words, montage progressed retrogressively, going from an engagement with the modernity of things as they are, towards a Platonic universe of supersensual ideas. Interestingly, Eisenstein tried to ground this conception of history in the national character of both American and Russian cultures:

> We refer to the *close-up*, or as we speak of it, the 'large' scale.

> This distinction in principle begins with an essence that exists in the term itself.

> We say: an object or face is photographed in 'large scale', i. e. *large*.

> The American says: *near*, or 'close-up'.

> We are speaking of the qualitative side of the phenomenon, linked with its meaning (just as we speak of a *large* talent, that is, of one which stands out, by its significance, from the gen-

eral line, or of *large* print [bold-face] to emphasize that which is particularly essential or significant).

Among Americans the term is attached to *viewpoint*.

Among us – to the value of what is seen. . . .

In this comparison, immediately the first thing to appear clearly relating to the principal function of the close-up in our cinema is – not only and not so much to *show* or to *present*, as to *signify*, to *give meaning*, to *designate*. (Eisenstein 1957: 237–8)

Eisenstein here tries to explain this difference in terms of the class-consciousness of Soviet artists, but this explanation is obviously forced. You cannot explain by class-consciousness the use of the word 'large'. Behind this attempt is an evident effort to present an archaic essentialism as super-modern, and to denigrate a modern capacity to see things by reducing them to pure appearances. Eisenstein dedicated thousands of pages to such explorations. The very intensity of his theoretical labours betrays the deep anxiety he must have experienced in relation to the problematics of modernity and anti-modernity. His theoretical Odyssey shows how national tradition reappropriates deviant phenomena into its mainstream. Stylistically, the later Eisenstein's films are very different from the films of his colleagues, but the premodern concept of the image has gained, in his late work, an undisputed dominance. The extravagant beauty and power of *Ivan the Terrible* (1944) is partly the result (as it was in Bauer's case) of this backward progress.

Notes

1. Tsivian's text is the best and the most serious recent attempt to date to describe the main stylistic characteristics of the early Russian cinema. It was published three times in different versions. The first version was in *Silent Witness: Russian Films, 1908–1919* (1989). The second version appeared as 'Some Preparatory Remarks on Russian Cinema' in Taylor and Christie's collection *Inside the Film Factory* (1991). The most recent version appeared as 'New Notes on Russian Film Culture Between 1908 and 1919' in Grieveson and Krämer's *The Silent Cinema Reader* (2004). Each time Tsivian corrected his text, the most radical corrections being in the last version. These changes concern the interpretation of the data that Tsivian provides. He is without doubt the most outstanding connoisseur of the early Russian cinema, so I will rely heavily on his data, but I will give my own interpretation of them, which differs significantly from his.
2. Tsivian: 'Some Preparatory Remarks on Russian Cinema', p. 8.
3. Tsivian: 'New Notes on Russian Film Culture Between 1908 and 1919', p. 342.
4. Ibid., p. 347.
5. Benjamin noticed that Russian cinema's main audience were peasants and 'that the rural audience is incapable of following *two simultaneous narrative strands* of the kind seen countless times in film. They can follow only a single series of images that must unfold chronologically, like the verses of a street ballad' (Benjamin 1999: 14).

6. Burch thinks that *benshi* contributed to the immobility of the early Japanese cinema: 'The voice was there, but detached from the images themselves, images in which actors were thereby all the more mute and were confined, moreover, in many instances, to remarkably static visual rendering of the scenes unfolding through the voice, much like the dolls or, to a lesser extent, the kabuki actors of the Edo stage' (Burch 1979: 78).

7. Tsivian: 'New Notes on Russian Film Culture Between 1908 and 1919', p. 344.

8. *Facingness* is a painting's ability to face a spectator with a kind of new, modern kind of theatricality, and refers to a painting's capacity to offer itself to a spectator, almost erotically. See Daniel Arasse (2000: 163–8). Fried (1996) calls the distanced piece of a closed representation a *tableau* and associates it with 'slowness' and 'penetratingness'. He shows that the tableau was historically opposed to the *morceau*, the latter being characterised by 'instantaneousness' and 'strikingness'.

9. Nevertheless, Tzvetan Todorov (2000) suggests that the changes to observational modes of representation can be found in portraits, first appearing in illuminated mansucripts and then in Flemish-Burgundian paintings. He argues that theologians in the Neoplatonist tradition inadvertently opened up the possibility of thinking about, and thus representing, objects and people as 'individuated' rather than merely as bearers of an inner essence, and that, after regimes of 'mixed' representations, the Italian city states appropriated and developed some of the tendencies pioneered by the Flemish painters, even hiring the painters to come and teach the 'new style' to Italian artists.

10. This attack on 'formalists' was made in a book with a significant title: *A Cinema for the Millions* (1935); it was adopted as a manifesto for the new party line.

11. One of the best theoretical works of the 1930s, written by Eisenstein's student and an eminent cameraman, Vladimir Nilsen, was a call for the restoration of pictorialism. He wrote that: 'Photography lost one if its most valuable qualities – its artistic picturesqueness. The wholesale photo, which was merely a mechanical reflection, a reproduction of a fortuitous subject, lost all right to be called an artistic production' (Nilsen 1959: 141).

12. This reference to Plato is omitted from the English translation of *Montage 1937*.

References

Alpers, Svetlana (1983), *The Art of Describing*, Chicago: Chicago University Press.

Arasse, Daniel (2000), *On n'y voit rien*, Paris: Denoël.

Benjamin, Walter (1999), 'On the Present Situation of Russian Film', in *Selected Writings 2: 1927–1934*, Cambridge, MA: Harvard University Press.

Benjamin, Walter (2003), 'The Work of Art in the Age of Reproducibility', in *Selected Writings 4: 1938–1940*, Cambridge, MA: Harvard University Press.

Blumental, A. E. and Tamarin, I. (2002), 'E. F. Bauer: Materialy k istorii russkogo svetotvorchestva', *Kinovedcheskie zapiski* 56: 236–71.

Burch, Noël (1979), *To the Distant Observer: Form and Meaning in the Japanese Cinema*, London: Scolar Press.

Eisenstein, Sergei (1957), *Film Form*, edited by Jay Leyda, Cleveland: The World Publishing Company.

Eisenstein, S. M. (1991), *Selected Works, Vol. 2: Towards a Theory of Montage*, London: BFI.

Eisenstein, Sergej (2000), *Montazh*, Moscow: Muzej kino.

Fried, Michael (1978), 'The Beholder in Courbet: His Early Self-Portraits and their Place in His Art', *Glyph* 4, Baltimore: The Johns Hopkins University Press.

Fried, Michael (1996), *Manet's Modernism or the Face of Painting in the 1860s*, Chicago: University of Chicago Press.

Galassi, Peter (1981), *Before Photography: Painting and the Invention of Photography*, New York: Museum of Modern Art.

Grieveson, Lee and Krämer, Peter (eds) (2004), *The Silent Cinema Reader*, London: Routledge.

Jay, Martin (1988), 'Scopic Regimes of Modernity', in Foster, Hal (ed.), *Vision and Visuality*, Seattle: Bay Press.

Kuleshov, Lev (1987), *Sobranie sochinenij v triokh tomakh*, vol. 1, Moscow: Iskusstvo.

Loraux, Nicole (1999), *La voix endeuillée. Essai sur la tragédie grecque*, Paris: Gallimard.

Nilsen, Vladimir (1959), *The Cinema as a Graphic Art*, New York: Hill and Wang.

Phillips, Christopher (ed.) (1989), 'From the Painting to the Photograph', in *Photography in the Modern Era*, New York: The Metropolitan Museum of Art.

Stanislavsky, Constantin (1948), *An Actor Prepares*, New York: Theatre Arts Books.

Stanislavsky, Constantin (1961), *Stanislavsky on the Art of the Stage*, introduced and translated by David Magarshack, NY: Hill and Wang.

Taylor, Richard and Christie, Ian (eds) (1988), *The Film Factory: Russian and Soviet Cinema in Documents 1896–1939*, Cambridge, MA: Harvard University Press.

Taylor, Richard and Christie, Ian (eds) (1991), *Inside the Film Factory*, London: Routledge, 1991.

Todorov, Tzvetan (2000), *Éloge de l'individu: Essai sur la peinture flamande de la Renaissance*, Paris: Adam Biro.

6 National Cinema in Ireland

Martin McLoone

Three fundamental and interlinked factors – economic prosperity in the South, the peace process in the North and a new engagement with emigration and diasporic culture generally – have transformed Ireland and Irish culture in the last fifteen years. This transformation has stimulated an intense cultural debate that has influenced and impacted on all the arts, and initiated a continuing process of cultural reimagining and reappraisal. This renewed concern with Irish emigration and the cultural achievements of the Irish abroad has had the effect of broadening and extending the very definitions of Irishness itself, from a once narrow and purist notion of identity to a concept that now has a global reach.

One of the many cultural consequences of the changes of recent decades has been the emergence of state-sponsored indigenous film industries in Ireland, north and south (McLoone 2000; Pettitt 2000; Barton 2004). Between them Ireland and Northern Ireland now produce ten to fifteen features a year as well as a steady output of short live-action and animation films. This new cinema has played an important role in reimagining Ireland and the Irish and has visualised on the screen and in a popular idiom many of the transformations, renegotiations and aspirations that have characterised a rapidly changing society. Ireland's is an emerging cinema culture and as such offers many interesting local counterpoints to the more general debates about national cinemas.

Theorising Irish National Cinema

Historically, cultural debate in Ireland emerged as a nationalist response to colonial domination and, after independence from Britain in 1922, successive Irish governments followed a cultural strategy that mirrored the nationalist parameters of this debate. Government policy reflected the conservative religious ethos and weak economy of the emerging Irish state. The development of a cinema industry was deemed neither economically viable nor ideologically desirable. The prevailing ethos, in other words, was one of protectionism, and while this might have been primarily designed with native industry in mind, it did not include a native film industry. Indigenous film-making was neither encouraged nor promoted. On the contrary, when the protectionist mentality was extended to include culture, the result was a heavy censorship regime that banned literature extensively and banned or cut incoming cinema with more zeal than any other European country (Rockett 2004).

This overly essentialist imagining of Irish cultural nationalism gave rise, especially in the years from the 1920s to the 1960s, to a narrow and restrictive national culture. While church and political leaders may have worried about the impact of American cinema, for the general Irish audience these films were positively liberating, giving them the scope to imagine and to dream. This is very much the theme, for example, of the film *This is My Father* (1998), written, produced, directed and performed by the Quinn brothers – Paul, Declan and Aidan – in homage to their Irish and Irish-American heritage. When one's own national culture is so narrowly defined, and in many cases so class-ridden as European cultures in general have been, the democratic address of American cinema was a welcome relief.

In recent years, however, Ireland has reinvented itself as a prosperous European nation at the cusp of contemporary global politics, enjoying a prolonged period of economic growth. Such has been the scale and pace of this economic growth that in the 1990s Ireland earned for itself the sobriquet 'Celtic Tiger'. This new prosperity was driven by inward investment from Europe and America, fuelling an extraordinary growth in the IT and chemicals industries. Tourism (much of it 'roots' tourism) boomed, and Ireland finally began to cash in on a century and a half of emigration. The Irishness of the original imagining – an Ireland of thatched cottages and a self-sufficient peasantry, a romantic rural Ireland of myth and immemorial antiquity – has been forgotten in 'Celtic Tiger' Ireland itself, except where it is packaged and sold as commodity kitsch.

Today, debate in Ireland, while predicated to some extent on the legacy of its nationalist past, is more concerned with the country's place in the culture of global capitalism. In the rush towards European affluence and sophistication, has something precious been lost? Terry Eagleton characterises the dominant impulse in contemporary Ireland in just these terms: 'For some [i]t would seem that Ireland will have assumed its distinctive place among the nations when it ends up looking exactly like Switzerland' (1998: 312).

The emergence of an Irish cinema in such a period of unprecedented prosperity and at a time of global Hollywood domination has refocused older concerns onto the more contemporary debates about American cultural imperialism and the threats posed to small nations in general by globalisation, in both economics and culture. As Ireland has been fully integrated into the global marketplace, Irish culture in general and Irish cinema in particular now inhabits some ill-defined space between the particular and the universal, between essentialist irrelevance and global insignificance. Coupled with the longstanding 'special relationship' between Ireland and the USA that is the result of emigration, the Ireland of the new millennium is a culture caught between its nationalist past, its European future and its American imagination. Irish cinema has emerged in a cultural space bounded by local, regional, national and global factors.

And yet, this space is also a site of considerable potential. It is an interface analogous to that space identified by Kenneth Frampton as 'critical regionalism', an *arrière-garde* which 'has the capacity to cultivate a resistant, identity-giving culture while at the same time having discreet recourse to universal technique' (1985: 20). In this respect, Irish cinema can be regarded   **89** as a form of critical regionalism, the end result of a *pas de deux* involving the particular and the universal – a cinema where the native themes and concerns are worked onto an international style.

Another way of theorising the space of Irish cinema is to consider it through the filter of post-colonial theory. This has been used in two ways. Firstly, linked to concurrent debates about globalisation, post-colonial theory has argued for a post-national cultural politics, asserting that nationalism itself, the construct originally of the coloniser, is inadequate to contemporary global society and that Ireland's rapid modernisation and increasingly European character has rendered obsolete the imagining of Irish nationalism. This imagining, anyway, was built on essentialist notions of Irishness and, in its narrowness and exclusivity, it oppressed as much as it liberated. Its malign influence on the present has been as much a factor in the problems facing contemporary Ireland as has the legacy of colonialism. Consequently, much Irish cinema has been concerned to move beyond nationalism and to create images of a globalised Ireland at the cusp of an international culture.

Conversely, though, the same theoretical framework has also been used to mount a radical defence of nationalism. The increasingly global nature of contemporary capitalism and the homogenising nature of the consumerist culture that it promotes, poses a considerable threat to the 'difference' of indigenous cultures everywhere. It also makes necessary a political and cultural response based on nationalist imaginings. This is the only way in which the great diversity of human cultures can be maintained against the cultural imperialism of capitalism and especially the popular culture of the USA. As Ireland is fully integrated into the global economy and takes its place among the nations of the European Union, Irish national identity is, if anything, more important now than at any time in its colonial past. To jettison wholesale the narratives of Irish nationalism is to bow to the destructive power and cultural domination of international capital.

Both of these positions identify and analyse real issues. Together they represent a dilemma for national politics everywhere – a seemingly impossible choice between a self-defeating essentialism and a self-abusing capitulation. Irish cinema occupies just such a post-colonial space and the cinema that has grown out of it reflects the culture and the aspirations of such a space. Indeed, in introducing the package of measures to stimulate film culture in Ireland in 1993, the then-minister, Michael D. Higgins, identified his project as the integration of 'indigenous energy' and the 'commercial space that tax incentive creates' (Higgins 1995). In fact, it was a total support strategy for all aspects of film production, education and training (a smaller-scale version of this scheme was attempted later in Northern Ireland without the benefit of Higgins' eloquent theorisations). Each element of an elaborate infrastructure was put in place: the Film Board for indigenous production; the Screen Commission for location promotion; the Film Institute for educational and archival activity; and Screen Training Ireland to co-ordinate all aspects of training. The package was designed to allow for three levels of film funding and film activity, from mega-budget Hollywood location shoots through mid-budget Irish co-productions and small-scale low-budget indigenous films. Each of these has its own implications at the level of film content, commercial viability and visibility to audiences, both at home and abroad. This suggests that there is a useful analogy between the way in which Irish cinema, as it has developed in the sense of film practice, might be analysed and the debate about 'Third Cinema' (as opposed to the cinema/s of the 'Third World').

In the 1960s and 1970s, radical political film-makers from Latin America tried to define what a political cinema should be. The initial theoretical concerns were laid out by the Argentinian film-makers Fernando Solanas and Octavio Getino in an essay which, first published in 1969, was to be hugely influential to oppositional film-makers the world over (Solanas and Getino 1976). Their argument was that the political and oppositional cinema represented by post-revolutionary Cuban cinema or by their own *La Hora de los Hornos* (*The Hour of the Furnaces*) (1968) was a 'third cinema' not because it spoke specifically to the so-called 'Third World' (though this was the context out of which it grew), but because it marked a clear aesthetic and political difference to what they saw as two dominant modes of film-making. 'First cinema' was big-budget, mainstream Hollywood feature film-making, 'destined to satisfy only the ideological and economic interests of the *owners of the film industry*, (Solanas and Getino 1976: 44; original emphasis). 'Second cinema' was a more modestly budgeted 'auteur' cinema, independent to some extent from the economics and aesthetics of the Hollywood model but nonetheless caught up in the ideology and politics of the establishment – 'at best the "progressive" wing of Establishment cinema' (Solanas and Getino 1976: 45).

Third Cinema is a revolutionary form of oppositional film-making, anti-imperialist and decolonising in its politics, artisanal and collective in its working methods, and geared towards raising political questions of its audience, rather than merely offering ideology marketed as entertainment. In his later discussion of the concept, Paul Willemen notes how Solanas revised his original formulation to take account of the fact that the idea of a Third Cinema was being adopted throughout both the 'First' and the 'Third Worlds' to meet the needs of oppositional film-making in diverse social and economic contexts (Pines and Willemen 1989: 1–29). The defining characteristic of the three cinemas is their relationship to dominant aesthetics, politics and ideologies. Thus the kind of intimate auteur cinema that in a production context might belong to the Second Cinema could and should be considered as First Cinema if its political effect is to reproduce unquestioningly the dominant representations of that cinema. As Solanas explains: 'So-called author cinema often belongs in the second cinema, but both good and bad authors may be found in the first and the third cinemas.' It is useful to quote Solanas' reformulation:

[T]hird Cinema is the expression of a new culture and of social change. [It] gives an account of reality and history. It is also linked with national culture. [I]t is the way the world is conceptualised and not the genre nor the explicitly political character of a film which makes it belong to Third Cinema. [T]hird Cinema is an open category, unfinished, incomplete. (Quoted in Pines and Willemen 1989: 11)

In Solanas as in other formulations of Third Cinema, there is an agreed assumption that this cinema will promote a socialist consciousness, both stimulating debate and finding a space within and without dominant culture where this can take place. Its object is not to foreclose such debate through dogmatic assertion, but to provide analyses and explorations that would be worked through by 'the people' themselves.

If we return to the three levels of state support for film-making in Ireland we can make some observations about the kinds of film that have emerged there over the last fifteen years or so. In big-budget USA productions, like Ron Howard's *Far and Away* (1991), artistic control has remained outside of Ireland itself (with implications for meaning and representation), while the level of studio and big-star involvement has meant that the films have received wide international exposure. These films are clearly part of what Solanas called First Cinema, for they are tied to the consumerist thrust of commercial cinema and offer no challenge to existing representations. However, still at this level, non Irish-themed films like *Braveheart* (M. Gibson, 1995) or *Saving Private Ryan* (S. Spielberg, 1998), which availed themselves of the tax incentives merely to take advantage of Irish locations, allowed for a spin-off to the general economy and to the infrastructure of film-making. This is the 'trickle down' economics of Higgins' original package. Written by Higgins into the tax incentives were provisions for training requirements for Irish personnel and, as we noted, Higgins himself characterised this part of the strategy as exploiting the 'commercial space' for the benefit of 'indigenous energy' (Higgins 1995). So, while these films are undoubtedly First Cinema, Irish state policy has attempted to engage with them at a production level in order to create the opportunities for more specific and more relevant indigenous film-making. The 'liminal spaces and interstices' where the local meets the global are being explored.

With medium-budget films – often the result of co-production partnerships – the incentives and other state-support mechanisms have allowed a greater level of artistic control to remain in Ireland, despite the need to secure a large part of their budgets from outside. These films are subsequently more interesting and, as a rule, more complex (as, for instance, the films of Neil Jordan, Thaddeus O'Sullivan or Jim Sheridan). Their critical impact has tended to outweigh by far their commercial achievements. In these cases, it is not easy to read off reductively the artistic concessions that have been made as a result of foreign financial arrangements, though it is tempting nonetheless to do so. Thus with a film like Sheridan's *In the Name of the Father* (1993), an interesting question emerges as to the extent to which the displacement of a political story onto an Oedipal father/son story is the result of the American backers of Sheridan's own way of inhabiting genre conventions.

Ireland has also attracted the attentions of American and British film-makers in whose films, although more modestly budgeted than blockbusters, the film-makers have retained artistic control to a degree that makes it difficult to regard the films as indigenous in any meaningful way. For example, despite the fact that both films were financed largely outside of Ireland, a distinction needs to be made between Neil Jordan's *The Crying Game* (1992) and John Sayles' *The Secret of Roan Inish* (1994). The source of the financial backing is not primarily the issue here. Rather, Sayles' film is extraneous to Ireland in a more crucial manner: it draws little on Irish creative talent other than in the employment of Irish actors. Jordan's film, on the other hand, is creatively dependent on the director's Irish sensibility and on his obsession with exploring the interface between sexuality and violence in Ireland. This

The Secret of Roan Inish (John Sayles, 1994)

does not, of course, mean that Sayles fails some kind of 'purity' test – his film is about Ireland; it was set and shot in Ireland, and it interacts in telling ways with Irish themes and iconography. However, its artistic genesis does impact on the kind of film that it is, and this, in turn, moulds the nature of this interaction.

In these medium-budget films, we can see the porous nature of the three-way distinction alluded to by Solanas. The determinedly independent Sayles may well occupy a clear Second Cinema position in regard to his American theme films, but in his commitment to collective political opposition (*The Return of the Secaucus Seven*, 1979, *Matewan*, 1987), in his exploration of American memory and myth (*Lone Star*, 1996), and his concern to represent marginal, ethnic experiences (*Lone Star* and *Hombres Armados*, 1997) he comes close to the Third Cinema category. However, his Irish film, *The Secret of Roan Inish*, moves perilously close to the dominant ideology of First Cinema in the way in which it recycles some of the hoary old myths about Ireland and the Irish.

So too does Kirk Jones' *Waking Ned* (1998), which trades on a blatant recycling of outrageous clichés and old myths about rural Ireland. Despite its modest budget, the film, in its relationship to the status quo, is clearly 'first cinema'. Some friction with dominant Hollywood ideology is staged via the film's treatment of age, and in the film-maker's bold decision to cast two seventy-year-olds as the heroes. How the film is received, therefore, depends on the cultural context of consumption – who sees the film and in what context. For the Irish who read this 'first cinema' film in a 'second' or 'third cinema' way, it is an insult (Linehan **93**

1999: 46). By contrast, for 'Help the Aged' groups it may well have the capacity to trigger a debate about ageism. It might, in other words, achieve some of the objectives outlined by Solanas in relation to moving individuals from passive spectators to active participants (though hardly in the socially, aesthetically and politically transforming manner which he envisaged). As a rule, however, medium-budget Irish film-makers are more oppositional to the dominant modes of Hollywood representation than that. In some instances (as for Jordan) the degree to which their films exhibit both thematic and formal innovation moves their work closer to a Third Cinema perspective. The most significant, and therefore the most 'Irish', films are those that explore the complex realities of contemporary Ireland, interpellating audiences by challenging dominant and sedimented notions about Ireland and the Irish.

The value of examining film-making in Ireland through the lenses of the Third Cinema debate does not lie simply in the fact that it resonates with the three-tier funding strategy outlined by Michael D. Higgins. More importantly, the debate on Third Cinema provides a pathway through the vexed question of what exactly constitutes an Irish film. In one regard, both *Far and Away* and *The Secret of Roan Inish* are Irish films, and as representations of Irish themes they are quite rightly discussed as part of a study of 'film and Ireland'. They have also played their role in generating the necessary infrastructure in Ireland that can sustain indigenous film-makers. The critique offered here is not that they are, by dint of their production contexts, less 'Irish' than those, say, of Jordan or Sheridan (after all, Jordan's *Michael Collins*, 1996, had a First Cinema budget), but that their representation of Ireland is extremely problematic. They interconnect with contemporary Ireland in regressive aesthetic, ideological and political ways. This may indeed be a result of their creative distance from Ireland and the Irish. The judgment here, however, is a critical, not an ethnic or an economic one – a position informed by aesthetic and political concerns about the films' relationship to dominant representations, and to the socio-political complexities, of contemporary Ireland.

The third category of films produced wholly within Ireland has tended to be low-budget films. These are films that are very particular in their concerns and the making of which is dominated by younger writer/directors determined to hold on to artistic control of both form and subject matter. This is especially the case for the earlier period of Irish film-making, in the 1970s and early 1980s – the closest Ireland came to a Third Cinema in the original sense with the politically charged cinema of Bob Quinn, Joe Comerford, Cathal Black and the feminist cinema of Pat Murphy – but also with the Film Board strategy since 1993, particularly with regard to first-time directors. This cinema is relatively unknown outside the country and, with the exception of a few films, largely unseen in Irish cinemas either. The films have made some impact at festivals around the world, but their main exhibition channel has been Irish or British television.

Irish Cinema – Themes and Contexts

The Irish film industry resembles that of most other medium- and small-scale European industries, in that film production is the result of a complex structure of national and transnational funding initiatives. As in other European industries, in Ireland state support for film production is designed to promote an indigenous film industry and to develop a more pluralist film culture in a country where cinema screens are dominated by Hollywood films. Ireland, however, differs from most other small-scale European national film industries in one major respect. Although the native language (Irish Gaelic) is still spoken in small pockets of the country, Ireland reflects its status as a former colony of Britain in the fact that it is now an overwhelmingly English-speaking culture with an anglophone cinema. In this regard, Irish cinema closely resembles the 'non-nation-state' cinemas of Wales and Scotland while being peculiarly exposed to the Hollywood behemoth, with which it shares a language. And yet, somewhat ironically, precisely because Irish cinema is anglophone, there is always the hope that Irish films will break through into the American market, with the consequent danger that production strategies are geared towards that eventuality. So far, only Neil Jordan's *The Crying Game* and Jim Sheridan's *My Left Foot* (1989) (both largely British financed) have really done so, but, as is the case with British cinema, the temptation to compete, rather than to live with Hollywood cinema, is always there.

The Irish experience is peculiar also in another way. The fact that film-making in Ireland is a fairly recent phenomenon should not disguise the fact that Ireland and the Irish have maintained a major presence in American and British film-making since the beginnings of cinema. This presence has been manifest in terms of personnel, especially actors and directors, but also and most specifically in terms of theme, setting, character and plot. The extraordinary high levels of migration from Ireland after the Famine years of the late 1840s to the 1920s meant that the Irish and the Irish-Americans made up a significant percentage of early cinema audiences in the USA, particularly in the cities on the east coast. In the early silent era producers pandered to these audiences with sentimental tales and romantic adventures set in Irish-American communities or in Ireland itself. These early two- and three-reel films attracted a range of Irish and Irish-American actors who perfected the stereotypes that would define the cinematic image of the Irish for decades after. The films were peopled by amiable drunks and aggressive brawlers, corrupt politicos and honest but dumb cops, Catholic priests and angelic nuns, long-suffering mothers, feisty colleens and vulnerable, naïve maidens. Although established in the earliest days of the silent cinema, these stereotypes continued to populate American genre cinema throughout the twentieth century – played by a range of character actors and stars who were either native-born Irish or who had an Irish ancestry that they could draw upon when necessary (especially when called upon for studio publicity purposes).

The relatively high profile of Irish themes and stereotypes in American and British cinema has ensured that the representation of Ireland and the Irish has been a major concern for film studies in Ireland. Two traditions in particular have been identified. On the one hand, Ireland has tended to be represented in romantic rural terms with great emphasis placed on its beautiful landscapes and stirring seascapes. This has been the enduring cinematic tradition and one that has recurred with remarkable consistency down the years (Rockett, Gibbons and Hill 1987). On the other hand, Ireland has also been portrayed as an urban hell, where violence and sectarian hatreds seem to form part of the Irish character and to have locked the Irish into an endless and meaningless cycle of murder and revenge. In the 1970s and 1980s, when political violence in Northern Ireland escalated, this image appeared with more regularity (Hill 1987; McIlroy 1998; McLoone 2000).

The fact that indigenous film-making was slow to develop meant that these two domi-nant trends went largely unchallenged and were left to circulate as markers of a general Irish identity. When indigenous film-making finally developed in both parts of Ireland, at the end of the twentieth century, these iconographic trends and the recurring images that went with them marked an important point of departure. Both are referred to, directly and indirectly, in much recent Irish film-making. In other words, the cinematic debate in Ireland is as much about the traditions of representation in the films of other countries as it is about the films produced in Ireland. The Irish cinema that has emerged over the last fifteen years or so is a cinema – again like the cinemas of Wales and Scotland – that reflects both inherited native and dominant external cultural tropes played out in a global arena (McLoone 2002).

This is evident in recent films that have explored aspects of the city in Irish culture. In a constellation that has been dominated by images of the rural, Irish urban life has been largely absent from the screen until relatively recently. However, with the growth of indigenous film-making, the Irish urban experience gradually became a recurring theme. With the economic boom of the 1990s, films that probed violence and organised crime in Dublin became especially popular. For example, three film versions were about real-life Dublin gangster Martin Cahill – John Boorman's *The General* (1997), Thaddeus O'Sullivan's *Ordi-nary Decent Criminal* (2000) and a BBC Northern Ireland television film *Vicious Circle* (1999). Each of these films was concerned to contrast the violence of organised crime in Dublin with the paramilitary violence more typically associated with Ireland. There is an ironic ref-erence to this in the title of O'Sullivan's film, while in *Vicious Circle* the parallel is clearly articulated by one of the investigating police officers: 'Dublin is turning into Dodge City', he says to a suitably sleazy politician, 'and the IRA have nothing to do with it'. There have been also two versions of the story of Veronica Guerin, the investigative crime reporter shot dead in 1996 by the Dublin gangsters she tenaciously pursued through her newspaper columns – John MacKenzie's *When the Sky Falls* (1999) and the big-budget Hollywood ver-sion *Veronica Guerin* (J. Schumacher, 2003) use Guerin's story to probe Dublin's organised crime culture and to valorise the kind of self-help determination that Guerin represented.

This concern with the Cahill and Guerin stories was part of a process of reclaiming the city from representational neglect. Thus in some of these films, Cahill becomes a kind of Robin Hood or Jesse James character, while Dublin is presented as a contemporary urban environment much like anywhere else. The emphasis the films lay on the contrast between 'ordinary' gangsterism and paramilitary violence is part of this reclamation process, an attempt to 'normalise' the cinematic image of Ireland not as a backward and rural place nor as run by the IRA – even if this means showing that urban Ireland suffers from much the same kinds of problems that cities in other developed countries do, including drug-related organised crime.

While these were all relatively high-profile productions, throughout the 1990s a number of low-budget indigenous films also probed crime in contemporary urban life, again drawing attention to the drug culture as a feature of city life. In Paul Tickell's *Crushproof* (1996), a raw and edgy Dublin of endless suburbs and grim housing projects is populated by dysfunctional teenagers and alcoholic or drug-addicted adults. The 'Dodge City' factor is evoked by the incongruous horses the teenage boys look after and ride around on. In Joe O'Byrnes' *Pete's Meteor* (1999) the devastation caused by drugs and drug-related AIDS provides a realistic contrast to the fantasy world that twelve-year-old Mickey constructs around the meteor that lands in his back garden. Grim, earth-bound realities are juxtaposed to the heavenly promise of transcendence. Even in John Lynch's *Night Train* (1999) the romance between middle-aged Michael and Alice is threatened by Michael's previous crimes, which come back to haunt his present.

There is a problem in all this. Ireland has been dominated by images of romantic rural life, and part of the attraction of this myth is that it provides escape from urban alienation and disharmony. In a society dominated by such myths, the otherwise understandable desire to represent the city and its problems can prove counter-productive. Regressive attitudes and prejudices against the city and urbanisation, implicit in rural romanticism, might well be confirmed rather than challenged. For many of the younger film-makers who emerged in the 1990s, however, the city is a cause for celebration, not a source of anxiety. This might well explain the preponderance, in recent years, of another kind of urban-based film – what might be called a cinema of 'hip hedonism'. This is a cinema that celebrates, even glorifies, an urban lifestyle dressed in the signifiers of contemporary global youth culture and populated by the beautiful people of Celtic Tiger Ireland. They are Irish, certainly, but they epitomise a kind of trans-global 'cool'. Drugs and crime still form part of the background, but these are now presented as lifestyle choices or get-rich-quick schemes removed from any social consequences. Most importantly, these films are much lighter in tone than the more political films, as well as being driven by a deliberately irreverent humour.

The Dublin that is portrayed here is a city of luxurious apartments and well-appointed offices, beautifully decorated rooms looking out onto spectacular cityscapes, conspicuous consumption in modern art galleries, trendy restaurants, stylish coffee and wine bars, and modernist pubs. This is also a Dublin of promiscuous sexual abandon, the new cinema's final affront to the values of the old Ireland. These films seem to suggest that Catholic, nationalist Ireland is now merely a faded memory passed down to the young population from their grandparents (or gleaned from those Irish films that seem to be obsessed by this dead past). Three films in particular epitomise this new hip hedonism – Gerry Stembridge's *About Adam* (2001), Liz Gill's *Goldfish Memory* (2003) and John Crowley's *Intermission* (2003) – although many more Dublin-based films display some of these characteristics, constituting a significant and identifiable trend in recent Irish cinema. Interestingly, *About Adam, Goldfish Memory* and *Intermission* have multiple story lines and circular plots – contemporary Irish versions of Arthur Schnitzler's nineteenth-century play *La Ronde* and Max Ophuls' 1950 film of the same name. The characters play games with one another in pursuit of love and sex while the film-makers play a game with the audience of circular plots that weave around coincidences and overlapping encounters. In *Goldfish Memory*, all possible combinations of sexual coupling are explored – straight, gay, lesbian and bisexual – and played out against a highly stylised   **97**

Dublin that was shot originally on digital video and later enhanced through computer imaging. This post-production process suffuses the final film with enhanced colours – oranges, soft blues and warm greens – creating an almost subliminal sense of well-being, a visual 'feel good' factor that makes the city of Dublin appear uncharacteristically bright and attractive. Just as the film explores alternative love possibilities so too the stylised cinematography reimagines an alternative Dublin, providing an almost impossibly attractive contemporary milieu for the film's daring sexual politics.

These are also films in which the camera seems to have become obsessed by good looks and designer clothes, lovingly dwelling on the beautiful and handsome faces and bodies that inhabit the reconfigured city. The cast of *Goldfish Memory* in particular is uniformly young and attractive, but the same could be said of *About Adam*, which is dominated by the charismatic performances of Stuart Townsend as the film's handsome serial seducer, and of Kate Hudson and Frances O'Connor as two of his attractive lovers. Similarly, Fintan Connolly's *Flick* (1999) explores a lifestyle of hedonistic excess, even if this view of contemporary Dublin has more rough edges than *About Adam* and *Goldfish Memory*. Centred on middle-class drug dealer Jack Flinter, played by David Murray, *Flick* seems at times mesmerised by Murray's presence. As it follows Jack through long sequences where he is seen buying, selling and imbibing his drugs in the clubs and pubs of contemporary Dublin, the camera seems to prowl along, eyeing him with almost voyeuristic zeal. The (young) audience is invited to look and to empathise. To some extent, then, these films' self-obsessed narcissism and their designer-label chic may well be a reflection of one aspect of Celtic Tiger Ireland – the rampant consumerism that comes from economic success and greater affluence. Their strength lies in their reimaging of Ireland, in their enactment of a luxurious facelift to the old artwork of Irishness.

Of course it is not just the old artwork of urban Ireland that has been revisited by recent cinema. The image of rural Catholic Ireland was literally blown up in Neil Jordan's *The Butcher Boy* (1997) in a memorable sequence that imagines an atomic explosion in the rural splendour of small-town Ireland. The religious ethos that underpinned Catholic Ireland has been effectively undermined also by a host of films exploring the abuses of Catholic institutions and ideology – for example, in Syd Macartney's *A Love Divided* (1999), in Peter Mullan's Scottish-financed *The Magdalene Sisters* (2002), a film that was also immensely popular in Italy, and in Aisling Walsh's *Song for a Raggy Boy* (2003). The same is true for the once dominant image of paramilitary Northern Ireland, which has also been considerably reconfigured in recent cinema (for instance, by David Caffrey's *Divorcing Jack*, 1998). Cinematic Belfast has been given the same kind of 'wine bar' facelift as Dublin has been in the hip hedonist films (in Michael Winterbottom's *With or Without You*, 1999, and in Declan Lowney's *Wild About Harry*, 2000).

Conclusion

Ireland's small-scale indigenous film-making is a national cinema in the sense that it problematises the concept of Irishness itself. It is a cinema that inhabits a contradictory space between the local and the global and which negotiates conflicting definitions of the national.

98

It is an *arrière-garde* cinema that captures a post-colonial dilemma over the legacy of the past and the challenges of the future. It is a national cinema in the sense that it is a cinema of national questioning, rather than a cinema of bland assertion. In its more political and confrontational moments, it is clearly a kind of 'third cinema', but in its negotiations with the global marketplace it is a cinema that straddles the divide between national specificity and a kind of international meta-style. Finally, in its relationship to an already existing tradition of representation, it is a cinema of inevitable intertextuality and internal reference.

References

Barton, Ruth (2004), *Irish National Cinema*, London: Routledge.

Eagleton, Terry (1998), *Crazy John and the Bishop and Other Essays on Irish Culture*, Cork: Cork University Press.

Frampton, Kenneth (1985), 'Towards a Critical Regionalism: Six Points for an Architecture of Resistance', in Foster, Hal (ed.), *Postmodern Culture,* London: Pluto Press: 16–30.

Higgins, Michael D. (1995), Public interview, National Film Theatre, London, October.

Hill, John (1988), 'Images of Violence', in Rockett, Gibbons and Hill (1987): 147–93.

Linehan, Hugh, (1999), 'Myth, Mammon and Mediocrity: The Trouble with Recent Irish Cinema', *Cineaste* xxiv (2–3) Contemporary Irish Cinema Supplement: 46–9.

McIlroy, Brian (1998), *Shooting to Kill: Film-making and the 'Troubles' in Northern Ireland*, Trowbridge: Flicks.

McLoone, Martin (2002), 'Internal Decolonisation? British Cinema in the Celtic Fringe', in Murphy, Robert (ed.) (2002): 184–90.

Pettitt, Lance (2000), *Screening Ireland: Film and Television Representation*, Manchester: Manchester University Press.

Solanas, Fernando and Getino, Octavio (1976), 'Towards a Third Cinema', in Nichols, Bill (ed.), *Movies and Methods: an Anthology*, Berkeley: University of California Press: 44–64.

7 British Cinema as National Cinema[1]

John Hill

Following the Oscar-winning success of *Chariots of Fire* (H. Hudson, 1981) on 23 March 1982, the film was re-released and shown successfully across Britain in the weeks which followed. On 2 April, the Argentinians invaded the Falklands/Malvinas islands and, three days later, the Thatcher government despatched a naval task force from Portsmouth which successfully retook the islands in June. In a sense, the coincidence of Oscar-winning success in Los Angeles and subsequent military victory in the Falklands seemed to link the two events together and the idea of a national resurgence in both cinema ('the British are coming') and national life became intertwined. Indeed, Hugo Young reports that David Puttnam, the producer of *Chariots of Fire*, was a subsequent guest of the prime minister at Chequers and that there was 'much talk in the Thatcher circle about the desirability of something similar being put on to celluloid to celebrate the Falklands victory' (Young 1990: 277).

There are, however, two factors which complicate this story. Despite its reputation, *Chariots of Fire* is a more complex work than is commonly suggested. Indeed, for a film which is reputedly so nationalist, it is surprising how conscious it is of the complexities of national allegiance, focusing as it does on the running careers of two 'outsiders': Abrahams, a Jew of Lithuanian background, and Eric Liddell, a Scotsman born in China. If *Chariots of Fire* did become identified with renascent national sentiment, then this was probably not so much the result of the ideological outlook which the film itself manifests as the moment at which its success was achieved. The other complicating factor is that when the film was re-released it was as a part of a double-bill with *Gregory's Girl* (B. Forsyth, 1980). While this double-bill was undoubtedly intended to showcase the range of new British cinema, there is also something a touch subversive in the way in which these films were coupled. For while both are British, they also represent rather different kinds of British cinema.

Although not a big-budget film, *Chariots of Fire*, at a cost of £3 million, was a comparatively expensive film for 1980. And, although it was strongly identified with 'Britishness' and the early 1980s 'renaissance' of British film-making, it was actually funded from foreign sources, including the Hollywood major, Twentieth Century-Fox. *Gregory's Girl*, by contrast, cost less than one-tenth of *Chariots of Fire* (about £200,000) and was financed from local sources, including the government-funded National Film Finance Corporation and Scottish

Television. A clear contrast in formal approach is also apparent. Thus, despite some play with temporal relations, *Chariots of Fire* employs a relatively straightforward narrative structure, organised around goal-oriented action and positive heroes. *Gregory's Girl*, however, opts for a much looser, more episodic form in which surface realism, comedy and domesticated surrealism are combined (in a way which successfully fuses British comic traditions with a modernist sensibility). These differences also extend to content. Thus, while *Chariots of Fire* is focused on the past, *Gregory's Girl* is resolutely of the present. The version of the past which *Chariots of Fire* constructs, moreover, is strongly identified with the English upper classes and male achievement while *Gregory's Girl* is set among the suburban middle and working class and gently subverts conventional stereotypes of male and female roles. And if both films are 'British', it is evident that *Chariots of Fire* is very much an 'English' film whereas *Gregory's Girl* is equally clearly 'Scottish'.

So while both films are, at least partly, set in Scotland, there is also a significant difference between the representations of Scotland which they provide. *Chariots of Fire* tends to look at Scotland from the outside (or rather from the metropolitan English centre), associating it with the 'natural' and the 'primitive'. *Gregory's Girl*, on the other hand, uses the 'new town' of Cumbernauld to avoid the conventional signifiers of 'Scottishness' and, in doing so, suggest an altogether more complex sense of contemporary Scottish identity. This, in turn, has

Chariots of Fire (Hugh Hudson, 1981)

links to what might be characterised as their differing modes of cultural address. *Chariots of Fire*, with its enthusiasm for the past and links with conventional notions of English 'national heritage', offers an image of Britain which generally conforms to the expectations of an international, and especially American, audience. *Gregory's Girl*, on the other hand, is a much more obviously local and idiomatic film. It too has an international appeal but for an audience more likely to be European than American. And, while it is *Chariots of Fire* which is conventionally taken to be the landmark in the revival of British cinema, it may, in fact, be *Gregory's Girl* which was to provide the more reliable indicator of the way in which British film-making was developing.

For what the two films also represent are somewhat different models of 'national cinema'. Since the 1980s, the conditions of production and reception of British films have changed significantly: the numbers of British films made has fallen, cinema audiences have been in long-term decline and British cinema screens have been increasingly dominated by films from Hollywood. As a result, it has often been argued that the British cinema has become a much more marginal cinema than hitherto and one which has lost much of its former connection to British national life. The prospect which the success of *Chariots of Fire* held out, in this respect, was that it might help to encourage the revival of a more genuinely popular national cinema. However, while there is something to this argument, it is also too simple and fails to capture some of the more complex aspects of the relationships involved between cinema and the 'nation'. By comparing some features of British cinema of the past with more recent British cinema, I want to suggest what these might be and at least question some of the standard assumptions which are often made about British cinema as 'national' cinema. In order to do so, I want to consider three main issues. These have to do with:

- production and the relationship between production strategies and 'national' cinema;
- consumption and the relationship between British films and the 'national' audience; and
- representation and how British films may be seen to represent the 'nation'.

Production

If the relationship of British film production to national life may be seen to have altered in recent years this is primarily the consequence of changing economic circumstances and the shift in film-making orientation which this has entailed. Since the end of World War I, it has been the case that one national cinema – that of the USA – has dominated virtually all others (India has been the main exception). This has meant that the cinemas of most other countries have in some way or other had to accommodate to the realities of a world film industry dominated by the output of another country. British cinema in the 1980s may be seen, in this regard, to have returned to the position in which it found itself in the 1920s when the government first introduced a quota for British films. In 1924 some 25 per cent of films exhibited in British cinemas were British but by 1925 this figure had dropped to 10 per cent and by 1926 to 5 per cent (*Cinematograph Films Act 1927*: 5). The vast bulk of films shown were, of course, from the US. Following the abolition of the quota in 1983, the percentage of British films on British screens dwindled to similar proportions. Thus, in 1992 the US had a 92.5 per cent share of the British exhibition market while British films accounted for only 4 per cent (*Screen Digest* Dec. 1993: 280).

The responses to US domination which have been open to the production sector of the British film industry in the 1980s and 1990s are, however, different from the 1920s. In his essay on the conceptualisation of national cinemas, Stephen Crofts identifies a number of strategies available to national cinema production. In terms of the British cinema, the most important are what he describes as the imitation of Hollywood, competition with Holly-wood in domestic markets, and differentiation from Hollywood (Crofts 1993: 50). The imitation of Hollywood involves the attempt to beat Hollywood at its own game and this has been attempted at various junctures in the history of British cinema: by Alexander Korda in the 1930s, by Rank in the 1940s, by EMI in the 1970s and then Goldcrest in the 1980s. Given the competitive advantage which Hollywood enjoys over other national industries by virtue of its scale of production, size of domestic market and international distribution and exhibition network (among other factors), this has proved an economically unviable strategy and, despite some success with individual films, all such attempts have resulted in financial disaster. It is therefore the second strategy which has constituted the traditional bedrock of British cinema.

As a result of the quota (and later some additional forms of state support), the existence of a commercial British cinema which did not compete with Hollywood internationally but only in the domestic market proved possible from the 1930s to – just about – the 1970s. The basis of this cinema, however, was a size of audience sufficient to sustain a domestic film industry. As cinema audiences began to decline, especially from the 1950s onwards, the com-mercial viability of a cinema primarily aimed at British audiences began to be threatened. As a result, regular British film production (characteristically popular genre film-making) aimed at the domestic market came to a virtual halt after the 1970s when Hammer horror, the *Carry On*s and the *Confession* films all ceased to be produced. While it had previously been possible for British films to recoup their costs on the home market this became an exception from the 1970s onwards. Only a minority of British films achieved a domestic gross of over £1 million during the 1980s and even an apparently popular success such as *Buster* (D. Green, 1988), which grossed £3.7 million in 1988, failed to recover its production cost of £3.2 million from British box-office revenues (given that only a fraction of these actually returns to the producer).

In consequence, the place of British cinema within the international film economy has had to change. Writing in 1969, Alan Lovell argued that, unlike its European counterparts, the British cinema had failed to develop an art cinema (or at any rate that the documentary film had served in its place) (1969: 2). During the 1980s, however, it was art cinema which was to become the predominant model of British film-making. The category of 'art cinema' is not, of course, a precise one and it is used here in a relatively generous sense. David Bor-dwell (1979), for example, has attempted to define 'art cinema' as a distinctive 'mode of film practice' characterised by realism, authorial expressivity and ambiguity. His definition, how-ever, is too tied to the 1960s and fails to do justice to the range of textual strategies employed by art cinema in the 1980s and 1990s. Thus, in the case of Britain, the category of art cinema may be seen to include not only the 'realism' of Ken Loach and Mike Leigh and the postmodern aesthetic experiments of Derek Jarman and Peter Greenaway, but also the aesthetically conservative 'heritage' cinema of Merchant-Ivory. In this last case, the 'art' of 'art cinema' is defined less in terms of the authorial presence of the director or the distance from classical narrational and stylistic techniques which such films display than the cachet of 'high art' which such films borrow from extra-textual literary or theatrical sources.

For Crofts, art cinema is the prime example of a national cinema avoiding direct competition with Hollywood by targeting a distinct market sector. This model, he argues, aims 'to differentiate itself textually from Hollywood, to assert explicitly or implicitly an indigenous product, and to reach domestic and export markets through those specialist distribution channels and exhibition venues usually called 'art-house' (Crofts 1993: 51). In this respect, the adoption of aesthetic strategies and cultural referents different from Hollywood also involves a certain foregrounding of 'national' credentials. The oft-noted irony of this, however, is that art cinema then achieves much of its status as national cinema by circulating internationally rather than nationally. While this means that art cinema (as in the case of Greenaway) may be as economically viable as ostensibly more commercial projects aimed at the 'popular' audience, it is also the case that successful British films have often done better outside of Britain than within. A particularly notorious example of this was Ken Loach's *Riff-Raff* (1991) which, at the time it won the European Film Award for Best Film in 1991, had been seen by more people in France than in the UK, where it had received virtually no distribution at all. Even in the case of the heritage film, it is international audiences, especially American, which have become a key source of revenues as well as prestige. As a result, it has become an attractive option to open such films in the United States before a release in Britain, as was the case, for example, with both *The Madness of King George* (N. Hytner, 1994) and *Sense and Sensibility* (Ang Lee, 1996).

In both these cases – the cinema *d'auteur* which circulates in Europe and the heritage film which appeals to the US – it can be argued that the changed economic circumstances of the British film industry have led to a certain decline of 'national' cinema insofar as the national address which earlier commercial British cinema appeared to have is no longer so evident. In this respect, much of the lamenting of the current state of the British film industry registers a sense of loss of the connection which it is assumed the British cinema once had with a national popular audience. There is a further twist to this argument, however. For, if the decline in domestic cinema audiences has made British film production increasingly dependent upon international revenues, it has also increased its reliance on television for revenues and production finance as well. The increasing interrelationship between film and television which has resulted has then had consequences for how film is consumed and thus upon the way in which it may be judged to be 'national'.

Audience

As has been argued, the changing character of British cinema in the 1980s may be explained **104** in terms of the new production strategies which emerged in the wake of declining cinema audiences. In 1946, cinema admissions reached an all-time high of 1,635 million but then steadily fell until 1984 when admissions reached as low as 58 million. There has, of course, been a subsequent increase, such that admissions reached over 123 million in 1994. However, this was still a figure lower than any year previously recorded prior to 1974. It is these figures which provide the backdrop to perceptions of cinema's declining national role. For if the British cinema of World War II is still regarded as a watershed in national cinema, it is not only as a result of the films which were then made but because of the size of the cinema audience which attended them. In 1940, admissions topped 1,000 million for the first time and, partly due to a lack of alternatives, provided the most popular form of entertainment. In this respect, wartime cinema is regarded as pre-eminently 'national' due both to the size and also the range of the audience which it addressed.

However, it is possible to over-state this argument. For, even at its peak, the cinema audience was never fully representative of the nation. A survey of the British cinema audience in 1943, for example, revealed that 30 per cent of the population didn't go to the cinema at all and that certain social groups were more likely to attend the cinema than others (Moss and Box 1943). Women went to the cinema more than men, the manual working class and lower middle class went more than managerial and professional groups, town-dwellers went more than country-dwellers. Most strikingly of all, the cinema audience was characteristically made up of the young rather than the old. Hence, the under-45s accounted for 85 per cent of the cinema audience but only 68 per cent of the overall population. Cinemagoing declined significantly with age and 60 per cent of the over-65s are reported as never going to the cinema at all. It is evident therefore that the 'national' audience for British films, even during the 'golden age' of British cinema, was neither as homogeneous nor as socially representative of the nation as is sometimes assumed. Moreover, it is also fair to assume that, even among cinemagoers, the appeal of British films was not necessarily uniform but also likely to vary according to gender, age and class.[2]

These issues of audience are also relevant when considering the subsequent decline of the cinema. For, if the cinema audience has become a smaller proportion of the overall population and cinemagoing no longer occupies the central place in leisure activities which it once did, the social character of the audience and its cinema-watching habits have also undergone change.[3] Thus, cinemagoing has become even more heavily concentrated among the young, particularly among the fifteen to thirty-four age group who accounted for 78 per cent of cinema attendances in 1990 (but only 37 per cent of the population). By comparison, only 11 per cent of the over-45s attended the cinema despite representing 46 per cent of the population. The class basis of cinemagoing has also altered. Cinemagoing is no longer a predominantly working-class activity and, in 1990, social classes ABC1 accounted for 59 per cent of cinemagoers (while representing 42 per cent of the population) (Grummitt 1995: 1). One explanation for this is the growth of multiplexes which, since 1985, have been responsible for reviving the cinemagoing habit, especially among car-owners.[4] Multiplexes have also made the cinema more attractive to women who, following a decline in attendance in the 1950s, have accounted for about 50 per cent of the cinema audience in the 1990s. In a sense, from the 1950s onwards, the working-class **105** cinema audience has been in decline and has been replaced by an increasingly young and more affluent one. This is in line with more general trends in cinemagoing which have seen an increase in the importance of the fifteen to twenty-four age group (which, it has been estimated, amounts to as much as 80 per cent of the worldwide cinema audience for English-language films) (James Lee in Scottish Film Council 1993: 44). This audience demography is clearly significant when thinking about national cinema: for what is most popular at the cinemas is not necessarily popular with a fully representative section of the 'nation' but only a relatively narrow segment of it.

What further complicates this argument is that while these trends are fairly clear with regard to cinemagoing, it is no longer the case that cinema is the primary site for viewing films. Despite the global decline in cinema attendances, it is argued by Douglas Gomery that the watching of films is more popular than ever (1992: 276). Films may no longer be watched in the same numbers in the cinemas but they are watched in increasing numbers on television and video and this is especially so in the UK where TV and video penetration is very high by world standards. Some comparisons are appropriate. In 1994, for example, total cinema admissions for 1994 amounted to 123 million. In the same year, video rentals (which are dominated by feature films) amounted to 194 million (a considerable drop, in fact, from 328 million the previous year) and video retail transactions accounted for 66 million (*BFI Film and Television Handbook* 1995: 34, 47). In the case of television, the contrast is even more striking. First, there are considerably more films on TV than in the cinemas. Thus, in 1994, 299 features were released in UK cinemas, of which thirty-five were 'wholly' British.[5] In the same year, 1,910 films were screened on terrestrial TV, of which 413 came from Britain (*Screen Finance* 11 Jan. 1995: 13; 8 Feb. 1995: 12). Films on TV are also watched by considerably more people as well. In 1994, the viewing figures for the top ten films on TV alone matched the total audience for all 299 films shown in the cinemas. This also means that individual films, including British films, are seen by significantly more people on television than in the cinemas. Thus, the most popular 'wholly' British film of 1992, *Peter's Friends* (K. Branagh, 1992), was seen by approximately four times as many people when it was shown on television in 1994 than when it was shown in the cinema (*Screen Finance* 24 Feb. 1993: 9).[6] A commercially unsuccessful film such as *Waterland* (S. Gyllenhaal, 1992) was seen by nearly thirty-four times as many people when it was shown on television in 1994 and, if its viewing figures of 3.3 million had been converted into cinema attendances, this would have put it in the box-office top ten for 1992.

A number of points may be made about these figures. First, it is evident, for example, that the number of people watching film on television and video is significantly higher than in the cinemas. Moreover, it is also an audience which is probably more representative of the 'nation' as a whole. Thus, the group which is over-represented in the cinemas – the sixteen- to twenty-four-year-olds – is under-represented in the television audience and those groups which are not heavy cinemagoers – the over-45s, social groups DE, country-dwellers – are much more likely to see films on TV. Barwise and Ehrenberg, for example, provide television viewing figures for 1985 which indicate that only 10 per cent of the television audience for films is aged sixteen to thirty-four while the over-55s account for 40 per cent

(1988: 29).[7] In this respect, the 'national' reach of cinema is the greater as a result of television and, although it is often seen as responsible for the demise of cinema, television may in fact be making it more accessible than ever before. While the figures do not exist to permit full precision, it does seem to be the case that many contemporary British films which are not regarded as especially 'popular' are nonetheless seen (on television) by as many people as 'popular' British films of the past. Thus, if the 7.8 million people who watched *Mona Lisa* (N. Jordan, 1986) on its first television screening in 1989 had gone to see a British film at the cinema in the 1940s, it would undoubtedly have been to a popular film. To put it deliberately provocatively, it may in fact be the case that a British cinema which is generally regarded as being in decline is nonetheless producing films which are often being seen by as many, and sometimes more, people as films made during the 'golden age' of British cinema.

There are, of course, provisos. As has often been argued, the cinema experience and the television viewing experience are dissimilar, and watching films on TV or video is characteristically less concentrated than in the cinema. Watching films on TV is also more likely to be part of a 'flow' of viewing and so provide less of a discrete experience than in the cinema.[8] As a result, the numbers watching films on TV may be substantial but their impact and significance for audiences may be much less than when watched in the special circumstances of the cinema. However, it is also worth noting how habitual cinemagoing was in its heyday. Browning and Sorrell, for example, report that in 1946 nearly three-quarters of those who went to the cinema more than once a month did so whatever films were being shown and without choosing between cinemas (1954: 146). Cinemagoing was only exceptionally an 'event' and, in a number of respects, television has taken over the cinema's former function of catering to the 'regular cinemagoer'. However, while this is true of the bulk of television scheduling of films, it is also the case that television can use film as an 'event', breaking up the televisual flow and offering a 'special' experience separated out from the rest of television. This is most commonly the case with the first screening of a big Hollywood blockbuster but would also be true, for example, of Channel Four's heavily trailered first screening of *Four Weddings and a Funeral* (M. Newell, 1994), which attracted an audience of 12.38 million viewers in 1996.[9]

Although films can achieve very high audience figures on television, it is, nonetheless, the case that other forms of drama (especially serial drama) achieve even higher figures. In this respect, the national reach of film is generally less than that of television drama. Indeed, John Caughie has expressed an anxiety that the growth in involvement of television in film production has led to an increased investment in drama on film aimed at the international market at the expense of more local forms of television drama. In doing so, he contrasts the work of Ken Loach in the 1960s and 1990s. '*Ladybird, Ladybird* (K. Loach, 1994)', he argues, 'circulates within an aesthetic and a cultural sphere which is given cultural prestige (and an economic viability) by international critics' awards, whereas *Cathy Come Home* (K. Loach, 1966) circulated as a national event and functioned as documentary evidence within the political sphere' (1996: 219). His point is well made but it also sets up too stark an opposition. For if television drama circulates less as a 'national event' in the 1980s than it did in the **107**

1960s, this is not simply the consequence of television's involvement in cinema. It has more to do with the transformations which broadcasting as a whole has undergone, especially the increase in channels (both terrestrial and non-terrestrial), the rise of video (and its opportunities for alternative viewing and time-shifting) and the fragmentation of the national audience which has resulted. If the capacity of both television drama and film to function as a national event has lessened, this is partly because the national audience for television does not exist in the same way as it did in the 1960s and because neither individual television programmes nor films can lay claim to the same cultural dominance within the entertainment sphere which they once could. In this regard, the national audience is, in fact, a series of audiences which are often addressed in different and diverse ways. At the same time, the representations which British cinema then makes available to them may also be seen to have themselves become much more complex and varied.

Representation

There is a scene in David Hare's *Strapless* (1988) which is suggestive in this regard. In this, a doctor, working for the NHS, addresses a group of assembled hospital workers and speaks up on behalf of 'English values'. It is a scene with loose echoes of wartime movies such as *In Which We Serve* (N. Coward and D. Lean, 1942) or *Henry V* (L. Olivier, 1944) in which morale-boosting speeches which uphold traditional English virtues are delivered to an assembled group (in these instances, sailors and soldiers). There are, however, significant differences. In *Strapless*, the speech is delivered not by an English man but by an American woman and the group to whom she speaks is not the homogeneous white male group of the earlier films but one which is visibly differentiated by gender and ethnicity. By having an American defend the 'idea of Englishness', the film acknowledges the difficulty which such a speech presents for a contemporary British film and attempts to sidestep the irony which would, almost inevitably, have had to accompany its delivery by an English character (and, even yet, there is still a hint of pastiche in the way in which the scene is realised). The difficulty of speaking for England is indicated, however, not only by the nationality of the speaker but even more strikingly by the composition of the group to whom the doctor speaks. Unlike the earlier films, there is no confident assumption of who represents 'Englishness'. Rather the vision of the 'national' community which the film provides is remarkably plural and diverse and there is clearly an effort in this scene to 'make strange' traditional conceptions of 'Englishness' and reimagine a more inclusive version of national identity (and identities within the nation).

It is a significant scene because, within writing on British cinema, it is the relationship between film and national identity which has often been taken to be especially close. Important works on British cinema by Jeffrey Richards (1984) on the 1930s, Charles Barr (1977) on Ealing and Raymond Durgnat (1970) on the post-war period have all uncovered in British films an effort to tell stories which invite audiences to interpret them in terms of ideas about the 'nation' and 'national identity'. More recently, Andrew Higson (1995) has identified what he regards as a characteristic way of 'imagining the nation' as a 'knowable, organic community' in British films which he links to a typically 'national style', characterised by episodic narratives involving multiple characters, a distanced observational view-point and a non-narrative use of space. Clearly, there is a danger that such arguments under-estimate the variety of British cinema and are too ready to make pronouncements about all British cinema on the basis of a selective sample of films (in Higson's case, his book deals with only five in any detail). Nonetheless, it is equally evident that, if not all British cinema then, at least significant strands of British cinema (such as wartime cinema and Ealing com-edies) have evolved an aesthetic and a way of telling stories which clearly display a national-allegorical import.[10]

However, if this is so, then it is also apparent that the certainties concerning the nation upon which such films relied have, since the 1960s, increasingly dissolved. The strategy of national allegory, in this respect, has not so much been abandoned as refashioned to express a new sense of difference, diversity and even conflict. Hence, films such as *My Beautiful Laundrette* (S. Frears, 1987) and *Sammy and Rosie Get Laid* (S. Frears, 1988) continue to employ, with a few postmodern embellishments, the stylistic features of British national cinema which Higson identifies and, in doing so, clearly invite the individual stories of its characters to be read in terms of an 'allegory' of the 'state of the nation'. They do so, how-ever, not to project a unified notion of national identity and culture but rather a much more fluid, hybrid and plural sense of 'Britishness' than earlier British cinema generally did. To this extent, such films are responding to the more complex sense of national identity which has been characteristic of modern Britain and have deployed the new space occupied by British cinema – as both art cinema and public service television – to develop a more critical relationship to 'British' culture.[11] In this respect, the interests of the art film (which are often individual and subjective) may be seen to have merged with the preoccupations of public service television (which are characteristically more social and 'national' in scope). As a result, the alliance between film and television which Caughie sees as lessening the local dimensions of *television* may also be read as a strengthening of the local aspects of *cinema*.

This is particularly the case in what has been a significant aspect of British cinema during the 1980s. Writing of the strong sense of 'national identity' apparent in British wartime films, Jeffrey Richards has observed how this sense of identity 'derived almost entirely from Eng-land, which was often used interchangeably with Britain to describe the nation' (1989: 44). Much the same conclusion is reached by Raymond Durgnat (1970) who describes the 'British movies' from 1945 to 1958 which he discusses as providing a 'mirror for *England*' (my italics). Since the 1980s, however, it can be argued that not only has British cinema articu-lated a much more inclusive sense of Englishness than previously but that it has also accorded a much greater recognition to the differing nationalities and identities within Britain (including, for example, the emergence of a distinctive black British cinema). In this respect, British national cinema now clearly implies Scottish and Welsh cinema as well as just Eng-lish cinema. Indeed, two of the most successful British films of the mid-1990s – *Shallow Grave* (D. Boyle, 1995) and *Trainspotting* (D. Boyle, 1996) – have been very clearly Scottish. This has implications, however, not only for the inclusiveness of the representations of Britain which British cinema provides but also, as the example of *Gregory's Girl* indicates, the way in which issues of national identity are then addressed. **109**

Graeme Turner, for example, writing of Australian cinema in the 1990s, has noted the suspicion which often accompanies discussion of both the nation and national cinema due to the socially conservative versions of national identity which these tend to imply. He argues, however, that the post-colonial status of Australia means that its discourses of the nation are much less settled and that it is possible for Australian films to provide 'a critical [b]ody of representations within mainstream Western cinema' (1994: 203). In the same way, the peculiar historical circumstances of Scotland and Wales – which may have gained economically from the British colonial enterprise but nonetheless encountered subordination culturally – provides an opening for a more complex negotiation of the discourses around the 'nation' than English/British cinema has traditionally provided.[12] *Trainspotting* is an interesting example in this regard. One of the most commercially successful British films of 1996, it was fully financed by the public service broadcaster, Channel Four, and combines an interest in social issues (drug-taking, AIDS, poverty) with a determinedly self-conscious aesthetic style reminiscent of the French and British 'new waves'. In experimenting with cinematic style, however, it also plays with the inherited imagery of England and Scotland. Thus, when the film's main character Mark Renton (Ewan McGregor) arrives in London, the film cheerfully invokes the most clichéd images of London in an ironic inversion of the touristic imagery which commonly accompanies the arrival of an English character in Scotland.[13] In a similarly iconoclastic manner, the film escorts its main characters to the Scottish countryside. It does so, however, not to invoke the 'romantic' beauty of the Scottish landscape but to provide Renton with the occasion for a swingeing attack on 'being Scottish' ('We're the lowest of the fucking low ... It's a shite state of affairs and all the fresh air in the world will not make any fucking difference'). So while *Trainspotting* may speak with a voice that is decidedly Scottish, it also does so in a way which avoids simple pieties concerning Scottish, or 'British', identity (even if its treatment of gender may be rather less self-reflective).

Conclusion

I have argued, elsewhere, that the idea of British national cinema has often been linked, virtually by definition, to discourses of nationalism and myths of national unity (Hill 1992).[14] However, this formulation of a national cinema underestimates the possibilities for a national cinema to reimagine the nation, or rather nations within Britain, and also to address the specificities of a national culture in a way which does not presume a homogeneous or 'pure' national identity. Indeed, as Paul Willemen has argued, the national cinema which genuinely addresses national specificity will actually be at odds with the 'homogenising project' of nationalism insofar as this entails a critical engagement with 'the complex, multidimensional and multidirectional tensions that characterise and shape a social formation's cultural configurations' (1994: 212). In a sense, this is one of the apparent paradoxes that this article has been addressing: that while British cinema may depend upon international finance and audiences for its viability this may actually strengthen its ability to probe national questions; that while cinema has apparently lost its 'national' audience in the cinemas it may have gained a more fully 'national' audience via television; and that while the British cinema may no longer assert the myths of 'nation' with its earlier confidence it may nonetheless be a cinema which is more fully representative of national complexities than ever before.

Notes

1. This essay originally appeared in Murphy (1997).
2. It is also the case that the films which have been most valorised in terms of their celebration of 'national' virtues were not necessarily those which were, in fact, the most popular with audiences. As Browning and Sorrell rather snootily put it, noting the difference in class and educational background between critics and audiences: 'reflection upon the composition of the average audience suggests some explanation of why it is that box-office successes are not invariably films that find favour with the critics'. (1954: 146).
3. Browning and Sorrell indicate that in the years 1950–2 the cinema accounted for over 83 per cent of all taxable admissions on entertainment (including theatre, sport and other activities) (1954: 135). In 1992, by comparison, spending on cinema admissions accounted for less than 6 per cent of household expenditure on entertainment (Monopolies and Mergers Commission: 1994: 90).
4. Between 1985, when the first multiplex was opened, and 1994 the number of multiplexes grew to seventy-one sites (incorporating 638 screens). By the end of 1993, about 40 per cent of all visits to the cinema were to multiplexes (Monopolies and Mergers Commission 1994: 96).
5. *Screen Finance* defines films as 'wholly' British when they were made solely by British production companies.
6. I've estimated admissions for individual films by dividing 1992 box-office revenues by the average realised seat prices for 1992 identified in Monopolies and Mergers Commission (1994: 102). Television viewing figures may be found in *BFI Film and Television Handbook* (1995: 57).
7. Barwise and Ehrenberg's figures also indicate that social groups C2DE watch marginally more films on TV than groups ABC1 and that women watch more films than men. It is also the case that the renting and buying of pre-recorded videos is highest among the 'lower' social grades, especially the C2s (BMRB International Report 1993: 21).
8. It is, of course, also the case that, as in the cinema, the bulk of films watched by British audiences on television and video are American. However, British audiences have always watched more American films than British, even during those periods when British films have attracted their greatest audiences. It is worth noting, too, that television not only shows more British films than the cinema but that, as the films it shows are from different periods, the circulation of British cinema for the modern audience also possesses a historical dimension. Thus, in 1995, to take just one example, almost as many people watched Ken Loach's *Kes* (1969) as the same director's *Raining Stones* (1993) (*Screen Finance* 24 Jan. 1996: 16–17).
9. These viewing figures made *Four Weddings and a Funeral* Channel Four's third most-watched broadcast ever (*Broadcast* 8 Dec. 1995: 24).
10. The idea of 'national allegory' has been employed, somewhat controversially, by Fredric Jameson (1986) in relation to 'third world' literature. For discussions of his argument, see Aijaz Ahmad (1987) and Kathleen Rowe (1991).

11. Wimal Dissanayake suggests that whereas popular cinema is more likely 'to reinforce the idea of an essentialized and unitary nation-state', art cinema tends to be more critical of national institutions and discourses (1994: xvi). However, while it is clear that the space which art cinema occupies can, partly because of its more obviously 'personal' character, encourage a critical relationship with ideologies of the nation, it is also the case that art films such as heritage cinema may reinforce relatively conservative notions of national identity as well.

12. This is a view to which Colin McArthur (1994) gives forceful expression.

13. The script refers to this interlude as a 'contemporary retake of all those "Swinging London" montages' (Hodge: 1996: 76).

14. In this essay, I also explore the implications of a critical theory sceptical of conventional constructions of the nation and national cinema when the implementation of film policy is still the responsibility of national government or sovereign state (through, for example, the Department of National Heritage, subsequently the Department for Culture, Media and Sport).

References

Ahmad, Aijaz (1987), 'Jameson's Rhetoric of Otherness and the "National Allegory" ', *Social Text* 17 (Autumn).

Barr, Charles (1977), *Ealing Studios*, London: Cameron and Tayleur.

Barwise, Patrick and Ehrenberg, Andrew (1988), *Television and its Audience*, London: Sage.

BFI Film and Television Handbook 1996, London: BFI, 1995.

BMRB International Report (1993): CAVIAR 10, 3 *Report of Findings*, Feb.

Bordwell, David (1979), 'The Art Cinema as a Mode of Film Practice', *Film Criticism* 4 (1) (Autumn).

Browning, H. E. and Sorrell, A. A. (1954), 'Cinemas and Cinema-Going in Great Britain', *Journal of the Royal Statistical Society* 117 (2).

Caughie, John (1996), 'The Logic of Convergence', in Hill, John and McLoone, Martin (eds), *Big Picture, Small Screen: The Relations Between Film and Television*, Luton: John Libbey Media and University of Luton Press.

Cinematograph Films Act, 1927: Report of a Committee Appointed by the Board of Trade (1936), London: HMSO.

Crofts, Stephen (1993), 'Reconceptualizing National Cinema/s', *Quarterly Review of Film and Video* 14 (3).

Durgnat, Raymond (1970), *A Mirror for England: British Movies From Austerity to Affluence*, London: Faber and Faber.

Gomery, Douglas (1992), *Shared Pleasures: A History of Movie Presentation*, London: BFI.

Grummitt, Karsten-Peter (1995), *Cinemagoing* 4, Leicester: Dodona Research.

Hill, John (1992), 'The Issue of National Cinema and British Film Production', in Petrie, Duncan (ed.), *New Questions of British Cinema*, London: BFI.

Hodge, John (1996), *Trainspotting and Shallow Grave*, London: Faber and Faber.

Lovell, Alan (1969), *The British Cinema: The Unknown Cinema*, BFI Mimeo.

McArthur, Colin (1994), 'The Cultural Necessity of a Poor Celtic Cinema', in Hill, McLoone and Hainsworth (1994).

Monopolies and Mergers Commission (1994), *Films: A Report on the Supply of Films for Exhibition in Cinemas in the UK*, London: HMSO.

Moss, Louis and Box, Kathleen (1943), *The Cinema Audience: An Inquiry Made by the Wartime Social Survey for the Ministry of Information*, London: Ministry of Information.

Richards, Jeffrey (1984), *The Age of the Dream Palace: Cinema and Society 1930–1939*, London: Routledge & Kegan Paul.

Richards, Jeffrey (1989), 'National Identity in British Wartime Films', in Taylor, Philip M. (ed.), *Britain and the Cinema in the Second World War*, Basingstoke: Macmillan.

Rowe, Kathleen K. (1991), 'Class and Allegory in Jameson's Film Criticism', *Quarterly Review of Film and Video* 2 (4).

Scottish Film Council (1993), *Movie Makers: Drama For Film and Television*, Glasgow.

Turner, Graeme (1994), 'The End of the National Project? Australian Cinema in the 1990s', in Dissanayake (1994).

Young, Hugo (1990), *One of Us*, London: Pan Books.

8   Ozu and the Nation

Kathe Geist

Nearly twenty years have elapsed since David Bordwell exhaustively explored Ozu's art in terms of both style and context. Although Bordwell resists specific interpretations of Ozu's work, he suggests ultimately that the work is so dense as to provide viewers with a multitude of interconnected levels from which to read the films (Bordwell 1988: 178). Nevertheless, Ozu's relation to the 'national' might seem, at best, tenuous. Ozu worked within a highly developed studio system; he is more often associated with aesthetics, whether Zen or Bordwell's 'parametrics,' than with message; and for over a decade his work was subjected to official censorship and has, at times, been construed as propaganda for either the Japanese war effort or the American occupation.

Why then study Ozu in light of a concept like the national? For one, Ozu's compatriots considered him the 'most Japanese' of all their directors (Richie 1974: xi). Just what that 'Japaneseness' consists of has been the subject of much debate. Ozu's connections to Buddhism and to Zen and other native aesthetic systems is well established as are the liberties he took with classical Hollywood film style.[1] Still, aesthetics and evidence of tradition may have less to do with Ozu's 'Japaneseness' than his ability to minutely evoke the quotidian, the feelings of ordinary Japanese and the manners and nuances of their everyday lives. Bordwell writes:

> Whenever Ozu's postwar characters sit recalling life before or during the war, the scene's force comes not only from the director's experience but also from the way in which that experience exemplifies what millions of other Japanese did and suffered. To an extent unparalleled in Western cinema, this director lives along with his audience. (1988: 10)

In 'living along with his audience', Ozu not only experienced their sufferings and hardships, but also their pleasure in being Japanese, their ambivalence about it, and their longing to escape. His films express both the tension that has existed in Japan between the modern (Western) and traditional since Perry's Black Ships pried open a closed and relatively static society, and the longing to escape a way of life circumscribed by geography, hierarchy, elaborate forms of courtesy, and a much greater degree of rigidity than we know in the West.[2]

Ozu worked for a leading Japanese studio, Shochiku, and some question whether studio films, being part of a dominant economic structure, can truly represent the national. Thinking more in terms of film-making's economic structuring today than that of fifty to seventy years ago, Paul Willemen has written that 'a cinema positively yet critically seeking to engage with the multi-layeredness of specific socio-cultural formations, is necessarily a marginal and a dependent cinema . . . this marginal and dependent cinema is [t]he only form of national cinema available.' (1994: 212). I would argue that in the far more localised world of the 1930s–1950s, studio films frequently engaged critically 'with the multi-layeredness of specific socio-cultural formations'. What we mean when we refer to a 'golden age' of cinema in one country or another may encompass not simply the quality and quantity of films in a specific period but also a national ethos of hope, longing and identity expressed in that body of films as well as a critical consciousness that questions as much as it endorses the status quo.

From 1939 to 1952 Ozu's work was subjected to military censorship, first by the Japanese military government and, after 1945, by the American occupation authorities (SCAP).[3] Some concrete evidence exists of how his work was affected: one script was rejected in 1939 for being too frivolous, while another, the 1947 *Nagaya Shinshiroku* (*Record of a Tenement Gentleman*), was criticised by SCAP censors, who felt the young boy in the film was treated too harshly. (In the end, however, the objectionable scenes remained in the film.) Edward Fowler imagines Ozu striking back by including in the film a futon, upon which the young boy pees in his sleep, endowed with a vague resemblance to an American flag (2001: 283). The dark rectangle with light polka dots in the upper left-hand corner on both sides of the futon is very likely *not* fortuitous, although Fowler overstates the significance of other aspects of the film as critical of the occupation – scenes of wartime rubble, reminiscences of better times, and a critique of the *après-guerre* (that is to say, Westernised) female, all of which are variations on stock Ozu motifs from the 1930s: the self-centred *moga* (modern girl), the ugly industrial landscape of films such as *Tokyo no yado* (*An Inn in Tokyo*) (1935), and the ever-present longing for better times, be they past or future.[4] It is impossible to say how Ozu's films might have changed had he not worked within the constraints of censorship, but it is more relevant for the purposes of this essay to ask if he was still able to grapple critically with his preferred themes, including the tension within Japanese culture between East and West, the resulting ambivalence, and the longing to escape. The four films I will discuss below, which Ozu made at critical junctures in Japanese history, suggest that censorship did not deform his ability to penetrate these issues.

Because the United States casts such a long shadow over cinema generally, understanding the national in another country's cinema means coming to terms with the American influences. In the early silent period, Japanese film developed along fairly independent lines, ignoring contemporary developments in continuity editing and grafting elements from native theatrical forms onto the new medium. Even when the general form of the Hollywood film had become the norm, Japanese were sufficiently aware of the native flavour in their cinema to brand, for example, the films of one director, returned to Japan after a stint in Hollywood, as *buta kusai*, that is, too Western, or, literally, 'smelling of butter' (Anderson and Richie 1982: 53).[5]

Ozu spent a sizeable portion of his youth skipping school and watching American movies. As a young man he absorbed the finely crafted narratives of Chaplin's *Woman of Paris* (1923) and Lubitsch's *The Marriage Circle* (1924), and, after the war, he enthused about *Citizen Kane* (1941), which he had screened while stationed in Singapore. Whereas Asian narratology does not necessarily demand a 'well-made plot', in the Western sense of a continuously progressive storyline headed towards a climax and followed by a resolution and denouement, Ozu, however low-key his stories, almost always followed this formula. And whereas Asian narratology does not always demand character development – stories may be driven more by a sense of 'karma', in which a person's actions and eventual fate are determined by character traits that will not change – Ozu's characters, albeit some more than others, develop: experience change of heart, self-knowledge, reformation and understanding. The 'most Japanese' director had a very Western sense of narrative.[6] Ozu, morever, adopted the optimism of American movies. Most of his films, for example, have happy or reasonably happy endings, even when the resolution to a character's problems seems forced, as in *Tokyo no gassho* (*Tokyo Chorus*) (1931).

Using Western narratology as his starting point, Ozu undercut its straighforwardness with narrative strategies and a cutting style that confounded viewers' expectations and undercut classical Hollywood norms. Such flaunting of Hollywood convention had its roots in the disregard of continuity editing in early Japanese silents and in the stylistic flamboyance of Japanese films from the late 1920s. Ultimately, however, the style was Ozu's own invention. It influenced his contemporaries, and it conveyed his dislike of authority. He might have worshipped at the altar of Hollywood, but he would not take orders from it! Ironically, Ozu's independence is itself more American than Japanese, hence the ambivalence one finds in so many of his films between a love of things Japanese and a pull towards the West – an ambivalence that seems to have resonated with his audience.

The films I will discuss in this essay were all made at times of crisis in Japan: *Tokyo no gassho* during the Depression; *Todake no kyodai* (*The Brothers and Sisters of the Toda Family*) (1941) the year before Pearl Harbor; *Banshun* (*Late Spring*) (1949); and *Bakushu* (*Early Summer*) (1951) during the American occupation. Ozu offers neither a radical critique of nor radical solutions to these times and the problems they present. Instead he nudges his audience along through the minefields of choices that test his characters' values.

The only extant Ozu film devoted entirely to the subject of middle-class unemployment, *Tokyo no gassho* was Ozu's first major critical success, winning third prize in Japan's most prestigious film competition, the annual *Kinema Jumpo* awards. Okajima, an insurance company employee, is fired when he protests the layoff of an older worker and spends the rest of the film looking for suitable employment. The film makes very specific references to the Depression. For example, when Okajima receives his bonus, he comments, 'Hoover's politics haven't affected us', although this turns out to be wishful thinking. After Okajima is fired, a title dubs Tokyo 'City of Unemployment'. When Okajima visits an employment bureau, the camera remains on two unemployed labourers, one of whom grabs the cigarette butt that Okajima drops. 'Even a gentleman like him is jobless,' **116** he comments.

Although influenced by Japan's left-wing 'tendency' films, which had introduced the *shomin-geki* (films about the lower-middle and working classes) and were popular in the 1920s, Ozu's never actually advanced a political agenda but coalesce around the personal affairs, values and choices of their protagonists.[7] Ozu, nevertheless, enjoyed deflating bourgeois pretentions, here requiring Okajima and his wife to give up various claims to status before a new job arrives at the end of the film. When, for example, the Okajimas' fortunes worsen because their daughter falls ill, the mother realises only after the child's recovery that her husband has sold all of her good kimonos to pay for the hospital. Ozu shows her trying not to cry as the family plays a circle game, celebrating the girl's return. Mrs Okajima is less understanding when she discovers her husband marching in the street, carrying banners advertising his former teacher Omura's new curry restaurant. Mortified, she confronts him but eventually comprehends his own humiliation and struggle to provide for them.

Within this scene, Okajima looks out at the smoke stack at the back of the house. Sitting down next to his wife, he looks in another direction, this time at laundry drying in front of the house. 'I feel I'm getting old,' he says. 'I've lost my energy.' He continues to look out. She follows his gaze, and the scene concludes with a two-shot of both looking at the laundry, then bowing their heads. The sequence echoes one early in the film, which begins with brief scenes of Okajima's student days, in which Okajima, reprimanded by Omura for being late to morning exercises, remains behind to smoke a cigarette. He looks up, and Ozu cuts to a shot of trees, which appear above the schoolyard gate. Freedom looms beyond the gate, but not, as it turns out, beyond graduation.

Ozu's epitome of subjugation, apart from school, a necessary evil redeemed by producing the life-long bonds that ultimately save Okajima, is the life of the 'salaryman'. Ozu's disdain for the salaryman escalated from film to film through the 1930s and 40s, until, by the late 1950s, he simply accepted such employment, like death, as inevitable.[8] In *Tokyo gassho*, the salarymen are equated with children and in *Umarete wa mita keredo* (*I Was Born*), *But . . .* (1932) with children and lackies. In *Chichi ariki* (*There Was a Father*) (1942), the father's great sacrifice, after deeming himself unworthy to continue his career as a teacher, is to become a salaryman. In this film Ozu pioneered the shot he would use in film after film to symbolise the life of the salaryman (or office lady): a close-up of an office building from the outside – a grid of windows in a cul de sac – flat, repetitive, uniform and going nowhere.

Although the Okajimas suffer, Ozu suggests that losing a job in the business sector confers freedom on a number of levels. Okajima's reverses, for example, allow him to throw off bourgeois pretentions, make choices based on values like humility, loyalty and determination, and establish more equal and democratic relationships with his wife, his children, and former teacher Omura. The job offered him at the end of the film is one teaching English – more creative and individualistic than his former job as an office worker, though it requires the sacrifice of leaving Tokyo.

Leaving Tokyo is seen as a sad fate, and the Okajimas console themselves that they will be able to return one day. The eponymous Tokyo Chorus, the former classmates gathered for a reunion in Omura's restaurant at the end of the film, sings a nostalgic graduation song that almost reduces Okajima and Omura to tears. Tadao Sato calls the ending tragic (Bordwell **117**

1988: 222), but one has to imagine, by the large number of Ozu characters condemned to it, that leaving Tokyo signifies more than an additional disappointment to which characters must resign themselves, that it also constitutes a form of escape. Since three of the four films under discussion in this essay involve protagonists who leave Tokyo, I will defer discussion of its significance to the end of my essay.

Ozu's wartime films, *Todake no kyodai* and *Chichi ariki* are frequently a source of worry to Western critics because they quite blatantly reinforce Japanese wartime ideology, and Western academics have a hard time accepting Ozu's being on the wrong side of history. Joan Mellen (1976: 155), in her polemical 1976 survey of Japanese film, accuses him of 'gently tak[ing] the unthinkable for granted' in *Todake no kyodai* while Bordwell (1988: 282ff) and Richie (1974: 228) defend him as having either ignored or even subtly undermined the official ideology of the time. Darrell William Davis included *Todake* as an example of 'monumental style', Japanese cinema's answer to the 'back to Japan' impulse of the 1930s and 40s, in a 1989 article but omitted it from his subsequent book on the subject (1996). Indeed, it is hard to imagine any Ozu film as an 'epic, ponderous [c]elebration of the national character and heritage' (1989: 16), but Davis correctly describes a more rigorous, austere style in *Todake*. 'Individuating elements of each shot are pared down until only the most minute details [a]re left to graphically differentiate one shot from another' (1989: 23), while Bordwell notes that 'Ozu frames figures in long-shot and holds establishing and re-establishing shots much longer than in his previous work' (1988: 287). Both Davis (1989: 24) and Mellen (1976: 152) see the patriarchal figure of father Toda, who dies early in the film but whose picture recurs again and again, as reinforcing the wartime ideology that valorised the Japanese family in its Confucian incarnation, that is to say, patriarchal and hierarchic. This hierarchic relation of father to spouse and children was the declared model for Japan's relation to its colonies (Davis 1989: 24; Dower 1986: 280).

Todake's story concerns a grown family of two brothers and three sisters, who lose their father shortly after a family reunion. Three of the siblings, two sisters and the elder brother, are married and well-off, but the mother and the youngest, unmarried sister Setsuko are thrown on their siblings' charity when the family discovers that the father had numerous debts and left no money to support his remaining dependents. Mother and daughter move in with the elder brother Shinichiro, whose responsibility they are in terms of Confucian morality. His pretentious, self-centred wife resents the intrusion, however, and mother and daughter move on to live with eldest sister Chizuko. She, too, finds them burdensome, so they take up residence in the family's delapidated villa by the seashore. Meanwhile, the youngest son Shojiro, introduced to us as an easy-going loafer, but moved by his father's death to make something of his life, decides to emigrate to Tianjin (Tientsin) in Japanese-occupied China to find work. This story element, which endorses the Japanese occupation of China and, by extension, an incredibly brutal war there, troubles Western critics most. 'Shojiro returns', fumes Mellen, 'in Chinese clothes, as if he had indeed fully integrated himself into the Chinese environment, and as if this were a natural and morally acceptable thing to do' (1976: 155).

Having colonies, even occupying large tracts of China, was, by European standards, still perfectly acceptable in 1941, and many Japanese were undoubtedly unware of the brutality of their troops in China. Ozu, on the other hand, had served in China, even in Nanking at the time of its infamous Rape. How, one wonders, could he have possibly reconciled the atrocities he had witnessed with his likeable hero's career move to China? I do not know, of course, but I imagine he justified it the same way imperialists everywhere justify their violence: by the supposition that after the bloodshed a more advanced or enlightened civilisation will emerge in a backward nation. The Japanese government stated this intent, and John Dower records a few instances of Japanese occupiers making contributions in Southeast Asia for which residents were actually grateful (1986: 285). Shojiro's Chinese clothes undoubtedly signal that he is a 'good' Japanese occupier, willing to fraternise and learn from the Chinese, much like the 'good' Americans who go native in *The Ugly American*.[9]

Whatever his rationale, Ozu neatly fitted China (although we never see it) into a role paralleling that of the frontier in American Westerns. Like the American frontier or, indeed, European colonies, China was a place on which a whole society could pin its hopes for a second chance. When *Todake's* Shojiro, having made good in Tianjin, returns to Japan, he is understandably shocked to find his mother and sister living in the old villa. He castigates his siblings for their selfishness and persuades Mrs Toda and Setsuko to return to China with him, where his hard work and inevitable prosperity will certainly be sufficient to provide for them. Not only they, but the elderly maid Kiyo as well as Tohiko, Setsuko's unpretentious, hardworking school friend, whom Setsuko intends as Shojiro's bride, will go along, too, to start new lives in a China administered by Japan.

Ozu may have endorsed national policy in this film, but one feels that the hopes pinned on China come from beneath, not simply from above. Although most of Ozu's films have reasonably happy endings, these are usually qualified by some form of nostalgia: the pain of parting, the inevitability of growing old. *Todake no kyodai* is the *only one* without such qualification. Anyone who has been an expatriate knows how strong nostalgia for the homeland can be, but Ozu, master of nostalgia, never alludes to it. Instead, the film has Ozu's most optimistic ending: Shojiro running down the beach, ostensibly to escape the *omiai* (arranged meeting of potential marriage partners) with Tohiko. The audience knows he won't escape this obligation forever, but he will escape the confines of Japan. As the film's final image, it creates powerful testimony to the importance of China as a colony, not merely, I would argue, in the eyes of the government, but in the popular imagination. Mellen rightly notes that 'China is seen as a place of refuge and salvation' (1976: 155) and functions in the film as much more than an unfortunate allusion to Japan's wartime status. The colonisation of China is central to the hope and happiness the film projects.

As well as winning the *Kinemo Jumpo* first prize, *Todake* was Ozu's first box-office hit. *Chichi ariki*, released five months after the bombing of Pearl Harbor, ends with the father's death and, although supportive of the war effort – its theme is personal sacrifice – is opposite in spirit from *Todake*. Though not exactly 'epic and ponderous', the film is highly nostalgic and severe in its demand that individuals sacrifice personal feeling for duty. (This *ninjo/giri* conflict is a common theme in Japanese film, but rarely occurs in Ozu's work.) **119**

The toll of total war on the national spirit, the cost of the imperialism so cheerfully celebrated in *Todake*, becomes evident in *Chichi ariki*.

In excoriating *Todake*, Mellen also notes Shojiro's references to Hitler and Siegfried, almost interchangeable figures in 1941. Protesting marriage, Shojiro says he will marry when Hitler does. Later, still protesting and using shyness as an excuse, he insists that all men have a weakness: Siegfried had a weak back. These are not simply jokes, as Bordwell suggests (1988: 288), but indications of a close identification with Germany, again by ordinary Japanese. 'We are both young nations fighting our way up, and it is not easy to win a place in the sun. And yet I do believe that we will win in the end,' writes Hilda Stolz from wartime Germany to Sachiko Makioka at the end of Tanizaki's classic *Sasameyuki* (1957: 465). The words resonate with irony, since the novel was first published after the war, but they surely capture the warm feelings and identification ordinary Japanese had with Germany. Moreover, Shojiro's positive, if irreverent, reference to Hitler echoes a remark he makes earlier in the film when he jokes that 'Father's telescope made him look like Admiral Tojo'. Ozu unapologetically delegates Shojiro to bear the torch for New Japan. Bordwell is right to insist that *Todake* is 'about the real guardians of tradition, the young' (1988: 288), but the young, who 'see through bourgeois hypocrisy', were staples of both communist and fascist propaganda at the time, in Japan as well as in Europe.

If *Todake* reflects the positive face of fascism and imperialism in the New Japan of the early 1940s, ambivalence negates any wholehearted endorsement of Japanese tradition, and, contrary to the contentions of both Mellen and Davis, the film does not ultimately resurrect the patriarchal family in a substantive way. Among its directives regarding subject matter, the new Film Law required an emphasis on filial piety, including respect for older brothers, and an avoidance of stories about the upper class. *Todake*, in which the effete older brother proves incapable of fulfilling his filial obligations, violated both of these tenets. Perhaps they cancelled each other out.

Images of traditional Japan in the film are associated with the Toda parents. They live in a traditional samurai-style villa and are connected to a variety of Buddhist images, including ceremonies at the time of and one year after the father's death. Meanwhile, the mother moves about with a caged myna bird and a potted orchid (traditional hobbies) and a picture of father Toda.

The Toda children, however, are associated with Western influences: *fusuma* (sliding screen doors) in Shojiro's room are decorated with Western notes and musical instruments, another has cupids on it, and elsewhere in the room we see examples of Western modernism. Elder brother Shinichiro's ambivalence about his role is characterised by his house, which resembles a European-style hunting lodge but has the traditional suit of samurai armour, indicating the family's lineage, in the front hallway along with *noren* (the traditional three-piece curtains that hang in doorways) with the family crest.

Although Ozu would, in later films, become much more serious about the evocation of Buddhism than he appears to be in this film (Geist 1997), the Buddhist embellishments in *Todake*, while underscoring the unpretentious sincerity of Mrs Toda and Setsuko, seem 120 eclipsed by the film's emphasis on youth and its rush to the future. Ozu's own ambivalence about traditional culture at this point in his career is summed up in the scene in which Mr Toda's art collection is sold. In a room filled with traditional art, whose deceased owner is bankrupt, Shojiro reads from a list of titles, 'Viewing waterfall'. Then adds, 'Who's viewing it?' thus poking fun at academic tradition. Although this is still the pre-Tianjin, unregenerate Shojiro, one senses Ozu's own voice behind the jab at classicism.

Masculine power, reasserted by Shojiro upon his return from Tianjin, is restored; but, always ambivalent about patriarchy, Ozu damps it down considerably by allowing Setsuko to share decisions with her brother – he will decide on her husband, but she will decide on his wife – and by showing Shojiro fleeing from her at the end. Moreover, Shojiro, as the younger brother, is not really the patriarch, and the family he would lead is not really intact.

Like the Western cowboy hero that he slightly resembles, Shojiro will disappear back to China, taking with him, to be sure, a remnant of the family, but thereby both splitting and displacing it. The contradiction is not merely Ozu's, but the nation's as a whole. Japan was flinging itself at too many targets, gearing up for a war programme it could not sustain, substituting spirit for substance. The young Todas are rich in spirit, but still lacking a cohesive family unit.

Ozu made six films in the occupation period, the first two, *Nagaya Shinshiroku* and *Kaze no naka no mendori* (*A Hen in the Wind*) (1948), concerned with the suffering and dislocation of the early post-war years. Most celebrated from this period, however, are *Banshun* and *Bakushu*, films in which a young woman named Noriko, who has waited rather long to marry (played in both films by Setsuko Hara), finds a suitable mate.

The American occupation brought to Japan many of the longed-for freedoms, particularly for women, but at such a dizzying pace that finding an identity amid the tidal wave of democratic reform and Americanisation, not to mention post-war hardships, became the new challenge. Although *Bakushu* (1951) deals most specifically with the liberation of women, a number of critics see *Banshun* (1949) as the quintessential occupation film. David Bordwell (1988) and Kristin Thompson (1988) feel Noriko's father's sweetness, his refusal to order Noriko to marry, and his lack of regard for the continuity of his *ie* (family line) constitute an affirmation of occupation reforms. Eric Cazdyn (2002) sees *Banshun* as reflecting the disappointment Japanese felt when promises of democracy and reform were not kept, as the occupiers co-opted Japan into the Cold War and shelved many of the reformist programmes of the early occupation.

Banshun is clearly an occupation film, but not for the reasons given above. The best example of Cazdyn's thesis (but one he fails to mention) is the scene in which the father, Somiya, corrects his friend Onadera's confusion over the direction of various locations: the sea, the shrine, Tokyo, even 'East'. Onadera points one way only to have Somiya point in the opposite direction. However tempting to think Ozu had the occupation's 'reverse-course', as the changed policies were dubbed by the Japanese press, slyly in mind, such play with reversals in Ozu's oeuvre is not unique to this film or to Japanese history. Japan had, after all, been reversing course every ten or twenty years since the Meiji Reformation. Moreover, Noriko's own 'reverse course', her decision, finally, to marry, is presented as both progressive and inevitable and thus hardly parallels the occupation's reverse-course.

Banshun (Yasujiro Ozu, 1949)

Likewise Bordwell and Thompson conveniently ignore the continuity between all of Ozu's characters, his sweet males and his spunky, independent females. *Todake*, after all, ends with Setsuko ordering her brother, the restored 'patriarch,' to marry! Bordwell and Thompson misunderstand, moreover, the notion of the *ie* in modern Japanese society. Without going into the relative unimportance of the *ie* to urbanites like Somiya (ultra-nationalist propaganda notwithstanding), it suffices to say that a daughter could not perpetuate her father's *ie*. She marries *out*, and that, of course, is the reason for the enormous sadness in these marriage films and the daughters' reluctance to enter into marriage.[10]

Many elements, however, mark *Banshun* as an occupation film. The most obvious, perhaps, are references to baseball. Introduced in the Meiji era, baseball had been popular in Japan but died out during the war years to be reintroduced by the Americans during the occupation. Contrary to those who see him as especially critical of the occupation, Ozu seems happy to show us 'MacArthur's children', young boys playing a baseball game from which Noriko's nephew has withdrawn. Noriko's groom is supposed to resemble Gary Cooper in 'that baseball film'. Released in 1943, *Pride of the Yankees* (S. Wood) would not have been seen in Japan until it arrived with the Americans after the war.

Less sanguine are references to wartime and post-war hunger. Somiya attributes Noriko's illness (anaemia), which has kept her from marrying, to 'forced labor during the war and spending all her holidays scrounging for food'. Despite food shipments from the United States, such scrounging, hunger and malnutrition went on well into the post-war period, due in large part to the inability of Japanese officials to curb the black market (Dower 1999: 94ff). It had only, finally, abated by 1949, the year *Banshun* was made. Against this background, Somiya's seemingly absurd argument with his sister Masa about whether she would eat at her wedding if she were a contemporary bride – 'You'd eat!' he insists – makes sense: the 'coarsening' of contemporary youth has a material cause.

Many observers have noted the way in which post-war Japanese immediately cast themselves into the role of victims, thereby relieving themselves of responsibility for the suffering they had caused so many others (Dower 1999: 29ff). Within the first twenty minutes of *Banshun*, Ozu echoes this popular sentiment. 'She was a victim!' says Onadera when Somiya describes Noriko's wartime hardships.

As an occupation era film, however, *Banshun* is as remarkable for what it does not say about the era as for what it says. With the abatement of widespread hunger, 1949 marked a return to relative normality in Japan, and Ozu, whose realist films about post-war suffering had failed at the box office, imagines a happy bourgeois family, seeking and finding, without much difficulty, a husband for the daughter. Based on a story by Kazuo Hirotsu from 1939, the marriage theme also evokes Tanizaki's *Sasameyuki* (1957), which concerns a bourgeois family's lengthy search, in the late 1930s, for a sister's marriage partner. This vision of life based on pre-war norms was no doubt comforting to a recently traumatised population, for, even in 1949, marriages for women of Noriko's generation were not easily made. John Dower writes about the *shuudan miai*, marriage markets, arranged so that large numbers of young men and women could simultaneously find partners, that were held in the late 1940s because young women, for a variety of reasons, could no longer depend on their families to arrange marriages.

> Young women of marriageable age [f]ound themselves in the most desperate circumstances, for the demography of death in the recent war had removed a huge aggregation of prospective husbands. [A] large cohort of women, most of them born between 1916 and 1926, confronted the prospect not merely of coping with postwar hardships without a marriage partner, but of never marrying at all. (1999: 106–7)

Dower includes a picture of a *shuudan miai* which took place in 1948 at the Hachiman Shrine in Kamakura, the same shrine that Somiya and Masa visit to pray for luck in matching Noriko and her Gary Cooper lookalike. Thus, while *Banshun* projects the 'good old days' onto its present, the marriage that the Noriko heroine of *Bakushu* arranges by herself is, in fact, more realistic for its time and far less shocking than critics have heretofore assumed.

Banshun seems to be an act of salving, evoking, as it does, a pre-war image of bourgeois matchmaking as well as illustrating a compendium of traditional Japanese arts: tea ceremony, **123**

Noh drama, the Hachiman shrine, the Kiyomizu temple, and Ryoanji's Zen garden. All but the Noh – a drama about jealousy, an emotion that overcomes Noriko during the performance – are presented in a fairly light-hearted context, but no one jokes about them. In this film, traditional Japan is a refuge for audience and characters alike.

Yet the film's project goes beyond merely presenting a fantasy of tradition and normality. Of the four films under consideration here, *Banshun* is the only one in which the protagonist doesn't leave Tokyo at the end, the only one in which she wants to cling to the past instead of embracing the future. The problem the story presents is prying the daughter loose from her father, loose from her childhood, loose from the past and persuading her to grow up. On some subliminal level, the film seems to be urging a nation on the cusp of recovery to go forward.

With *Bakushu* Ozu returned to a strong protagonist who refuses to settle for the status quo. Embodying post-war reforms for women, insisting 'We [women] are normal now', this Noriko helps to support her family, has, as a school girl, admired Katharine Hepburn,[11] and eventually shocks family and friends by agreeing to marry her widowed neighbour Yabe, raise his child, and move with him to northerly Akita. Asked why she has chosen this less financially secure and socially acceptable match, when her boss and family had proposed a wealthier man, she replies that she trusts a man with a child more than one who has remained single until forty (!). 'Poverty doesn't worry me like it does other people,' she says and assures her sister-in-law that she has no qualms about loving another woman's child. Here Ozu points to what many at the time began to perceive as a national character-flaw: an inability to feel compassion for those who were different. The war had multiplied such individuals enormously: war widows, orphans, cripples and *hibakusha* (survivors of the nuclear blasts) all suffered discrimination and neglect (Dower 1999: 61–4). Noriko's willingness to fill this breach, albeit within her bourgeois milieu, marks her depth of character. The film endorses women's post-war liberation, but doesn't rest there. Liberated, Noriko has choices, and Ozu is as concerned with those choices as he is with her liberation.

In a nation 'revaluing all values' (Dower 1999: 245), Ozu is careful to distinguish between truly liberated values and Western bourgeois values as empty as their Japanese counterparts. Noriko's friend Aya names them: a Western-style house with a picket fence, a covered porch and a tiled kitchen, a refrigerator full of Coca-Cola, a white sweater and a terrier. Noriko's forty-year-old prospect, meanwhile, comes from a prosperous family that 'keeps their home in the best traditional style'. She shuns both, offering instead to raise a motherless child and compete with her sister-in-law in thriftiness. Yabe, her groom, embraces the opportunity to go to Akita, not simply to advance his career, but to pursue his medical research 'on local problems'. In accompanying him, Noriko tacitly supports this worthy purpose.

Explaining her sudden realisation that Yabe would make a good husband, Noriko echoes Dorothy in the *Wizard of Oz* (V. Fleming, 1939): 'You look for something all over the place and find it was right in front of you all along.' For the second time she is identified with a strong American film heroine. Unlike her friends, she is never shown wearing a kimono; unlike *Banshun's* Noriko, she is never seen in her wedding kimono. Like Shojiro in *Todake*, she has seized the future. Although, unlike Shojiro, she weeps copiously at the thought that she is breaking up her family, she is rarely associated with old Japan. Although her brother and, to some extent, her sister-in-law hold old prejudices, traditional Japan – kabuki, scroll painting, caged birds and a trip to Kamakura's *Daibutsu* (Great Buddha) – is associated with her parents and, particularly, 'Uncle', the father's much older brother. Uncle lives in Yamato, the family seat, and, after Noriko's marriage, the parents join him there. 'Yamato' is the name for ancient, pre-Chinese-influenced Japan;[12] thus the cleavage between old and new, past and present, is fairly complete in this film. In a scene devoted entirely to the father, he goes out to buy more bird food and sits to wait for a passing train. A sign near the tracks – in English becase this is still the occupation – reads: 'Caution, automatic alarm is out of order.' In a world with new rules and new values, Japanese, like Noriko, will need to think for themselves, construct their own identity and their own happiness.

These four films escorted their contemporary viewers through troubled times, offering solutions based on progressive, often Western, even specifically American, values. *Todake*, infatuated with German fascism, might seem the exception, though the solution as presented in the film, enlightened imperialism, was certainly not at odds with Western values. Evocations of traditional Japan offer comfort, but never solutions. Even the job – teaching English – that *Tokyo gassho*'s Okajima finds in rural Japan looks westwards. For all that Ozu admired and practised traditional Japanese aesthetics, particularly in their reductiveness and play with space, his films never point '*back* to Japan', but always to the future, even when the modern world seems bleak, or, as in *Ohayo* (1959), television threatens to create '100 million idiots'.

The longing for freedom, evident in all the films considered here except *Banshun*, results in the characters leaving Tokyo at the end. Some might read this as Ozu's version of 'Be careful what you wish for', but I believe he saw these departures for the provinces as an escape from the superficiality and distractions of the city that would free his characters to cultivate essential values. *Soshun* (*Early Spring*, 1956) is the only Ozu film that actually follows its protagonists, a young couple, into exile, where they commit to repairing their marriage away from the frustrations and temptations of Tokyo. *Todake* is the only film that allows us to observe the effect of exile: Shojiro leaves a wastrel and comes home a responsible adult. After graduating from middle school, Ozu had himself experienced a year-long exile to a mountain village, where he worked as an assistant teacher. We know little of his experience there, except that he was lonely and drank a lot, but it may well have been the crucible in which a spoiled boy developed enough inner strength to become a great artist.

A motif like 'freedom-in-exile' was typical of Ozu, whose films are structured around reversal, contradiction and ambivalence. These give them a dialogic rather than a purely ideologic quality, as though Ozu were not just 'liv[ing] with his audience', but conversing with them – teasing, cajoling, preaching in various measures, sometimes reinforcing, often challenging their perceptions. Was it his style, his sometimes elegiac evocation of Japanese life and traditions that made him the 'most Japanese' director? Or was it this dialogic quality, this refusal to be defined that captured best the essence of Japan?

Notes

1. For Ozu's connections to Buddhism and traditional arts, see Burch (1979), Geist (1994 and 1997), Richie (1974), Schrader (1972), Vasey (1980), Yamamoto (1987) and Zeman (1972). For a detailed analysis of the liberties he takes with conventional Hollywood cutting and narrative techniques, see Bordwell (1988), Thompson and Bordwell (1976), and Thompson (1977 and 1988).

2. Films suggesting entrapment like *Hadaka no shima* (*The Island*) (Kaneto Shindo, 1960) and *Suna no onna* (*Woman in the Dunes*) (Hiroshi Teshigahari, 1963) appealed to Western, existentialist thought as describing the essential human condition, but they described the Japanese condition first!

3. Censorship has existed in Japan since the Tokugawa period. (The eighteenth-century *ukiyoe* artists were persecuted by censors and even today their explicitly sexual works must be altered before being sold in Japanese bookstores.) Film censorship began in 1917 and policed mainly communism and lewdness, examining only finished films, not scripts. Only in the late 1930s did the Home Ministry begin to 'request' nationalistic themes. The Film Law of 1939, however, based on the Nazis' *Spitzenorganization der Filmwirtschaft*, regulated every aspect of the industry, demanded nationalistic themes and Confucian morals, and examined scripts as well as finished films (Davis 1996: 62ff).

4. An entire genre dubbed *Trümmerfilme*, films shot against wartime rubble, emerged in Germany in the occupation period with the Allies' blessing. SCAP censors forbid the mention of the atomic bombings of Japan, scenes of Tokyo's burnt-out districts, and visual or verbal references to the occupation itself, but not references to the lifestyle or the general misery that engulfed Japan after the war.

5. Anderson and Richie describe the difficulties Japanese studios had in modernising (i.e. Americanising) their methods, despite importing Japanese directors and technicians from Hollywood: 'The invasion from America [h]ad failed not only because the Japanese audience preferred the *benshi* (live commentator) films, but also because subject and treatment of the new-style films were considered "too American," the Japanese crews plainly disliking all of these foreign connections and much preferring to work in a "pure Japanese" style. This anti-foreignism held little political implication, but has always been a definite part of the Japanese film' (1982: 43).

6. Ozu's penchant for Western narratology was not only conditioned by American films. He admired many Japanese authors from the Taisho period who had been influenced by Western literature, among them Junichiro Tanizaki, Ryuunosuke Akutagawa, Naoya Shiga and Ton Satomi.

7. Anderson and Richie attribute this to Ozu's studio Shochiku, which was oriented to a female audience, presumably more interested in the personal than the political and not yet equating the two (1982: 67).

8. Ozu made two films about a father pushing his daughter into marriage. In the first, *Banshun* (1949), the father is a college professor; in the second, *Samma no aji* (*An Autumn Afternoon*) (1962), he is a business executive, and while the early film concentrates on the daughter about to begin a new life, the late one concentrates on the father, whose next stop on the life cycle is death.

9. William J. Lederer and Eugene Burdick (1958), New York: W. W. Norton. The war film *Nishizumi Senshacho-den* (*The Story of Tank Commander Nishizumi*) (1940) shows ideal commander Nishizumi aiding Chinese civilians. Anderson and Richie call this 'prewar humanism' (1982: 128), but, in fact, such humanitarianism was national policy. (That humanitarians also make good imperialists is illustrated by the model for one of the heroes of *The Ugly American*, Edwin B. Hillandale, who excels in 'going native'. Hillandale was based on Edward G. Lansdale, architect of the Vietnam War.)

10. In an extreme example of what Paul Willemen calls a 'cultural cross-border raid' (1994: 211), Robin Wood (1992) recasts Ozu as a postmodern, radical feminist, insisting the director viewed marriage as essentially tragic. While Japan has never fostered a romantic view of marriage and Ozu had no illusions about its challenges or the sacrifices women made for it, he saw it as natural, progressive, and essentially positive. For a more cultural-contextual view of marriage in Ozu's films, see Geist 1989 and 1992.

11. Criterion's new subtitles for its 2004 DVD release of the film wrongly identify the 'Hepburn' referred to by Noriko's friend Aya as 'Audrey' instead of 'Katharine'. (Audrey was still a child when the fictional Noriko was collecting her 'Hepburn' pictures.)

12. The 'great Yamato race' was a Japanese catchphrase from the war years equivalent to the Nazis' notion of a pure Aryan race, indicating Japanese superiority and their consequent right to subjugate Chinese and other Asians. This may be another reason why Ozu and his scriptwriter relegated 'Yamato' so firmly to the past.

References

Anderson, Joseph and Richie, Donald (1982), *The Japanese Film: Art and Industry*, Princeton: Princeton University Press.

Bordwell, David (1988), *Ozu and the Poetics of Cinema*, Princeton: Princeton University Press.

Burch, Noël (1979), *To The Distant Observer: Form and Meaning in the Japanese Cinema*, Berkeley: University of California Press.

Cazdyn, Eric (2002), *The Flash of Capital: Films and Geopolitics in Japan*, Durham: Duke University Press.

Davis, D. William (1989), 'Back to Japan: Militarism and Monumentalism in Prewar Japanese Cinema', *Wide Angle* 11 (3): 16–25.

Davis, Darrell William (1996), *Picturing Japaneseness: Monumental Style and National Identity in Japanese Film*, New York: Columbia University Press.

Dower, John (1986), *War without Mercy: Race and Power in the Pacific War*, New York: Pantheon Books.

Dower, John W. (1999), *Embracing Defeat: Japan in the Wake of World War II*, New York: W. W. Norton.

Fowler, Edward (2001), 'Piss and Run: Or How Ozu does a Number on SCAP', in Washburn, Dennis and Cavanaugh, Carole (eds), *Word and Image in Japanese Cinema*, Cambridge: Cambridge University Press.

Geist, Kathe (1989), 'The Role of Marriage in the Films of Yasujiro Ozu', *East-West Film Journal* 4 (1): 44–52.

Geist, Kathe (1992), 'Narrative Strategies in Ozu's Late Films', in Nolletti, Arthur Jr and Desser, David (eds), *Reframing Japanese Cinema, Authorship, Genre, History*, Bloomington: Indiana University Press.

Geist, Kathe (1994), 'Playing with Space: Ozu and Two-Dimensional Design in Japan', in Ehrlich, Linda C. and Desser, David (eds), *Cinematic Landscapes: Observations on the Visual Arts and Cinema of China and Japan*, Austin: University of Texas Press.

Geist, Kathe (1997), 'Buddhism in Tokyo Story', in Desser, David, *Ozu's Tokyo Story*, Cambridge: Cambridge University Press.

Hirano, Kyoko (1992), *Mr Smith Goes to Tokyo: Japanese Cinema under the American Occupation, 1945–1952*, Washington, DC: Smithsonian Institution Press.

Mellen, Joan (1976), *The Waves at Genji's Door: Japan through its Cinema*, New York: Pantheon Books.

Richie, Donald (1974), *Ozu: His Life and Films*, Berkeley: University of California Press.

Schrader, Paul (1972), *Transcendental Style in Film: Ozu, Bresson, Dreyer*, Berkeley: University of California Press.

Tanizaki, Junichiro (1957), *The Makioka Sisters*, New York: Alfred A. Knopf.

Thompson, Kristin (1977) 'Notes on the Spatial System of Ozu's Early Flms', *Wide Angle* 1 (4): 8–17.

Thompson, Kristin (1988), *Breaking the Glass Armor: Neoformalist Film Analysis*, Princeton: Princeton University Press.

Thompson, Kristin and Bordwell, David (1976), 'Space and Narrative in the Films of Ozu', *Screen* 17 (2): 41–105.

Vasey, Ruth (1980), 'Ozu and the Noh', *Australian Journal of Screen Theory* 7: 88–102.

Willemen, Paul (1994), *Looks and Frictions*, London: BFI.

Wood, Robin (1992), 'The Noriko Trilogy', *Cineaction* 26–7: 60–81.

Yamamoto, Kikuo (1987) 'Ozu and Kabuki', *Iconics* 1: 147–60.

Zeman, Marvin (1972), 'The Serene Poet of Japanese Cinema: the Zen Artistry of Yasujiro Ozu', *The Film Journal* 1 (3–4): 62–71.

9 The Break-up of the National Body

Cosmetic Multiculturalism and the Films of Miike Takashi[1]

Mika Ko

Film Comment (2002: 35) introduces Miike Takashi as one of the 'new Japanese New Wave' who built his international reputation largely on the success of the psycho-thriller *Audition* (1999). Born in 1960 into a working-class family with a history of displacements to China and Korea, Miike studied film-making at the film school founded by Imamura Shohei, but he admits that he seldom went to classes. Although he worked as an assistant on Imamura's *Zegen* (1987) and *Kuroi Ame* (*Black Rain*) (1989), as well as assisting a few other directors such as Onchi Hideo and Kuroki Kazuo, Miike initially worked mostly in television. His first work as a film director was a made-for-video feature, known as V-cinema in Japan, *Toppu Mini Pato Tai* (*Sudden Gust of Wind: Miniskirt Patrol*) (1991). Since then, he has made more than forty films, including feature-length video releases. While having made quite a few feature films since his first theatrical feature *Shinjuku Kuroshakai: China Mafia Senso* (*Shinjuku Triad Society: China Mafia War*) (1995), the release of these films has been rather limited and the films earn back most of their cost through video rentals (Rayns 2000: 30).

Because of the 'new Japanese New Wave' label given by *Film Comment*, and the fact that he was a student as well as an assistant of Imamura, in Miike's films one might expect strong connections or influences from the Japanese New Wave movement of the 1960s. However, although it is possible to find some common elements, there is a fundamental difference between Miike's films and those of the Japanese New Wave in the 1960s, such as the work of Imamura, Oshima Nagisa and Hani Susumu. Miike's films seem to be neither particularly politically motivated nor progressive. As I argue below, his films are not nationalistic or nostalgic for some 'old Japan', but neither are they anti-nationalist. This is not to say that Miike's films do not tell us anything about contemporary Japanese society or politics. Like any other cultural product, films (whether political or not) are shaped by the social and historical constellations within which, and for which, they are made. It is in this sense that Miike's films can be read and interpreted in relation to the socio-historical context of contemporary Japan. Here I examine how one fundamental and structuring element of Miike's films, namely 'body-metaphors', suture precisely that relation between the films and their socio-historical context.

Miike's films are commercial: as a film director he works within the generic conventions of, largely, the gangster and, occasionally, the horror film. At the same time, as for any other film auteur, it is often impossible to pigeonhole his films into any one single genre. If Tony Rayns (2000: 30) is to be believed, Miike seems to refuse to bend to widely accepted norms of narrative and film style and grammar. Similarly, *Film Comment* (2002: 39) suggests that Miike is an 'ultra-prolific and stylistically unpredictable' film-maker of contemporary Japan. And yet, for all their 'unpredictability', Miike's films display three key characteristics. The first of these is the presence of foreigners and mixed-race groups. Although it is true that 'foreigners in Japan' has been one of the themes that, since the late 1980s, attracted many Japanese film-makers, and while it also true that in some of Miike's films there are no foreigners at all, his films remain unusual among the work of contemporary Japanese film-makers for their constant inclusion of non-Japanese characters and mixed-race groups. Abe Kashou (2000: 318) takes this characteristic to mean that Miike practises an 'Asian cinema', that is to say, a cinema that may well be set in Japan but which embodies a notion of 'Asia' in which the Japanese landscape, especially that of Tokyo, is 'Asianised'. For Abe, Miike's films exceed the narrow category of 'Japanese cinema': by including many non-Japanese Asian characters Miike 'de-Japanises' the local landscape (Abe 2000: 350). Abe also argues that the concept of 'Asia is One' is a thread running through Miike's gangster films (Abe 2000: 350). Very much in the same vein, Tony Rayns argues that Miike's films 'not only take it as given that Japan is as "Asian" as any of its neighbours', but also imply that 'a bit of cross-cultural fertilisation does Japan's uptight mainstream culture a power of good' (Rayns 2000: 31).

With the inclusion of many non-Japanese characters, Miike's Tokyo does assume a certain Asian, or more precisely, cosmopolitan character. If, however, as Abe and Rayns suggest, Miike's films embody 'Asia', then it is a very peculiar notion of 'Asia' – one constructed by the Japanese, or seen from the perspective of a specific sector of the Japanese population. Secondly, although Miike's films deal with foreigners or mixed-race groups, they are not necessarily films about foreigners in Japan. Rather, what seems to be at stake is the self-representation of Japan, or how Miike conceives of Japanese society in relation to these foreigners.

The second key characteristic of Miike's films is the weakening of diegetic or narrative unity within his fictional worlds. For instance, at the opening of *Katakurike no kofuku* (*The Happiness of the Katakuri*) (2001), Miike inserts animation sequences which relate to the plot but interrupt the diegetic world of the film, while in *Shinjuku Triad Society*, the opening sequence is fragmented in narrative terms, juxtaposing images that may or may not be part of the same diegesis. In *Blues Harp* (1998), the opening credit sequence is also fragmented, beginning with cross-cutting between the performance of live music and a fight among gangsters. Later in this sequence, some other images, such as military planes in the sky, people on the street and images from a TV game, are inserted and juxtaposed, apparently at random. In addition, while the gangsters are punching each other, the sound accompanying the diegesis sometimes stretches the diegetic event. Like cartoon comics, onomatopoeia such as 'Boom!' and 'Biff!' appear as text on the screen against a black background in the fight scene. It is not clear whether this sequence does or does not have a diegetic unity as it is not always **130** possible to tell whether the images belong to a diegetic or to a non-diegetic world. Even though the soundtrack in such sequences does tend to provide a cohesive continuity of sorts, it is evident from such examples that Miike destroys the integrity of the fictional worlds he stages. This breaking open of diegetic homogeneity is one of the key characteristics of many of his feature films.

The third key characteristic of Miike's films is the repeated use of the metaphor of the body or, more precisely, a concern with images staging 'a lack of bodily integrity'. This, in turn, links to a different but related notion of fragmentation. Fragmentation of the body, such as a severed human head, fingers or arms, are evident in many of Miike's films, including *Audition* (1999), *Gokudo Sengokushi: Fudo* (*Fudo: The New Generation*) (1996) and *Shinjuku Triad Society*. In *Fudo* freshly severed human heads repeatedly appear throughout the film. In one of the more surreal scenes, little boys are playing football with a chopped-off human head. The opening sequence of *Shinjuku Triad Society* also contains a diegetic image of a severed head as well as a non-diegetic image of a pig's head. In *Audition*, the severing of body parts plays a prominent role in that it constitutes the heroine's main act of revenge. 'Lack of bodily integrity' here means a collapse of bodily boundaries, with things coming out of or going into bodies, blurring not only the contours of bodies, but also the boundaries between that which is (or ought to be) either inside or outside the body. Again, in *Fudo* one of the female characters (although she is actually a hermaphrodite) is showered with sulphuric acid while stripping in a club, removing a whole layer of her skin and flesh. As an image suggesting dissolution of bodily boundaries, this scene could not be more explicit. Excessively spouting blood evident in most of Miike's films may also be cited as an example of this characteristic, as can the pervasive scenes of drug injections, eating and drinking or the forced insertion of objects into people's bodies. Activities of forced or voluntary but always excessive ingestion tend to be followed by equally virulent eruptions or ejection from bodily orifices.

These three characteristics are not, of course, Miike's single-handed monopoly. My argument is that in Miike's films the presence of non-Japanese characters within the Japanese body politic of his films, the breaking open of diegetic homogeneity and narrative integrity, and the constant emphasis on the transgressing of body boundaries, connect to, and echo, each other. That is to say, these three aspects of his films, reinforced by others at the thematic and acting levels, constitute a kind of basic constellation, a matrix that organises important dimensions of his films and which we may read as a preoccupation with the homogeneity of Japan – or its lack – as a socio-political entity. Miike's films tell us about a particular conception of 'Japaneseness' in the context of a contemporary Japan allegedly concerned with questions of multiculturalism.

The body-integrity constellation may be seen clearly at work in Miike's *Dead or Alive-Hanzaisha* (*Dead or Alive*) (1999). The film is set in Shinjuku, central Tokyo. The story basically consists of the battle between Jojima, a Japanese police detective, and Ryuichi, a gangster who is *chugoku-kikokusha* (a returnee from China) and half-Japanese, half-Chinese.[2] In *Dead or Alive* many characters, such as Ryuichi and his comrades, are of non-Japanese (mainly Chinese) and mixed-race groups. In addition, the film presents various examples of the relevance of the body-metaphor as well as of the stretching of 'narrative coherence'.

The opening sequence offers a good example of the lack of unity within, or the fragmentation of, the film's narrative world. More than five minutes long, it consists of various image strands juxtaposed in ways that prevent the formation of a unified narrative world: a naked woman with a bag of cocaine in her hand falling from a building onto a street; strip dancing; an act of sodomy in a public toilet; a man snorting a long line of cocaine; a man eating a huge amount of noodles at the Chinese restaurant; the retrieval of a gun from a supermarket fridge and several killings. Comprising twenty scenes and more than a hundred shots, this sequence sets the plot in motion and introduces most of the main characters, but each shot is edited abstractly, in quick tempo, with full use of jump-cuts and abrupt location changes. Apart from the soundtrack, which constructs a continuous 'sound space', there is hardly any spatial or narrative coherence across the shots. Unlike *The Happiness of the Katakuri* and *Shinjuku Triad Society*, where diegetic unity is disrupted by the insertion of animation and non-diegetic images, the opening of *Dead or Alive* seems to maintain some sort of potential diegetic coherence. However, the narrative that animates this world does not possess a coherent unity and is drastically fragmented.

Thirdly, this sequence resorts to metaphors of the 'lack of bodily integrity': when the man eating noodles at the restaurant is killed, the noodles he was eating erupt from his stomach and scatter over the screen (by way of computer graphics with animation-like rather than realistic effect), signalling the loss of 'bodily integrity' and the breakdown of 'bodily boundaries'. Another striking example of such a collapse of bodily boundaries appears later in the film when Ryuichi's girlfriend Kaoru dies at the hand of a Japanese yakuza. Kaoru is killed in a pool of her own bodily excreta after being injected with a narcotic, raped and given an enema. Such an excessive excretion clearly suggests a loss of control of bodily boundaries.

Body-related metaphors of various kinds return in the middle of the film's end-sequence, which shows the confrontation between Jojima and Ryuichi. Coming out from a crushed car with steel rods sticking into his stomach, Jojima wrenches off his own injured arm. When, having shot at each other several times, Jojima and Ryuichi are about to collapse, the camera alternates between each of their tortured faces. At this point, the film suddenly abandons verisimilitude altogether: a bazooka comes out of Jojima's back, which he aims at Ryuichi. This is followed by a cut to a shot of Ryuichi extracting what looks like a burning sphere from his chest. After staring at the fireball in his hand, Ryuichi throws it at Jojima while Jojima fires his bazooka. As the fireball and bazooka collide, there is an explosion that obliterates the images on the screen. The following shot shows an image of the earth seen from space, with Japan clearly visible. The fireball explodes in the Tokyo area. This apocalyptic ending evokes a nuclear explosion, blowing up Japan and, with it, the world. While both the bazooka and the burning sphere may invite various possible readings, it is neither possible nor important to bestow a single fixed meaning on them. What is important here is that by breaking down genre conventions and verisimilitude, the film takes the confrontation of individuals (a policeman and a gangster) to another level: the confrontation between Japan/ese and 'others' which leads to the obliteration of Japan.

The work of the anthropologist Mary Douglas provides a useful framework to understand the connection between, on the one hand, the three characteristic aspects of Miike's films as exemplified in *Dead or Alive*, and, on the other hand, the socio-historical context of contemporary Japan. In her essay 'Do Dogs Laugh?' (1975) Douglas identifies an analogy between the relation of the spoken word to non-verbal communication and the relation of the written word to the physical materials and visible manner of its presentation. Just as the physical embodiment of the written word, such as typography, the arrangement of footnotes, or the layout of the margins of a written document indicate a set of implicit meanings about the realm of discourse to which it belongs, Douglas argues that bodily functions, such as posture, voice, articulation and speed, support and contribute to the meaning of a spoken communication as well as indicating the social sphere to which it is directed. Douglas is not the first to claim the importance of the unspoken part of any discourse or to identify an analogy between society and the body. The important aspect of her work is, however, her attempt to reverse the usual organic analogy by which society is seen as a body. Instead of seeing society as a body, Douglas identifies the body as a site of information, a coding and transmitting machine, arguing that 'the body communicates information for and from the social system of which it is a part' (Douglas 1975: 83). For Douglas, the body expresses the relationship of the individual to the group and it both represents and contributes to the social situation at a given moment. In addition, it should be noted here that the body is as Douglas points out, 'not always under perfect control' (Douglas 1975: 86).

In addition to the 'real' bodies that may appear in a film, Douglas allows us to look at a filmic text or a diegetic world also as a body. How the story is told, and how it is presented in the films, are as important as (or sometimes more important than) 'what' is told. How the film treats (whether consciously or unconsciously) its own body (the filmic text) and the way the actual body and bodily functions are presented in the films can also be seen, according to Douglas' argument, as embodying a notion of the contemporary Japanese society to which it belongs and which it 'figures'. As mentioned earlier, Miike's films are not about foreigners but rather about Japan's understanding of itself in relation to these foreigners. In that sense, the lack of bodily integrity (literally – as in actorial bodies – or figuratively – as in the 'body' of the text) in Miike's films dramatises the break-up of the nation or, more appropriately, the break-up of the national body or *kokutai* of Japan.

Writing on Tsukamoto Shinya's cult film *Tetsuo* (*Tetsuo: The Iron Man*) (1989) and Oshii Mamoru's animated film *Kokakukidotai: Ghost in the Shell* (*Ghost in the Shell*) (1995), Eric Cazdyn (2003: 243) argues that these two films are about the body and subjectivity, and that they allegorise the break-up of the nation (Japan) by narrating the break-up of the individual. Establishing an analogy between the 'I' of the 'Cyborg' and the relation of the 'Nation' to the 'Global', Cazdyn argues that the problematic of the 'I' and its instability in the cyborgian body in *Tetsuo* and in *Ghost in the Shell* represent the problematic of the 'Nation' and its instability in relation to 'a world in which "Japan" no longer exists' (Cazdyn 2003: 250). Although not referring to Mary Douglas, Cazdyn's argument seems to be a good example of Douglas' anthropological framework for reading the relation between body and society applied to films. However, while Cazdyn's analogy refers to the individual body and the nation (Japan), my argument here focuses on the relationship of the body (both real body **133** and filmic body) to a myth or ideology of 'Japaneseness', that is to say, to the *kokutai* ideology which specifies notions of Japaneseness in terms of body homogeneity.

Kokutai is an ideology that was invented to unite Japan as a modern nation-state under the emperor in the late nineteenth century. It claims that Japan is a racially homogeneous organic unity and that all Japanese are linked by blood to a single imperial family. In addition, the myth of Japaneseness stresses the notion of 'boundary' as it conceives of Japan as an organic unity in which outside and inside can be clearly demarcated. Although the term *kokutai* is no longer used or heard in Japan, the myth, or the ideology, of Japan as a racially and culturally homogeneous country has continued, serving as a dominant self-portrait of Japan and as the bedrock of Japanese nationalism. Although often translated as 'national essence', literally rendered the Japanese characters that form the word *kokutai* would read 'national body' (*koku* = national, *tai* = body). By the repeated use of metaphors emphasising a lack of bodily integrity, the breakdown of bodily boundaries and the fragmentation of the body, Miike's films seem to allegorise the break-up of the mythical national body of Japan as a racially homogeneous organic unit.

By using the metaphors of bodily disintegration, Miike's films can be seen to attempt to deconstruct the myth (or ideology) of a homogeneously unified Japan. However, this is not necessarily a critically progressive deconstruction. In fact, Miike may well be presenting a nostalgic nationalist discourse lamenting the loss of *kokutai*, or he may merely be registering the breakdown of any notion of *kokutai* without attaching positive or negative meaning to it.

In one sense, the fragmentation of the body may be read as a progressive deconstruction of *kokutai* ideology, or of the traditional notion of Japaneseness. Like modernist works of art, especially those of the avant-garde, which challenge the notion of an apparent natural or given, self-evident unity, Miike splits up the narrative world or the body of the films in the opening sequences of *Dead or Alive* and goes beyond the conventional boundaries of generic unity in the end-sequence. If we look only at these aspects and at the fact that there are many non-Japanese (including mixed-race characters) in the films, it may be possible to argue that, by splitting apart and breaking up the coherent unity of the filmic body, Miike's films attempt to subvert or deconstruct the idea of the unified body or the mythical national body of Japan. However, in his films, de-construction does not involve re-construction. Put differently, the deconstruction of the ideology of *kokutai*, or the notion of a homogeneous unified Japan, does not involve the radical project of a reconstruction of a new 'Japan' characterised by cultural and racial diversity. Rather, as the apocalyptic ending of *Dead or Alive* suggests, the break-up of the national body leads to the obliteration of Japan.

Such a 'non-productive' deconstruction may also be found in the way mixed-race groups are treated in the film. In *Dead or Alive*, as well as in other Miike films, such as *Shinjuku Triad Society*, mixed race is represented as an erosion of the boundaries of the Japaneseness – that is to say, as a contamination of Japanese blood. In *Dead or Alive*, there is a scene in which Jojima and his colleague visit a small town where there seems to be a community of *chugoku-kikokusha* (returnees from China) and where Ryuichi obtained a reputation as a trouble-maker when he was a teenager. Jojima and his colleague approach two young men and ask about Ryuichi. One of them refers to Ryuichi as 'our' hero. Jojima's colleague asks him what he means by 'our' or who 'us' is. The two young men reply, 'Us, we look Japanese, but we ain't. Then again, we look Chinese, but we ain't. That is us who are not really anything.' Here mixed-race people, or people with two different cultural backgrounds, are not presented in a positive way: Japanese and at the same time Chinese, producing a new Japanese culture through what Paul Gilroy (1987: 154) calls 'cultural syncretism'. Rather, as the two of them say, they are not anything. While the *kokutai* ideology presents Japaneseness as linked to a single imperial family by blood, the metaphor of 'Japanese blood' is an important element in the affirmation of Japanese identity. The erosion of 'Japanese blood' by foreign blood symbolised as 'mixed race' causes the difficulty or the impossibility of constructing a stable, clearly defined identity. Like the ending of *Dead or Alive*, which suggests that the break-up of the boundary is associated with the 'destruction' of Japan, here, rather than being associated with multiple and hybrid subjectivities, the break-up of national identity is associated with the production of a subjectivity which is described as 'nothing'. The way these two men are presented also makes them anonymous: the camera captures them in a static long shot and even when they talk about 'who they are', the camera never moves close to them. Once they realise that Jojima and his colleague are policemen, they start running away. Then there is a cut which catches one of them from behind running along a railway line. He runs but the camera does not follow, and there is no reverse angle shot showing what he is running away from. Just as they say they are not 'anything', so the camera does not tell us who they are either. They remain anonymous 'others'.

In another sense, then, while in Japanese film history a mixed-race protagonist is unconventional, and although in Miike's films there are many non-Japanese Asian characters, neither *Dead or Alive* nor any other Miike film featuring non-Japanese characters seems to actually subvert the ideology of Japan as a homogeneous unified country. While these films do not present a nostalgic vision of old mythical Japan, they still suggest a sense of 'loss'. The disintegration of a national body and the loss of control of bodily boundaries seem to be conceived as the tragedy (probably comedy as well) of Japan. Moreover, it is foreigners and mixed-race groups which appear to dramatise the break-up of the national body, or the loss of control of bodily boundaries.

The metaphor of the lack of bodily integrity or the breakdown of bodily boundaries is often discernible also in those of Miike's films that do not deal with foreigners at all. This may well mean that in Miike's work the loss of a unified national body or boundary is not necessarily attributed only to foreigners. And yet, the many of Miike's films which do deal with foreigners clearly mobilise foreigners or mixed-race characters as an active factor in a narrative strategy that dramatises the break-up of a notion of the national through the device of dramatising the loss of control over bodily boundaries.

Since the late 1980s, in Japan as in other countries, there has been a trend in which cultural diversity is praised under the banner of 'multiculturalism'. If, at first glance, the discourse of multiculturalism seems to challenge the ideology of Japan as a homogeneous nation, in the light of Miike's films, the question can be raised as to whether this is in fact the case.

Tessa Morris-Suzuki (2001: 185) describes the recent trend of 'multiculturalism' in Japan as 'cosmetic multiculturalism': the diversity of a culture is not only enjoyed on a superficial level, but also used as the means to exemplify the generosity of Japan as well as its capacity to accommodate other cultures. More often than not, claims for the recognition of their political and economic rights by the bearers of these 'other' cultures are ignored. Positioned in Japanese culture as 'objects', these 'other' cultures are acknowledged only to the extent that they are to be seen, enjoyed, spoken of and consumed (Morris-Suzuki 2001: 186). The demarcation or boundary between Japan as the host culture and the 'other cultures' remains firmly in place as the mark of 'permitted' cultural diversity. The effect is a rigid hierarchy between dominant Japanese culture and 'other cultures'. From this perspective, the celebration of multiculturalism in recent Japan can be seen as self-congratulatory or self-indulgent culturalism which celebrates the capacity of the allegedly unique Japanese culture to absorb the cultural forms and practices of 'others'. Indeed, for Morris-Suzuki multiculturalism in contemporary Japan may be seen as a form of Japanese nationalism (Morris-Suzuki 2001:186) – this time around a reconstructed nationalism designed to pay lip service to political correctness in the era of so-called post-colonialism and globalisation without, for this, losing nationalism's dominant position within older, even pre-Meiji discourses of the nation. To conclude, the discourse of multiculturalism may well seem to challenge the ideology of Japan as a homogeneous nation and the positive aspects of it should not be underestimated. Yet, in the context of contemporary Japan, Morris-Suzuki's criticism of the current trend of 'cosmetic multiculturalism' is particularly pertinent. This concept allows us to understand how foreigners and mixed-race groups are handled in Miike's films. Miike may not present non-Japanese (including half-Japanese) characters as stereotypically threatening 'others' in a simple binary of 'good' Japanese and 'evil' foreigner. Although it is true that non-Japanese characters in Miike's films are, in many cases, extremely nasty, violent and atrocious, Japanese characters are not any better. As Abe Kashou (2000: 320) puts it with regard to *Shinjuku Triad Society*, it is 'multiple' and 'multinational' evil which is presented in Miike's films. Miike's films do dramatise, insistently and graphically, how the loss of body integrity also 'figures' the destruction of any notion of a stable Japanese identity, as well as any notion of both social and aesthetic homogeneity. While this breakdown of bodily integrity generates intense energies which pervade his films at all levels, it is also linked explicitly with pain and even with the destruction of Japan as a coherent geopolitical image.

In this respect, Miike's films present a special case of 'cosmetic multiculturalism': these films do not lament the loss of Japanese 'essence' and homogeneity as, for instance, some of Kitano Takeshi's films do (for instance, *Hana-Bi* [1998]). Rather, they merely register it and note its destructive impact while savouring the energies released by this destruction. Nor are they xenophobic, for the break-up of the national body in Miike's films is not registered as something that needs to be, or even can be, counteracted or restored. The breakdown is dramatised without, however, envisaging an alternative conceptualisation of Japan, as was the case, for instance, in Hani Susumu's films of the 1960s and 1970s (*Buwana-Toshi no uta* [*Buwana Toshi*], 1965, or *Andesu no hanayome* [*The Bride of The Andes*], 1966), where the

oppressive aspects of the Japaneseness discourse and its attendant myths of exceptionalism and unity were put to the test. On the other hand, while accommodating ethnic diversity by including many of the previously underrepresented Asian and mixed-race figures, Miike's films do not actively disrupt the dominant structure and definition of Japaneseness. Instead, it is the films' lack of formal homogeneity, their multi-tiered and shattered discursive figurations, which bear the brunt of Miike's encounter with the core metaphor that incarnates Japanese exceptionalism: the unified body of the *kokutai*.

Notes

1. An earlier version of this article appeared in *New Cinemas: Journal of Contemporay Film* 2 (1).
2. Following the Manchuria Incident in 1931, many Japanese settled in northeastern China as a part of the Japanese government's Manchuria development promotion scheme. Amid the confusion of the former Soviet Union's entrance into the Pacific War in August 1945, and following Japan's surrender, many of these Japanese, especially small children and young women, were left behind in Manchuria. Those Japanese who grew up in China after being separated from their families at the end of World War II are called *zanryu-houjin*. Because of the Cold War and ruptured diplomatic relations between China and Japan, these Japanese had no choice but to stay in China by marrying Chinese people or being adopted by Chinese families as orphans. It was not until 1981, nine years after the normalisation of diplomatic relations with China, that the Japanese government began an investigation to identify these Japanese and launch a repatriation project (in a slow and ineffective way) for those who wished to return to Japan. *Chugoku-Kikokusha* (Japanese returnee) refers to those people who were *zanryu-houjin* and their offspring who returned to Japan from China. It has been reported that, after coming back to Japan, many of them have experienced difficulties in adapting to Japanese society because of language, customs and cultural differences.

References

Abe Kashou (2000), *Nihon eiga ga sonzai suru (Japanese Films Exist)*, Tokyo: Seidosha.
Cazdyn, Eric (2003), *The Flash of Capital: Film and Geopolitics in Japan*, Durham: Duke University Press.
Douglas, Mary (1975), *Implicit Meanings: Essays in Anthropology*, London: Routledge and Kegan Paul.
Film Comment (2002), January/February.
Gilroy, Paul (1987), *There Ain't no Black in the Union Jack*, London: Hutchinson.
Morris-Suzuki, Tessa (2001), '"Posutokoroniarizmu" no imi wo megutte (Discussion over the meanings of post-colonialism)', *Gendai Shiso – Special issue* 29: 183–7.
Rayns, Tony (2000), 'This Gun for Hire', *Sight and Sound* 10 (5): 30–2.

10 Taiwan New Cinema, or a Global Nativism?[1]

Kuan-Hsing Chen

My central task in this short essay is to problematise the very notion of the Taiwan New Cinema (hereafter TNC), so as to propose a possible problematic for comparative cultural studies in the inter-Asia region. I shall demonstrate that the history of TNC was born out of, and participated in facilitating, the nativist movement.[2] However, when it was integrated into the functioning of another kind of TNC (transnational corporations, that is to say, in this case, Hollywood), it was swallowed up by the new nation-building and state-making project. Perhaps, as part of a general trend in 'world cinema', it will move into what I shall term a global nativism: a nativism predicated upon the commodification of the complicit dialectic between nationalism and transnationalism.

'TNC' refers generally to a range of cinematic practices from the early 1980s to the present and gathers together a whole set of activities (production, criticism, promotion, consumption). Disavowed by directors who were identified as key players, it was mainly a term first coined by critics and later accepted by a wider population as referring to an alternative cinema beginning with *In Our Time* (1982), co-directed by then four younger-generation directors, produced by the party/state-owned Central Motion Picture Company (CMPC), and dying with *All for Tomorrow* (1988), a political propaganda MTV film, co-directed with Chen Kuo-fu by the foremost director of TNC, Hou Hsiao-hsien. What has come later then can be termed 'post-TNC'. On the other hand, there is a continuity between the 'post-' and the 'new-' TNC: the 'post', while losing the TNC's defining commitment to alternative cinematic practices,[3] inherited its concern with the cinematic representation of Taiwan's local histories. The question then becomes: how does one position and understand this obsession with 'histories'?

Unlike most Third World places that participated in the post-World War II global decolonisation movement by way of a nativism mobilised by national independence movements, Taiwan's belated 'self-rediscovery' was blocked by the Cold War structure of the Kuomingtang (Nationalist or KMT) regime in alliance with the United States. Although it can be argued that the tradition of an oppositional nativist movement began from the end of Japanese occupation, especially after 28 February 1947 massacre, and was culturally crystallised first in the upsurge of Taiwanese language and dialect films in the late 1950s, after

Dien Bien Phu, and then again in the 'homeland' literary movement (*hsiang-tu wen-hsue yun-dong*) in the 1970s, the full-blown nativisation movement (*ben-tu-hua yun-dong*) did not come about until the late 1970s and early 1980s, when the late President Chiang Ching-Kuo, the son of Chiang Kai-shek, recognising that there was 'no hope of recovering the mainland' (*fan-kung wu-wang*), began to nativise (or more accurately, to ethnicise) his political regime as a strategy to maintain governing legitimacy. However, a caveat is in order here. From the point of view of the most deprived population in Taiwan, the aboriginals, the Han people are and have been the coloniser, no matter whether they came before or after 1945 when the Japanese handed the regime over to the Han Chinese. In the decade-long nativist-nationalist movement, aboriginals have been excluded and marginalised. The imposed categories classifying 'ethnic' groups as Taiwanese (*tai-wan-jen*) or Mainlander (*wai-shen-jen* or 'people coming from outside the province') in post-1945 eras, and into 'four big ethnic groups' (the dominant *min-nan-jen*, the Hakka or *ker-jia-jen*, the *wai-shen-jen* and the aborigines) since the late 1980s, have been contested by the aboriginals. For them, it's not so much an ethnic difference between aboriginal Taiwanese and Han Chinese, but a racial one. In short, the nativisation in political practices, oppositional or otherwise, refers in fact to a 'Min-Nan-isation'.

When the political sphere opened up and the export-oriented national economy was fully incorporated into the structure of global capital to become an often-exaggerated member of the four tigers, TNC, along with other cultural forms (literature, music, dancing, painting, academic production, religion and so on), began to look back at the historical formation in search of a Taiwanese rather than a Chinese 'lost self'. In this sense, the cinematic writing or invention of histories became one of the central sites where a new sense of 'self' could be constructed and contested.

However, this wider social mood and ideological structure of feeling alone cannot explain the birth of TNC. One must also grasp the inner logic of the film industry and the cinematic apparatus. As part of its particular version of the Cold War and aiming to foster anti-communist films in Hong Kong, in the 1950s the Taiwanese government had exempted Hong Kong cinema from restrictions pertaining to imported films, allowing its stronger industry to become dominant in distribution and exhibition in Taiwan. This, together with an intrusive but inconsistent domestic regulation of cinema, disadvantaged the Taiwanese film industry. From the mid-1970s, Taiwan's film industry lost its game to a Hong Kong that had gradually become the little Hollywood of the region. The formation of a TNC movement was thus in part to revive local film industry. As critic Tung Wa explained in 1986, 'TNC was born in the chaotic situations of demand-supply dysfunction in the local market and defeat in the external market' (1986: 31). In addition, with the so-called 'Taiwan Miracle', a 'consumer society' was taking shape in the late 1970s, and the new generation of moviegoers responded to films more directly connected to their own experiences. This created difficulties for directors belonging to an older generation. In short, the formation of TNC was historically overdetermined by economic and political forces.

What was essentially new about the TNC since the 1980s was, in my view, this reclaiming of the 'real' home space from which to construct a popular memory of people's lives on **139** the island, especially in the post-war era. The critics' call for an alternative 'national cinema', although deliberately formulated against Hollywood's global expansion (Tung Wa, 1986: 34), was not a xenophobic blocking out of cultural resources from the outside, but a political move. As Tung Wa argued in the context of a drive to construct a 'national' cinema, 'it is not a bad thing for Third World Cinema and other non-mainstream cinemas to learn from each other' (1986: 34). In the early stage of TNC, Tung Wa's concern was expressed within the context of constructing a 'national cinema'. The nativist language movement reached a new high point in the late 1980s not so much as a stubborn continuation of the 'dialect' film wave of the late 1950s, but rather as a critical re-examination of that phase in Taiwan's cultural production (such as the *gezaixi* theatre performance troupes) that accompanied the childhood years of many TNC directors and writers. Hou mixed different local languages in his earlier films and *Hill of No Return* (Wang Tong, 1992) was spoken entirely in Min-Nan.

In sharp contrast to the pre-TNC, as Wu Chi-yen (1993: 7) summarised it, the newness of the TNC expressed itself on two levels: in the use of historical 'materials from the local, with a sense of reality', and in 'the exploration and creation of new cinematic languages', referring to aspects of *mise en scène*, cutting, narrative structure, sequence shots, non-linear narrative and critical social realism. Whether TNC possesses its own language in the history of world cinema remains an open question. The critic Cheng Chuan-shing once observed that if there is one, it is a 'parrot' language, collaging elements without any identifiable coherence, rather like the rest of Taiwan's export-oriented economy. In my view, the crucial point about TNC is perhaps not so much its aesthetic forms, but its strategic-ideological functioning within the wider cultural history of Taiwan, or more precisely, its deliberate 'historical turn' to the discovery and construction of a Taiwanese 'self'.

There is a general consensus among critics that TNC was born in 1982, when the CMPC released the low-budget film, *In Our Time* (Edward Yang, Tao Te-chen, Ko I-cheng and Chang Yi, 1982). The success of *In Our Time* provided the incentive for the party-owned CMPC to produce *The Sandwich Man* (Hou Hsiao-hsien, Zeng Zhuang-xiang and Wang Jen, 1983), by rewriting three short stories from the 'homeland literary movement'. This borrowing from nativist literature constituted one of the defining features of the TNC throughout the 1980s. What can be termed as *Bildungsroman* narrative, expressed in *Ah-Fe (Rape Seed)* (1983), *Boys from Fengkuei* (Hou Hsiao-hsien, 1983), *Growing Up* (Chen Kunhuo, 1983), *Summer at Grandpa's* (Hou Hsiao-hsien, 1984), *Dust in the Wind* (Hou Hsiao-hsien, 1986), *Taipei Story* (Edward Yang, 1985), *The Time to Live and the Time to Die* (Hou Hsiao-hsien, 1985), *Banana Paradise* (Wang Tong, 1989) and *A Brighter Summer Day* (Edward Yang, 1991), not only constituted a retracing of 'how we, the post-war generation, grew up', but also charted the trajectories of changing political and economic environments. In this sense, the TNC obsession with history signals the change from one era to another: from an agricultural to an industrial society, from a poor rural life to an urban one, from a political identification with China to one with Taiwan. In short, TNC conveyed a struggle over the construction of (popular) memory. Perhaps because the ethnic background of the directors as well as that of those who

were in control of the film industry was largely that of 'mainlander' (*wai-shen-jen*), the longer term of historical memory did not extend as far back as the era of Japanese occupation. This happened only recently, with films such as *Hill of No Return*, *The Puppetmaster* (Hou Hsiao-hsien, 1993) and *A Borrowed Life* (Wu Nien-chen, 1995).

Along with the explosion of identity politics in various kinds of social movements (women, labour, aboriginals, veterans, lesbians and gays, and youth) from the late 1980s on, there emerged a set of movies that concerned themselves with the politics of identity, such as *Banana Paradise* (one of the most critical films to date, analysed in Wu 1993 and Chen 1991), *Two Painters* (1990), *Rebels of the Neon God* (Tsaï Ming-Liang, 1992), *Dust of Angels* (Hsiao-ming Hsu, 1992), *The Wedding Banquet* (Ang Lee, 1993) and *Vive L'amour* (Tsaï Ming-Liang, 1995). However, it has to be noted that unlike in Hong Kong cinema, which had women directors such as Ann Hui and Clara Law, TNC has been a predominantly male affair. Tsaï Ming-liang can be seen as the first explicitly gay director with *Vive L'amour*. What is more interesting for the gay and lesbian movement is the appearance of a 500-page, almost encyclopaedic collection of gay films from all over the world, compiled and commented on in campy form by the most insistent critic, Lee You-shing (Youth-Leigh 1993).

Two moments of heated debate mark the TNC's place in Taiwanese film history, one surrounding *All for Tomorrow* and one focusing on *A City of Sadness*. On 24 January 1987, a *Manifesto for Taiwan's Cinema* was co-signed by fifty cultural workers to express their discontent with, and to reform, cinematic policies, stating at the top of their proclamation their demand for a 'film policy that supports film culture. [I]f the relevant administrative office in control of the film policy supports commercial films and films for political propaganda, it should explicitly say so, and those who are willing to devote themselves to the activities of cinematic culture can then abandon all hope for state support.' The next year, 1988, key players of the TNC such as the directors Hou Hsiao-hsien and Chen Kuo-fu and scriptwriters Hsiao Yeh and Wu Nien-chen, jointly produced *All for Tomorrow*, an MTV-style promo for recruitment to the military school funded by the Ministry of Defence. This association between TNC and militarism came as a shock. The sense of betrayal generated a series of attacks in the popular press, and the literary supplement page of the *Independently Daily* also ran a series of articles (the debates were collected and documented in Mi-Chou and Liang 1991: 33–79). The critic and scholar Cheng Chuan-shing framed the debate on cinema and politics:

> Before the appearance of *All for Tomorrow*, there was still a distance between TNC and politics, although the latter through different forms and mechanisms attempted to shorten that distance in order to put the former under total surveillance and control; therefore, in essence, they opposed each other. [If] before *All for Tomorrow*, there was still talk of political cinema and of the politics of cinema, there is no doubt that afterwards the phrase 'cinema is politics' is no longer merely a matter of rhetoric or theory, but a reality. Cinema is now entirely swallowed and assimilated by politics. (1991: 67–9)

In response to these criticisms, Hou re-emphasised that his cinema 'never talks about ideology' and that he never sought to endow his films with either a progressive or a conservative ideol-   141 ogy, making such criticism irrelevant. Hsiao Yeh went further and stigmatised the criticisms as 'media violence and fascism'. Critics' interventions, of course, could not change the course of TNC, which 'ideologically' originated as an alternative cultural movement, and by then had become co-opted into the establishment. This debate led critics to announce the death of TNC.

Perhaps the death of TNC as a conscientious intellectual project was inevitable. TNC never operated outside the prevailing system of production, distribution and consumption. The party/state-owned CMPC had been TNC's production base. In effect, the launching of the TNC could be read as a generational struggle over power, manifested in the 1987 Cinema Manifesto, drafted and signed by this new generation when the means of production appeared to become available to them. Once they had learned to survive within the commercial industry and to live with the 'irresistible' market forces, the project was over and done with.

By far the most politically controversial debate on history centred around *A City of Sadness* (1989) directed by Hou. Departing from the *Bildungsroman*-mode typical of TNC, *A City of Sadness* attempted to deal with a then taboo episode of political history: the 'white terror' (*bai-se kung-bu*) of the 1940s, especially the 28 February 1947 massacre, when at least 30,000 people were killed and which later defined the shape of post-war mainstream politics built on an ethnic mobilisation typical of Third World nationalisms. The event crystallised the structure of feeling under the authoritarian regime, saturating every corner of social life. The entire leftist tradition was completely wiped out as surviving dissidents were jailed, some for over thirty years, which partly explains the relative weakness of Taiwan's contemporary critical intellectual formation. The universally implemented surveillance technology to control allegedly pro-communist thought or any politically dissident views has shaped 'distorted personality types', views on society often having to be conveyed in a circuitous and ambiguous way. More than any other film, *A City of Sadness* called upon larger sectors of society to respond to its address of this key moment. The then young critic, Mi-Chou, opened the attack, on 10 October 1989 in the *Independent Daily*, commenting on the alliance between the director and critics at a panel discussion staged by the press in an attempt to depoliticise the reading of the film. The attack called for another 'epistemological break' in film criticism (1991: 113). Through this emotionally charged film-event, the debate took on board a wide range of issues, including the problem of historical narration (who has the power to write history, in what directions, to what ends), and the prevailing industrial regime of cinema and the system of film reviewing (as journalists, in alliance with the production enterprise, become part of the public relations mechanism to control the film's meanings). The debate addressed questions of history, context and text; the cinematic apparatus, history and popular memory. As Mi-Chou and Liang (1991: xii) put it, the film triggered a 'sudden explosion' of issues which forced critics to face problems of cinema that had been neglected. It can be argued that TNC's contribution has precisely been its ability to cut into the social fabric, interpellating cultural identities of different constituencies, triggering the suppressed collective flow of desire and offering itself as a sounding board to articulate affective responses.

The TNC's entry into the international circuit was accidentally staged by this seemingly taboo film, *A City of Sadness*. In 1987, martial law was lifted, but the habitual mood of self-censorship did not immediately dissolve. The 28 February massacre was highlighted in the overseas promotional materials (previews, advertising, poster, press conferences). In order to avoid being censored by the state, the production team developed the strategy to first win international fame before coming home, hoping to embarrass the state into passing the film. As the 'packager' of the film, Tsan Hung-chih characterised his strategy: 'Promote expansively overseas, play low key back home' (quoted in Mi-Chou 1991: 109). The film, as expected, won the Golden Lion award in the 1989 Cannes Film Festival. Since then, the state has not only offered the victimised families of the 28 February financial compensation, it also erected a memorial statue in Taipei New Park in 1995, and a memorial museum was opened by the Taipei city government in 1997.

On the other hand, the success of the strategy made the producers realise that there was a potential market overseas to sell its nativist or exotic alienness. This new discovery (by the local and international industry) marked a shift in TNC. For instance, *A Brighter Summer Day* was produced in co-operation with Japanese investment. At this point, the Taiwanese state's ideological project to join the United Nations (in order to win more bargaining chips with the Chinese state) also discovered the marker of TNC to register the name of 'Taiwan' in the American mind, hoping to win US support. In 1992, the Government Information Office, in charge of international propaganda and local censorship, signed a contract with Warner Bros. to circulate TNC. To further facilitate the process, the diasporic director, Ang Lee, resident in New York for over a decade, was hired to generate films such as *Pushing Hands* (1991) and later *The Wedding Banquet*, both of which were funded by the Central Studio and set in New York's diasporic Chinese community. With the release of *Sense and Sensibility* (1995), Ang Lee almost became a national hero in Taiwan's transnationalisation effort. For the state, what matters is not so much the ideological content of the film, but whether it will disseminate 'Taiwan', to make sure the worldwide audience is able to distinguish, for instance, Taiwan from Thailand. The crew of *The Wedding Banquet* was warmly received by President Lee Teng-hui, the film's engagement with homosexuality being, of course, completely ignored. From then on, the production of TNC was no longer simply locally oriented, but also with a sensitive eye on the foreign market. *The Wedding Banquet* became the first TNC circulated in Hollywood's theatres in the US and elsewhere. This transnationalisation aimed, firstly, to expand TNC's market; secondly, to attract foreign investment; and thirdly, to bolster the state's new nation-state building project.

The political economy of the TNC may not be unique in this respect. A global nativism, though contradictory in terms, dedicated to the circulation of duly exoticised images of natives and national-local histories or signs, appears to be on the rise as a selling point, a trend sailing under the flag of 'World Cinema'. In recent events, such as the 1995 San Francisco International Film Festival, one could no longer distinguish the 'nationality' of certain highly acclaimed films, being co-produced by three or four nations, with directors coming from different national locales, with no sense of a specific local audience being addressed, not to mention concerns for local history and politics. Perhaps this development will call into 143 question notions of 'national cinema' in the classic sense of the term. Lii (1998), for instance, drew attention to what he calls the 'yielding' production strategies adopted by Hong Kong producers, incorporating demands from various foreign distributors into the very fabric of the films. Even Hollywood's distribution system appears ready to circulate some selected nativist products, strengthening the trend towards an address of globalised (mainly English-speaking) audiences.

Whether nation-states are in decline and transnational corporations (TNCs) are taking over, is an issue to be debated. But there is no sign that nationalism is disappearing; quite the contrary: transnationalism and nationalism seem to be bonded together. In this respect, TNC may indeed be seen as a kind of TNC. What is urgently needed is not only to recognise the hegemonising power of the nation-state and TNCs to incorporate the radical potential of nativist movements, but also to actively discover the heterogeneity and positive energy of nativist elements. As Mi-Chou put it in a letter to me dated 25 August 1996: 'What should be done is to actively sort out, analyze, and make use of these heterogeneous elements and turn them into resources of resistance; rather than throwing them away, which would merely be a gift to the hegemonic project of the nation-state. What is needed now is perhaps not a totalizing, but a counter-reading strategy.'

Postscript

In the year 2000, the Democratic Progressive Party (DPP) defeated the KMT. The fifty-year-long monopoly of Taiwan state power thus ended. What has supported the oppositional 'democratic' politics in a wider social context was indeed the nativist movement of which TNC was an integral part. Looking back, the continuity of cultural nativism and political ethnic nationalism has been the driving force of Taiwan's democratisation movement since the 1980s. However, the problem is that after the DPP took over, the society is no more democratic. To remain in office, the DPP regime continues to play on ethnic divides,[4] mobilising one sector against the other, leaving social and political reforms largely untouched. The new regime, building on the existing nativist ground and the long-term established anti-communist/pro-American sentiment, launched a de-sinicisation project that constructs China as the enemy in order to push further the Taiwan Independence Movement and to win the election in 2004. The mystical gun-shot right before elections day over-turned the result. Chen Shui-bian won by a small margin and remained in office.[5]

Sensing the escalation of ethnic conflicts mobilised by the two rival political candidates, during the election and in order to ease the fascistic tendency of the tension, a group of intellectuals emerged to form an Alliance for Ethnic Equality. One figurehead of the group is Hou Shiao-hsien.[6] Having contributed to the rise of the nativist movement and with no political ambition, Hou Shiao-hsien thinks the direction has gone too far astray against the democratic ethos and he has to take action to correct it.[7] The opposition between the DPP and the KMP is a binarism in the same direction – towards the right – that leaves no space for any other mode of thinking. After the election, a third force, leaning towards liberal social democracy, is called for by the wider social forces. Hou and the Alliance members thus formed a new Democratic School, so that a second wave of democratic movement can be initiated. As the first Head of the School, Hou was reported by the mainstream media as using his expertise to 'direct' a new political narrative, only that this 'film' is a live perform-ance on the political stage. Is this the new life of TNC? Let's hope so.

In this context, the issue of democratisation has been addressed eloquently by the stun-ning *Goodbye Dragon Inn* (*Bu San*) (2003), by Malay-born author Tsaï Ming-Liang. Perhaps one of the director's most uncompromising films, *Goodbye Dragon Inn* focuses on the life of the once popular Fu Ho Theatre, a cinema about to close down but still functioning as a ghostly place for the marginalised – an old man, a crippled woman, gay men. Dwelling at leisure on the almost empty auditorium, Tsaï Ming-Liang's direction conveys effectively and wittily the sense of a space-in-waiting, where every detail and every sound resonates with questions. Turning the camera back at the audience (we hardly ever see the screen), *Goodbye Dragon Inn* asks that we think about cinema as *our* space.

Tsaï Ming-Liang has been making that claim quite vociferously and for some time now, in and outside his films. As he explained in an interview in the late 1990s:

> Over the last ten years, if you have been able to see many quality Taiwanese films which have won prizes at international festivals, it's thanks to the system of government subsidies. Today there are many problems with that system. [Taiwanese production companies] have taken their investments off to Hong Kong and China. Hong Kong because there they are still making Hollywood-style films, and China because it's the same thing, it's like a Hollywood system. As the film industry in Hong Kong has also been in a downturn for some years now, all these investors have set up distribution companies for Hollywood films. [W]hat is even worse is that they too are starting to apply for [government] subsidies. They are very influential and control most of the unions. So now they are starting to form pressure groups to ask the government to subsidize commercial films too. The problem is that the people in government who are in charge of cinema don't know much about culture, and they are also very pally with these press-ure groups, so they allowed them to get subsidies. That's why I have started working with foreign producers. (Rehm, Joyard and Rivière 1998: 117)

Notes

1. This essay, first written in October 1997, is dedicated to Wang Fei-ling and Wu Chi yen who were friends and comrades, critics of the Taiwan New Cinema. Both died of cancer in their late thirties and early forties respectively. I wish to thank Robert Chen Ru-hsio and Ray Jing for giving me English titles of the films, Tung Wa and Cheng Chun-shing for critical discussions, and Nai-fei Ding and Shang-jen Lii (Mi-Chou) for commenting on the earlier draft of the manuscript. Being a 'native informant' on Taiwan New Cinema will inevitably draw criticism for an infinity of unforgivable absences, factional biases and privileged subject positions. These are the risks that I have to take.

2. By nativist movement (*ben-tu-hua yun-dong*), I am not only referring to the 'self-rediscovery' movement in Taiwan, but to a general historical reaction to the end of colonial domination. I use the term as an analytical designation with both positive and negative dimensions of the concept. **145**

3. 'Alternative' here refers both to a political critique of the dominant ideology of the KMT state in the form of a cinema that is alternative to the state-sponsored cinema, and to an alternative cinematic idiom to the dominant narrative modes, namely psychological realist dramas and genres. In Taiwan, the TNC may thus also be 'alternative' because it adopted an 'art cinema' modality that is to the dominant Hong Kong and Hollywood mass-market-oriented films. Art cinema is not necessarily critical of the state, unless, that is, the state dictates narrative modalities and excludes art cinema from its approved, fundable menu. This appears to be the case in Taiwan – a suspicion confirmed by the Manifesto cited below and by the ability of Hou Hsiao-hsien to make a military recruitment film in response to the CMPC's refusal to sponsor TNC art cinema.

4. For a more detailed account of ethnic politics in Taiwan, see Chen (2002).

5. For a detailed account of the election and the history of Taiwanese politics, see Anderson, 2004.

6. About the Allliance, see the interview in *New Left Review* (II) 28 (2004) with Hou et al.

7. Personal conversation, March 2004.

References

Anderson, Perry (2004), 'Stand-off in Taiwan', *London Review of Books*, 26 (11) (3 June).

Chen, Kuan-Hsing (1991), 'A City of Sadness in Banana Paradise: The Problematic of the National-Popular Memory', unpublished manuscript.

Chen, Kuan-Hsing (2000), 'The Formation and Consumption of KTV', in Chua, Beng Huat (ed.), *Consumption in Asia: Lifestyle and Identities*, London: Routledge.

Chen, Kuan-Hsing (2002), 'Why is "Great Reconciliation" Impossible? De-Cold War/Decolonization, or Modernity and its Tears', *Inter-Asia Cultural Studies* 3 (1): 77–99.

Chen, Robert R. S. (1993), *The Historical and Cultural Experiences of the Taiwan New Cinema*, Taipei: Wan-hsiong Company, in Chinese.

Cheng, Chuan-shing (1991), 'Ventriloquist's National Anthem', in Mi-Chou and Liang, Hsing-Hua (eds) (1991): 66–74, in Chinese.

Chih, Rung-jen (1993), 'Farewell "the New Cinema": Wish for the Coming of "Alternative" Cinema', in Mi-Chou and Liang, Hsing-Hua (eds) (1991): 53–9, in Chinese.

Lii, Ding-tzann (1998), 'A Colonized Empire: Reflections on the Expansion of Hong Kong Film Industry in Asian Countries', in Chen, Kuan-Hsing (ed.), *Trajectories: Inter-Asia Cultural Studies*, London: Routledge.

Hou Shiao-hsien, et al. (2004), 'Tensions in Taiwan', *New Left Review* (II) 28.

Memmi, Albert (1967), *The Colonizer and the Colonized*, Boston: Beacon Press [1957].

Mi-Chou (1991), 'The Foggy Discourses Surrounding *A City of Sadness*: On the Problems of Film Criticism', in Mi-Chou and Liang, Hsing-Hua (eds) (1991), in Chinese.

Mi-Chou, and Liang, Hsing-Hua (eds) (1991), *The Death of New Cinema: From* All for Tomorrow *to* City of Sadness, Taipei: Tonsan Books, the War Machine series 3, in Chinese.

Mi-Chou, and Liang, Hsing-Hua (eds) (1994), *After/Outside the New Cinema*, Taipei: Tonsan Books, the War Machine series 13, in Chinese.

Rehm, Jean-Pierre, Joyard, Olivier and Rivière, Danièle (eds) (1998), *Tsaï Ming-Liang*, Paris: DisVoir.

Tung, Wa (1986), 'Language Law and Color Pen: Notes on the 1985 Taiwan New Cinema', *Film Appreciation Journal* 22: 29–36.

Wang, Fei-ling (1994), *An Unfinished Film Dream: In Memory of Wang Fei-ling*, edited by Chien Cheng, et al., Taipei Klim Publications, in Chinese.

Wu, Chi-yen (1993), *Underdeveloped Memories*, Taipei: Tonsan Books, the War Machine series 8, in Chinese.

Wu, Chi-yen (1996), *Marginal Angle*, edited by Chang Jing-pei, Taipei: Wan-shiong Book Company, in Chinese.

Wuo, Young-yie (1993), 'Hong Kong, Pig King, Nation: Mainlander's National Identity in Home Coming Films', *Chung Wai Literary Monthly* 22 (1): 32–44, in Chinese.

Youth-Leigh, Alphonse (1993), 'Histoire de P (P comme penis) or Films of, by and for gay men', Taipei: Ji-wen, in Chinese.

11 From National Cinema to Cinema and the National

Chinese-language Cinema and Hou Hsiao-hsien's 'Taiwan Trilogy'

Chris Berry

During my first trip to Taiwan almost fifteen years ago, I was shown a majority of the feature films made there and in Hong Kong the year before. On my return, I wrote some essays noting that many of these films were returning to history to question nationalist orthodoxies and trace the complex affiliations produced by post-colonial experience. I asked whether a 'postnational' cinema might be emerging (Berry, 1992, 1992/3, 1993). As I will discuss further below, instead of the fading away of the national, our current era seems to feature *both* rising economic globalisation *and* rising political nationalist tensions. This is certainly the case in Taiwan and throughout what is sometimes called the Greater China region.[1] So, it seems I spoke too soon, or at least that I need think more about what I meant by 'postnational.'

My primary site for this reinvestigation will be Hou Hsiao-hsien's 'Taiwan Trilogy', composed of *Beiqing Chengshi* (*A City of Sadness*) (1989), *Ximeng Rensheng* (*The Puppetmaster*) (1993) and *Hao Nan Hao Nü* (*Good Men, Good Women*) (1995). At this time of high political polarisation around independence issues, it is unclear whether anyone in Taiwan is interested in returning to films like these, which, as I explain below, complicate and resist drawing clear lines between the national collective self and others. Indeed, those who insist that Taiwan is in no way Chinese and that Taiwan films should not be considered under any kind of 'Chinese cinemas' rubric whatsoever will have no patience with my project. However, writing from outside Taiwan and Greater China, the complexities of these texts make them a useful site for the re-examination of the national in film theory. If that also helps in however small a way to make alternatives to the lethal either–or game of territorial nationalism more conceivable, I will not be unhappy.

I argue here that if I was hasty in my use of the term 'postnational' fifteen years ago, my error was not one of observation, but one of interpretation. Since that time, I have worked more on theories of the national in the cinema (Berry 2000; Berry and Farquhar 2001).[2] A 'national cinema' approach is too invested in territorial nationalism to adequately account for films such as these. It is in this sense of the national grounded in the modern territorial nation-state that these films might be considered 'post-'. However, as my observations about the current era indicate, the national may not be what it once was, but neither has it disappeared altogether. Like 'national cinema', the term 'postnational' is still too deeply tied to the ideology of modernity – which only acknowledges the territorial nation-state – to account for the contemporary upsurge in both the transnational and the national. Instead of abandoning the national, we need to rethink it. To fail in this regard would be to perform an ideological short circuit. In the case of film studies, we need to place the 'national cinema' approach and transnational cinema with a larger framework of issues around cinema and the national. Within this framework, the national is no longer confined to the form of the territorial nation-state but multiple, proliferating, contested and overlapping.

Assumptions that many of us made a few years ago about the waning of the national and the waxing of the transnational are being challenged in three areas relevant to this essay: the general political and economic realm, film production and film studies. Yet the form of that challenge appears contradictory. In all three cases, the transnational continues to grow. But the national persists, often indeed stimulated by the very same transnational forces that we thought might be making it obsolete.

First, in the general political and economic realm, the forces of economic globalisation and so-called free trade are continuing unabated, apparently making the nation-state obsolete as they dismantle trade barriers and integrate the planet. On the other hand, new nation-states and new national disputes are proliferating, often stimulated by the very same forces of globalisation. The most obvious formation that incarnates both these tendencies simultaneously is the new American unilateralism. On the one hand, it signifies a withdrawal from engagement with the world and an aggressive reassertion of territorial nation-state sovereignty. On the other hand, it also signifies a new global American empire that equally aggressively denies or destroys all difference.

Similar apparent contradictions are also strengthening in Greater China. On the one hand, more people are travelling and trading between Hong Kong, Taiwan and the People's Republic of China than ever before, creating an increasingly interdependent and integrated economic zone. One ironic example of this interconnection is the video piracy industry (Wang 2003). However, at the same time, nation-state nationalism is intensifying in both the People's Republic (putatively including Hong Kong) and Taiwan. Furthermore, in Taiwan the situation is producing ever greater social and political polarisation, as manifested in the assassination attempt drama during the 2004 Taiwan presidential election campaign.

Second, in film production, including Chinese-language film production, the idea of a national film industry seems obsolete in the face of burgeoning co-production and transnational distribution and exhibition. From blockbusters like *Wo hu cang long* (*Crouching Tiger, Hidden Dragon*) (Ang Lee, 2000) and *Yingxiong* (*Hero*) (Zhang Yimou, 2002) to low-budget independent films like *Zhifu* (*Uniform*) (Diao Yinan, 2003) and *Shijie* (*The World*) (Jia Zhangke, 2004), increasing numbers of Chinese films are transnational productions. Neither their production nor their consumption circumstances match the idea of films produced within a territorial nation-state to express national culture for national audiences – which was the practice in the People's Republic for most of the Maoist period. Instead, they have international financing, actors and crews from across the Greater Chinese realm and beyond, and they are intended for a wide variety of audiences all over the world. On the other hand, **149** there continues to be anxiety about local film production and film culture in the face of increased Hollywood imports, not only in the People's Republic of China, Taiwan and Hong Kong, but all over the world. And increased co-production and global circulation has not reduced the use of national labels in marketing films and interpreting them.

In film studies itself, the 1990s saw something of a shift away not only from the 'national cinema' model but from issues of the national in general, and a corresponding growth of interest in all that might be marked as 'transnational'. For example, in his provocative and insightful introduction to *Transnational Chinese Cinemas*, Sheldon Hsiao-Peng Lu is prompted by the growth of Chinese regional co-production I have just noted to reconsider the history of Chinese cinema from its earliest days as an import, and to argue that it was already transnational (Lu 1997). In response to this growing awareness of the transnational in Chinese cinema, a variety of new terms has also appeared in Chinese film studies. 'Chinese cinemas' (for example, in the title of Lu 1997), 'Chinese-language film' (for example, in the title of Lu and Yeh, forthcoming), and others manifest the pressure to acknowledge and accommodate difference within transnational Chineseness.

The apparent contradiction between the national and the transnational that I have been highlighting here also appears in Hou Hsiao-hsien's Taiwan Trilogy. On the one hand, as is well known, all three films present stories from local history that had been excluded from public discourse during the period of KMT (Kuomingtang) Nationalist martial law that only ended in 1987. *A City of Sadness* follows the fate of a local Taiwanese family in the period

150 *A City of Sadness* (Hou Hsiao-hsien, 1989)

immediately after the end of fifty years of Japanese colonial rule, during which one of the four Lin brothers has disappeared in Japanese military service and another has gone insane. The much awaited return to Chinese rule also disappoints, and the 28 February Incident in which the local populace resists the KMT government only to be massacred occurs. By the end of the film, one of the two surviving brothers has died and the other's fate also seems sealed.

The Puppetmaster mixes together dramatisation and documentary interview segments to tell the biography of the eponymous Li Tienlu, also known through his appearance as the father in *A City of Sadness*. Significantly, the film focuses on the period of Japanese colonialism. While it does not represent Japanese rule as positive, nor does it represent the Japanese as monstrous. In the light of earlier KMT-sponsored representations, this is an important change.

Finally, *Good Men, Good Women* intertwines a contemporary story with events from the 1950s and earlier. A young Taipei actor is rehearsing a play in which she appears as a leftist from the 1950s. Although deeply patriotic, the leftist and her husband suffered twice at the hands of the KMT. During the Pacific War, they made their way to the mainland in an effort to join the anti-Japanese resistance, only to find themselves suspected of being spies by the KMT. Later, when the White Terror begins, her husband is seized for suspected ties to the communist government on the mainland and she becomes a widow.

By themselves, these stories have potential to be mobilised for Taiwanese political nationalism. They provide the 'logic of the wound' that typically imagines national history as beginning from some sort of low point of crisis when the integrity and survival of the national body comes under threat (Chow 2000: 4–5). In the Chinese context, the idea and practice of 'speaking bitterness' (*suku*) also works according to the logic of the wound. Ann Anagnost has examined this as a powerful trope in Chinese revolutionary discourse that transforms local stories of personal suffering into collective narratives of blood and tears based on class identity. In the class-based nation of the People's Republic, it simultaneously constructs nation and subject, blending individual stories into collective memory that claims – or counter-claims – to be 'truth written in blood' (Anagnost 1997). Examples range from the anchoring of the modern Zionist narrative in the biblical flight from Egypt, to 1066 and the foundational status of the Battle of Hastings in English history. By themselves, the stories told in the Taiwan Trilogy have the potential to operate according to the logic of the wound for a future Taiwanese nation-state.

However, many critics sympathetic to the nationalist cause were dissatisfied with Hou's trilogy.[3] To explain this, we need to consider how the stories are told. If the *énoncée* – or the events narrated – could be used for Taiwanese nationalism, the *énonciation* – or the way the events are narrated – articulates a very different perspective on these events. This perspective is not focused on the space of the nation-state itself. For example, although the main characters in *A City of Sadness* are deeply affected by the 28 February Incident, it is never shown on screen. The film's characters do include some based on real participants in the uprising, such as the teacher who leads the rebels when they retreat to the hills. But they are secondary, and the main focus is on the fictional Lin family. In *The Puppetmaster*, Li Tienlu's life is decisively shaped by Japanese colonialism, but events we hear about, such as air raids on

Taipei, remain off screen while the film focuses more on his family life and its complications. The same screen absence of nation-state events, no matter how important to the protagon-ists, is also true of *Good Men, Good Women*.

In each case, the focus of the film is on domestic and everyday life, rather than the grand events in public space that are usually considered to make up national history. In *A City of Sadness*, it is the life of the Lin family, and in *The Puppetmaster*, it is Li Tienlu's domestic arrangements that take the spotlight. In the case of *Good Men, Good Women*, the film oscil-lates between past events that could be told as national history and the actress's present-day pain and memories of her relationship with a now dead gangster.

All three films establish a tension between the space of domestic, everyday life and public national history. A particular, much-noted scene in *A City of Sadness* expresses this very clearly. The fourth brother is deaf and mute. For communication, he is dependent on his fiancée Hinomi, who writes notes to him. When her brother and his friends come to visit they engage in an energetic discussion of the politics of the day. The camera focuses on the animated debaters for a long time. But then, at a moment when we may have forgotten about the fourth brother or his inability to hear what is being said, the camera pans slowly over to where he is sitting with Hinomi, on one side of the main group. The conversation fades away on the soundtrack as we watch them engage in their own conversation through an exchange of notes. Those notes appear on the screen in the manner of intertitles, becom-ing more and more detached from the conversation of the brother and his friends and draw-ing us into the intimate space of their romance. Some see this as suggesting that the couple's romance is more important than politics. But there is another way of understanding this. While the brother and his friends are not aware of the contents of the notes, and the couple is increasingly detached from the debate, we see both. In this way, the film does not construct the Taiwanese experience as a monolithic, unified, abstracted and seemingly objective national history, but as a multiplicity of distinct experiences, sometimes shared, sometimes separate.

Not only is there a tension between the domestic everyday and the national public spaces in Hou's Taiwan Trilogy, but also the national often appears as that which destroys and damages the domestic. The deaths of all four Lin brothers in *A City of Sadness* can be related to national and international events, as can the twists and turns in Li Tienlu's domestic life. The connection between the present and the past in *Good Men, Good Women* is more com-plex and probably requires a study in its own right. But the actress's failure to relate her situ-ation to the events she portrays at the same time as the film intertwines them suggests a blindness to history rather than a genuine lack of connection.

In addition to the tension between the domestic everyday and national history in the films, the Taiwan Trilogy also articulates what Nick Browne calls 'the poetics of landscape'. Focusing on scenes of nature that draw us away from human life altogether, Browne considers that 'the natural, not the political, history of Taiwan is the significant cultural subtext of this oeuvre', and concludes that 'In sum, the category of "history" in *The Puppetmaster* is more genealogi-cal than political. [P]olitics has real effects and consequences, but they are viewed as incidental and temporary against the landscape and the larger pattern of life' (Browne 2005).

Browne's observations are meticulously made. However, I am not so sure about interpreting the tension between the world of human events and nature as an opposition between politics and nature. In the same way as describing these films as 'postnational' relies on a very limited sense of what the national can be, this may also limit the political too much. Indeed, there are ways of seeing the cosmology that Browne describes as another kind of politics and another kind of national culture. To explain this, we need to understand how the national appears differently from within modernity and postmodern post-coloniality. In the process, the apparent contradictions between the national and the transnational (and Browne's contradiction between politics and nature) are reconfigured. The shift from national cinemas to cinema and the national is also part of the perspective change or paradigm shift.

The territorial nation-state is not only a product of modernity, but it is also a concept that naturalises itself. In other words, its rhetoric denies its own history and claims absolute and exclusive legitimacy. Writing with events like the Opium Wars in mind, Prasenjit Duara points out that, 'it was only territorial nations with historical self-consciousness which, in the world of competitive capitalist imperialism in the late nineteenth and early twentieth centuries, claimed rights in the international system of sovereign states. Such nation-states claimed the freedom, even right, to destroy non-nations such as tribal polities and empires' (Duara 1998).[4]

To legitimate this struggle with other polities like the monarchy or the dynasty, both in Europe and elsewhere, the modern nation-state produced an ideology that denied its own contingency. As is well known, Benedict Anderson's pioneering work traced the emergence of the modern nation-state as an invention of modernity. He distinguishes between the modern nation-state as one form of imagined community and others, including the dynastic empire. For example, he points out that empires are defined by central points located where the emperor resides, whereas nation-states are defined by territorial boundaries. Those living in empires are subjects with obligations, whereas those living in nation-states are citizens with rights, and so forth. Furthermore, it imagines itself as unified and homogeneous, working to erase all internal differences (Anderson 1983: 20–8).

However, this history of its own invention is precisely what the nation-state necessarily occludes to legitimate itself against other forms of polity. In an essay entitled 'Narrating the Nation,' Homi Bhabha (1990: 1) also cites Benedict Anderson (1983: 19). 'If nation states are widely considered to be "new" and "historical",' Bhabha points out, 'the nations to which they give expression always loom out of an immemorial past and . . . glide into a limitless future'.[5] In other words, modern national narratives that operate on the logic of the wound along the lines already discussed imply that the nation is always already existent, waiting to be fully realised in the form of a strong, unified and integral nation-state.

The model of the territorial nation-state traced by Anderson also underlies many assumptions in the long history of writing about 'national cinema', and in particular the idea that any given nation must have a national culture and a cinema through which to express it. Deconstruction of the seeming naturalness of the idea of the nation underlying it has been a powerful force within film studies. In a survey of writing on national cinemas Michael Walsh **153** finds that, 'of all the theorists of nationalism in the fields of history and political science, Anderson has been the only writer consistently appropriated by those working on issues of the national in film studies' (Walsh 1996: 6).

As a result, the old assumptions about 'national cinema' have been dislodged. Mitsuhiro Yoshimoto pointedly notes, 'Writing about national cinemas used to be an easy task: film critics believed all they had to do was to construct a linear historical narrative describing a development of a cinema within a particular national boundary whose unity and coherence seemed to be beyond all doubt' (Yoshimoto 1993: 338). Once, it might have been possible to produce a list of elements composing something called 'traditional Chinese culture' or 'Chinese national culture,' or even some characteristics constituting 'Chineseness'. Then we could have tried to see how these things were 'expressed' or 'reflected' in Chinese cinema as a unified and coherent Chinese national identity with corresponding distinctly Chinese cinematic conventions. This would then have constituted a 'national cinema', but this is no longer possible.

As a result, various theorists have moved away from the classic 'national cinema' model. Andrew Higson's much-cited work is evidence of the growing awareness of the dependence of nationally based film industries upon export markets, international co-production practices, and the likelihood that national audiences draw upon foreign films in the process of constructing their own national identity. After working through these various factors using Britain as his primary example, he turns away from the established 'national cinema' emphasis on production to advocate examination of cultures of national cinema consumption (Higson 1989). Other writers have even claimed that with the discrediting of any assumption that the cinema expresses national identity, it would be better to abandon the examination of cinema and national identity, and move to a formalist approach where one speaks about common cinematic tropes and patterns as 'conventions' within the cinema of certain territorial nations (Walsh 1996). And indeed, as already noted, my impression is that there has been a turn away from the national to the transnational.

However, to turn away from the national in the current era is to confuse deconstruction with destruction. Anderson does not help in this regard. Because he does not engage with other forms of nationality, such as cultural belonging outside of any political state formation, he does not make the multiplicity of the national visible. However, if the idea of the territorial nation-state as a transcendent and exclusive ideal form is no longer tenable, that does not mean either that the form or issues of the national disappear. This is the lesson of the current upsurge in both globalisation and nationalism in various forms. And to abandon the national altogether with the deconstruction of the modern nation-state's pretensions to exclusivity also runs the risk of ignoring what is most crucially at stake in all textual constructions of the national – their power to mobilise collective affiliations with very real political and social consequences.

Just as Mickey Mouse chops up the magic broom in Disney's *Fantasia* (1940) only to find himself confronted by thousands of little brooms, deconstructing the national only proliferates it. And unlike Mickey Mouse, who is confronted with thousands of replicas of a single

154 original, we face innumerable different Chinese senses and instances of the 'national' in Chinese cinema. Any attempt to account for the national in Chinese cinema must engage with the potentially endless project of distinguishing and explaining each of these senses and instances.

Now we can return to the Taiwan Trilogy with this idea of a framework of cinema and the national in mind and consider it as a textual site that invokes specific senses and instances of the national. One of these, as we have already noted, is the concept of a Taiwanese modern territorial nation-state, with its own history and its own logic of the wound. Because this conforms to the exclusive model of the national we are all familiar with from modernity, it has been relatively easy to recognise this.

However, the realms of the domestic and the natural that the Taiwan Trilogy uses to establish a tension with the events of this Taiwanese nation-state history can also be seen as national, but in a different sense. Where Browne (2005) notes a tension between the domestic and the natural realms, I argue that this tension itself combines to constitute a cosmology invoking a Chineseness that is trans-'national' in the sense of the nation-state, but national in the sense of a culture. The belief that humanity and human affairs are fleeting within a larger world of nature is not exclusively Chinese, by any means. Not only Taoist but also Buddhist cosmologies in general could be claimed to share these beliefs. But when this is combined with a situation where the world of the family is set in tension with the state, and the maintenance of family lineage is a central concern for the family, then we have something that could be claimed as a larger Chinese cultural pattern.

This is precisely what is articulated in the Taiwan Trilogy. In *A City of Sadness*, the four brothers and their families symbolise the potential prosperity of the Lin family. The film opens with the birth of the eldest brother's son at the same time as the Japanese emperor announces his surrender on the radio. This combination promises a new start and a harmonious relationship of the state to the lives of the ordinary people. The deaths of all four brothers symbolise the failure to realise that promise. In *The Puppetmaster*, poverty and the difficulties of Japanese occupation and war force Li Tienlu to do the reverse of what is usually held up as appropriate behaviour for a Chinese man: instead of finding a bride to bring into his family and continue the family line, he marries out into the family of a woman without a son, to continue their family line. And in *Good Men, Good Women*, the actress returns repeatedly to her desire to have her dead lover's child.

In these circumstances, instead of seeing a tension between the national and the transnational in the Taiwan Trilogy, or a move towards the postnational, or a tension between nature and politics, we can see these films as articulating a tension between two types of national belonging. One is the modern nation-state order and specifically the potential Taiwanese nation-state. The other is a larger cultural order that can claim to pre-exist the modern nation-state and is often asserted – although not directly within the films – as the basis for a supra-state Chinese cultural affiliation.

By manifesting both these national perspectives at once, it could be argued that the Taiwan Trilogy satisfies neither of the existing outlooks of the two main constituencies on the island. The local or *benshengren* community that has been there for centuries remembers Japanese colonialism and suffered particularly at the hands of the new KMT regime that took over in 1945. This is the group that is most likely to understand its national affiliation in terms of a proto-Taiwanese state. On the other hand, the descendants of those who came with the KMT – the *waishengren* or 'outside the province people' – are more likely to affiliate to a larger Chinese culture, especially given their antipathy to both the People's Republic and any putative independent Taiwanese nation-state.

Chen Kuan-Hsing has explored these two communities and the different cultural memories that make 'great reconciliation' impossible (Chen 2002). However, I would conclude by suggesting that reconciliation is only impossible so long as both outlooks are grounded in the quest for the modern nation-state – be it a nostalgic or future-directed quest. What makes the Taiwan trilogy powerful for me is its ability to articulate a vision that accommodates both *benshengren* memories and cultural affiliations that *waishengren* do lean towards and *benshengren* could also claim. But of course, this is a complex national articulation that exceeds that of the nation-state and requires new visions, visions that films like the Taiwan Trilogy may help to create.

From the point of view of film theory, I hope that this reframing of the Taiwan Trilogy has shown two things. First, approaches grounded in the old national cinema model that locates films in relation to the assumed singular culture of a nation-state are blind to some of the national dimensions of films. And second, only an approach that sees cinema and the national as a multidimensional problematic can move beyond the national cinemas approach without losing sight of the national altogether and in the process, capture the complexity of the national in the transnational era.

Notes

1. For further information on this concept, see Uhalley Jr (1994).
2. The latter essay has been incorporated into our forthcoming book (Berry and Farquhar 2006). I want to thank Mary for stimulating me to think more about these topics and all her many ideas that are now inextricably fused with my own.
3. The reaction is discussed in Chi (1999), and a sophisticated example of this critique available in English is Liao (1999).
4. Partha Chatterjee has traced the same defensive logic in the Indian move from Puranic to nationalist historiography in chapters four and five of *The Nation and its Fragments* (1993).
5. Unfortunately, this is misquoted in Bhabha, with 'nations' appearing as 'nation states'.

References

Anagnost, A. (1997), 'Making History Speak', in *National Past-times, Narrative, Representation and Power in Modern China*, Durham: Duke University Press: 17–44.

Anderson, B. (1983), *Imagined Communities: Reflections on the Origin and Spread of Nationalism*, London: Verso.

Berry, C. (1992), 'Heterogeneity as Identity: Hybridity and Transnationality in Hong Kong and Taiwanese Cinema', *Metro* 91: 48–51.

Berry, C. (1992/3), 'These Nations Which Are Not One: History, Identity and Postcoloniality in Recent Hong Kong and Taiwan Cinema', *Span* 34 (5): 37–49.

Berry, C. (1993), 'A Nation T(w/o)o: Chinese Cinema(s) and Nationhood(s)', *East-West Film Journal* 7 (1): 24–51, republished in Dissanayake, W. (ed.) (1994), *Colonialism and Nationalism in Asian Cinema*, Bloomington: Indiana University Press: 42–64.

Berry, C. (2000), 'If China Can Say No, Can China Make Movies? Or, Do Movies Make China? Rethinking National Cinema and National Agency', in Chow, R. (ed.), *Modern Chinese Literary and Cultural Studies in the Age of Theory: Reimagining a Field*, Durham: Duke University Press: 159–80.

Berry, C. and Farquhar, M. (2001), 'From National Cinemas to Cinema and the National: Rethinking the National in Transnational Chinese Cinemas', *Journal of Modern Literature in Chinese* 4 (2):109–22.

Berry, C. and Farquhar, Mary (2006), *China On Screen: Cinema and the National*, New York: Columbia University Press.

Bhabha, Homi K. (ed.) (1990), *Nation and Narration*, London: Routledge.

Browne, N. (2005), 'Hou Hsiao-hsien's *Puppetmaster*: The Poetics of Landscape', in Berry, C. and Lu, F. (eds), *Island on the Edge: New Taiwan Cinema and After*, Hong Kong: Hong Kong University Press. Originally published in *Asian Cinema* 8 (1) (1996): 28–38.

Chatterjee, P. (1993), *The Nation and its Fragments: Colonial and Postcolonial Histories*, Princeton: Princeton University Press.

Chen, Kuan-Hsing (2002), 'Why is "Great Reconciliation" Impossible? De-Cold War/Decolonization, or Modernity and its Tears', *Inter-Asia Cultural Studies* 3 (1): 77–99 and 233–51. Forthcoming in an abridged form in Berry, C. and Lu, F. (eds).

Chi, R. (1999), 'Getting it on Film: Representing and Understanding History in *A City of Sadness*', *Tamkang Review* 29 (4): 47–84.

Chow, R. (2000), 'Introduction: On Chineseness as a Theoretical Problem', in Chow, R. (ed.), *Modern Chinese Literary and Cultural Studies in the Age of Theory: Reimagining a Field*, Durham: Duke University Press: 1–24.

Duara, P. (1998), 'The Regime of Authenticity: Timelessness, Gender, and National History in Modern China', *History and Theory* 37 (3): 287–99.

Higson, A. (1989), 'The Concept of National Cinema', *Screen* 30 (4): 36–46.

Liao, P. (1999), 'Passing and Re-articulation of Identity: Memory, Trauma, and Cinema', *Tamkang Review* 29 (4): 85–114.

Lu, S. (1997), 'Historical Introduction: Chinese Cinemas (1896–1996) and Transnational Film Studies', in Lu, S. (ed.), *Transnational Chinese Cinemas: Identity, Nationhood, Gender*, Honolulu: University of Hawaii Press: 1–31.

Lu, S. and Yeh, Y. (forthcoming), *Chinese-Language Film: Historiography, Poetics, Politics*, Honolulu: University of Hawaii Press.

Uhalley Jr, S. (1994), '"Greater China": The Contest of a Term', *Positions* 2 (2): 274–93.

Walsh, M. (1996), 'National Cinema, National Imaginary', *Film History* 8 (2): 5–17.

Wang, S. (2003), *Framing Piracy: Globalisation and Film Distribution in Greater China*, Lanham, MD: Rowman and Littlefield.

Yoshimoto, M. (1993), 'The Difficulty of Being Radical: The Discipline of Film Studies and the Postcolonial World Order', in Miyoshi, Masao and Harootunian, H. D. (eds), *Japan in the World*, Durham: Duke University Press: 338–53.

12 'We're in the Money!' A Brief History of Market Power Concentration and Risk Aversion in the American Film Industry from the Edison Trust to the Rise of Transnational Media Conglomerates

David A. Cook

The American motion picture industry's production and distribution of feature films generated nearly $40 billion in theatrical revenues worldwide in 2003 (Cook and Wang 2004: 1). If 'ancillary' revenues for video and television programmes are added, the figure rises dramatically to over $75 billion (Kanninen 2004: 1). By one account, the American majors control three-quarters of the entire international distribution market, and since 1997 entertainment has been the United States' second-largest export industry, after aerospace. The lion's share of this money goes to seven huge global media conglomerates, listed here in descending order of assets: AOL Time Warner, owner of Warner Bros. Pictures, Castle Rock Entertainment and New Line Cinema, as well as the Turner Broadcasting System (CNN, TNT, TCM and the Cartoon Network) and HBO/Cinemax; the Walt Disney Company/Buena Vista, owner of Walt Disney Pictures, Touchstone Pictures, Hollywood Pictures, Miramax Films and Dimension Films, as well as the ABC Television Network; Rupert Murdoch's News Corp., owner of 20th Century-Fox, Fox 2000 Pictures and Fox Searchlight Pictures, as well as the Fox Broadcasting Company; Viacom, Inc., owner of Paramount Pictures, as well as the MTV networks, BET networks and Showtime networks, the CBS Television Network, the UPN network and Blockbuster Video; Sony Corp./Columbia Pictures, owner of Columbia Tri-Star Films and Sony Pictures Classics, in addition to being one of the world's largest electronics manufacturers; Vivendi-Universal, SA, owner of Universal Pictures and Canal+ (France), as well as the USA Network, Echostar Communications and several of Europe's largest telecommunications companies; and MGM/UA, which owns MGM Pictures and United Artists Pictures, as well as television stations and satellite networks in the UK, Germany, France, Spain and New Zealand. Many of the larger conglomerates also have holdings in book, magazine and newspaper publishing, as well as theme parks and resorts. Together, the filmed entertainment components of these companies – which are still known as 'studios', but very obviously consist of much more – comprise the membership of the Motion Picture Association of America, the industry's major lobbying and advocacy group. These same companies belong to an export cartel, the Motion Picture Association (formerly the Motion Picture Export Association) that acts as the sole export agent for its members, setting prices and terms of trade for each foreign country. Their combined might is truly awesome: as of 2003, with the sole exceptions of the People's Republic of China, Iran and Cuba, there was no film-producing nation on earth that could compete with the American majors in its own domestic market, and even the most aggressively protectionist among them (such as France) was able to control no more than a 30 per cent share.

Yet two news stories from the autumn of 2004 illustrate the paradox of the majors' power. The first one was headlined 'Sony's Profit Surges on Strength of *Spider-Man 2*' (S. Raimi, 2004) and told us that the corporation reported 'a 61 percent increase in net profit for the most recent quarter, as *Spider-Man 2* pulled in big profits for the company's movie division and helped conceal a slide in its consumer electronics and video game businesses' (Zaun 2004: W1). The other, titled 'A High-Wire Act at Warner Bros.', explains that the 'poor opening' of *Polar Express* (R. Zemeckis, 2004), which grossed just $23.5 million in its opening weekend, 'was a blow to a studio that has staked its success . . . [o]n star vehicles and event films that spare no expense, whether the Harry Potter series or *Troy* [W. Petersen, 2004]. [W]arner Bros. has pursued its high-risk, high-reward strategy partly because of its deep pockets as part of Time Warner and its rich, revenue-producing library of films.' The article goes on to say that, unlike other major studios, Warner generates about $500 million a year from its library, enabling it, in the words of Morgan Stanley media analyst Richard Bilotti, to 'swing for the fences' on production; furthermore, the studio has recently sought to insulate its risk by sharing production costs with

Spider-Man 2 (Sam Raimi, 2004)

co-investors (Waxman 2004: L1). In the case of Sony, we have a major multinational conglomerate whose third-quarter profitability rests on the box-office success of a single film; and in the case of Warner Bros., a company that takes multiple large risks and subsidises them by licensing archival film rights and seeking co-investment from other studios (and, sometimes, individuals: it shared *Polar Express*'s $170 negative cost with real estate magnate Steve Bing). These two articles suggest a fundamental tension between risk-taking and risk aversion that has characterised the American film industry since its inception.

As is clear from even a cursory survey of its history, the American film industry has tended from the very outset towards greater and greater concentration of ownership and monopoly control. As a capital-intensive technology, the motion pictures have been the subject of patents wars extending from the Edison Trust in the period 1908–13 to Microsoft's attempts to control proprietary CGI software in the early twenty-first century. This has given rise to the popular mythology – knowingly cultivated by industry publicity – that the production and distribution of feature films is a risky business. Yet, in each of its historical eras, the major studios were able to develop sophisticated strategies to eliminate competition and lay off the risk of their business on other parties. In fact, one of the distinguishing features of the American film industry has been the maintenance of a competitive advantage by balancing the intrinsic liability of a business that must constantly appeal to public taste against practices of risk aversion that enable it successfully to hedge its bets. Here I will briefly examine the manifestation of this characteristic in three distinct historical periods: that of the Edison Trust (1908–13), the classical Hollywood studio system (1934–53), and the post-Paramount years of 1954–88, before addressing the industry's current domination by way of global media cartels.

Before the formation of the Edison Trust, or Motion Picture Patents Company, the biggest patent litigation was between Edison and Biograph over basic camera and projector technology (Biograph's didn't use sprockets), which was exacerbated when the Supreme Court ruled in early 1908 that both patents were valid (Litman 1997: 61). Film-makers aligned themselves with one patent or the other until a truce was called, resulting in the creation of the Motion Picture Patents Company (MPPC) on 18 December 1908, with Edison, Biograph, Vitagraph, Essanay, Selig Polyscope, Lubin, Star Film (Méliès), Pathé Frères and Klein Optical pooling sixteen key motion picture patents and contracting for raw stock exclusively with Eastman Kodak. In 1910, the General Film Company was added, thus integrating licensed distributors into the single corporate entity. The American film industry was controlled for several years within this tight circle centred in the New York–New Jersey area, until independent distributors organised and fought back aggressively. In the end, however, it was the Trust's own risk aversion that destroyed it. The MPPC's relentless commitment to the production and distribution of one-reel films and its ban on publicity for creative personnel put it at disadvantage once the public's taste for the multiple-reel feature with star talent had been stimulated by independent distributors such as William Fox and Adolph Zukor.

Shortly after the MPPC was formed, independents organised their own trade association in January 1909: the Independent Film Protective Association (later called the National Independent Moving Picture Alliance), with ten original members. More effective at combating the Trust was the Motion Picture Distributing and Sales Company, which began operations in May 1910 in a direct challenge to General Film, and which eventually came to serve forty-seven exchanges in twenty-seven cities. For nearly two years, independents were able to present a united front through the Sales Company, which finally split into two rival camps in the spring of 1912: the Mutual Film-Supply company, which distributed for the a group of independent producers at the rate of about twenty reels per week; and the Universal Film Manufacturing Company. By imitating MPPC practices of combination and licensing, the early independents were able to compete effectively against the Trust: in the Trust's first three years, the independents netted about 40 per cent of all American film business. Their product, the one-reel short, and their modes of operation were initially the same as Edison's. But later independents, such as William Fox (1879–1952) of the Greater New York Film Rental Company, and Adolph Zukor (1873–1976) of the Famous Players Film Company, would revolutionise the industry by adopting the multiple-reel feature, with higher rentals and slower turnover rates, as their basic product and by promoting stars and celebrity directors by name (and paying them higher salaries into the bargain) (Litman 1997:62).

Meanwhile, Fox filed an anti-trust suit against the MPPC, which was joined by the Department of Justice. The case was tried in a district court in 1915. At issue was whether legally granted patents could be cross-licensed, thus creating a government-sanctioned monopoly eliminating competition. The Trust argued that it had the same right as an individual patent holder to exploit or license patents. But, applying the Sherman Act, the court held that a group could not legally form a vertical combination to monopolise an industry and exclude non-members in constraint of trade. The court ordered the restructuring of the motion picture trust, as it soon would for the tobacco trust, the Standard Oil trust and others, but the MPPC had lost its competitive edge to the independents through its conservative risk-aversion practices years before this ruling (Litman 1997: 63).

By the time the MPPC was declared illegal, the independents had established themselves at the head of a feature film industry in southern California. Forbidden monopoly by their own suit against the Trust, they turned famously to oligopoly and created the classical Hollywood studio system. The formative studio oligopoly of the 1920s was comprised of the 'Big Three' and the 'Little Five'. The former were Zukor's Famous Players Film Company (which had merged with Jesse L. Lasky's company to become Famous Players-Lasky Corporation, then acquiring Paramount Pictures as its distribution and exhibition wing in 1916; commonly known as Paramount); Loewe's Inc., the national theatre chain owned by Marcus Loewe that had moved into production with the acquisition of Metro Pictures and Louis B. Mayer Productions (founded in 1915 and 1917, respectively) in 1920, becoming the parent company of Metro-Goldwyn-Mayer in 1924; and First National Exhibitors Circuit (after 1921, Associated First National), the company founded in 1917 by twenty-six of the nation's largest exhibitors to combat Paramount's practice of block booking. First National was able to eliminate block booking (temporarily) by 1918 and sign an exclusive distribution deal with Charlie Chaplin, the industry's number-one star. Paramount responded by aggressively, entering the exhibition sector by buying up first-run houses all over the country. By 1921, Paramount owned 303 theatres compared to First National's 639. **161**

The Little Five were Universal Pictures, founded by Carl Laemmle in 1912; Fox Film Corporation (becoming 20th Century-Fox in 1935); Producers Distributing Corporation (PDC); Film Book Office (FBO); and Warner Bros. Pictures. United Artists was basically a paper corporation formed by D. W. Griffith, Charlie Chaplin, Mary Pickford and Douglas Fairbanks to distribute their own pictures in 1919. Below these were about thirty thinly capitalised minor studios, of which only Columbia, Republic and Monogram would survive the coming of sound. Of the Little Five, Fox and Universal had joined Zukor in the race to acquire theatres, with Fox buying the large Midwestern Publix Theater chain and Universal acquiring a healthy international distribution exchange and several chains of sub-run theatres. United Artists acquired first-run theatres in Los Angeles, Detroit and Chicago, but sold them in 1935 (Cook, 2003:169–270). During this stage of the oligopoly, risk involved vertical integration *within* competing companies. Horizontal integration would not come until the conversion to sound.

In one sense, the coming of sound represents an incursion by the electronics industry (radio and telecommunications) into the film industry. The major oligopolists had no practical use for sound. By the mid-1920s, their studio assembly lines were humming along quite lucratively without it. It was the electronics sector that dangled the prospect of sound recording before the Big Three. In 1925, Western Electric, the R&D subsidiary of American Telephone and Telegraph Corporation (AT&T), attempted to market a sound-on-disc system called Vitaphone to each of the three majors in turn, but only the small (but aggressively expanding) Warner Bros. studio signed on, with the idea of using Vitaphone to provide canned orchestral accompaniment for its features. Meanwhile, William Fox had secured the American rights to a sound-on-film, or optical sound system derived from the German Tri-Ergon process, aiming to produce talking newsreels. The astonishing popularity of Warners' first Vitaphone films in 1926 and 1927 forced the entire industry towards conversion by the end of the year. As early as February 1927, the Big Three and the largest of the Little Five, Universal and the Producers Distributing Corporation, signed an accord (known somewhat confusingly as the 'Big Five Agreement') to adopt a uniform sound system if and when conversion became necessary. At the beginning of 1928, when the American public had clearly chosen sound, there were three competing recording and playback technologies from which to chose: Vitaphone, which was marketed by AT&T's non-telephone subsidiary, Electrical Products Research Incorporated (ERPI); Fox Movietone (a variable-area optical process); and RCA Photophone, a variable-density optical process developed by General Electric for the Radio Corporation of America from patents held by Lee De Forest. Although all three proprietary systems were used to produce sound films in the early years of the conversion, none of them was compatible with the others, which meant that any first-run theatre hoping to capitalise on the American audience's new craze for sound had to install all three systems at an approximate cost of $50,000 per system. Because they held a virtual monopoly on first-run exhibition (owning more than 70 per cent of the first-run houses in the ninety-two largest cities in the country, that is to say, those with populations of 100,000 or more), the majors were able to shift the cost of converting sub-run theatres to their owners, although for several years they supplied both silent and sound versions of their films to accommodate those theatres which had not yet been wired (Crafton 1997: 165).

The wiring of theatres proceeded at a much slower pace than conversion in the production tier, where the costs were easier to amortise (Crafton 1997: 165). Nevertheless, the majors undertook prodigious borrowing to convert their studios (in excess of $300 million, or easily four times the market valuation of the entire industry in 1928) and they colluded to stabilise the market in 1930 by pooling their patents and adopting a single industry standard: sound-on-film (either RCA or Western Electric, which had developed its own variable-density system in 1928), although the competition between the variable-density and variable-area systems continued until 1942 when the former became the standard. The wholesale borrowing that enabled the conversion represented an enormous financial risk for the studios, which they sought to minimise by avoiding a patents war of the sort that had plagued the industry in the early years of the century. Their collusion on sound set the pattern for the horizontal integration of the mature oligopoly.

The conversion itself ended in an industry-wide shakeout that left the Big Five and the Little Three to dominate the Hollywood studio system. In descending order of market power, the majors were MGM (backed by Chase National Bank), Warner Bros. (which had absorbed both the Stanley Theater and First National Theater chains in its rise as the catalyst for sound), Paramount (financed by Kuhn, Loeb and Company), Fox (backed by the John F. Dryden–Prudential Insurance Group)[1] and RKO (Radio-Keith-Orpheum, formed in 1929 by RCA to exploit its Photophone process). The minors were Universal (backed by Shields and Company), Columbia (founded by Harry Cohn in 1924) and United Artists (founded in 1919). Each of the majors was vertically integrated but none was self-sufficient in terms of production and exhibition capacity. Each depended on the others to launch nationwide releases and to keep their theatre screens turning over with feature films. During this period of the mature oligopoly, 1934–53, there was virtually no downside risk to production. The five majors owned some 2,600 first-run theatres between them, only 16 per cent of the national total of theatres, but they were the ones that generated 75 per cent of the box-office revenue because they held their films the longest and charged the highest prices. They colluded with the three minors, who owned no theatres and were dependent on the majors for first-run bookings, to set rental rates, ticket prices and release patterns uniformly across the nation. Together, they operated a run-zone-clearance system of distribution that divided the country into thirty markets, each subdivided into zones whose theatres were classified as first-run, second-run and subsequent-run; clearances of fourteen to forty-two days were required before a film could move to the next zone, enabling the Big Five to wring maximum profit from each release, regardless of its quality or popularity (Cook 2003: 239). Despite the national hunger – actively stimulated by studio publicity and marketing machines – for the 'Hollywood of the Stars', production throughout the 1930s and 1940s accounted for only 5 per cent of total corporate assets, with another 1 per cent going to distribution. As Douglas Gomery has pointed out, with 94 per cent of total investment allotted to the exhibition sector, the five majors during the studio era could best be characterised as 'diversified theater chains, producing features, shorts, cartoons, and newsreels to fill their houses' (Gomery 1985: 124).

The studio system could exist only as long as the majors maintained their monopoly on exhibition: without a guaranteed weekly audience, their films would have to compete on the **163** open market and be subject to dynamic pricing. The fact that the system was a totalising, vertical and horizontal monopoly was recognised by the Justice Department when, in July 1938, it began litigation against the five major and three minor studios for combining and conspiring to restrain trade unreasonably in order to control the production, distribution and exhibition of motion pictures in the United States. When war seemed imminent in 1940, the court issued a consent decree permitting the studios to retain their exhibition chains, but *The United States v. Paramount Pictures* was reactivated in 1945 and concluded in May 1948 when the US Supreme Court ruled that the majors, with the collusion of the minors, had violated federal anti-trust statutes through vertical integration. The Big Five were ordered to divest themselves of either distribution or exhibition, and they naturally chose to retain distribution where control over product resides. The divestiture order itself came in the form of consent decrees, widely known as the 'Paramount decrees', requiring the majors to spin-off their theatre chains over a five-year period. Although they were still free to set clearances and minimum admission prices (and to limit the supply of features at the exhibitors' expense, a frequent ploy in the post-Paramount environment), the studios lost their ability to generate automatic box-office receipts for every film. Risk had entered the realm of production as never before.

Industry-wide restructuring ensued. The minors, who had lost nothing to the Paramount decrees because they owned no theatres, were suddenly able to compete with the majors on something like an even playing field, with the result that they all became majors themselves by the end of the 1960s. RKO, always undercapitalised, was bankrupted in 1956 and extra-mural corporations began buying up the studios to gain control of their film libraries (increasingly valuable with the advent of television) and the real estate. MCA bought Universal in 1962; Gulf + Western Industries acquired Paramount in 1966; Transamerica bought United Artists in 1971; Kinney National Services (soon to become Warner Communications, Inc., or WCI) bought Warner Bros. in 1969; and Las Vegas financier Kirk Kerkorian bought MGM in 1970 and gutted it. On balance, according to Tino Balio, the mergers benefited the industry by reviving dying management, stabilising operations and forcing the industry to adapt to television (Balio 1990: 40). Yet, the steady, orderly pursuit of profits that had characterised the high studio era was now a thing of the past. Increasingly, the profitability of a studio came to rest on the success of a single film, whether it was a big-budget spectacle like MGM's *Ben-Hur* (W. Wyler, 1959) and Universal's *Spartacus* (S. Kubrick, 1960), or a low-budget sleeper like Paramount's *Psycho* (A. Hitchcock, 1960) and Warner Bros.'s *Bonnie and Clyde* (A. Penn, 1967).

Between 1969 and 1980, profits for the most successful motion pictures rose from the hundreds of thousands to the hundreds of millions. Veteran industry leadership had been replaced by a melange of agents, lawyers, bankers and business executives who saw film-making primarily as an investment strategy, not unlike commodities trading, which combined the risks of high-stakes speculation with a virtually limitless potential for corporate tax-sheltering. The shift from production to finance and distribution had occurred gradually in the wake of the Consent decrees, but it was accelerated to the point of near completion **164** during the 1970s. Formerly, banks and other lending institutions had negotiated revolving

credit agreements with the studios, leaving the companies free to allocate the funds themselves, but in 1971 banks began to extend loans on a picture-by-picture basis, with the films
themselves as collateral.

One significant factor in these changes was the government subsidies allocated to the
industry, enabling it to overcome its 1969–71 financial crisis. Two major developments
assisted the recovery, both expedited by the Nixon administration at the urging of the
industry leadership: (1) Federal income tax credits on losses; and (2) a 7 per cent investment
tax credit on domestic production, backed up by a provision written into the Revenue Act
of 1971 for the creation of offshore studio subsidiaries called Domestic International Sales
Corporations, which could defer taxes on profits earned from exports by reinvesting them
in domestic production. In fact, tax shelter and other tax-leveraged investment became the
key mode of production finance for the rest of the decade. Both the 'purchase' tax shelter
and the 'production service company' tax shelter financed 20 per cent of all film starts
between 1973 and 1976. Entertainment attorney Tom Pollack estimated that, all told, tax
shelters added about $150 million in production money between 1971 and 1976 (quoted in
Laskos 1981: 13–14). The combination of risk-free loans and artificial losses through accelerated depreciation prompted Alan Hirschfield, then president of Columbia Pictures, to tes-
tify before Congress, quoted in *Variety* (14 August 1974: 5) that the 'availability of this kind
of financing is the single most important occurrence in the recent history of the industry'.

The effect of the investment tax credit was less spectacular but ultimately more significant, since it allowed 7 per cent of production investment to be deducted from a studio's
overall corporate tax up to a 50 per cent limit, with carry-forward provisions for seven years.
Furthermore, a tax court ruling in a 1973 Walt Disney Production case made the credit
retroactive to 1962 through 1969. *Variety* (6 June 1973: 3, 6) estimated that an American theatrical film production investment of $3.5 billion from 1962–9 would yield a total of 7 per
cent tax credit of about $250 million against the majors' overall corporate taxes. As Martin
Dale pointed out, such extensive Federal tax breaks amounted to a government subsidy for
the industry during the 1970s and early 1980s (Dale 1997:157).

The injection of public funds was accompanied by a sharp drop-off in production as studios came to shape their schedules around a handful of potential blockbusters or 'event'
movies, any one of which might produce windfall profits and send their stock soaring on
Wall Street, with the expectation that the rest would break even or fail. This 'blockbuster
mentality' radically increased the risks of film-making and led the industry to pursue a variety of risk-reduction strategies whose net effect was to take production finance out of studio
hands (Cook 2000: 1). During the 1970s, in addition to receiving massive subsidies, production came to be funded also by pre-sale agreements with television and cable networks,
advance exhibitor guarantees through such practices as 'blind-bidding', and ancillary merchandising tie-ins such as books, toys and soundtrack albums. Conglomerate ownership, as
experienced at the time by Warner Bros., Paramount, Universal and United Artists, offered
the benefits of synergy, allowing diversified components of a company (film-making, publishing, recording and merchandising) to cross-market the same product or 'franchise' in
mutually enriching ways. But the ultimate effect of the blockbuster syndrome, and of the **165**

outside money it both attracted and required, was to raise the ceiling on industry costs across the board. Average negative costs inflated from $2 million in 1972 to nearly $10 million in 1979, an increase of 450 per cent in less than seven years. Even more alarming, marketing costs exceeded negative costs for the first time in the industry's history, the costs of promoting a film actually exceeding the cost of producing it, often by 100 per cent (Cook 2000: 2).[2] Advertising went from local to national via expensive prime-time network campaigns, and distributors turned to the practice of saturation booking, or 'wide opening', formerly the precinct of exploitation film, to build product awareness and maximise the available audience. During the studio era, marketing had never been a determining issue because market hegemony, broken by the Paramount decrees, was implicit in the majors' control of exhibition. By the 1980s, however, marketing and distribution executives had come to dominate studio production policy, and projects were selected for their marketing potential, demographic appeal and ability to hedge risks, rather than for any intrinsic merit as entertainment (Cook 2000: 3).

As negative and marketing costs began to soar during the 1970s, it became increasingly important for the majors to develop ancillary income streams (Cook 2000: 24–93). Foreign markets and television sales both helped to amortise production, but by mid-decade they had become insufficient to guarantee the profitability of blockbusters, and the home video market had yet to emerge. Soon, however, in addition to the government subsidies, three significant new sources of revenue appeared on the horizon: merchandising, product placement and, most crucially, home video.

In merchandising, income derives from the sale of licences to manufacture goods tied to film characters, plots and themes. Merchandising in its current state can be traced back to the exponential success of products associated with *Star Wars* (G. Lucas, 1977), which demonstrated that if a film had characters that can be made into toys or video games, or marketed in conjunction with fast-food products, the producer/distributor can reap handsome profits risk-free, since the licensee incurs all manufacturing and distribution costs and the studio typically receives an advance payment, plus royalties of 5–10 per cent on gross merchandising revenues to retailers. Soundtrack albums and novelisations had brought income to the studios since the 1950s, but Disney alone among the majors had established merchandising as a major source of income and production capital, licensing its branded cartoon characters to a wide range of international product manufacturers since the 1930s. The profitability of merchandising for live-action features was demonstrated irrefutably by *Star Wars*, whose spin-off toys, posters, T-shirts, clothing, candy, watches and other products earned more money by the end of the decade (reportedly $1 billion) than the film took at the box office. In the 1980s, the success of films such as *The Empire Strikes Back* (G. Lucas, 1980), *E. T.: The Extra-Terrestrial* (S. Spielberg, 1982), *The Empire Strikes Back: Return of the Jedi* (G. Lucas, 1983), *Superman III* (R. Lester, 1983), *Ghostbusters* (I. Reitman, 1984), *Who Framed Roger Rabbit?* (S. Spielberg, 1988), *Batman* (T. Burton, 1989) and *Dick Tracy* (W. Beatty, 1990), helped to confirm this new calculus. As a hedge against risk, merchandising came to assume an important role in blockbuster production, and it also helped to stimulate the mass consciousness necessary for blockbuster marketing. Since film-related product lines are promoted at the expense of the licensee, merchandising functions as a form of free national advertising for the film, even if the product itself fails. In 2002, film licensing revenues worldwide were estimated at $2.6 billion (Wasko 2003: 139).

Because successful merchandising depends on audience familiarity with easily identifiable characters (a lesson learned from Disney), its proliferation has contributed to the seemingly endless cycle of repetitions (sequels), re-releases and remakes that afflicts much of American cinema today. As Stephen Prince points out, films are increasingly shaped by the economic imperatives of merchandising, so that during the 1980s, for example, the need to feed ancillary merchandising drove the production of film fantasies featuring cartoon or mechanical characters that lent themselves to reproduction as toys and games (Prince 2000: 139). Furthermore, the multinational recognition factor of these characters across several different media helped to sell their parent films globally and stimulate overseas markets for the vertically integrated, multinational corporations that produced them.[3]

Another income stream first tapped in the late 1970s was product placement: a producer accepts a fee or in-kind service to feature a manufacturer's product(s) in a film. After a modest beginning, in which only two companies, one in Hollywood and one in New York, specialised in getting 'product identification' props into movies, product placement developed into a full-blown industry during the 1980s. By 1986, there were more than twenty-five product placement firms in Hollywood alone. In 2004, there were about forty of them. They have their own trade organisation, the Entertainment Resources & Marketing Association (ERMA, founded in 1991). As Janet Wasko notes, a very specific process for product placement has developed in the intervening years involving studios, corporate advertisers and product placement agencies, in which studio and advertising executives review and sometimes reshape scripts for product placement opportunities. The agencies broker these transactions for fees averaging about $24,000 per placement, so that in most high-profile Hollywood films, as one agency director put it, 'Virtually everything you see, other than background stuff, is a negotiated deal' (Miller 2001:155).

Most important among the new sources of revenue was, of course, home video, introduced to the American consumer market in December 1975 by the Sony Betamax (SL-7300).[4] This was a half-inch, helical-scan videotape recorder/player whose immediate success in early 1976 spurred JVC (owned by Matsushita Electric but independently operated) to introduce its competing VHS format that same year. Sony initially promoted the Betamax for 'time-shifting' purposes, but the majors saw it as a vehicle for film piracy over the airwaves, and Universal and Disney filed suit on their behalf against Sony for copyright infringement in November 1976. In 1979, a federal District Court in California ruled in favour of Sony, but the majors appealed all the way to the US Supreme Court, which in January 1984 upheld the lower court's decision (Cook 2000: 5). For Sony it was a pyrrhic victory, because by the mid-80s, VHS, although technically inferior to Beta, had won the format war, in large part because the majors supported it to the exclusion of the Sony system.[5] Furthermore, as 'Universal vs. Sony' wound its way through the legal system, film industry resistance to the new technology gradually faded and consumer video came to be seen as a vast new market for Hollywood product. As early as 1977, Fox made a historic deal with Andre **167**

Blay's Magnetic Video of Farmington Hills, Michigan, for non-exclusive video rights to fifty pre-1972 titles, and Allied Artists licensed a hundred titles for distribution on pre-recorded cassette the following year. By 1981, the annual sale of VCRs increased to 11 million from 800,000 the year before, and all of the Hollywood studios had set up video divisions to exploit their film libraries. In 1986, revenues from video sales and rentals exceeded those from the theatrical box office for the first time, and by the end of 1987 they had nearly doubled theatrical revenues ($7.5 billlion video; $4 billion theatrical). By the end of 1989, the unthinkable occurred: home video income outstripped box -office revenue by 120 per cent ($11 billion video; $5 billion theatrical). Home video had become Hollywood's second window of release, just after theatrical exhibition (which then, as now, 'sets' a film in all ancillary markets) and Wall Street analysts had begun to use home video revenues as a basis for evaluating studio stock. As Stephen Prince notes, home video not only changed the industry's expectations about the sources of its revenues, but multiplied those expectations exponentially and reinforced the blockbuster syndrome in the process, since home viewers overwhelmingly paid to watch on video the same films that were big hits in the theatres (Prince 2000: 97, 116). The tail was suddenly wagging the dog. But the dog itself had assumed a more protean form.

Diversification was another risk-reduction strategy begun in the 1970s, as the studios became the major suppliers of network television programmes and expanded into related businesses such as camera equipment (Warners/Panavision), recording (Columbia/Arista), theme parks and resorts (Disneyworld, the Universal Studios tour, the MGM Grand hotel and casino). During the 1980s this trend led to ever larger mergers in which Coca-Cola bought Columbia (1982) and sold it to Sony (1989); real estate magnate Marvin Davis bought Fox (1981) and sold it to Rupert Murdoch's News Corporation (1985); Transamerica spun off United Artists in the wake of Cimino's *Heaven's Gate* disaster (1981) and UA merged with what was left of MGM; Ted Turner bought and briefly held MGM-UA to gain control of its 3,300-title film library (to programme his super-stations TNT and TCM); Time, Inc. bought WCI and became Time Warner (1989); Gulf + Western spun off its non-media holdings to become Paramount Communications (1989); and Matsushita Electrical bought MCA (1999). Two of these mergers, Sony-Columbia and Matsushita-MCA, were undertaken with the specific purpose of creating a synergy between software (films) and hardware (television sets, VCRs, DVD players), while the others worked to build media conglomerates on a truly global scale. The mergers of the 1990s created three of the largest media combines on earth when Viacom acquired Paramount Communications (1994), Disney bought ABC/Capital City Broadcasting (1995) and AOL merged with Time Warner.

Between 1990 and 1995, studio marketing costs rose by 92 per cent, star salaries doubled and production costs experienced double-digit growth, at the same time that box-office revenues increased by only 9 per cent. Concurrently, the profit margins for features shrank to 14–15 per cent. This dramatic inflation of costs threatened the industry in a major way, as did an increase in the number of films released, from 167 to 212 (Litman, 1997: 192). In 1995, in fact, an industry financial analyst wrote that 'this is the worst time to be producing motion pictures in the history of the business' (Collette 1997: 122). By this time, only 35 per cent of industry earnings came from theatrical release (both domestic and foreign, the latter now exceeding the former), the remainder came from ancillary markets (Chapman 2003: 155). Wide releases became the order of the day: 130 films played in at least 800 theatres in 1994 (rising to 153 in 1995) and accounted for $4.9 billion (94 per cent) of that year's $5.2 billion theatrical revenues (Litman 1997:193). Now it is not uncommon for a major studio release to open on 2,000 or even 3,000 screens. Such wide openings have the effect of negating theatrical sub-run options and put an inordinate emphasis on the three-day grosses for a film's opening weekend which are used to set the values for the film in all of its subsequent windows. These windows are opening faster now than ever before, especially since the new practice of global wide release means that there is no value in delaying a film's clearance to video and DVD, except for its theatrical run. As product moves every more rapidly through the system, more and more product must be produced to meet rising demand. At present, however, DVD region coding prevents DVDs released in any one of eight Hollywood-defined international markets from playing on machines manufactured for use in others. This is a form of digital 'run-zone-clearance' system that works to maintain the exclusivity of the majors' films in foreign markets by keeping them from entering those markets as DVDs before their theatrical release. (The regions correspond to the majors' international releasing clock as it sweeps across the hemispheres from east to west.)

The American film industry of the early twenty-first century has become a crucible for the creation of franchises and brands through the synergistic interaction of corporate parts. A franchise involves the creation of an infinitely exploitable entertainment product, such as the *Star Wars*, *Superman* or the *Alien* series. An entertainment brand has been described as 'a lump of content [w]hich can be exploited through film, broadcast and cable television, publishing, theme parks, music, the Internet, and merchandising', like the spokes of a wheel radiating from the branded product so that exploitation both produces an income stream and further strengthens the brand (*The Economist* 1998: 57). Examples of this kind of cross-promotion would be the synergies created by News Corp's *The X-Files* (1993–2002), Time Warner's *Batman* or Viacom's *Rugrats* (1991–2004). The effect is to re-purpose material created initially for feature film production into other media or to re-purpose material created for other media into films. Often, the reproducibility of a film's brand is the key to obtaining production finance. According to Michael Allen, synergy has come to define the modern conglomerate-controlled film industry: 'It is the scale of supplementary product and the level of interaction that differentiate the modern period of American mainstream film-making from its predecessor', suggesting that film subjects are now chosen and developed specifically for their possible connections with other media (Allen 2003: 139). For motion picture studios like Disney, Paramount and Warner, parts of diversified entertainment conglomerates owning broadcast and cable networks, there is an outlet for their media content which diversifies the opportunities into other markets demanding branded products (Collette 1997: 139). Thus, American films, like other forms of mass media, are no longer simply commodities, but advertisers and creators of additional commodities as well. As Stephen Prince has put it, 'Understood in strict economic terms, production by the majors [is] about the manufacture and distribution of commodities (not films) on a national and global scale' (Prince 2000: 40).   **169**

The United States has the great advantage of sustaining the largest home market for motion pictures in the world: with 37,000 screens, American audiences account for 44 per of the global box office. Relative to the world market, infinite exploitability translates into 'infinite exportability', that is to say, given that a film's highest costs (those incurred in production) are often amortised in the domestic market, American film revenues abroad can translate into pure profit. In 2001, for instance, it was estimated that worldwide video/DVD revenue may earn up to eight times the negative cost of a film (Chapman 2003: 155). For this reason, the films can be under-priced relative to nationally produced ones and maintain a competitive edge (some would maintain, an unfair one) against foreign national cinemas. Global markets are increasingly important to the transnational entertainment conglomerates that dominate the US film industry (Wasko 2003: 172). International distribution has grown from a source of supplemental income to an economic necessity (Litman and Ahn 1997: 194). Recent examples abound: *Troy*, which Warner Bros. released in May 2004, made $133 million in the US, but nearly three times that, $363 million, internationally. Dreamworks' *The Terminal* (S. Spielberg, 2004) earned a disappointing $77.2 million domestically but another $96.3 million abroad. Disney's *King Arthur* (A. Fuqua, 2004) earned only $51.8 million in the US but $149.8 million abroad. Some American producers are even shaping their films with the foreign market in mind: *Ocean's Eleven* (S. Soderbergh, 2001) was deliberately set and filmed in Amsterdam, Paris and Rome to enhance its international appeal (Lippman 2004: 12.). Risk reduction practised on a global scale has replaced the guaranteed theatrical success offered by the Edison Trust and the cartelised studio system, but concentration of market power by the American majors has never been stronger, or more disturbing in its totalising nature, than it is today.

Notes

1. Fox had briefly attempted to control the motion picture industry of the entire English-speaking world by buying a controlling interest in Loewe's Inc., owner of MGM, a 44 per cent share of Gaumont British, England's largest producer/distributor/exhibitor, and a 50 per cent share of the newly formed Columbia Broadcasting System (CBS). Together with Fox's Publix theatre chain, the 'Fox Loew's Corporation' would have been the largest motion picture company on earth. The Hoover Justice Department and the stockmarket crash of 1929 prevented this from happening.

2. Marketing costs rose at an average annual rate of more than 12.5 per cent throughout the decade.

3. The relationship between Hollywood and one licensed product – video games – has grown particularly close, because game developers have come to rely heavily on movies for their characters, themes and plots. Within the past decade, moreover, films were increasingly based on video games (such as *Super Mario Brothers* [R. Morton, 1993], *Lara Croft: Tomb Raider* [S. West, 2001], *Final Fantasy: The Spirits Within* [Sakaguchi Hironobu and Sakakibara Moto, 2001], *Resident Evil* [P. W. S. Anderson, 2002]) and cross-licensing income between the two industries by 2000 had reached an estimated $1 billion for each. More recently, Peter Jackson (*The Lord of the Rings* trilogy, 2001–3) and Ridley Scott (*Gladiator*, 2000; *Blackhawk Down*, 2001) have formed their own companies to produce original video games, from which, presumably, filmed adaptations will also flow.

4. Perfected by electronics companies during the 1960s, the first half-inch videotape system available to consumers was actually Cartrivision Television, whose 1972 rollout attracted little public interest.
5. The reasons for this had less to do with corporate rivalry than with the fact that Betamax produced manifestly better copies than VHS, and was therefore perceived by the majors to present the greater threat of movie and programme piracy over the airwaves.

References

Allen, Michael (2003), *Contemporary US Cinema*, London: Longman.

Balio, Tino (ed.) (1990), *Hollywood in the Age of Television*, Cambridge, MA: Unwin Hyman.

Chapman, James (2003), *Cinemas of the World: Film and Society from 1985 to the Present*, London: Reaktion.

Collete, Larry (1997), 'The Wages of Synergy: Integration into Broadcast Networking by Warner Brothers, Disney and Paramount', in Litman, Barry R. (1997).

Cook, David A. (2000), *Lost Illusions: American Cinema in the Shadow of Watergate and Vietnam, 1970–1979*, vol. 9, *History of the American Cinema*, New York: Scribner's.

Cook, David A. (2003), *A History of Narrative Film*, New York: W. W. Norton.

Cook, David A. and Wang, Wenli (2004), 'Neutralizing the Piracy of Motion Pictures: Reengineering the Industry's Supply Chain', *Technology in Society* 20.

Crafton, Donald (1997), *The Talkies: American Cinema's Transition to Sound, 1926–1931*, vol. 4, *History of the American Cinema*, New York: Scribner's.

Dale, Martin (1997), *The Movie Game: The Film Business in Britain, Europe and America*, London: Cassell.

Gomery, Douglas (1985), *The Hollywood Studio System*, New York: St Martin's.

Kanninen, Morgan (2004), 'Motion Picture Association Sues Movie Downloaders', *The California Aggie*, 23 November.

Laskos, Andrew (1981), 'The Hollywood Majors', in Pirie, David (ed.), *Anatomy of the Movies*, New York: Macmillan.

Lippman, John (2004), 'Bombs-Away! Some Big Hollywood Duds Rake up Profits Overseas', *The Wall Street Journal*, 19 November.

Litman, Barry R. (1997), *The Motion Picture Mega-Industry*, Boston: Allyn and Bacon.

Litman, Barry and Ahn, Hoekyun (1997), 'Predicting Financial Success of Motion Pictures', in Litman, Barry R. (1997).

Miller, Toby, Maxwell, Richard, Goril, Nitin and McMurria, John (2001), *Global Hollywood*, London: BFI.

Olson, Scott Robert (1999), *Hollywood Planet: Global Media and the Competitive Advantage of Narrative Transparency*, Mahwah, NJ: Lawrence Erlbaun.

Prince, Stephen (2000), *A New Pot of Gold: Hollywood under the Electronic Rainbow, 1980–1989*, vol. 10, *History of the American Cinema*, New York: Scribner's.

'Size Does Matter', *The Economist*, 23 May 1998.

Wasko, Janet (2003), *How Hollywood Works*, Thousand Oaks, CA: Sage.

Waxman, Janet (2004), 'A High Wire Act at Warner Bros.', *The New York Times*, 15 November.

Zaun, Todd (2004), 'Sony's Profit Surges on Strength of *Spider-Man 2*', *The New York Times*, 27 October.

13 National and Postnational French Cinema

Martine Danan

Film is not, is no longer, a national product. Film today is by definition a transnational product.
Jean Dondelinger (EC Commissioner responsible for audiovisual and cultural affairs)
(1991: 87)

'The French cultural exception is dead. [It] is simply a Franco-French archaism.
Jean-Marie Messier (director Vivendi Universal)[1]

'Cultural diversity', which has replaced the supposedly too self-serving 'cultural exception' in the numerous official French speeches and reports discussing France's national cinema, seems to be more than ever an essential theme in French cultural policy, if one believes the numerous official documents discussing France's national cinema. However, in spite of this visible continuity in the defence of French culture, a closer examination of cinematographic policies implemented since the late 1980s reveals that France's attitude towards its national cinema may in fact be changing to the point of affecting the prevalent mode of film practice among French film-makers. In particular, the state is now openly encouraging the making of English-language superproductions in the hope of capturing a larger share of the global market. To comprehend this apparent contradiction, I will first trace the evolution of French cinema since the 1920s, when a similar search for successful international formulas was undertaken by European film industrialists, although at that time the state had little interest in cinema affairs. A first turning point led to the disappearance of the 1920s 'prenational' cinema and to the creation of a 'national' cinema as a protected cultural and economic institution. A second transformation in the relationship of the French state to cinema started occurring in the mid-1980s, with the emergence of a 'postnational' cinema which shares some (but not all) of the features of the 'prenational' model. Today a distinctive national cinematographic production still persists concurrently with the postnational approach, as I will also show. But is this coexistence a transitional phase until national cinemas and nations themselves eventually become obsolete? Or is this complex evolution part of a changing 'cultural logic' as nations adapt to the growing demands of global capitalism? This is the question this paper will ultimately try to address.

'Prenational' Search for an International Model in the 1920s

In the early 1920s, in an effort to regain control of world markets dominated by Hollywood since World War I, several important French film industrialists turned to a strategy of international alliances, with the hope of producing 'international' films that could appeal to a European or even an American audience. Gaumont, for example, chose to ally itself with Hollywood, which in essence transformed Gaumont primarily into a distributor of American films, while another group formed more successful alliances with European – especially German – producers (Sadoul, 1975b: 312, 315). The creation of a united European industry, whose goal was to override the specificity of national cultures, was judged necessary to reach markets larger than national ones and amortise the huge costs of movie-making. As early as in 1924, Louis Aubert, the head of a powerful French film company, and Erich Pommer, the leader of the German cartel UFA, signed a reciprocal distribution agreement and expressed the urgent need for close co-operation among European producers. The ultimate goal of this co-operation was to produce economically competitive 'continental' films easily marketable throughout Europe and able to resist Hollywood's economic hegemony (Sadoul 1975a: 37, 434).

European film industrialists were learning from their American competitors that cinema required greater concentration of capital and significant market expansion to remain economically successful. Practical proposals to set up a 'Film Europe' were even made at the Paris and Berlin international film congresses in 1926 and 1928 (United States 1929: 11). Furthermore, to be on par with American cinema, films had to acquire an essentially international character, not only on the financial level but also from an artistic point of view, in order to become commodities appealing to a world audience. The co-production policy for prestige international films was perhaps facilitated in the latter half of the 1920s by the development of a new genre, 'the modern studio spectacular', whose popularity soon surpassed that of another profitable genre – the 1920s historical epic (Abel 1984: 38). Studio spectaculars, relying on a 'fantasy of internationalism' which negated the past and the specificity of national cultures, sought to emulate American films by representing characters in a stylised European decor that seemed to symbolise the material well-being of an emerging class of urban consumers. They conspicuously depicted affluent younger men and women (often played by an international cast), indulging in the good life, on an ultramodern and neutral backdrop of nightclubs, resorts and Art Deco mansions (Abel 1984: 71, 205–6). By 1927, the genre was so popular that it became the main model for commercial film-making until the advent of sound (Abel 1984: 210–14, 216).

The success of these European superproductions and the attempt to create European alliances striving to control economic competition on an international scale led to a note of concern on the American side, afraid that a truly united Europe could challenge the American hegemony (United States 1929: 11–12). However, it was not this emerging European cinema that really came to challenge Hollywood, but rather the creation of a national cinema as the result of growing pressure from film industrialists demanding protectionist legislation. The first legislative measures were soon followed by the coming of sound, which drastically changed the importance of cinema as a cultural institution. **173**

Obstacles to Internationalisation: The Creation of a 'National' Cinema

The initial turning point in the French state's attitude towards cinema affairs can be traced back to 1928 when, as a result of two years of pressure by some of the same industrialists who were seeking European alliances and demanded protectionist measures against American imports, the French government passed the first cinema statute. Thanks to this statute, cinema was proclaimed a 'protected national institution', and the principle of state intervention into the affairs of the film industry was finally established. The first task assigned the Control Commission, representing most government ministries and the main cinema professions, was to protect French cinema by defining it, differentiating it from foreign films, and attempting to impose import quotas (Léglise 1969: 70, 262). The presence of industry representatives in the Control Commission indicated the government's willingness to seek consensus in a divisive matter of national importance since not all film industrialists, divided by diverging interests, agreed on direct state intervention in the film industry. Even within the government itself, those who believed that purely economic considerations should prevail opposed those who felt that national economic and cultural goals should not be dissociated.

The advent of sound less than a year later most decisively altered the relationship of cinema to the national public and to the state. Sound introduced a realistic dimension to cinematographic expression, which significantly increased its appeal as a form of entertainment for the mass audience. Part of this appeal in France derived from the French spectators' nationalistic pride in images and dialogues which, grounded in their own culture, strengthened their sense of identity (Danan 1996: 112–13). The French public's enthusiastic reactions to national films, in turn, made political leaders more fully aware of the social impact of cinema. Unlike the prenational stage, when the French state had refused to take an active interest in the film industry because it viewed cinema as a weak and disorganised industry of negligible cultural significance for the nation, by the late 1920s government officials became determined to prevent private industrialists or foreigners from entirely controlling national cinema affairs (Gomery 1980: 81–2).

By the early 1930s, it had become clear to many intellectuals and politicians that reconciling the cultural and economic aspects of cinema was a national necessity which required direct governmental involvement to achieve a profound reorganisation of the film industry. As a result of the newly perceived significance of movies, the state endeavoured to transform cinema into a true 'national' institution, namely an institution defined in relation to the larger cultural, economic and political system of the nation in which it functioned. Thus, cinema became progressively integrated into the structure of the nation-state, which in its strongest, nationalistic forms, relies on centralised power in the hands of the ruling classes, on differentiation from external elements likely to threaten national sovereignty, and on internal unification to achieve consensus among competing interest groups. However, it took a coercive power to put an end to all the disputes over state intervention in the film industry, which dissenting groups in civil society kept on opposing. World War II enabled the Vichy government to impose widespread state control and the creation of a national cinema centre, which in 1946 took the name of Centre National de la Cinématographie (CNC).

Through the CNC, every single industrial practice has been codified by the state in order to control the film industry, defend it against external attacks, and turn it into an agent of transmission of national culture through a series of production, distribution and exhibition incentives. For over half a century, this mixed economy system, in which economic and cultural objectives, private and public interests are intertwined, has allowed French cinema to combat internal crises, withstand strong external competition, and contribute to the cultural unity needed to strengthen the capitalist nation-state (Miège and Salaun 1989: 55–7). The main measures, which were elaborated in the 1950s and early 1960s, have essentially remained unchanged ever since. A support fund, subsidised by a tax on all ticket sales from French and foreign films (and increasingly since 1985 by a tax on television earnings), has financed and regulated the film industry by automatically redistributing internal resources within the various branches of the French film industry. In addition, to remedy the cultural limitations of the automatic aid scheme and ensure that cinema also fulfils its high cultural mandate, the CNC has allocated part of the fund resources 'selectively', on the basis of 'quality' criteria, most notably by giving unknown young auteurs a chance to contribute to the renewal of a national high culture, clearly differentiated from mass-appeal Hollywood movies (Neale 1982: 14, 37). However, encouragement to both national mass culture through automatic subsidies, and to high culture through selective aid schemes should not be viewed as a contradiction but rather as the necessary means to maintain the vitality of a closed national system. If only high culture is encouraged, it runs the risk of becoming artificially cut off from mainstream culture, losing its potential for self-renewal and its impact on the majority of the citizens. And mass culture which does not find a source of inspiration in the official culture is likely to escape the state's control. Thus, until recently, the strength of French cinema may have largely derived from a perpetual symbiosis between high and mass culture, a symbiosis necessary to the vitality of the 'national popular' culture (as theorised by Gramsci).

Towards a 'Postnational' Model

The government's interventionist and protectionist approach, which successfully transformed the French film industry into a quasi-closed system, corresponded to a redistribution of resources within a protected economy with a sufficient domestic market. Globalising counter-forces, such as the search for international markets through co-production agreements since 1949 or significant post-war American investments in French productions through the 1960s did exist but never prevented French cinema from functioning as an important national institution (Jäckel 2001a: 74). However, the thrust towards globalisation has become so strong since the mid-1980s that France's previous emphasis on a nationally oriented film policy may have finally been superseded, giving way to a 'postnational' cinema supported by an increasing number of film professionals and government officials (although it is still being contested by many others).

The globalising forces to which the national cinema system is now confronted result in part from the intensified pressure of international competition and the increased interdependence of capitalist economies, which has affected the financing and distribution of films. For instance, the merging of Hollywood film studios within enormous media conglomerates able to orchestrate massive marketing campaigns on a world scale has helped American block- **175** busters secure over 50 per cent of French admissions since 1989 (CNC 1993: 24; CNC 2003: 6). The French majors, in turn, have sought alliances with American companies in order to maintain their power. Most importantly, the creation in 1993 of Gaumont Buena Vista International (GBVI) and in 1995 of UGC Fox Distribution (UFD) has transformed the two vertically integrated French majors into the main importers of American films rather than producers of French films (Barbotin and Meignan 2003). Even the semi-public pay television channel, Canal+ (launched by the Havas media group), which has financed 80 per cent of French film production since 1984, has invested in American films through its production company Studio Canal+. Most recently, Canal+ has become part of NBC Universal, the second-largest media/communications conglomerate (after AOL Time Warner) with the merging of NBC and Vivendi Universal Entertainment in May 2004 ('NBC and Vivendi' 2004). In addition, the 1996 and 1997 launches of the French satellite digital pay-TV platforms CanalSatellite and TPS have led to increased competition for American films, perceived as choice programming (Pardo 1999: 29). American films, dubbed and re-exported to other French-speaking countries by companies such as StudioCanal and TF1 International, also bring in additional revenue to the most powerful French multimedia groups (CNC 2002: 22). Thus, even when they are based in France, these conglomerates operate far beyond a national framework. With a vested interest in the commercial success of French *and* American cinema, their ambitions are bound to clash with a traditional protected economic system subject to state-imposed cultural objectives (Miège and Salaun 1989: 59).

Far from stopping these globalising forces, the French government has felt compelled to embrace a film policy encouraging the pursuit of the global market and attempting to compete with Hollywood on its own terms. Report after report since the mid-1980s has stressed the need to encourage film exports and, to that effect, encourage new modes of film practice. In possibly even stronger words than in earlier documents, a 2001 report to the Foreign Affairs Commission of the House of Representatives pointed out that globalisation was the key challenge for the survival of French cinema, which can no longer rely 'on a cultural exception removed from economic realities' (Blum 2001: 66). Stated even more bluntly, French cinema has reached the limits of its 'Franco-French logic', according to a representative of Unifrance, the organisation responsible for the promotion of French film abroad (Ammar 2000: 67). Most recently, the report written in 2003 by Jean-Pierre Leclerc at the request of the Minister of Culture and Communication concluded with a series of recommendations to make French cinema more competitive and increase its international presence (Leclerc 2003: 119):

> [The recommended] modifications are a reminder that cinema cannot completely escape general economic rules, for example by regularly producing a number of films which cannot be viably exhibited in theatres. These recommendations also intend to stress that cinema cannot remain limited to its national horizon, as it is sometimes tempted to do, and that it cannot escape the general movement toward globalization.

As one of the first reports on this issue noted in 1988, purely cultural considerations, such as **176** the defence of the French language, had to be left to less commercially ambitious films

(Court 1988: 54–5). By the late 1980s, such experts' recommendations resulted in a major policy shift stressing that the correlation between commercial success, English, and big-budgets was unavoidable since English-language film-making appeared as the necessary step to overcome the resistance of the American public, considered the most important target audience and the key to global success. In particular, a 1989 decree made it possible for English-language films to receive the *agrément* that confers French nationality to a film, thus entitling its producer to aid from the national support fund. The greater than expected number of English-language co-productions in the wake of the 1989 measures forced the government to issue new decrees in 1992 and 1993 to slow the trend towards the use of English. But some observers were quick to point out that the use of English combined with careful planning at the pre-production stage had been preconditions for massive international success. Indeed, since 1989, English-language films, with the exception of *Le Fabuleux destin d'Amélie Poulain* (*Amelie*) (Jeunet, 2001) have dominated French film exports. Milos Forman's *Valmont* (1989), Jean-Jacques Annaud's *L'Amant* (*The Lover*) (1992), Luc Besson's *Le Cinquième element* (*The Fifth Element*) (1997) and *Jeanne d'Arc* (*The Messenger: The Story of Joan of Arc*) (1999) have brought in the highest export revenues (CNC 1999: 28). As a result of such unprecedented successes, the latest (1999) legislation reversed the trend once more by making optimal subsidies available to English-language co-productions, even if French-language films are entitled to a bonus (France 1999).

The perceived need to shoot high-budget films in English may only be the most blatant strategy for emulating the hegemonic Hollywood model while minimising national cultural specificities, which often appear to have become obstacles to global success. High-budget films are usually entrusted to well-established directors (such as Luc Besson), who have mastered the art of well-crafted, technologically perfect simplified narratives with widespread appeal, and to prestige producers (like Claude Berri, who co-produced *Valmont* and *L'Amant*). Above all, by focusing on excess spectacle, the 'postnational' mode of production erases most of the distinctive elements which have traditionally helped define the (maybe) imaginary coherence of a national cinema against other cinematographic traditions or against Hollywood at a given point in time: for example, an implicit or explicit world view, the construction of national character and subjectivity, certain narrative discourses and modes of address, or intertextual references (Higson 1989: 36, 38, 43–4). Instead, these 'New Holly-Wave' films attempt to downplay their 'Frenchness' as they depart from Hollywood productions only through the presence of iconic French elements or the choice of subject matter.

As the result of the newly acquired importance of subject matter as the main differentiating element since the late 1980s, French producers have turned their attention to numerous lavish costume productions, often drawing on canonical literary culture and revisiting the nation's past – especially selected periods of French history brought to the fore by contemporary events (Vincendeau 1995: 31). In particular, 'heritage films' have focused on the French Revolution and its aftermath (as in *Valmont*), the nation's colonial past (as in *L'Amant*) and some glorious moments of European history (as in Besson's *Jeanne d'Arc*), which have all attracted the attention of the media.[2] But as in Hollywood superproductions, heri- **177** tage films benefiting from extensive marketing campaigns are intended for both domestic and international consumers sensitive to production values, technological progress and pleasurable cultural representations.

Even the French-language international hit *Le Fabuleux destin d'Amélie Poulain*, touted by a *Le Monde* journalist as the proof that the 'French cultural exception had never been so evident' (Sotinel 2001), played into this blurring of genres and images. This supposedly quintessential French film, which became the most exported French film after *Le Cinquième élément,* is in fact a French-German co-production that blends stereotypical, nostalgic images of French culture while combining romantic comedy, mystery and poetic realism reminiscent of the 1930s (Lequeret 2002: 73). Moreover, images are heightened by special effects which erased any signs of modern life in Paris (Haun 2001: 14). It may be worth noting that its director, Jean-Pierre Jeunet, known for his quirky dark comedies, also directed *Alien Resurrection* (1997) in Hollywood.

In the most extreme cases, there may be nothing French at all in an English-language production considered 'French', as with *Le Cinquième élément,* although many reviewers, possibly influenced by Luc Besson's well-known name, often stressed the film's 'French' look with its costumes by superstar fashion designer Jean-Paul Gaultier, production design (including space creatures) by graphic illustrator Mœbius, and cityscapes by art director Jean-Claude Mezières. In keeping with the regulations stipulated in the 1999 decree, a film with minority capital can be considered French as long as its producer and director are French citizens (France 1999: 2902), hence the recent controversial decision to subsidise Oliver Stone's *Alexander* (2004), an English-language 180-million-euro co-production primarily financed by Warner Bros. In addition, the CNC has recently eased co-production regulations by removing the strict distinction between purely financial co-productions (based on investment reciprocity) and traditional co-productions (with mandatory artistic and technical collaboration between partners). In 2002 France also ratified the European Coproduction Convention facilitating multilateral financial co-production agreements, which makes it easier to finance high-budget films and distribute them in several countries (CNC 2002: 41–2). Consequently, the number of co-produced films soared, representing in 2003 over 50 per cent of French production and nearly 50 per cent of French investments, compared to less than one quarter in 2001 (CNC 2004: ch. 5).

Persistence of National Elements

In spite of the danger of simply turning the French cinema fund into an international source of financing for business ventures, the French government is claiming that support for internationally oriented films is the only way to keep the French film industry afloat and, therefore, to generate the financial resources needed to maintain the mixed economy system set up by the CNC. One of the main objectives of France's film policy, according to an earlier CNC report, is 'to refine the balance between an opening up to international projects and the defense of a nationally-based production'. This report states that such a goal can only be achieved by securing a significant place for French cinema in the global market while preserving a 'French-style economy' through an independent production bound to the nation's cultural objectives (Wallon 1993: iii, 23, 44).

In short, postnational films allow the CNC to pursue its multifaceted policy in favour of culturally oriented French films, and indeed, the number of low-budget films (under 1 million euros), in direct opposition to the blockbuster trend, has jumped from seven in 1994 to over forty since 2001. Numerous officials have been quick to stress the vitality of French cinema, with its 35 per cent domestic market share and its flourishing production. Since 2002 yearly film production in France has risen to over 200, from a low of 115 in 1994; new talents keep on emerging regularly as first and second films, often produced with subsidies from the CNC, represent over 50 per cent of the annual production; and independent French films, as in the past, garner prizes and critical acclaim in national and international festivals (CNC 2004: ch. 5; Leclerc 2003: 26).

France's renewed commitment to a diversified approach to production has contributed to a marked rebirth of creativity, especially among younger film-makers in their thirties and forties, which seems to support the government's claim that its policy is achieving the declared cultural objective. Since the mid-1990s especially, this young cinema with little-known or sometimes non-professional actors has revived a form of realism and social consciousness often neglected since the New Wave. Films by the younger generation of directors often aim at a harsh social commentary about characters beset with problems of unemployment, violence and racism in provincial settings or underprivileged environments, especially suburbs (in a genre that has been labelled 'cinéma de banlieue'). Although most auteur films are made primarily for a specialised public of cinephiles, many esoteric productions from the last decade have also succeeded in attracting much critical attention *and* in broadening their appeal with a relatively large domestic (and sometimes international) public. One of the most successful and best-known examples of the 'cinéma de banlieue' genre is probably Mathieu Kassovitz's *La Haine* (*Hate*) (1995), a 2-million-dollar film made with unknown actors. It won numerous French and international prizes while becoming a domestic box-office success and one of the most discussed film events of the year (Jäckel 2001b: 224–5). A number of other films about social exclusion or marginal characters have met with commercial success and were well received by critics: for example, Manuel Poirier's *Western* (1997), staging a Spanish travelling salesman crossing paths with a Russian hitchhiker/drifter on the roads of Brittany; Erick Zonca's *La Vie rêvée des anges* (*The Dream-life of Angels*) (1998), about the encounter of two working-class girls in the industrial north of France; Robert Guédiguian's *Marius et Jeannette* (1997), which portrayed the growing bond between a poor single mother and the lonely guard of an abandoned factory in the south of France. Most recently *Etre et avoir* (2002), a documentary by Nicolas Philibert about a rural single-classroom school, even achieved significant national and international success (CNC 2004: ch. 3).

Such films seem to indicate that France may be achieving its official goal of protecting 'cultural pluralism' against the 'perverse effects of globalization and cultural homogenization', therefore resisting the homogenisation which threatens cultural representations because of Hollywood's hegemony, as former culture minister Catherine Trautmann stated (1998a). However, sites and forms of consumption rather than production may be truer indicators of progress towards cultural pluralism. Not only do nations need to **179**

Être et avoir (Nicolas Philibert, 2002)

preserve pluralistic forms of cultural production, but they must also facilitate 'democratic access to culture', because both priorities are essential in order to bring together 'the diverse people of the nation' and 'keep a society alive'(Trautmann 1998b). Nevertheless, in spite of culture ministers' repeated commitment to cultural democratisation and the fact that some critically acclaimed films have been relatively successful, admissions remain primarily concentrated on a handful of well-advertised American blockbusters, and to a lesser-extent, a few mainstream French films. With independent or esoteric subtitled films from lesser known foreign cultures normally geared to a cosmopolitan public in Paris and a few other major urban centres, in 2002 only half of the film production proved to be profitable, and one third of French films were exhibited in fewer than ten movie theatres (Leclerc 2003: 35–6). Instead of greater access to a pluralistic culture, therefore, only audiences with already a higher 'cultural capital', to use Bourdieu's phrase, seem to avail themselves of the wide spectrum of films and truly benefit from state-subsidised culture, while the tastes of the majority, shaped by the market, are narrowing (Harbord 2002: 111). Consequently, one may wonder whether the apparent continuity in French film policy support for film culture is masking a profound rift between an old elite devoted to a traditional high culture seemingly removed from direct economic considerations and a new elite converted to the homogenising culture of capitalist expansion. Or is there a new logic that reconciles the apparent contradiction between old and new cultures in such a way that heterogeneity and homogenisation need to coexist?

A New Postnational–national Dialectic

Part of this new logic since the 1990s may be the growing transformation of cinema into a large-scale cultural industry, to be integrated into a whole media network encompassing theatres, video and DVDs, thematic cable channels, satellite and digital television. Film is more and more conceived as a consumer product to be commercialised, marketed and sold in these multiple venues (Pailliart and Miège 1996: 133, 138). Consequently, traditional theatre spectatorship constitutes only a small portion of profits derived from film production within the larger audiovisual landscape. Film consumption is also turned into a more complex operation as images create more needs and entertainment meets the demands of fragmented markets through multiple sites (Creton 1997: 28–31; Harbord: 2002: 2). For example, low- and medium-budget foreign films provide the many cable and satellite TV channels with the variety programming needed worldwide for their niche audiences (Danan 2000: 359–60). Above all, with its powerful dissemination of images, cinema plays a powerful symbolic role (Creton 1997: 31). The noticeable presence of French independent 'art' films in international festivals and the fame of French auteurs contribute to the international prestige of France, since such films seem to demonstrate that France remains *the* country of film aficionados and the uncontested defender of artistic diversity. Thus, these films represent a cultural capital which transcends the actual market value of traditional art objects. In short, French cinema, like other prestigious products, has become an internationally known brand of exceptional value for France, according to a report entitled *The Desire for France: The International Presence of France and Francophonie in the Information Society* (Bloche 1998): '[French cinema] has its public everywhere in the world and especially in the United States. Although it is a niche audience, it is also an elite audience, given that our films have such a reputation for being intellectual, perhaps a little verbose and complicated. Our cinema is a brand.' Such brands are helping culture 'made in France' keep its distinctiveness and 'quality label' as one of the strategies for worldwide exports. In a 2003 statement, Jean-Jacques Aillegon, former Minister of Culture, reiterated the importance of cinema as a cultural industry which, by reinforcing France's prestige, is essential for national economic prosperity: 'For French cinema the conquest of foreign publics must be a priority objective: first because of its cultural impact, but also because external markets can become one of the sources of its economic prosperity.'

In this perspective, exporting 'art' cinema as well as postnational films becomes part of France's 'diplomatic arsenal' in the 'culture wars' which support a nation's 'struggles for political rights and recognition' in the world economy (Smith 1990: 185). Thus, France's dual policy in favour of postnational and auteur films no longer appears as a contradiction but rather as a synergetic battle for international visibility within an integrated approach in favour of global economic expansion. Like art films, postnational films do not simply bring in direct economic gains but promote a positive image of France. These top-of-the-line, most commercially viable products, which represent a large share of French film investment money and are most heavily advertised, also convey the image of a competitive European film industry leader whose products are capable of high production values and technological sophistication. The image of French cinema as a film industry leader, in turn, is a reminder that France is still a leading inter- **181** national economic power (the fourth) and major force in the global economy. Therefore, both components of this policy with its two-pronged global/national approach result from a new form of state practice dependent upon the making and dissemination of images in our 'spectacle society' with the assistance of new technology. And both encourage identification with global consumer culture while reasserting the specificity of the nation.

Thus, the homogenisation of cultural representations fostered by postnational cinema and more generally by global mass culture becomes part of a complex dialectic between national identity and globalisation. Althusser had earlier theorised that 'uneven development' explains the contradictions and struggles between areas dominated by an outmoded type of economic organisation and those areas influenced by more advanced forms of capitalism (Althusser 1979: 209–15). In the current stage of capitalistic development, the 'historical blockage' preventing the full development of advanced capitalism in industrialised countries may finally have been overridden. But this stage may have been achieved without completely superseding the national space of monopoly capitalism and transforming heterogeneity into obsolete remnants, as Fredric Jameson had predicted in the early 1990s (Jameson 1991: 412). Rather, as Stuart Hall has argued (1991: 28), capital expansion must operate through or even enhance national differences to achieve its globalising objective, as it 'is now a form of capital which recognizes that it can only, to use a metaphor, rule through other capitals, rule alongside and in partnership with other economic and political elites. It does not attempt to obliterate them; it operates through them.'

Political elites are indeed eager to profit from globalisation while preserving their hegemonic interests within the nation-state by maintaining the cultural specificities that structure the lives of citizens and maintain social unity. To achieve this dual and often contradictory goal, a nation's leaders must encourage 'a loyalty to market economics' among selfish individualistic consumers, while forming selfless, collective 'cultural citizens, docile but efficient participants in that economy and society mix', in a continual dialectical tension. The current role of a state's cultural policy, therefore, is to produce this consumer-citizen so as to foster a sense of individual subjectivity as well as communal belonging (Miller 1993: xii, xvi, 26). In its current intensified phase especially, capitalist expansion relies on this constant tension within nation-states, caught between the openness of capital and the closure of particular social structures, as Raymond Williams had demonstrated over twenty years ago when discussing 'The Culture of Nations' (1983: 192)

> Thus an ideal condition is relentlessly pursued. First, the economic efficiency of a global system of production and trade, to include a reorganised and efficient 'national' sector within an open and interpenetrating market flow. But at the same time a socially organised and socially disciplined population, one from which effort can be mobilised and taxes collected along the residual but still effective national lines.

The globalisation phenomenon has therefore not superseded national cultures but transformed them into increasingly complex manifestations complicating the role of the nation-state as it endeavours to maintain a delicate balance between homogenization and heterogeneity, or the universal and the particular, as Arjun Appadurai has further theorized (1990: 307). As manifestations of globalisation 'are absorbed into local political and cultural economies', these manifestations may 'be repatriated as heterogeneous dialogues of national sovereignty'. French film policy may be one of the most visible manifestations of this 'repatriation of difference' in an environment that may accommodate heterogeneity but is still dominated by the commercial logic of globalisation.

Conclusion

The national cinema system set up after World War II has served the interests of the traditional nation-state, whose capitalist organisation relied on boundaries reinforced by culture. This nation-centred cinema framework prevented film industrialists from further pursuing the internationalisation of cinema started in the 1920s and, in a sense, forced the film industry back into an already outmoded form of production, which delayed the integration of cinema into a more advanced capitalistic system. However, as a result of the growing pressure of economic globalisation in recent years, the French state has begun actively to encourage the development of a postnational cinema capable of competing with Hollywood for a share of global markets. With the export success of globally oriented films, and in light of statements emphasising short-term economic goals rather than cultural considerations, one may speculate that governmental support for France's postnational strategy will remain the dominant mode of film practice. However, while facilitating postnational productions, the French state continues simultaneously to support modes of film practice which appear to resist the homogenising effects of globalisation. Yet, even this heterogeneous film production, which could foster a pluralistic society while attesting to the persistence of distinct local cultures, also fully participates in France's effort to benefit from global capitalist expansion. Ultimately, what appears to be a direct opposition between culture and commerce, national manifestations and global pursuits, or heterogeneity and homogenisation, is part of a capitalistic dialectic redefining the role of nations as they face changing economic demands. In its effort to adapt to these demands, France may be more concerned with what cinema, through its dissemination of powerful images, can do for the nation's ranking in the world than with encouraging democratic plurality and preserving the 'cultural diversity' it had vowed to defend.

Notes

1. Messier was director of the Vivendi Universal group in 2001, when he made this statement reported in 'Messier et l'exception culturelle', *AlloCiné*, 19 December 2001. He left in July 2002. All translations from the French are the author's.
2. For a more detailed analysis of *Valmont* and *L'Amant*, see my contribution to Catherine Fowler (2002).

References

Abel, Richard (1984), *French Cinema: The First Wave, 1915–1929*, Princeton: Princeton University Press.

Aillegon, Jean-Jacques (2003), 'Communication du Ministre de la culture et de la communication sur la politique de l'Etat en faveur du financement du cinéma', 30 April; web reference: <www.culture.gouv.fr/culture/actualites/communiq/aillagon/cinema-texte300403.htm>.

Althusser, Louis (1979), 'On the Materialist Dialectic', in *For Marx*, London: Verso: 161–218.

Ammar, Alain (2000), 'L'industrie cinématographique française s'exporte mieux', *Le MOCI* 1449, 6 July: 67.

Appadurai, Arjun (1990), 'Disjuncture and Difference in the Global Cultural Economy' in Featherstone (1990): 295–310.

Barbotin, Laurent and Meignan, Géraldine (2003), 'UGC/Gaumont: Le duel des majors françaises', *L'Expansion* 29 October.

Bloche, Patrick (1998), *Le désir de France: La présence internationale de la France et la francophonie dans la société de l'information*, Rapport au Premier Ministre, 7 December; web reference: <www.internet.gouv.fr/français/textesref/rapbloche98>.

Blum, Roland (2001), 'Rapport d'information déposé par la commission des affaires étrangères sur les forces et les faiblesses du cinéma français sur le marché international', 26 June; web reference: <www.assemblee-nationale.fr/rap-info/i3197.asp>.

CNC (1993), *Bilan 1992*, Special issue of CNC *info* 246, April–May.

CNC (1999), *Bilan 1998*, Special issue of *CNC info* 272, May.

CNC (2002), *Rapport du groupe de travail sur le financement de la production cinématographique*, July; web reference: <www.cnc.fr/b_actual/r5/ssrub4/prodcine/fin_prodcine.pdf>.

CNC (2003), *Bilan 2002*, Special issue of CNC *info* 287, May.

CNC (2004), *Bilan 2003*, Special issue of CNC *info* 290, May.

Court, Jean-François (1988), *Le cinéma français face à son avenir: Rapport au Ministre de la Culture et de la Communication*, Paris: La Documentation française.

Creton, Laurent (1997), *Cinéma et marché*, Paris: Armand Colin.

Danan, Martine (1996), 'A la recherche d'une stratégie internationale: Hollywood et le marché français des années trente' in Gambier, Y. (ed.), *Les Transferts linguistiques dans les médias audiovisuels*, Lille: Presses Universitaires du Septentrion, 109–30.

Danan, Martine (2000), 'French Cinema in the Era of Media Capitalism', *Media, Culture and Society* 22 (3): 355–64.

Dondelinger, Jean (1991), 'Les rencontres cinématographiques de Beaune' (17–20 October), unpublished proceedings.

Featherstone, Mike (ed.) (1990), *Global Culture: Nationalism, Globalization and Modernity,* special issue of *Theory, Culture and Society* 7, London: Sage.

Fowler, Catherine (ed.) (2002), *The European Cinema Reader*, London: Routledge.

France (1999), Ministère de la culture et de la communication, 'Décret no 99-130 du 24 février 1999 relatif au soutien financier de l'industrie cinématographique', *Journal Officiel de la République française,* 47, 25 February: 2902.

Gomery, Douglas (1980), 'Economic Struggle and Hollywood Imperialism: Europe Converts to Sound', *Yale French Studies* 60: 80–93.

Hall, Stuart (1991), 'The Local and the Global: Globalization and Ethnicity', in King, A. D. (ed.), *Culture, Globalization, and the World System: Contemporary Conditions for the Representation of Identity*, London: Macmillan: 19–39.

Harbord, Janet (2002), *Film Cultures*, London, Thousand Oaks, New Delhi: Sage.

Haun, Harry (2001), 'Fantasy in Paris', *Film Journal International*, November: 14–16.

Higson, Andrew (1989), 'The Concept of National Cinema', 'Introduction: Over the Borderlines', in *Over the Borderlines: Questioning National Identities, Screen* 30 (4): 36–46.

Jäckel, Anne (2001a), 'Shooting in English? Myth or Necessity', in Gambier, Yves and Gottlieb, Henrik (eds), *(Multi)Media Translation,* Amsterdam, Philadelphia: John Benjamins Publishing Company: 73–89.

Jäckel, Anne (2001b), 'The Subtitling of *La Haine*: A Case Study', in Gambier and Gottlieb (2001): 223–35.

Jameson, Fredric (1991), *Postmodernism or the Cultural Logic of Late Capitalism*, Durham: Duke University Press.

Leclerc, Jean-Pierre (2003), 'Réflexion sur le disposif français de soutien à la production cinématographique', January; web reference: <www.ladocumentationfrançaise.fr/brp/notices/ 034000061.shtml>.

Léglise, Paul (1969), *Le cinéma et la IIIe République*: *Histoire de la politique du cinéma français,* vol. 1, Paris: Lherminier.

Lequeret, Elisabeth (2002), 'La dernière vague est une lame de fond', *Cahiers du cinéma*, May: 70–4.

Messier, Jean (2001) 'Messier et l'exception culturelle' in *AlloCiné* 19 December.

Miège, Bernard and Salaun, Jean-Michel (1989), 'France: a Mixed System: Renovation of an Old Concept', *Media, Culture and Society* 11: 355–64.

Miller, Toby (1993), *The Well-Tempered Self: Citizenship: Culture and the Postmodern Subject,* Baltimore: Johns Hopkins University Press.

'NBC and Vivendi Universal Entertainment Unite to Create NBC Universal' (2004), 12 May; web reference: <www.finance.vivendiuniversal.com/finance/news/00001398.cfm>.

Neale, Steve (1982), 'Art Cinema as Institution', *Screen* 22 (1): 11–39.

Pailliart, Isabelle and Miège, Bernard (1996), 'Les industries culturelles', *Institutions et vie culturelle: Les notices*, Paris: La documentation Française: 133–8.

Pardo, Carlos (1999), 'Le cinéma français, otage de la télévision', *Le Monde diplomatique*, 29 May.

Sadoul, Georges (1975a), *Histoire générale du cinéma, 5: L'art muet 1919–1929*, vol. 1, Paris: Denoël.

Sadoul, Georges (1975b), *Histoire générale du cinéma, 6: L'art muet 1919–1929*, vol. 2, Paris: Denoël.

Smith, Anthony D. (1990), 'Towards a Global Culture?' in Featherstone (1990): 171–91.

Sotinel, Thomas (2001), '2001, millésime d'exception pour les films français, *Le Monde,* 28 December.

Trautmann, Catherine (1998a), 'Allocution à l'occasion de l'ouverture du Colloque "La Culture française à l'horizon de l'an 2000"', *Discours et communiqués*, Ministère de la Culture et de la Communication, 16 April; web reference: <www.culture.fr>.

Trautmann, Catherine (1998b), 'Budget de la culture', Conférence de presse, Ministère de la Culture et de la Communication, 9 September; web reference: <www.culture.gouv.fr/culture/actualites>.

United States Department of Commerce Bureau of Foreign and Domestic Commerce (1929), *European Motion Picture Industry in 1928*, Trade Information Bulletin 617, Washington: Government Printing Office.

Vincendeau, Ginette (1995), 'Unsettling Memories', *Sight and Sound* July: 30–1.

Wallon, Dominique (1993), *Pour un nouveau développement de l'industrie des programmes,* Rapport à Monsieur Jacques Toubon (Ts), Paris: CNC.

Williams, Raymond (1983), *The Year 2000*, New York: Pantheon Books.

14   From Cine-mania to Blockbusters and Trans-cinema

Reflections on Recent South Korean Cinema[1]

Kim Soyoung

Part I

Various factors have contributed to the recent proliferation of all kinds of film festivals in South Korea. There is, to begin with, cine-mania, the Korean version of cinephilia. Second is the enactment of a local self-government system. Third, there has been a shift in the site of Korean activism from the politico-economic to the cultural sphere. And finally, there is the ambitious project of *Saegaehwa*, the Korean version of globalisation. *Saegaehwa* was initiated with the establishment of civil government in 1991. In 1997 it reverberated in this way:

> As the newest member of the Organisation of Economic Cooperation and Development and as one of the world's strongest trading nations, the Republic of Korea will further accelerate *Saegaehwa*, its ambitious economic liberalization effort aimed at greater globalization. *Saegaehwa* will open the Korean market to foreign trade and investment and will further strengthen corporate Korea's role on the international business stage.[2]

In a breathless and condensed narrative of *Saegaehwa* and civil society, cultural critics often mention a paradigm shift as having occurred in the 1990s. Their argument is that the social change of the 1980s triggered by a massive labour movement in alliance with student protests is being severely damaged by a retreat from the notion of class. The problem with this rhetoric is that it fails to perceive not only emerging social forces and new political agents, but also the transformation of class identities.

Facing the need for a new direction in a social movement that no longer appears totally grounded on a proletarian class perspective, groups composed of feminists, gay/lesbian activists, some members of youth sub-cultures and civil activists have initiated film festivals as public platforms from where to address their rights and concerns. The desire to be represented or recognised in public prevails in the various modes of festivals. It seems that these various film festivals have become not only a space of negotiation among different forces but also a cultural practice that links the audience to the specific agendas raised by new identities, subject positions and organisations.

Generally speaking, these film festivals can be classified into three categories. First, there are those stemming from a coalition of state, local governments, corporations and intellectuals equipped with film expertise – as exemplified by the Pusan International Film Festival and Puchon International Fantastic Film Festival. Second, there are corporate-sponsored festivals, such as the Q Channel Seoul Documentary Film and Video Festival and the Samsung Nices Short Film Festival. Third, there are festivals organised by new and old activist groups.

In a social formation where state intervention into every aspect of people's lives is still highly visible, even the second kind of festival needs to compromise with the power of the state exerted through censorship and exhibition laws. The third kind of festival is relatively autonomous from the state and the corporate sector. For this reason, it offers an interesting example of how the new social movement of the 1990s is taking tentative steps away from the labour-based social movement of the 1990s.[3]

In this third category, the discourses of the 1980s and 1990s are simultaneously operative. The similarities and continuities, as well as the differences and ruptures between the two periods become visible when the different film festivals are examined closely. Further, by examining the politics of these festivals, the notion of identity politics and the possible formation of alternative public spheres may be tested against the civil society claimed by the present government and the mainstream media. So far, the third category has included the Women's Film Festival in Seoul, the Seoul Queer Film and Video Festival, the Human Rights Watch Film Festival (organised by an ex-political prisoner previously jailed for violation of the National Security Law), IndeForum (held by young film-makers) and various other small-scale festivals that take place on college campuses, in videotheques, and so forth.

The way the three categories of film festival operate may be viewed as an index to the new contours of cultural specificity in the 1990s. The notion of the public sphere and the alternative public spheres in which each film festival is located (or dislocated) has to be taken into consideration vis-à-vis the inauguration of the civil government, the retreat of the labour movement as the privileged force of social change, and the concomitant endeavour to find new agencies for social change. Around the same period, the discourse on nationalism has been re-mobilised with the discourse of *Saegaehwa* in order to dictate a social programme marked by a bourgeois project of appealing to unity in order to neutralise class conflict. The international-scale film festivals in particular thrive on the manifold manifestations of the global and the local, as well as the national and the local. The local is a fragmented site contested by central and newly formed local governments. As noted above, the film festival provides a condensed space where different interests and ideologies all come into play at the contested intersection of residual authoritarian and emergent democratic modes. The negotiations and compromises between the state, the corporations, the intellectuals and the audiences betray how the different social forces are contesting with one another in this historical conjuncture.

The various film festivals tend to operate in a strategic way so as to render the festival occasion a cultural, political and economic site of ongoing recognition, negotiation and contest. The banning of festivals like the Seoul Queer Film and Video Festival, the Human Rights Watch Film Festival and the IndeForum Festival explicitly indicates pressure points in the hegemonic order. The organisation, exhibition and banning of film festivals reveals blockages, grey areas, niches and points of compromise, as well as possible directions towards alternative or oppositional platforms. Among the different matrixes of emerging groups, collectives and identities engaged in film festival politics some are not only recognised, but also heavily supported by the authorities, whereas others are refused recognition, yet others resist recognition by the authorities.

Desire for Cinema, Desire for Recognition

In Korea, loving cinema or desire for cinema has become a distinctive feature of youth culture since the early 1990s. Loving cinema is known as 'cine-mania' in the Korean cultural context, or cinematic scopophilia or cinephilia in the West. It seems that two things observed in relation to cinephilia in general are also relevant to an understanding the phenomenal increase of Korea's cinema-loving audience. One is a quasi-mystical aspect of cinephilia, which encourages the viewer to recognise her/his soul projected onto the screen or the soul of actors and directors. In other words, there is a moment of recognition related to the viewer's aesthetic as expressed in the concept of *photogénie*.

> It clearly sets in place a viewer's aesthetic. The defining characteristic of cinema is said to be something that pertains to the relationship between viewer and image, a momentary flash of recognition, or a moment when the look at [s]omething suddenly flares up with a particularly affective, emotional intensity. The founding aspect of cinematic quality, instead of its specificity, is located not in the recognition of an artistic sensibility or intentionality beyond the screen, as it were, but in the particular relationship supported or constituted by the spectatorial look, between projected image and viewer. (Willemen 1994: 228)

Since, in cinephilia, people are looking for something they desire to see that is not actually there to be seen, the mode of spectatorship allows for a diversity of reading activities. Along with the notion of recognition in relation to the viewer's sense of identity, cinephilia functions to unify different groups with different positions under the rubric of the desire for cinema. The growth of cinephilia in Korea is linked to the growth of film culture through the proliferation of film festivals, arthouse cinema theatres, cinematheques, videotheques, film magazines, journals and cinema groups housed both in cyberspace and real space.[4]

As is often noted, the quasi-religious energy of the 1980s Korean student movement – in fact a kind of youth culture – is hardly detectable on streets and campuses in the 1990s. Unexpectedly, and unlike in the 1980s, quasi-religious energy is found in film spectatorship. The fascination for cult movies, or a mode of cult spectatorship around American B-movies, European arthouse cinema, Hong Kong action movies and Wong Kar-wai in particular, are phenomenal in Korean youth culture. The term 'cine-mania' was coined in recognition of the large number of such spectators.

In my view, the present mode of spectatorship detected on the Korean cultural scene is a hybrid form of cinephilia and mania. Cine-mania connotes the swallowing up of incredible numbers of films. It is a frenzied mode of film consumption. Cine-maniacs are estimated at as many as 30,000, mostly in their twenties and thirties. This is the pool or potential audience available to fill festival seats, to subscribe to film magazines, and other similar activities. In fact, thematic film festivals like the Seoul Women's Film Festival and the Seoul Queer Film and Video Festival might be characterised as attempts to redirect the energy of mania into something that is grounded on a political agenda via the cinema.

Considering the presence of this movie mania, no one should be surprised to learn that the best-selling weekly magazine on the street kiosks is *Cine-21*, a mixed form publication fusing the fan magazine format with a touch of cinematic expertise. The success of *Cine-21* is noteworthy. As an allegedly politicised nation, Korea's best-selling magazines used to be monthly social/political commentary publications. Issued by the progressive newspaper *Hangyurae*, *Cine-21* has reshaped the magazine market and become the best-selling weekly. Does this indicate a replacement of political concerns with cinematic ones? Or is it rather the displacement of the real by representation? In response to this hasty and anxious diagnosis – one that laments the advent of a depoliticised postmodern age – I would argue that new political agency may be found in the topography of cultural politics.

Cine-21 magazine

In synchronicity with this outburst of cinephilia, Korean society has witnessed the emergence of new identities and subject positions that are usually considered the premise for identity politics and struggles for recognition. Nancy Fraser, in her argument on the politics of redistribution and recognition, makes a distinction between two areas of injustice. One is economic, the other is cultural, although the two are necessarily entwined. The remedy for economic injustice entails political-economic restructuring, which in turn requires 'redistributing income, reorganizing the division of labour, subjecting investment to democratic decision making, or transforming other basic economic structures'. The remedy for cultural injustice, she suggests, is cultural or symbolic change **189** that involves 'upwardly revaluing disrespected identities and the cultural products of maligned groups, the wholesale transformation of social patterns of representation, interpretation and communication in ways that would change *everybody's* sense of self'. She refers to this kind of remedy as 'recognition' (Fraser 1997: 15).

Identity politics or the politics of recognition as Nancy Fraser rephrases it, is likely to be positioned in the cultural sphere, which is not totally removed from the one inhabited by the cinephile. Along these lines, I would like to suggest that the problem of how to rearticulate the politics of recognition to the politics of redistribution might be rephrased as the question of how to rearticulate the emergence of group identities in the 1990s to the class problematic of the 1980s. As social fantasy, the cinematic apparatus seems to mediate two areas of concern.

Group identity dissociated from class identity came onto the scene with the appearance of the Orange Tribe in the early 1990s. The term was coined for a certain group in their twenties who were spotted in the most affluent and nouveau riche part of Apgujungdong in Seoul. In spite of their insignificant numbers, the mainstream media devoted a hysterical amount of space to stories about them. They were condemned as a morally and sexually corrupt, as well as an overspending group of young people. There was a tangible sense of collective envy directed at this handful of people who could afford such luxurious lifestyles thanks to their parents' money. Soon the Yata Tribe eclipsed the Orange Tribe. The linguistic use of the terms Orange Tribe and Yata Tribe is highly suggestive.[5] This was around the time when the consequences of the Uruguay Round were forcing Korea to import foreign agricultural products. Due to its high price, the Californian orange represented something expensive, upper class and American in flavour. The ownership of foreign cars and leisure time connoted by the term Yata Tribe indicates the upper classes. However, the pairing of the words Orange and Yata with a term – tribe – that carries explicit feudal connotations, reveals an interesting mixture of signifiers, pointing simultaneously to the postmodern and the pre-modern. Considering the current diffusion of postmodernism in both academic and mass media discourse as a replacement for Marxism in Korea, and the consequent naming of anything new as postmodern, these names effectively rearticulate the pre-modern onto the postmodern. Korea's alleged entry into the postmodern era since the 1988 Olympics is marked by group names invoking the feudal in the guise of the postmodern.

Subjected to the authoritarian gaze of the media and society, these groups were constructed as an imagined community of upper-middle-class consumers. With the expansion of consumerism, another identity, 'Missy', has been mobilised for certain targeted consumers. The term 'Missy' started as a commercial phrase used by a department store around 1993. Young housewives in their late twenties and thirties launched a particular mode of consumption for married women. These new identities were constructed only to offer identification for new consumers in the expanding economy.

At around the same time, but with a different twist, the notion of feminist subjectivity emerged. As feminism penetrated not only the socio-economic, but also the cultural, sphere, the use of the terms 'feminist' (in Korean, English pronunciation is used) gradually replaced the term 'women's movement activist' (*yosong undonga*) Whereas '*yosong undonga*' is generally associated with the agents of the social movement in the 1980s, in the case of 'feminist' this association is much more attenuated. Nineteen nineties feminism brought forth and dealt with the issues of feminine writing and feminist subjectivity, mostly in the domains of literature, theatre and film.[6] Towards the mid-1990s, gay/lesbian activists began to question the effects of cultural representations on the construction of identities. Again, cinema has since provided the space where these questions can be discussed. The circulation of feminist and women's films and films with gay characters has contributed significantly to raising related issues. With its certain distance from society, the cinema has facilitated the incorporation of gay/lesbian issues into a cultural discourse that absolutely refused to recognise these issues before.

However, it appears that in South Korea identity politics based on class, gender and race have not entered the cultural scene in full force yet. Different groups do exist, but the articulation of identity with politics still sounds strange. Identities are interpellated, but politics based on differences are not yet fully recognised in the political sphere. Many factors can be cited to account for this. First, there is a Confucian resistance to the notion of multiple identities. Second, the everyday linguistic habit of saying 'we' and 'our' (*uri*) blocks the notion of different identities. For instance, people tend to call their own partner 'our husband' or 'our wife'. Third, there is a refusal to recognise sexual and gendered identity because of a social norm which regards such matters as 'private' and hence not as part of public discourse. In this regard, it is telling that reactionary male critics choose not to use the term '*yosong*' when discussing women's issues, as this has a strong implication of feminine sexuality. Instead they use the more neutral term '*yosa*', which means simply a person who is born as *yosong*.

Last but most significant is the dominant force of national identity, safeguarded by the National Security Law, the narrative of the racially homogeneous nation, and the ever-present scenario of North Korean invasion. Any challenge to the fiction of the racially homogeneous nation is still a social taboo. Underneath the belief in the collective 'one true self' there lurks uneven regional development, the repression of gender differences and class divisions, and the exploitation of foreign workers. In a way, national identity claims exclusive appropriation of identity politics without referring to its politics, as the idea of one homogeneous race with a shared history and shared blood is unquestionably embodied in the understanding of Korean national identity. National identity in this context is never a 'production which is never complete, always in process and always constituted within, not outside, representation' (Hall 1994: 392). Rather, it always remains a trans-historical and essential notion. The hold of national identity disallows the dissemination of different identities into politics.

Certainly, this notion of national identity was used effectively against both the Japanese colonial discourse of the Greater Asian Co-Prosperity Sphere and American neo-colonial discourse. However, due to the appropriation of national identity by the military dictatorship from 1961 to 1990 as the ground on which to legitimise heavily centralised and oppressive regimes, the discourse of national identity has foreclosed the development of politics based on local and gender differences. National identity based on shared ancestry can be used as a strategic essentialism by a nation with a history traumatised by colonial and neo-colonial memories. But it becomes a problem, especially when the multinational corporations of that nation branch out to employ workers from other parts of Asia, such as Nepal, the Philippines and India.

In South Korea, any attempt to disrupt nationalistic discourse would be immediately taken as a violation of the National Security Law. In this regard, the emerging groups with an emphasis on gender, sexuality and local politics could be construed as a challenge to the sweeping discourse of national identity. The present government unwittingly proved this by banning film festivals such as the Seoul Queer Film and Video Festival, the Human Rights Watch Festival and the IndeForum Festival.

The notion of fragmented and multiple identities does not sit well with the claim to a 5,000-year-old nation-state based on a single race. Even the powerful class movement based in the student movement of the 1980s seldom questioned this construction of national identity. Indeed, the class movement often resorted to national identity or the discourse of nationalism to mobilise the people. Irrespective of class position, what has been always at stake is the mode of government, not nationalistic discourse. Furthermore, there is no doubt that the national identity propagated by the hegemonic discourse has primarily represented the middle-class male population. The presence of North Korea as immediate 'other' has also always provided an alibi and, ironically, contributed to securing the discursive stability of South Korean national identity.

In this opening, identity (*chongchae*) politics has not yet been grafted onto the social formation of Korea. Some might even argue that the topic itself is being imposed upon us as one of the problematics of travelling cultural studies. Despite the fact that identity politics does not provide the most privileged entry point for reading the cultural formation of Korea at this moment, this scarcely means that emergent different identity groups do not exist. Rather, the identity groups deploy a different rhetoric and different strategies to negotiate with the state apparatus and the mainstream media.

Finding themselves in the ever-shifting space between the residual authoritarian government of military dictatorship and hegemonic quasi-democratic government, the non-majority groups tend to employ the discourse of radical differences, less than the idea of universal humanism. The appeal to human rights reverberates through the array of feminist and gay/lesbian movements. Although pragmatic, there is a price for this practice. On the one hand, it has helped to reduce the risk of radical separation, but, on the other, it has barely touched the critical discourses and practices of nationalism, capitalism and the Confucian patriarchal notion of sexuality.

It is also true, however, that the general situation is unlike the 1980s, when the problematic of class dominated both intellectuals and the people (*minjung*). It might therefore be asked how other subject positions such as women, gays and lesbians have been able to emerge as political agents during the social transformation of South Korea. In the light of Confucian ageism, a feudal way of maintaining traditional hierarchy and order, the formation of youth culture in the form of cine-mania and rock-mania is also noteworthy in this regard.

Film Festival Politics and Identity Questions

Mapping film festivals allows significant understanding of Korean cultural politics in the 1990s. This is because organising festivals has turned into one of the major cultural practices for feminists, queer groups, young film-makers, college students, youth groups and citizen activists.

Local governments like Pusan and Puchon and multinational corporations like Daweoo and Samsung have also joined in. Desire for cinema and desire for globalisation, often encapsulated in the official discourse of *Saegaehwa,* converge in international-scale film festivals.

Simultaneously, the notion of national identity has re-emerged in 1990s Korea under the slogan of *Shintopuli,* meaning the non-differentiated sameness of the body and the native soil. This essentialised notion conflating the nation, the body and nature has arisen as a complicit counter-narrative to the anxiety generated by *Saegaewha.* Again, not unlike the term Orange Tribe, the allegedly postmodern discourse of *Saegaehwa* has come into being only by evoking the pre-modern Confucian notion of *Shintopuli.* Between *Saegaehwa* and *Shintopuli,* the notion of the modern remains somewhat abstract. So does the notion of the public sphere, never mind that of the alternative public sphere. In this highly contested force field where the synchronicity of the non-synchronous collides, new subject positions based on gender and sexuality have emerged.

However, the women's movement absolutely cannot be characterised as something new to the 1990s. From the colonial period (1910–45), women workers and intellectuals joined the social movement with demands for equal wages, the revaluation of housework and the denunciation of Confucian patriarchy. Until recently the women's liberation movement was located in the larger context of the class and national movement, with the possible exception of certain groups launched in the 1980s such as Another Culture (*Ttohanaui Munhwa*). The identity of activists from the women's liberation movement (*yosong haebang undonga*) of the previous period is considered to occupy a different position from that of the 1990s feminists. The discourse of the latter is often associated with cultural politics, but neither the women's movement nor feminist practice have problematised the discourse of nationalism or the notion of sexuality to any great extent. For instance, the 'comfort women' issue – about former Korean sex slaves of the Japanese army – has once again been reappropriated by the nationalistic cause because of the failure to bring out the tension between nationalism and women's issues. The 'comfort women' issue is often reinterpreted to produce an appeal to empower the nation via capitalism and militarism. In this case, discursive strategies reliant on universal humanism fail to problematise these issues. Admittedly, in a society that oscillates between the residual mode of an oppressive regime and a quasi-civil mode, the relative distance posited between women's issues and macro-politics has shielded feminist practice from the National Security Law. However, intervention has not been fully realised. By not problematising these issues, some feminists even find themselves performing in a space which is not only almost risk-free, but also profitable due to the service they provide for cultural industries geared to women consumers, such as television, publishing, theatre and movies. In this regard, the recent boom of professionally successful women's autobiographies has been astonishing.

The Seoul Women's Film Festival is located in this rather vague space, where a wide range of women's issues is shared. This has both negative and positive sides. On the one hand, a public platform like this festival can bypass the prescriptive and often dogmatic kind of feminist programme. On the other, it can be easily reincorporated into the hegemonic discourse by allowing itself as a momentary event to be one of the eccentric manifestations of the identity question via cinema.

The growth of cinephilia and the proliferation of theme-based film festivals, and the emergence of identity groups in 1990s Korea may be articulated with one another. There is something in cinephiliac culture that can facilitate the process of identity and subject formation, and festival politics. In cinephilia, people are looking for something they desire to see. In the same vein, film festivals based on themes and identities encourage and invite viewers who desire to 'share' a relatively vague object of desire they are collectively looking for. This situation may have useful political-cultural dimensions in that it both invites an active reading and a sense of a joint project. In this way, it simultaneously engages with group identity processes and individual creative reading activities, both focused on notions of desire defined in terms of cultural politics in given situations. The mode of festival spectatorship that includes discussion materials and seminars mobilises the process of identity and subjectivity formation. Since a film festival may provide a space for sharing between the viewers, programmers, academics and activists involved, it opens up the possibility of activating the viewers' subjective reading around the overall rubric put on the agenda by the festival. An air of eloquent inarticulateness pervades viewers as there is no dogmatically defined cultural-political project.

In the case of the Seoul Women's Film Festival, this is a preliminary process in the articulation of feminist identity and subjectivity, unevenly desired and searched for by female spectators with multiple positions. If this is part of the politics of recognition, it is not so much about recognition by authority, as about the recognition of difference among 'women'. Unlike the 1980s women's movement, which proposed a direct political agenda via the class movement, today's feminist practice is partly but significantly engaged with, and positioned in, a space of negotiation. As well as ticket sales, the festival was supported by an array of sponsorships, including donations from supporters' groups, the city of Seoul and Hyundai Corporation. This indicates where women's cultural politics in the form of the film festival is located.

In a way, the feminist movement is positioned at a conjuncture where emerging identities like queer, sub-cultural youth formations, residual class identity and hegemonic national identity converge in order to contest. How to rearticulate and dearticulate this array of social forces in relation to feminist issues remains an ongoing project. In a society where the notion of the public sphere is not highly valorised or established, the film festival provides an experimental space that might produce an alternative public sphere if not an oppositional one. The banning of the Seoul Queer Film and Video Festival, the Human Rights Watch Film Festival and the IndeForum Festival reveals the rhetoric about the alleged civil society as one which refuses to recognise emerging identities and agencies. From the Orange Tribe to queer, hybrid signifiers of pre-modern and postmodern identities exist. The unacknowledged demands of human rights and freedom of expression, however, demonstrate that the modern notion of the public sphere must not be bypassed. Indeed, the condensed process of locali-sation and *Saegaehwa* globalisation, together with the blend of pre-modern hierarchy and cel-ebratory postmodern consumerism, seems to demand 'going on theorising' by being attentive to the rise of new social movements.

Part II

The cinephiliac culture of 1990s continues even after the IMF crisis of 1997. The issues that now define the global and the local, gender and class, in dialogue with cinematic specificity, manifest themselves within the new public sphere known as the film festival. This is indeed both a cinematic society and societal cinema. The cinema provides a privileged site from where to read Korean society, and vice-versa.

But as the Korean version of the blockbuster hits the box office, both in the domestic and in some other Asian film markets, a certain desire brews at the heart of a Korean film industry that has been bombarded by venture capital. Reclaiming its position as something in-between the Hollywood, the Asian and the Korean cinema industries, South Korean blockbusters desperately seek ways in which an internal cultural incommensurability makes its peace within the optical and aural unconscious of its imagined audience. It is not surpris-ing that the existence of such an audience should largely depend on the use of digital effects, on promotion and marketing systems, and on saturation booking. But these factors alone cannot sustain the larger *cultural* ambitions of the blockbuster movie industry as it aspires to square its Asian targets and global markets with the excess of a guarded nationalism.

The South Korean blockbuster is clearly a compromise between foreign forms and local materials, a compromise itself often staged on a grand scale. This blockbuster offers both a voluntary mimicry of, as well as imagined resistance to, large Hollywood productions, play-ing off various logics of identity and difference in the global culture industry. Backed by the Korean nation-state and its national culture, the South Korean blockbuster presents itself as the cultural difference opposing the homogenising tendencies of Hollywood. But it is an opposition between what Jameson once called 'the Identity of identity and nonidentity' (Jameson and Miyoshi 1998) and, as such, the blockbuster in the South Korean mode incar-nates a contradiction.

As I have shown in my *Blockbuster in Korean Mode: America or Atlantis* (2001), film critics and scholars did note the huge impact of such recent popular cinema on society. This impact ranges from redefinitions of the role of cultural nationalism and globalisation to the new configurations of morality, desire and everydayness. The local film weekly *Cine-21* (2000) sums up the phenomenal success of local blockbusters in the following way:

'As Good as It Gets' succinctly describes the phenomenal success of recent Korean movies. *Chingoo/Friends* (Kyung-Taek Kwak 2001) took 38.3 per cent of the domestic market by drawing an eight million audience. During the summer season, local films like *Shinlaui Dalbam/The Moonlight on Shilla* (Sang-Jin King 2001) and *Yeopgijeogin geunyeo/My Sassy Girl* (Jae-young Kwak 2001) would be competing at the box office. There has been a speculation that local movies would dominate 40 per cent of the domestic market. It is not a slogan anymore, but a reality.

The key issue that local blockbusters bring to the fore lies not so much in the actual amounts of real profit they generate as in the investments they reveal in national cultural value. Since the 1990s, these investments have come alongside with the government's consistent emphasis on the virtues of the movie industry itself as something of an exemplary smog-free, post-industrial sector that sits well with the government's new purpose as presented to the popular imagination. Notwithstanding the often outrageous marketing fees and ticket sales, in 2001 the film industry as a whole made profits that were only equivalent to those of a medium-size corporation. Nevertheless, what the film industry in its blockbuster mode displays and informs are the popular imagining of the working of finance capital and mass investment culture. The 'Netizen Fund' set up on the internet by film companies finds enthusiastic investors, often with such volume of usage that people complain about accessibility. Both the blockbuster movies and the related dissemination of blockbuster culture appear to announce a cultural era of investment that plays a critical role in strengthening the hegemonic dominance of finance capital. This cultural intervention links the perceived interests of tens of millions of workers to its own by embedding 'investor practices' into their everyday lives and by offering them the illusion of a stake within a neo-liberal order.

Paralleling the emphasis among activists and intellectuals on the internet as an alternative public sphere, some film-makers turn to digital video, easily transferable to streaming technology on the net. Access to DSL service is both easy and cheap (approximately $15.00 per month per household) both at home and outside (less than $1 per hour at PC lounges). This kind of public access has introduced two independent but related phenomena into the home. On the one hand, we see a popularisation of cyber trading and stock investment; on the other, the formation of a new kind of public sphere sometimes claimed, perhaps hastily, as cyber democracy. Both activities, of mass investment culture and cyber democracy, stage the *mise en abîme* of the era of globalisation, as well as of what is also claimed to be the network society.

Glimpsing the possibilities of constructing a new critical space, most militant independent film and video groups, many of whom were connected to and have grown out of the 1980s labour and people's movements, have created their websites on which both demo versions and full-length documentaries are freely available. Recently, the female workers' network (www.kwwnet.org/) has been showing a documentary on the issue of how irregular employment was expedited after the IMF crisis. It claims that seven out of ten female workers are now employed as irregular and flexible labour without any benefits. *Patriot Games* (www.redsnowman.com) comes as a forceful attack on nationalism, a taboo area even among the progressive intellectuals of 1980s, not only because of the National Security Law but also because of the way it reflects on the post-colonial and neo-imperial impact of Japan and America. The makers of *Patriot Games* claim the net as a distinctive space for their counter-cinema. They refuse to sell their works on video and have very limited public screenings outside the net.

Trans-cinema

Taking a cue from the proliferation of digital cinema vis-à-vis new modes of activism, I would like to propose a notion of *trans-cinema*, or a cinema that should, I suggest, be attentive to the transformation of its production, distribution and reception modes as shown by independent digital film-making and its availability on the net. Trans-cinema proposes that digital and net cinema, LCD screens (installed in subways, taxis and buses) and gigantic electrified display boards (*Chonkwangpan*) should be seen as spaces into which cinema theories and criticism should intervene. The gigantic screens in downtown Seoul exist as a phantasmatic space permeating and simultaneously constructing the everydayness of the city.

By conceptually framing this new space as trans-cinema, one could further claim that it should not be used or taken solely as advertisement space, and indeed that such space should be opened up to issues concerning the public. Unlike the individual or family viewing patterns that characterise TV, the big monitors installed on the walls of tall buildings inevitably involve collective, public and momentary watching. People in transit get a glimpse of electric displays showing movie trailers, advertisements and news. Gigantic images looming on the walls of buildings certainly create *Blade Runner*-type (R. Scott, 1982) effects that bring differing registers of temporality and spatiality to existing urban space. In a word, in such space a heterotopia is being constantly invented.

In a project entitled the 'Clip City', under the section of City Vision, *Media City Seoul 2000* used these electric display boards to present experimental images by twenty-five media artists including Paik, Namjun. It was an eye-opening experience to watch a one-minute clip of experimental images in the midst of the usual commercials. The tone of festivity around the project was, however, suddenly changed when Song Ilkon's video, entitled *Flush* – a one-minute piece that captured a sequence where a teenage girl delivered and flushed a baby in a toilet – was found among abstract and experimental images on forty-three monumental electric boards (www.nkino.com/moviedom/online_sig.asp). *Flush* soon disappeared from the Clip City project, but it remains an event that used the city's electric display boards as space of public art.

Another, contrasting, example, is *Chonkwangpan*. It was almost an apocalyptic experience to watch the collapse of Songsu bridge and the Sampung department store (both icons of successful modernity) which claimed thousands of lives. *Chonkwangpan* disrupts the demarcations between cinema, TV and billboards. It also blurs the line between public art, commercials and public announcements. In terms of collective spectatorship, *Chonkwangpan* is closer to cinema, but its content – comprising of commercials, news and public announcements – is akin to the content of television. The City Vision/Clip City project shows a communicative and artistic dimension articulated within the public space. *Chonkwangpan* is the kind of trans-cinema and public television that expands existing notions of both cinema and television.

Trans-cinema is a curious entity, an unstable mixture. It cuts across film and digital technology, and challenges the normative process of spectatorship that followed the institutionalisation of cinema. As a successor and a critique of the pairing of world cinema with national cinemas, trans-cinema calls for the need to rethink the constellations of local **197** cinemas in the era of transnational capitalism. As such, trans-cinema, unlike trans*national* cinema, is also a recognition of, and a response to, the increasing rate of inter-Asia cultural traffics, including local blockbuster movies (Hong Kong, China, India and South Korea) and art-house cinema (Taiwanese and Iranian cinema). Inter-Asian blockbusters in particular offer an opportunity to revisit Hollywood-like global culture industry formations, as well as to rethink the ways in which local or regional circuits are simultaneously dearticulated and rearticulated. The genealogy of the cinematic apparatus is embedded in the culture of industrial capitalism. One might need to redefine this apparatus in relation to shifting political economies and their transformation into a global space. In order to articulate the cinematic apparatus in relation to a public sphere that encounters radically shifting socio-economic, political and cultural conditions, it is necessary to note both the persistence of diverse constituencies, as well as the emergence of new ones in cinematically aided 'public spheres'.

As South Korea is exposed to the gaze of powerful global forces, and as it, in turn, mimics this gaze with its desire to be a player in Asia, the dynamics of anxiety and desire that shape those aspirations manifest themselves and register in the Korean blockbusters, where they take unexpected forms. Paralleling the rise of a local popular culture known as the Korean Wave (*hanryu*, composed mainly of TV drama, music and fashion), which is now hitting other parts of Asia, blockbusters have taken to multinationalising their women characters: *Shwiri* (Je-gyu Kang, 1999) features a North Korean espionage female agent (code name Hydra); *Gongdong gyeongbi guyeok JSA* (*Joint Security Area*) (Chan-wook Park, 2000) employs a Swiss-Korean woman as an inspector to resolve a murder case at the JSA. *Failan* (Hae-sung Song, 2001) casts a Hong Kong actress to play a Chinese migrant worker in Korea; Zhang Ziyi (a heroine of *Wu hu cang long* [*Crouching Tiger, Hidden Dragon*], Ang Lee, 2000) plays a Ming princess in *Mus* (*Musa the Warrior*) (Sung-su Kim, 2001); in *Bichunmoo* (*Flying Heaven Martial Arts*) (Young-jun Kim, 2000) the heroine is cast as a Mongolian.

This type of inter-Asian characterisation is quite unprecedented. From the mid-1950s, South Korean films sustained themselves largely through representing women as terrains of traumas concerning modernity and the post-colonial condition. This is the case of, for instance, *Jayu bui* (*Madame Freedom*) (Hyeong-mo Han, 1956), *Miwodo dashi hanbeon* (*Love Me Once Again*) (So-Yeong Jeong, 1968), *Ggotip* (*Petal*) (Sun-Woo Jang, 1996) and *Seopyeonje* (Kwon-taek Im, 1993), to name but a few. When blockbusters feature South Korean women with central roles, these are usually associated with gangsters and monsters, recent examples being *My Wife is a Gangster* (*Chopog Manura*) (Jin-gyu Cho, 2001), *Shinlaui Dalbam* and *Soul Guardians* (*Toemarok*) (Kwang-chun Park, 1998). The disappearance, in these films, of South Korean women, and their transmutation into this new type of character is problematic, especially in circumstances where the identity of a fraternal collective is being reconstituted around notions of global citizenship. At the representational level, it appears that such a global citizenship now excludes South Korean women. The films mentioned above reveal a newly forming nationalism in conjunction with globalisation. In order to acquire a global façade, these films appear to suggest that one needs to make their local women invisible. Predictably the vanishing of South Korean women characters is offset by a new consolidation of homo-social bonding among men. And when Chinese migrant female labour is invoked in *Failan*, she carries the archetypal role of the innocent and self-sacrificing woman – a staple figure of the films and literature of the period of condensed industrialisation in the 1970s. The presumed virtue, now allegedly lost, of the South Korean woman of the recent past is projected upon a woman from a less global/ised sector. As South Korean women disappear, other women are summoned to meet the purposes of nostalgia.

Relegating women to the invisible, blockbusters mobilise male dominant groups such as the army, the Korean Central Intelligence Agency and organised gangsters so as to foreground homo-social relations. The relationships recognisable by and among male members in the group simply become opaque to female characters. The Swiss-Korean heroine in *JSA*, Sophie Chang, is dispatched by the Neutral Nations Supervisory Commission as an investigator to unravel the mystery around the murders of South Korean and North Korean soldiers at the North Korean camp located in the DMZ. The situation becomes totally impenetrable to Sophie. Her investigator's 'look' is constantly denied agency, presumably because the murder and its concealment is provoked, sustained and empowered by a brotherhood based on an ethnic nationalism that transcends the different ideologies that sustained the Cold War. In desperation, Sophie tries to connect to this situation via her deceased father, who had served in the Korean War but had defected to Switzerland after being detained in a prisoner of war camp. Her father's photograph does allude to the complexities of a modern history ravaged by the Cold War, division and migration, but it does not enable Sophie to see through the veiling of the murders among North and South Korean soldiers. Nor does her expertise in international law (Zurich law school graduate) or her half 'ethnicity' as Korean help her.

The disappearance of local women constitutes the structuring absence and a symptom in a new globalised national discourse. The orchestration of transparency and impenetrability bitterly resounding in the global and the national arena increasingly stages an orchestra without women players. A retreat of gender politics, indeed. And this retreat doesn't stop at the level of representation. Along with the official declaration of the collapse of public intellectuals and their replacement with twenty- or thirty-something young venture capitalists as the 'new intellectuals', the feminist intervention in the public sphere attuned to a globalised national is doubly denied.

Conclusion

These questions demand to be reviewed within a perspective distinct from the trinity of state, civil society and public sphere. They require a theorisation of an uncertain zone of political society, that is *min-jian* (*min* signifying, roughly, 'folk', 'people' or 'commoners' society' and *jian* meaning 'in-between' and 'space'). *Min-jian* is the space that has allowed 'the commoners' to survive, so that no radical break could take place following the violence of a modernising state and civil society.[7] Just as for the forked tongue used in the postcolonial context, one needs to be strategically dexterous with the use and promise of the public sphere. Historically, the notion of the public sphere has constantly made gestures towards including the sector of the excluded. Because of this hopelessly unattainable ideal, it accidentally redraws a map even though there is a limit. Being wary of contingent open- **199** ing in its true sense of *Öffentlichkeit* but certainly not being dependent upon it, one needs to make an 'event' out of the contingent and accidental opening of an episodic public sphere. Film festivals like the Women's Film Festival in Seoul, the Queer Film Festival, the Labour Film Festival and the Human Rights Watch Film Festival are such episodic instances. At the same time, attention must be drawn to the way in which normative notions of the public sphere fail to deal with and account for the persistence and transformation of political society and of *min-jian*. What is needed are frameworks that are attentive to the 'in-between' and emergent social/cultural movements.

Notes

1. This text originated as a paper entitled 'Look Who's Talking: Media and Public Sphere', presented at a UC Berkeley Conference. A revised version was delivered at the Asian Women's Forum at the 4th Seoul International Women's Film Festival and at the ICA Pre-Conference at Tokyo University. I thank Chris Berry, Kim Eunshil, Kang Myung-Koo and Yoshimi Shunya for their kind invitations. Thanks to their encouragement, this paper has become a trans-Asia project. My thanks also go to Naifei Ding, Kuan-Hsing Chen and Ashish Rajadhyaksha for their suggestions. Sections of Part I of this text originally appeared in an article entitled ' "Cine-Mania" or Cinephilia: Film Festivals and the Identity Question', *UTS Review* 4 (2) (Nov. 1998): 174–87.
2. This statement appeared in a South Korean government advertisement in the *International Herald Tribune*, 26–7 July 1997.
3. For instance, the Human Rights Watch Film Festival and the Labour Film Festival are organised by activists whose organisations are rooted in the 1980s People (*minjung*) movement, whereas the Seoul Queer Film and Video Festival is steered by a group of gay and lesbian activists who have emerged in the 1990s. The Seoul Women's Film Festival is located in and between these two categories.
4. The monthly magazines published by the major newspapers, such as the *Monthly Chosun* and the *Monthly Dongah,* usually deal with political and social issues, focusing on political leaders and scandals. The *Hangyurae Daily Newspaper*, set up in the late 1980s, issued the progressive weekly magazine *Hangyurae 21*, which became the leading magazine of its kind. It also replaced the dominance of monthly magazines with a weekly one.
5. The name of the Yata Tribe came from their style of starting a date: cruising the night streets in a fancy car, a male would signal his interest by shouting 'Yata!' (meaning simply 'get in the car'). There are many accounts of the origin of the Orange Tribe. One story claims that the alleged Orange Tribe starts a dating request by sending a cup of orange juice to the desired person. Yata and Orange tribe members have similar class affiliations and are both connected to the 1990s bubble economy.
6. The relevant issues have also been raised through cinema. Films such as *Orlando* (S. Potter, 1992), *Antonia's Line* (M. Gorris, 1995), *Thelma and Louise* (R. Scott, 1991) and local productions, such as *Nazen moksor* (*The Murmuring*) (Young-joo Byun, 1995), a film on the question of comfort women, or *Geudaneanui blue* (*The Blue in You*) (Hyun-seung Lee, 1992), on the conflict between marriage and profession, have contributed to the dissemination of these issues.
7. *Min-jian* is a concept developed by Chen, Kuan-Hsing (2002).

References

Chen, Kuan-Hsing (2002), 'Civil Society and Min Jian: On Political Society and Popular Democracy', unpublished paper.

Fraser, Nancy (1997), *Justice Interruptus: Critical Reflections on the 'Postsocialist' Condition*, New York: Routledge.

Hall, Stuart (1994), 'Cultural Identity and Diaspora', in Williams, Patrick and Chrisman, Laura (eds), *Colonial Discourse and Postcolonial Theory: A Reader*, New York: Columbia University Press: 392–403.

Jameson, Fredric (1998), 'Notes on Globalization as a Philosophical Issue', in Jameson and Miyoshi (1998).

Soyoung, Kim (ed.) (2001), *Blockbuster in Korean Mode: America or Atlantis*, Seoul: Hyunshil Munhwa Yongu.

15 The Hidden Conscience of Estimated Palestine[1]

Elia Suleiman

This epilogue (epitaph) is dedicated to the Palestinian TV to be. It is written in the manner a schoolchild writes, when asked by the teacher to do homework about his or her wish for what she or he wants to become, when he or she grows old and mature.

Here are some wishful thoughts, a chronicle of death foretold.

What I wish not to expect from switching on my national TV:

I wish when I switch on my TV not to mistake my national TV channel for other neighbour national TVs.

I wish not to contemplate our national flag for long or short pauses except if the authority insists, then at the end of the broadcast day. And when, and if, our national needs are met, then I will wish to use our national flag at the beginning of the broadcast day, but as colour bars.

I wish not to see the anchorwoman/man all dressed up, made up stressed up centred and giving petty news details such as the whereabouts of high officials. I wish her/him to speak in relaxed fashion, not to worry about control rooms, not the one nearby her studio nor the control room outside which is never so far. I wish her to speak in slang here and there not in the archaic Arabic that often sounds like nineteen hundred decorative verse lingo emptied of meaning.

I wish not to keep flipping the cable channels to return to our national TV still flickering shaking hand and smile images.

I expect our national TV to reach beyond our national needs and not to still be pleading for our national rights which are our national rights which we should not have to plead
for.

I wish our national TV to transmit images that undifferentiate colour, gender or race and melt them in the pot: images that bulldoze boundaries, not apply and conform them to existing ones. I wish these images to enter the site of transgression, interrogate the role of traditionalism, sexism and colonial discourses that have been inherited, willingly or unwillingly, by decades or shall I say centuries, of various levels and layers and other kinds of occupations, including that which eventually led to the occupation of the soul.

I wish our national TV not to over-folklorise. Considering the political shifts that are taking place, certain cultural codes, particularly those that have been employed for political manifestations, have to be reconsidered. One example is the Dabki, which in recent years seems to have been multi-functional; a Dabki for a solidarity conference, a Dabki for a protest. A Dabki for a national festivity. A love Dabki and a war Dabki. Dabki with a sickle and Dabki with a sword. And finally Dabki as art expression. In a semi-fata morgana of cultural production, primarily because of occupation, we were left with almost nothing but to chew on Dabki and re-store it in our hump of conscious memory.

I wish my national TV to open a cultural dialogue that would not cater to or be composed of the power hungry shops, some of whom took a free ride after the signing of the treaty, and others who are critical of it, yet all are running after the foreign funds, claiming they are cultural representatives. During the Intifada, these shops played the role of mediators for foreign TV companies who used them as trace guides and bought their kuffia credibility. They were used as front liners who went deep into the 'jungle' to gather footage. They also used other Palestinians who lived inside the 'jungle' itself to do the mission impossible in order to make it possible for political peeping toms. Small cameras were given to amateurs and the footage gathered was exoticised and sensationalised because of its immaturity and unprofessionalism, in its voyeuristic nature, because it was a look from within.

I wish our national TV not to over-sentimentalise land or at least remind its viewers every once in a while that earth is a fragment of the Earth. I wish our national TV not to over-emphasise our right to exist on this land. There are other ways of exercising this right. We can say that at least we know that we exist. The question is how to exist. And how can culture play a role in proposing other ways of existing. What culture can do is to create debate. And debate feeds on difference. We must expand difference, not uniform it, which is another way of saying freedom of expression.

I wish this TV to be wary of the ongoing 'Mass-Peaceteria' (derivative of peace hysteria) imposed on artistic expression. The so-called dialogue initiating co-productions; a funding McCarthyism that has been initiated lately whereby a vague or (in)visible guideline indicates that if you have no intention of including a moment of true love between an Israeli and a Palestinian, a soldier crying over spilt milk – in this case the blood of a Palestinian – or a terrorist gone vegetarian, you are not eligible. And you don't have to be against the peace process to be marginalised but by simply not reciting the declared constitution. **203**

This is not to speak of the dilemma of identity versus eligibility. Who is eligible to be Palestinian according to the present geopolitical reality is quite intriguing. I am from Nazareth, living in East Jerusalem, but it is only recently that I discovered that Jesus is from Gaza.

As a partial result of this funding constraint, I have noticed recently that the friendly match sport events have lent themselves to art as we have seen lately in a few assimilationist theatre productions: playing the Happy Ending already at the beginning of the play by a joint team of actors made of Israelis and Palestinians as they sing a song borrowed from Shakespeare, or calling a production 'Jericho something or another'. In one such production I was left with a nauseating feeling similar to that which I felt after I first heard the hypocritical song 'We Are The World'. I plead to such productions to give peace a chance.

An Egyptian director invited to the Haifa Film Festival was interviewed a few months ago on Israeli TV. The director was asked if he was not afraid to be put on the blacklist because of coming to Israel. The director, seemingly so enchanted, in a euphoria of reigning love and peace, replied that now it is those who are against peace who will be put on the blacklist. It might be a slip of the tongue or simple ignorance, or otherwise, a pure vulgar opportunism of the peace process. However, we ought to be wary of a potential state of reversed McCarthyism. There seems to be an undeclared war going on, a war between the ones who say there is a war and the ones who say there isn't.

Cultural codes need not be a didactic language; neither ideological nor pointed. Neither visual mobilisation of images, nor images for mobilisation. A re-reading of the concept of who is Palestinian is at this time more necessary than ever. One proposition is to employ interculturalism to re-examine notions of tribalism, in which nationalism is one of its outstanding features. The danger of being named Palestinian to fit a particular quota is admitting to a ghettoisation on a national level.

For that reason this TV may strategise Palestinianly while it lets itself loose and criss-crosses boundaries. We might discover that so many cultures and arts are just as Palestinian as the Palestinians. We as Other and Other as a constant presence.

Satire can be one of those cultural codes that can be employed. Externalising stereotypes is a conscious production of stereotypes which exhausts their essence. The danger is we protect the system from parody and critical humour. We ought to be wary of this kind of self-defence, also referred to as self-censorship. The latter can result in us becoming our own stereotypes.

Ridicule the image that we produce of ourselves and cancel out their power. Constitute new ones to avoid the danger of one clotted truth. A one truth is a stagnant truth. Real as it can get, it becomes our only reality and we become its prisoners. A diversity of potential truth, constantly shifting, proposes a diversity of choices of who we are and who we want to be.

If I summon the above stutters I uttered in a rather chaotic fashion, I can trace a text of a critical viewpoint by nature but which can only reflect my strong desire to belong.

Another layer of reading this text can reveal a subtext read between the lines which hints to my shifting positioning regarding the status quo. In another way of telling, and for this occasion, I appropriate an Anthem from the writings of Leonard Cohen.[2]

> The birds they sang
> at the break of day
> Start again
> I heard them say
>
> Don't dwell on what
> has passed away
> or what is yet to be.
>
> The wars they will
> be fought again
> The holy dove
> be caught again
> bought and sold
> and bought again
> the dove is never free.
>
> Ring the bells that still can ring
> Forget your perfect offering.
> There is a crack in everything.
> That's how the light gets in.

Notes

1. This article is an extract from a longer work, also called 'The Hidden Conscience of Estimated Palestine' and was originally published in *UTS Review* 2(2) (Nov. 1996): 163–7.
2. Cohen, Leonard (1973), 'Anthem', in *Stranger Music: Selected Poems and Songs*, New York: Pantheon Books: 373.

Part III Crossroads

16   Early Cinema and Modernity in Latin America[1]

Ana M. Lopez

The early years of the silent cinema in Latin America, roughly 1896–1920, are the least discussed and most difficult to document in Latin American media history. This period was overshadowed by wars and other cataclysmic political and social events and, subsequently its significance was eclipsed by the introduction and development of other media – the 'golden ages' of sound cinema and radio in the 1940s and 1950s, television in the 1960s and 1970s. These developments seem to 'fit' better with the narratives of Latin American modernity some scholars want to tell, be they tales of foreign technological and ideological domination and inadequate imitation (à la Mattelart 1983 and Schiller 1976), or contemporary chronicles of global mediations (à la Barbero 1987). Nonetheless, in this early period, we find not only complex global interactions but also extensive evidence of the contradictory and ambivalent transformative processes that would mark the later reception and development of the sound cinema and other media. These early forms of mediated modernities already complexly refracted and inflected the production of self and other imagined communities and, I argue, lay bare the central characteristics of the processes through which subsequent media engaged with and contributed to the specificity of Latin American modernity.

The Arrival

According to Paulo Antonio Paranguá, 'The cinema appear[ed] in Latin America as another foreign import' (Paranaguá 1985: 9). This is perhaps the most salient characteristic of the experience of early Latin American cinema: rather than developed in proto-organic synchronicity with the changes, technological inventions and 'revolutions' that produced modernity in Western Europe and the US, the appearance and diffusion of the cinema in Latin America followed the patterns of neo-colonial dependency typical of the region's position in the global capitalist system at the turn of the century.

[T]he cinematic apparatus – a manufactured product – appeared, fully formed, in Latin American soil a few months after its commercial introduction abroad. Subsequently, on the very same ships and railroads that carried raw materials and agricultural products to Europe and the US, Lumière and Edison cameramen returned with fascinating views of exotic lands, **209** peoples and their customs. Thus, in reference to Latin America, it is difficult to speak of the cinema and modernity as 'points of reflection and covergence' (Charney and Schwartz 1995: 1), as is the presumption in US and European early cinema scholarship. Rather, the development of early cinema in Latin America was not directly linked to previous large-scale transformations of daily experience resulting from industrialisation, rationality and the technological transformation of modern life, because those processes were only just beginning to occur across the continent. In turn-of-the-century Latin America, modernity was, above all, still a fantasy and a profound desire.

In Latin America, modernisation has been a decentred, fragmentary and uneven process.[2] As José Joaquín Brunner (1993: 41) has argued, modernity (and, simultaneously, postmodernity) in Latin America is characterised by cultural heterogeneity, by the multiple rationalities and impulses of private and public life. Unequal development led not only to 'segmentation and segmented participation in the world market of messages and symbols' but also to 'differential participation according to *local codes of reception*' that produced a decentring of 'Western culture as it [was] represented by the manuals'. In other words, Latin American modernity has been a global, intertextual experience, addressing impulses and models from abroad, in which every nation and region created, and creates, its own ways of playing with and at modernity. These 'spectacular experiments'[3] constituted what Angel Rama (1996: 99) called 'the momentous second birth of modern Latin America', which took place as *la ciudad letrada* or the lettered city – the nexus of lettered culture, state power and urban location that had facilitated the continent-wide colonising process – entered the twentieth century. Albeit intensely engaging with European and, later, US culture, the intellectual sectors Rama dubbed the *letrados* were nevertheless able to define local modernities.

Another crucial sign of Latin American modernity is a kind of temporal warp in which the pre-modern coexists and interacts with the modern, a differential plotting of time and space, and, subsequently, of history and time. In Anibal Quijano's words: 'In Latin America, what is sequence in other countries is a simultaneity. It is also a sequence. But in the first place it is a simultaneity' (Quijano 1993: 149). Rather than a devastating process that ploughs over the traditional bases of a social formation – all that is solid melting into air – Latin American modernity is produced via an ambiguous symbiosis of traditional experiences/practices and modernising innovations, such as the technologies of visuality epitomised by the cinema. To quote Brunner again: 'Not all solid things but rather all symbols melt into air' (Brunner 1993: 53). This warp has profound consequences for any historical project: because of temporal ambiguity and asynchronicity, teleological narratives of evolution become mired in deadends and failed efforts and do not do justice to the circuitous routes of Latin American modernity.

The cinematic apparatus appeared in Latin America quickly, less than six months after its commercial introduction in Europe. There is journalistic evidence that British Brighton School films (using the Vivomatograph) were premiered in Buenos Aires as early as 6 July 1896 (not surprising, given the ongoing neo-colonial relationship between Argentina and

England during this period). Confirmed screenings using the Lumière apparatus (the Ciné-matographe) took place shortly thereafter: in Rio de Janeiro (8 July 1896), Montevideo and Buenos Aires (18 July), Mexico City (14 August), Santiago de Chile (25 August), Guatemala City (26 September) and Havana (24 January 1897). Edison's Vitascope took only slightly longer to arrive. First was Buenos Aires (20 July 1896), followed by Mexico City (22 October), Lima (2 January 1897) and Rio de Janeiro (30 January).[4] These locations are not surprising, for they follow well-established routes of transatlantic commerce through the most advanced cities of the continent, which were already in the throes of modernisation.

Arguably, Buenos Aires was ahead of the pack. Looking at some of the most salient indicators typically used to assess modernisation, Buenos Aires was the centre of national industrial activity (through its ports flowed the wool, beef and leather that arrived on the British-sponsored railroad system linking the city to interior production centres; it housed 600,000 of the nation's four million inhabitants); it had an efficient electric streetcar system (since 1890), a reliable electrical infrastructure that serviced business interests, and two telephone companies (with more than 10,000 subscribers by 1900). Furthermore, its population was cosmopolitan; the government-encouraged waves of immigration from Europe, beginning in 1895, had changed the physiognomy of the city, producing a fluid constituency and sumptuous public works and private palaces that coexisted alongside *conventillos* (tenement housing) where labourers and poor immigrants resided. Also quite modern by continental standards, Rio had electric streetcars, telegraphs, telephones and electricity, although the latter was unstable until completion of a hydroelectric plant in nearby Ribeirão das Lajes in 1905. Like Buenos Aires, Rio's population was cosmopolitan: Rio (and later São Paulo) was a magnet for migrants from the northeast and immigrants from Europe. In contrast, a capital city like Lima was showing only the beginning signs of modernisation. Despite urban renewal, funded by the rubber boom that would eventually modernise the city (especially significant was the redesign of the principal urban arteries of La Colmena and the Paseo Colón), Lima lacked a reliable source of electricity and was the centre of a quasi-feudal state that historian Jorge Basadre calls the 'República Aristocrática'. Peru was a nation in which only 5 per cent of the population had the right to vote and in which that 5 per cent governed and suppressed all peasant protests and urban popular movements. Further, its Europeanised elites, not the nation's majority indigenous population, controlled the country. Thus, it is not surprising that the 'modernity' of early cinema echoed more resoundingly – and lastingly – in Buenos Aires and Rio than in Lima, since even the simple films shown at these first screenings already exemplified a particularly modern form of aesthetics responding to the specificity of modern urban life.

Porteños (Buenos Aires residents) took to the medium immediately; there is evidence that the first Argentine film – views of Buenos Aires – may have been produced as early as 1896. By the turn of the century, businessmen specialising in photography had mastered the new medium's technology and begun to produce a steady stream of actualities and proto-fictional shorts. Other impresarios included imported and national films in their popular public entertainment venues (theatres and, in the summer, open-air festivals) and, as early as 1901, **211** had even built dedicated movie houses. *Cariocas* (Rio de Janeiro residents) also became early enthusiasts, but despite a series of 'firsts' and the efforts of pioneers, the medium did not become established until reliable electricity was available in 1905. In contrast, the cinema acquired a foothold in Lima much more slowly. Although there is evidence that a national short may have been produced in 1899, the first confirmed filming did not take place in Peru until 1904; newsreel or actuality production was not consistent until 1909–15; dedicated movie theatres did not appear until 1909, the first fiction film was not produced until 1915, and the cinema did not develop beyond its first documentary impulses until the 1920s.

The diffusion of the cinema throughout the interior of Latin American countries followed a pattern determined by, among other things, the level of development of railroads and other modern infrastructures. In Mexico, for example, where a national railroad system was already well established by the turn of the century, the Edison equipment enchanted Guadalajara, the nation's second-largest city, in 1896, and by 1898 the Lumière apparatus had already appeared in Mérida, San Juan Bautista, Puebla and San Luis Potosí. Conversely, more inaccessible regions – that is, regions marginal to international trade – were not exposed to the new invention until significantly later. For example, residents of the remote community of Los Mulos in Cuba's Oriente province did not see movies 'for the first time' until the mid-1960s, made possible through the auspices of the Cuban film institute's (ICAIC) *cine-móvil* programme. The experience is documented in Octavio Cortàzar's short film *Por primera vez* (*For the First Time*) (1967).

212 *Por primera vez* (Octavio Cortázar, 1967)

More significant than the speed of diffusion of the technological apparatus is how it was used at various sites and locales – the process of adaptation, contestation and innovation in the context of the international cinematic marketplace. The cinema experienced by Latin Americans was – and still is – predominantly foreign. This is a factor of tremendous significance in the complex development of indigenous forms, always caught in a hybrid dialectics of invention and imitation, as well as in the development of the form of experience – mass spectatorship – necessary to sustain the medium.

Peripheral Attractions

The early films that arrived in Latin America alongside the new technology were part of what Tom Gunning and other film scholars have characterised as the 'cinema of attractions' (Elsaesser 1990: 56–62). Instead of the narrative forms that would later become hegemonic, the cinema of attractions (predominant in the US until 1903–4) was based on an aesthetics of astonishment; it appealed to viewers' curiosity about the new technology and fulfilled it with brief moments of images in movement. It was, above all, a cinema of thrills and surprises, assaulting viewers with stimulating sights; in Miriam Hansen's terms, it was 'presentational rather than representational' (Williams 1997: 137).

In Latin America, this aesthetics of astonishment was complicated by the ontological and epistemological status of the apparatus. In fact, the Latin American context, in which, despite all attempts to produce films locally, imported films tended to dominate the market and have usually been the most popular, leads us to pose the question, 'Indeed attracted, but to what?' The cinematic attraction is 'attractive' in and of itself *and* as an import. However, beyond any purported fit with the experience of modernity in local urban life, its appeal is – and perhaps first of all – the appeal of the other, the shock of difference. With its vistas of sophisticated modern cities and customs (ranging from Lumière's rather sophisticated workers leaving the factory and magnificent locomotives to Edison's scandalous kiss), the imported views could produce the experience of an *accessible* globality among the urban citizens of Latin America, many of them less than a generation away from the 'old world'. Fashion, consumer products, other new technologies, and different ways of experiencing modern life and its emotions and challenges[5] were suddenly available with tremendous immediacy: 'In its earliest days, [t]he cinema was an opening to the world' (Caneto et al., 1996: 31). But to the degree that that experience was desired and delightful, it also created profound ambivalence and was a source of anxiety.

The cinema's complex images of distance and otherness problematised the meaning of locality and self. Where were they to be found – these spectators of the 'new world' in this brave new 'other' world of specular and spectacular thrills? On the one hand, the cinema fed the national self-confidence that its own modernity was 'in progress' by enabling viewers to share and participate in the experience of modernity as developed elsewhere, to respond to the thrill. On the other hand, to do so, the national subject was also caught up in a dialectics of seeing: viewers had to assume the position of spectators and become voyeurs of, rather than participants in, modernity. To the degree that the cinema of attractions depended on a highly conscious awareness of the film image *as* image and of the act of looking itself, it also 213 produced a tremendously self-conscious form of spectatorship in that Latin America was almost immediately translated as the need to assert the self as modern but also and, more lastingly, as different, ultimately as a national subject. Thus, the earliest Latin American films recirculated the parameters of modernity as cinematically experienced elsewhere, while simultaneously enabling viewers to participate in and promote whatever forms of that modernity were available locally.

In its form and content, early Latin American cinema clearly resonates with the technological changes and innovations generally associated with modernisation, echoing how the intersection of cinema and modernity was evidenced in Western Europe and the US while demonstrating the desire to identify 'attractions' locally in order to exploit the incipient modernity of each site. For example, in response to the great impact of the Lumières' *Arrival of a Train at the Station* (1895), one of the films included in most 'first' Latin American screenings, local film-makers sought in the developed and/or developing national railroad and transportation systems an equivalent symbol and the duplication of the amazement produced by the French film. One of the first national 'views' filmed in Buenos Aires, screened in November 1896, was precisely of the arrival of a train at a local station, described pointedly in the press as 'the arrivals of our trains' (*El Diario* 7 November 1896, cited in Caneto et al. 1996: 34). Slightly later, in 1901, Eugenio Py chronicled the *Llegada de un tramway* (*Arrival of a Streetcar*), undoubtedly seeking a similar effect. In Brazil, Vittorio de Maio filmed *Chegado de um tren a Petrópolis* (*Arrival of a Train in Petrópolis*) and *Ponto terminal dal linha dos bondes* (*Streetcar Line Terminal*) in 1897; their exhibition at the Teatro Casino Fluminense in Petrópolis (a mountain resort city near Rio) in May 1897 was widely advertised.

The Novelty of Objectivity

The cinema's impulse towards display and spectacle was ambivalently linked with the technology's purported affinity with science, much lauded in Latin America[6] and aligned with then hegemonic positivist ideologies of progress. Positivism and modernity were themselves inextricably linked; the former was perceived as the theoretical matrix that would permit the achievement of the latter. The idea that 'scientific' rational knowledge could control the chaos of natural forces and social life was the intellectual rationale for the ideology of 'Order and Progress', the motto of more than one nation and a sublation that condensed the contradictory impulses of the evolving 'modern' rationalities of economics and politics in still overwhelmingly traditional societies. In fact, only a few early films documented 'scientific' projects. In Argentina, surgical pioneer Alejandro Posadas recorded two of his surgeries – a hernia operation and the removal of a pulmonary cyst – in Buenos Aires in 1900 (both films are extant). In Brazil, the preventive work of Oswaldo Cruz was the subject of *Erradicação da febre amarela no Rio de Janeiro* (*Eradication of Yellow Fever in Rio*) (1909), while a somewhat precarious dental extraction in Venezuela was the subject of what may be the earliest views shot in Latin America. The film, *Un célebre especialista sacando muelas en el Gran Hotel Europa* (*A Famous Specialist Pulling Teeth in the Gran Hotel Europa*), was made by Guillermo and Manuel Trujillo Duran and shown for the first time in January 1897. The cinema's veneer of scientific objectivity – its ability to display the physical world – perfectly rationalised its more thrilling appeals.

Also linked to the ideology of scientific rationality and progress was the insistence of local inventors on improving and expanding the medium. In 1898 Mexico, for example, someone 'invented' the 'ciclofotógrafo', a camera attached to a bicycle for travelling shots, and Luis Adrián Lavie announced his 'aristógrafo', which allowed spectators to see motion pictures in 3-D. In Argentina, three inventors patented a series of machines, among them the 'estereobioscopio', which produced moving images with depth. The cinema was welcomed first and foremost as a sign of and tool for expressing the rationalist impetus of the modern. It was thoroughly aligned with the civilising desires of the urban modernising elites and disassociated from the 'barbarism' of national 'others'.

In Mexico, it was, above all, the cinema's purported objectivity that first endeared it to the highly positivist intelligentsia of the Porfiriato, who were fully committed to its leader's 'Order and Progress' motto. Linking the cinema with the also new and booming illustrated press and arguing that it was against the medium's nature to lie, early commentators railed stridently against the film *Duelo a pistola en el bosque de Chapultepec* (*Pistol Duel in Chapultepec Forest*) (1896), a reconstruction shot by Lumière cameramen Bertrand von Bernard and Gabriel Veyre of a duel between two deputies, as 'the most serious of deceits, because audiences, perhaps the uninformed or foreigners [w]ill not be able to tell whether it is a simulacrum of a duel or a real honorific dispute' (de los Reyes 1972: 104). The concern over Mexico's image abroad is explicit; after all, the film was shot by Lumière cameramen charged with collecting foreign views for international distribution, at a time when the government was already beginning to organise its pavilion for the 1900 Paris Universal Exhibition. But the paternalism explicit in this commentary – the 'uninformed' (the national illiterate masses) – indicates the unstable relationship between the regime's much-touted 'progress' and those it had bypassed. For the majority of Mexico City inhabitants, 'progress' was experienced as entertainment, not science; they had already gathered in the streets to watch the installation of electrical power posts and a parade of new bicycles they still could not afford. The cinema was next in line, and, to the degree that it was adopted by the masses and developed its 'attractions' it was repudiated by the elites. Thus, the cinema functioned as a modernising force, not according to positivist scientific parameters but by consolidating the formation of a modern urban audience. Nonetheless, although abandoned by the *científicos*[7] and eventually given over to the masses as spectacle, the Mexican cinema remained bound to the myth of objectivity, to its value as 'truth'.

If at first the illusion of movement necessarily involved the disavowal of the frailty of our knowledge of the physical world, that thrilling anxiety was quickly sublimated into the still-shocking experience of seeing 'history' – near and far – as it happened. Stimulated by the surprise of being able to see imported images, whether real or reconstructed, of the Spanish-American war,[8] local film-makers throughout the continent exploited the ostensible objectivity of the medium to record current events. The attraction of history in the making allowed the still economically unstable medium to continue to attract audiences and develop commercially; as the novelty of the first shocks of movement wore off, the focus shifted to **215** monumental current events. In fact, it has been argued that locally financed and local interest actuality newsreels constitute the only consistent and unbroken cinematic tradition of early Latin American cinema. Beginning with the chronicling of the visit to Buenos Aires by the Brazilian president – *Viaje del Doctor Campos Salles a Buenos Aires* (*Trip of Dr Campos Salles to Buenos Aires*) (1900) – and, the next year, naval operations – *Maniobras navales de Bahía Blanca* (*Naval Operations in Bahía Blanca*) (1901) – the company of Argentine pioneer Max Glucksmann, Casa Lepage, which specialised in actualities, produced an outstanding record of the Argentine public sphere throughout the silent and sound periods. Joining in this endeavour were other entrepreneurs, among them Julio Irigoyen (*Noticiero Buenos Aires*) and Federico Valle. Valle entered the field shortly after his 1911 arrival in Argentina (after working with Méliès in France) and produced, among other films, the *Film Revista Valle* weekly newsreel from 1920 to 1930.

Actualities were also the mainstay of the early film business in Brazil. Antonio Leal in Rio and regional producers (especially in Curitiba) were soon joined by Marc Ferrez and his son Julio, Francisco Serrador, the Botelho brothers, and others in the provinces. In Brazil, however, the novelty of news also took on a spectacular character as sensational crimes, already popularised by the illustrated press, were meticulously restaged and shot on location. Films like *Os estranguladores* (*The Stranglers*) (Francisco Marzullo or Antonio Leal, 1908) and the two versions of *O crime da mala* (*The Suitcase Crime*) (Franciso Serrador and Marc Ferrez and son, respectively, both 1908) were wildly successful: the audience's familiarity with the crimes enabled the film-makers to tell their 'stories' efficiently without intertitles or internal continuity.

Another restaging of a news story, Antonio Leal's *O comprador de ratos* (*The Rat Buyer*) (1908) is of particular interest, as it unwittingly captures the idiosyncrasies of modernity in the midst of underdevelopment, thus serving as a particularly vivid example of the contradictions produced by 'misplaced ideas'.[9] During the Oswaldo Cruz-led campaign to eradicate yellow fever in Rio, the government announced that it would buy dead rats by the pound. The inhabitants of Rio's poor neighbourhoods found themselves in the midst of a thriving industry, breeding and fattening rats to sell to the government. In a brilliant allegory of modernity in Latin America, *O comprador* tells the story of a Niterói native who attempted to sell thousands of rodents until the scam was discovered.

Following the Lumière model, Mexican pioneers also took to current events, perhaps with the greatest enthusiasm after Salvador Toscano exhibited the actualities *Guanajuato destruido por las inundaciones* (*Guanajuato Destroyed by Floods*) (1905) and *Incendio del cajón de la Valenciana* (*Fire at the Valenciana Warehouse*) (1905). In 1906, both Toscano and his principal competitor, Enrique Rosas, rushed to chronicle an official trip to Yucatán by President Díaz, whose image was still of great interest to audiences; their films exhibited a preoccupation with formal structure that pushed them beyond the simplicity of the typical actuality. Following an excruciatingly linear logic dependent on editing, Toscano's film narrated the presidential trip from beginning (Díaz's departure by train from Mexico City) to end (his farewells to Yucatán), thus substituting a chronology that was absolutely faithful to the pro-

216 filmic event for narrative development.

Similarly, the Alva brothers' *Entrevista Díaz-Taft* (*Díaz-Taft Interview*) (1909), a report of the Díaz and William Howard Taft meetings in Ciudad Juarez and El Paso, employs the chronological 'record of a trip' structure, but it is mediated by two additional concerns: a visible effort to record both sides of the event (some of President Taft's trip as well as Díaz's) and a willingness to fiddle with the chronology of the pro-filmic event to augment the narrative impact. As Aurelio de los Reyes demonstrates, the film-makers altered the sequence of events towards the end of the film in order to have the film end on an apotheosis, with the image of both presidents on the steps of the customs building in Juarez. This image is the visual equivalent of their interview, but it is also strongly marked by an accidental pro-filmic action: as the presidents descend the steps, an observer waves a flag in front of the camera and, for an instant, the screen is filled by the flag and its large slogan, 'Viva la República', visually affirming the national despite the alleged impartiality of its treatment. In fact, the cinema's 'truth value' was selectively applied: the Porfirian cinema was basically escapist and did not record the more disagreeable aspects of national life, such as the bloody strikes in Cananea (1906) and Río Blanco (1907), the violence and poverty of urban ghettoes, or the injustices of rural life.

Attractions of Nationness

Beyond the drive to identify 'local' modern thrills – almost, but not quite, the same as those of the imported views – or to record current events, the new technology was used for the benefit of the imagined national community, to negotiate precisely the conflicts generated by the dilemmas of a modernity that was precariously balanced between indigenous traditions and foreign influences, between nationalist aspiration and internationalist desires. Thus, the fascination with the epiphenomenal manifestations of modernity and their perceptual thrills was inflected with explicit exaltations of nationness – these are not just 'our' railroads but symbols of our national *belongingness*, in a sense as 'modern' as the new technological forms themselves – linked in many instances to current events.

Following the non-chronological plotting of time and history suggested earlier, this process occurred both sequentially and simultaneously with the fascination with modern technology and current events described above. In late 1897, for example, a notice in the Buenos Aires newspaper *El Diario* announced not only a filming of local events but the time and location: 'The views will be photographed in the morning. The first will be of bicyclists in Palermo park at 7.30 AM. Those who would like to see their figures circulating on the screen of this theatre should take notice' (Caneto et al. 1996: 35). Similarly, a few months later, *La Nación* remarked in its column 'Vida Social':

The views shot in Palermo, which will be projected by the marvelous machine next Monday on the stage of the Casino theater, will perhaps be of greater interest that the landscapes and exotic scenes reproduced by the 'American Biograph'. We are assured that these views are as sharp as the European and that we shall clearly recognize many of our socially prominent citizens.[10]

Clearly invoking another kind of desire or 'attraction', these notices posited spectatorial position predicated on identification and self-recognition, which was but an embryonic form of cinematic nationness. It was also a process markedly aligned with the existing power structure, the appeal was not just that one would see ordinary Buenos Aires citizens but socially prominent ones – metaphorical stand-ins for the nation itself.

In Latin America as a whole, the cinema was, from its earliest moments, closely aligned with those in power, be they wealthy and socially prominent or simply in government, and this alignment was a first step towards nationalist projects. The first films, photographed in Mexico, for example, were not landscapes or street scenes but carefully orchestrated views of Porfirio Díaz (recently re-elected for a fourth presidential term), his family and his official retinue shot by Lumière cameramen von Bernard and Veyre in 1898. The young Frenchmen recognised the need to secure the dictator's goodwill to proceed in their commercial enterprises and arranged a private screening of the new technology for Díaz and his family in Chapultepec. During the five months they remained in Mexico, they filmed the president, who quickly recognised the propagandistic value of the new medium, at all sorts of official and familiar events. As one historian has remarked, Porfirio Díaz was, by default, the first 'star' (attraction?) of the Mexican cinema: his on-screen appearances were enthusiastically hailed with rousing 'Vivas!'.

Akin to the Mexican example, the first two views filmed in Bolivia were explicit paeans to the power structure. Both *Retratos de personajes históricos y de actualidad* (*Portraits of Historical and Contemporary Figures*) (1904) and the very popular *La exhibición de todos los personajes ilustres de Boliva* (*The Exhibition of All the Illustrious Characters of Bolivia*) (1909) were designed to align the new technology with those who effectively controlled and defined the nation *and* to display them for the enjoyment and recognition of the new audiences. In Mexico, however, the initial links between cinema and the urban power elites were short-lived. Production/exhibition pioneers, motivated by the 1900 closing down of Mexico City's exhibition sites – primarily *carpas* or tents – because of city safety regulations designed to curb the 'uncivilised' behaviour of popular spectators and to diminish the risk of fires, became itinerant and left Mexico City, taking the cinema with them (there were only a handful of film exhibitions in the capital between 1901 and 1905). They travelled throughout the national territory showing the films in their repertoires but also regularly producing local views to entice the various regional audiences. These views chronicled the activities of small cities and towns: the crowds leaving church after Sunday mass, workers outside factories and local celebrations and festivities. Rather than focusing on modern life and technology, this early cinema took a turn towards the people – positioned in their local landscapes and captured in their everyday activities. Its attraction was self-recognition: 'On premiere nights the improvised actors would come to the shows *en masse* to see themselves on film; the enthusiasm of each and every one when they saw themselves or their friends and relatives on screen was great' (Sanchez Garcia 1951: 18). But through that self-recognition these actors also began the process of producing an image of the nation based on its traditional sectors and ways of life – the peoples and customs of the interior rather than the modernity of the capital city –

and a more broad-based audience for the cinema.

The linchpin of the cinema-nation symbiosis coincided with the various centennial celebrations around 1910. In Argentina and Mexico (Chile also celebrated its centennial in 1910), film-makers competed fiercely to record the festivities, and their films were quickly exhibited to great public acclaim. Aurelio de los Reyes reproduces a telling photograph in his book *Filmografía del cine mudo mexicano, 1896–1920*: while President Díaz is placing the cornerstone of a monument to Louis Pasteur, three cameramen vie for the best angle. At least three film-makers – the Alva brothers, Salvador Toscano and Guillermo Becerril – competed to record the events that were the apotheosis and swan song of the Porfirian era.

Actualities such as *El desfile histórico del Centenario* (*The Historic Centennial Parade*), *Gran desfile militar del 16 de septiembre* (*Great Military Parade of 16 September*) and *Entrega del uniforme de Morelos* (*Presentation of Morelo's Uniform*) illustrated the magnificence of the events as well as the exuberance and optimism of the crowds. But the paroxysms of patriotism elicited by the centennials and their preparations also motivated film-makers in a different direction, away from current events and towards the reconstruction of key patriotic moments, in an effort to further mobilise the new medium in the service of nationhood.

National Narratives

Undoubtedly, Latin American audiences were already quite familiar with the post-1904 productions imported from the US and Europe – dubbed 'transitional narratives'[11] to highlight their status in between the cinema of attractions and full-fledged narrative cinema – and had begun to experience the appeal of a different kind of cinematic identification, one that film-makers sought to exploit for the national celebrations. Viewers were influenced less by the chase films and Westerns arriving from the US than by the theatrical adaptations filled with artistic aspirations produced by the Société Film d'Art and other European producers. The theatre was already an artform with an extensive history and of great elite and popular appeal throughout Latin America. As such, it was a natural source of inspiration for film-makers seeking to narrativise the medium. This process is most evident in Argentina, where the appeal of actualities of current events waned in comparison to the enthusiasm generated by a new series of proto-narratives, beginning with Mario Gallo's *La Revolución de May* (*The May Revolution*) (1909).

A perfect example of a transitional film, *La Revolución* has neither a self-sufficient nor an internally coherent narrative. To make sense of the film and understand the motivations linking the various tableaux, the spectator must have extensive knowledge of the historical event being represented, as the intertitles are identificatory rather than expository. Furthermore, the style is thoroughly presentational, ranging from direct address to *mise en scène* (theatrical acting and theatrical backdrops suggested depth and perspective rather than reproducing it). Its one purely 'cinematic' moment occurs in the last tableaux, in which a visual device effectively supplements the film's patriotic enthusiasm: while the patriot leader Saavedra speaks from a balcony to a throng, a image of General San Martín in uniform and wrapped in the Argentine flag appears unexpectedly over a painted backdrop of the Cabildo; the people and the army salute him and shout 'Viva la República' (according to the titles). Other Gallo historical reconstructions further developed this patriotic theme and style (utilising well-known **219** popular stage actors), as seen, for example, in *La creación del himno* (*The Creation of the National Anthem*) (1909), an homage to the writing and first performance of the national anthem, and *El fusilamiento de Dorrego* (*Dorrego's Execution*), *Juan Moreira*, *Güemes y sus gauchos* (*Güemes and his Gauchos*) and *Camila O'Gorman* (all 1910).

Humberto Cairo's *Nobleza gaucha* (*Gaucho Nobility*) (1915) further developed Gallo's narrative-nationalist impetus. This film most clearly exemplifies the nationalist sentiments and contradictions of this period and was perhaps the first to develop the city-countryside dialectic central to Latin America's modernity debates. Although much closer to a classical style than *La Revolución*, *Nobleza* is still a transitional narrative. Rather than depending on the audience's prior historical knowledge, however, its intertext is cultural; the intertitles cite the great Argentine epic poem *Martín Fierro* to recount the story of a courageous gaucho who saves his beautiful girlfriend from the evil clutches of a ranch owner who abducted her to his palatial city mansion. The ranch owner falsely accuses the gaucho of theft but dies when he falls off a cliff while being chased by the hero on horseback. Skilfully filmed – with well-placed close-ups, elegant lighting and diverse camera movements, including tracking shots from trains and streetcars – and acted naturalistically, the story line allowed Cairo to focus on the always appealing folklore of the countryside (songs, ranchos, gauchos and barbecues), as well as the modernity of the city: shots of Constitución Avenue, Avenida de Mayo, Congress, the Armenonville station and even night-time urban illuminations. *Nobleza* simultaneously exalts the traditional values of rural life – indulging in what Rey Chow (1995) calls 'primitive passions'[12] – while displaying in all its splendour the modern urbanity that would make it obsolete; the gaucho may have been the hero of the narrative, but he was already relegated to the status of a foundational myth like *Martín Fierro*. *Nobleza's* exploration of the crisis in national identity generated by the conflict between traditional experiences and values and the internationalisation endemic to modernity was extraordinarily well received: the film cost only 20,000 pesos to produce but made more than 600,000 from its many national and international screenings.

Thus, transitional narrative styles, in all their diverse forms, were almost naturally linked to the project of modern nation building. Once the cinema had exhausted its purely specular attractions and sought new storytelling possibilities, the task of generating narratives about the nation inevitably led to the problematisation of modernisation itself. The epidermal modernity of urban daily life – with its railroads, mobility and technology – had been exalted earlier. Narratives now required the exploration of the contradictions of that process at a national level. With few exceptions, the earliest successful Latin American films identified as 'narratives' were linked to patriotic themes. In Mexico, for example, Carlos Mongrand invoked well-known historical figures in *Cuauhtémoc y Benito Juárez* and *Hernán Cortés, Hidalgo y Morelos* (both 1904); later Felipe de Jesús Haro and the American Amusement Co. (sic) produced the elaborate (seven tableaux) *Grito de Dolores* (*The Shout of Delores*) (1907) which was usually screened with live actors declaiming the dialogue behind the screen. In Brazil, in addition to addressing historical events and figures (for example, Alberto Botelho's *A vida do Barão do Rio Branco* (*The Life of the Rio Branco Baron*) (1910), similar to *Nobleza Gaucha*), narrative was aligned with comedy and contrasted with urban and rural lives. Julio Ferrez's *Nhô Anastacio chegou de viagem* (*Mr Anastacio Returned from a Trip*) (1908), recognised as the first Brazilian fiction film, presents the misadventures of a country bumpkin newly arrived in Rio, including his encounters with urban modernity (railroads, monuments, etc.) within a mistaken-identity love plot. It engendered a series of similar comedies, focused on the conflicts between traditional rural ways and the modernity of cities filled with foreign immigrants and twentieth-century technologies. Throughout these comedies, which attempt to produce the discursive triumph of positivism, the traditional/rural is figured as nostalgically obsolete, a cultural remnant being willed into history, while the modernity of the metropolis is presented as inevitable, 'natural' and national.

Although problematised by differential chronologies, similar efforts occurred in other parts of the continent. On the one hand, it is as if developments that took place in, say, Argentina or Brazil, in the early-to-mid-1910s began to unfold in nations like Chile, Bolivia and Colombia in the 1920s. On the other hand, the films of the 1920s in Chile, Bolivia and Colombia were very much produced in the context of 1920s global trends – familiar through always-abundant imported films – and had, to some degree, already abandoned the parameters of the 1910s. Thus, instead of rough transitional narratives, the first Chilean, Bolivian and Colombian fiction films follow very closely the hegemonic representational parameters of the era – continuity editing, self-sufficient internal narration and feature length – yet return to the nationalistic concerns of the earlier era elsewhere. In Bolivia, for example, the conflict between indigenous/rural existence and urban life was explored in José María Velasco Maidana's *La profecía del lag* (*The Prophecy of the Lake*) (1925) and Pedro Sambarino's *Corazón Aymara* (*Aymara Heart*) (1925). In Colombia, we find skilful adaptations of foundational fictions mediated through the conventions of European-inspired film melodrama: *María* (Alfredo del Diestro and Máximo Calvo, 1921–2) and Di Doménico's *Aura o las violetas* (*Dawn or the Violets*) (1923). Chile's version of *Nobleza Gaucha*, *Alma chilena* (*Chilean Soul*) (1917), was directed by Arturo Mario, the star of the Argentine film, while Gabriella von Bussenius and Salvador Giambastiani's *La agonía del Arauco* (*Arauco Agony*) (1917) contrasted the Mapuche landscape and people with the melodramatic foibles of its urban protagonists, and Pedro Sienna's *El húsar de la muerta* (*The Hussar of Death*) (1925) chronicled the exploits of national hero Manuel Rodríguez.

The Chilean example highlights a curious characteristic of early Latin American cinema that perhaps explains, in part, its obsessive concern with nationness: throughout the continent, the overwhelming majority of early film-makers were first-generation immigrants. The evidence to support this assertion is too vast to summarise efficiently, so a few names must suffice: in Brazil, the Segreto family came from Italy, Antonio Leal from Portugal and Francisco Serrador from Spain. In Argentina, Enrique Lepage was Belgian, Federico Figner Czech, Max Glucksmann Austrian, Eugenio Py French, and Mario Gallo and Federico Valle Italian. In Chile, Salvador Giambastiani was Italian (and had worked in Argentina before arriving in Chile in 1915), and the Argentine actors Arturo Mario and María Padín became producers/directors in 1917. In Uruguay, the branch of Max Glucksmann's Argentine company was the principal producer of actualities between 1913 and 1931. Pedro Sambarino, an Italian, worked in Bolivia and Peru. Originally from Italy, the Di Doménico **221** family was instrumental in establishing the cinema in Colombia and Central America. After immigrating to Panama, they acquired film-making equipment from Europe and travelled through the Antilles and Venezuela, arriving in Barranquilla in 1910 and settling in Laz Paz in 1911, where they established a regional distributor/production company of great significance until the arrival of sound. Thus, the cinema was a medium not only of mobility but also of great appeal to the mobile, to immigrants seeking to make their fortunes in the new world through the apparatuses of modernity yet eager to assert their new national affiliations, and to those who restlessly travelled throughout the continent.

Peripheral Displacements

In complex negotiations between national events/traditions and foreign models and the demands of Westernisation, Latin America produced a series of 'spectacular experiments' that dialectically inscribed the cinema in national histories while simultaneously recognising it as the embodiment of always differential dreams of modernity. Parochial yet also of the 'world at large', the silent cinema was a key agent of both nationalism and globalisation. With few if any proprietary claims to technology (the technology remained primarily an import), early cinema nevertheless contributed to the construction of strong nationalistic discourses of modernity. As evidenced by this comparative analysis, throughout the continent and despite certain regional differences, filmic visuality came to define the necessarily ambivalent position of those caught in the whirlpools of change, whether because of the shift from rural to urban life, displacements caused by immigration, or the cataclysms of civil war. A mechanism for accessible globality, the cinema captured and accompanied the vertiginous modernisation of urban sectors, as well as the simultaneous inertia of other zones and territories: in the discursive struggle between the urban and the rural as icons of nationalisms, the cinema – the urban instrument par excellence – actively contributed to the postulation of the non-urban as a folkloric past or an anachronistic vestige.

Throughout the continent, national producers were faced with two significant changes in subsequent decades. The onset of World War I redefined the international cinematic marketplace; blocked from its usual markets and practices in Europe, US producers 'discovered' the potential of the Latin American market and moved in aggressively. They consolidated their presence throughout the continent and, in most instances, effectively precluded national production from prospering commercially. This was quite marked in Brazil, for example, where the end of the *bela época* (circa 1912) coincided with the development of a strong distribution/exhibition sector geared to imports[13] and the subsequent arrival of subsidiaries of US firms.[14]

This shift was soon followed by a far more devastating change: the arrival of sound. Aggressively marketed, sound films from the US quickly took over the exhibition and distribution sectors, while national producers scrambled for capital, technology and know-how. In some cases, the arrival of sound severed all cinematic activities: several nations – notably Bolivia, Venezuela and Colombia – were not able to resume film-making until nearly a decade after the introduction of sound. Others – principally Mexico, Argentina and Brazil –

by hook or by crook, invented, adapted and experimented, producing a different yet resonant version of early cinema. The sound cinema of the 1930s, 1940s and 1950s would become the principal interlocutor of Latin American modernity – as Carols Monsiváis says, where Latin Americans went not to dream but to learn to be modern (Monsiváis 1997).

Notes

1. Extracted from *Cinema Journal* (40) 1: 48–78 with permission of the author. All translations by the author unless otherwise indicated.

2. Whereas I use 'modernity' to refer to both the idea of the modern as well as a particular disposition towards lived experience that encompasses various ideological and discursive paradigms, 'modernisation' refers more specifically to the processes of change that result from the introduction of certain technologies into the various spheres of private and social life.

3. The term was coined by Arjun Appadurai in reference to the introduction of cricket to India (Appadurai 1996: 24).

4. For Argentine dates, see Caneto et al. (1996: 27–8); for Brazil, see Paranaguá (1987: 24); for Mexico see Dávalos Orozco, Federico (1996), *Albores del cine mexicano*, Mexico City: Clio: 12; and de los Reyes (1972: 40); for Uruguay see Hintz, Eugenío (1988), *Historia y filmografía del cine uruguayano*, Montevideo: Eds. de la Plaza: 11; for Cuba see Rodríguez, Raúl (1993), *El cine silente en Cuba*, Havana: Letras Cubanas: 27–31; for Chile, Peru and Guatemala see Paranaguá (1985: 10–11).

5. Aurelio de los Reyes's discussion of how the practice of kissing in Mexico changed after the circulation of explicit cinematic kisses and the innovation of darkened public spaces – movie theatres – in which they could be exchanged is especially relevant here. See his 'Los besos y el cine', in Estrada de Garlero, Elena (ed.) (1995), *El arte y la vida cotidiana: XVI coloquio internacional de historia del arte*, Mexico City: UNAM: 267–89.

6. All accounts of the new medium describe its technology in excruciating detail over and above its effects, giving precise technical information about how the illusion of movement was produced. See, for example, the description of the Cinématographe that appeared in the Buenos Aires newspaper *La Prensa* on 3 April 1896, cited in Caneto et al. (1996: 23), and the one published in the Mexican daily *El Mundo* on 23 August 1896, reproduced in its entirety in de los Reyes (1972: 217–22).

7. What Porfirio Díaz's closest advisers – the Mexican power elite – called themselves in reference to their conviction that Mexico would be transformed (that is, modernised through science and technology).

8. Soon after the sinking of the *USS Maine* in Havana harbour on 15 February 1898, US Edison and Biograph cameramen began to produce views and shots of the events unfolding in Cuba. Throughout 1898, and especially after the US entered the war, they extended the cinema's capacity as a visual newspaper (often in collaboration with the Hearst organisation) and, for the first time, used the medium to elicit patriotic sentiments in the US audiences, revealing the medium's ideological and propagandistic force. The difficulties of filming in real battles also led to many 'reconstructions' of famous events, most notoriously Albert E. Smith and J. Stuart Blackton's reconstruction of the Battle of Santiago Bay in New York, using a tub of water, paper cut-out ships, and cigar smoke. Many credit the enthusiasm generated by these films with the

revitalisation of the lagging motion picture business in the US, the ongoing production of a few firms set the commercial foundation for the US industry.

9. The term was coined by Roberto Schwarz to explain the juxtaposition of modernising ideologies such as liberalism within traditional social structures such as the slave-owning Brazilian monarchy. Misplaced or out of place 'ideas' lead to significant discursive dislocations, which critically reveal the fissures of allegedly universal concepts (1992).

10. *La Nación* 17 February 1898, cited in Caneto et al. (1996: 35). This is an astounding example of the speed of cinematic diffusion, not only of technology but also of modes of commercialisation and spectatorship. According to Charles Musser's research, American Biograph began its overseas expansion in 1897, establishing a London office in March. It was one of the characteristics of the Biograph operators to provide locally shot scenes to theatre operators in order to enhance the programmes' popularity (Musser, Charles (1990), *The Emergence of Cinema: The American Screen to 1907*, Berkeley: University of California Press: 157, 172).

11. According to Tom Gunning's periodisation, after the waning of the cinema of attractions's dominance (circa 1905), early narrative forms developed that enabled film-makers to experiment with the specific cinematic narrative language that would become standardised as the 'classic Hollywood narrative style' around 1915–17. This 'transitional' period of more than a decade was volatile and ambivalent; D. W. Griffith's narrative ambitions of the period were far from the norm (1998: 262–6).

12. The modernist effort to reconceptualise origins, which typically attributes to indigenous traditions the significance of a primitive past (Chow 1995).

13. Francisco Serrador, an early entrepreneur, expanded his business and, by the mid-1910s, had created what is often referred to as an 'exhibition trust'. He created the company Companhia Cinematográfica Brasileira in 1911 with a broad base of investors to focus on distribution and exhibition. It proceeded to acquire and/or build theatres throughout Brazil, especially in Rio de Janeiro. The company also became exclusive agent of the principal European producers and featured imports prominently (de Pasula Araujo 1976: 369–70, 396; 1981: 210–25).

14. Fox arrived in 1915, Paramount's Companhia de Peliculas de Luxo da America do Sul in 1916, Universal in 1921, MGM in 1926, Warner Bros. in 1927 and First National and Columbia in 1929 (Johnson 1997: 34–6).

References

Appadurai, Arjun (1996), 'Playing with Modernity: The Decolonization of Indian Cricket', in Breckenridge, Carol (ed.), *Consuming Modernity: Public Culture in a South Asian World*, Minneapolis: University of Minnesota Press.

Barbero, Jesús Martín (1987), *De los medios a las mediaciones*, Barcelona: Eds. Gili.

Basadre, Jorge (1968–70), *Historia de la República del Peru, 1822–1933*, Lima: Editorial Universitaria.

Brunner, José Joaquín (1993), 'Notes on Modernity and Postmodernity', translated by John Beverly, *Boundary 2* 20 (3).

Charney, Leo and Schwartz, Vanessa R. (1995), *Cinema and the Invention of Modern Life*, Berkeley: University of California Press.

Chow, Rey (1995), *Primitive Passions*, New York: Columbia University Press.

de los Reyes, Aurelio (1972), *Los orígines del cine en Mexico*, Mexico City: UNAM.

de Pasula Araujo, Vivente (1976), *A bela época do cinema brasileiro*, São Paulo: Perspectiva.

de Pasula Araujo, Vivente (1981), *Salles, circos e cinemas de São Paulo*, São Paulo: Perspectiva.

Gunning, Tom (1998), 'Early American Film', in Hill and Church Gibson (1998): 262–6.

Paranaguá, Paulo Antonio (1985), *Cinéma na America Latina: Longe de Deus e perto de Hollywood*, Porto Alegre: L&PM Editores.

Quijano, Anibal (1993), 'Modernity, Identity and Utopia in Latin America', translated by John Beverly, *Boundary 2* 20 (3).

Rama, Angel (1996), *The Lettered City*, translated by J. C. Chasteen, Durham: Duke University Press.

Sanchez Garcia, José Maria (1951) 'Historia del cine mexicano', *Cinema Reporter*, 30 June.

Schiller, Herbert (1976), *Communication and Cultural Domination*, White Plains, NY: International Arts and Sciences.

Williams, Linda (ed.) (1997), *Viewing Positions: Ways of Seeing Films*, New Brunswick, NJ: Rutgers University Press.

17 The Quest for/Obsession with the National in Arabic Cinema

Sabry Hafez

In a famous essay, 'Third-World Literature in the Era of Multinational Capitalism' (1986), Fredric Jameson suggests that Third World novels necessarily tell the 'narrative of national allegories'. Although there is truth in his insight, I have some reservations about his generalisation in regard to literature, but in relation to an investigation of Arabic cinema and the theorisation of the national in it, I find his remarks in that essay, as well as his concept of 'cognitive mapping' developed in two subsequent books (1991 and 1992), more appealing. For it is clear, from any serious investigation of Arabic cinema, that this cinema is motivated by a quest for, and obsessed with, the national, particularly when it is read allegorically or metaphorically. It is the impossible vision, often remaining below the surface, of social and cultural totality inherent in its many filmic genres, which any theory of the national in Arabic cinema should try to capture and articulate. Making films in an Arabic culture is never ideologically or cognitively neutral. Making an Arabic film is to create a specific product elaborating a locus of meaning and specifying an 'Arab' experience, to construct an art object that imparts certain knowledge about the region and its people, and to produce a knowledge that will be bound by that act of film production. Unlike literary narrative, which is only bound by the limits of an individual imagination and the ideological vision inherent in it, filmic narrative is bound in addition by 'the aesthetic technologies available for the crystallization of a particular spatial or narrative model of the social totality' (Jameson 1992: 4).

The modes of the crystallisation of social totality that makes cinema the realm in which a culture acts out its own fantasies and, at the same time, turns these fantasies and realities into commodities, can be probed and understood through 'cognitive mapping'. This concept originated in the work of urban architect Kevin Lynch to describe the way in which people make sense of their urban surroundings and to negotiate their way in the alienating urban intersection between the individual, the social/collective and the real in order to comprehend their own position in the urban totality. Jameson fine-tuned the concept, extended it to national and global spaces and gave it theoretical potency by extending it beyond the confines of urbanisation to mimesis in general. Combining the geographic and empirical aspects of Lynch's concept with the Althusserian redefinition of ideology as 'the representation of the subject's *Imaginary* relationship to his or her *Real* conditions of existence', Jameson pointed out that 'the cognitive map is not exactly mimetic in that older sense; indeed, the theoretical issues it poses allow us to renew the analysis of representation on a higher and much more complex level' (Jameson 1991: 51). Cognitive mapping allows us to pose the question of the relationship of films to the social and/or national totality since it requires 'the co-ordination of existential data (the empirical position of the subject) with an unlived, abstract conception of the geographic totality' (Jameson 1991: 52). The mobilisation of our awareness of the imaginary nature of our place in the 'real world' makes cognitive mapping a useful instrument in dealing with cinema, precisely because, due to its individualistic nature as art and its social organisation as an industry, it is an imaginary projection of the individual's relationship to the real. Cinema can thus be seen as an ideological instrument through which the national 'self' conceptualises its being-in-the-world.

Using the concept of cognitive mapping, the aim of this essay is twofold: to offer a theoretical paradigm of the national in Arabic cinema, and to provide the reader with a general survey of its development and the nature of its different trajectories both as a specific art-form and as popular cultural product. Cinema is one of many literary and artistic genres – such as the novel, the short story, drama and framed painting – which emerged in Arabic culture in the twentieth century as a result of a comprehensive process of change and cultural modernisation that occupied most of the nineteenth century. Elsewhere, in dealing with the emergence of new narrative genres in Arabic culture, I rejected the notion of cultural importation as too simplistic to account for cultural interconnections and posited instead the concept of *genesis* with its complex sociological process of cultural transition, 'world-view' transformation, and the emergence of new audiences with different needs (Hafez 1993). The socio-cultural transition which Arabic culture underwent from the early parts of the nineteenth century to the turn of the twentieth, involving complex interactions with various aspects of modernity, was responsible for and conducive to the genesis of Arabic narrative discourse. The introduction of a new educational system, alongside, rather than instead of, the traditional one, allowed for the education of women (a prerequisite for their emancipation), and created a new educated class with a different worldview. The accelerated urbanisation, the introduction of the printing press, the spread of journalism, and the modernisation of the economy and transport changed the Arabs' perception of time and space in a way that is inseparable from the emergence of a sense of nationalism in general (Anderson 1983) and in Arabic culture in particular. But this nationalistic verve developed more acutely in Arabic culture, because as soon as the process of modernity took root in the culture and started to yield its fruits, most of the Arab countries fell under the yoke of colonialism, and the struggle for independence became inseparable from the quest for national identity. The literary and artistic elaboration of this identity was a vital element in the process of cultural transition and motivated the constant interaction between nation and narration from the outset.

The accumulated effects of all these changes led to the gradual replacement of the traditional modes of social interaction with more modern ones conducive to urban and urbane living, a rational and quasi-liberal 'worldview', a new artistic sensibility, and the ability to express needs and views in new genres while consuming them. The new literary genres that started to emerge at the turn of the twentieth century introduced readers to the conventions of narrative and its internal rules of reference, accustoming them to its rubrics. This facilitated an interaction with the new cinematographic products a few decades later. Without a clear understanding of this comprehensive process of cultural transition, and its materialisation at different historical moments in different Arab countries, it would be difficult to understand both the uneven development of Arabic culture, and the success or even complete lack of cinematographic activities in some countries. For this comprehensive cultural transition is also the prerequisite for the emergence of cinema in Arabic culture, which, like most other narrative forms, cannot simply be imported, for it is a hybrid cultural product generated by the inner dynamics of social discourses and internal socio-cultural energies.

The national, whether in its purely political or socio-cultural dimensions, has been the mainstay of Arabic cinema since its inception. Its drive was at the heart of the genesis of Arabic narrative genres, and cinema is no exception. When one talks of Arabic cinema, the Arabic in this construct refers primarily to the language, for one is dealing here with cinema that is produced in the Arabic language and its different spoken vernaculars. It also denotes a large geographical area, some twenty countries or so, which extends from Iraq and the Gulf to Morocco and Mauritania, and from Syria to the Sudan. Some of these countries, such as Egypt and Lebanon, have long sustained a film industry, while many others have a significant film-making tradition. But there remain others without any significant cinematic output. The lack of cinematic activities in these countries cannot be explained by the lazy assumption that Islam is hostile to images. Egypt, a predominantly Muslim country, has produced more than 3,000 feature films since 1924. That Islam should be hostile towards 'representation' is an orientalist prejudice. Another equally lamentable myth is the commonplace that cinema requires a technical expertise that 'is only available in the West' (Kennedy-Day 2002: 372). Cinema is a product of the social, a genre of artistic expression that is inseparable from certain levels of cultural development and social modes of interaction.

By an instructive coincidence, the introduction of cinema into Arabic culture coincided with the inception of this new artform, as well as with its flirtation with the national and the orientalisation of the orient. The brothers Auguste and Louis Lumière showed some of their first films in Alexandria in 1896, making Egypt the third country, after France and Belgium, in which Lumière films were presented. In the following year, 1897, they filmed thirty-five films in Egypt, among which are *Muhammad Ali Square in Alexandria*,[1] *Saqqara Pyramid*, *The Three Great Pyramids*, *The Sphinx*, *The Bedouins*, *The Procession of the Cover of the Ka'ba* and *Dam on the Nile*. Although most of these films were seen as curiosities at the time, and many of their locations were selected for their exotic value and spectacular vista, they can also be seen as launching the battle for presentation and representation. Many of these films emphasised the eternal beauty of Egypt and its glorious past and sparked a sense of national pride,[2] something the French expedition to Egypt had emphasised a century earlier.[3] But others, like those that were filmed at the time in Jerusalem, Bethlehem, Beirut and Damascus, represented the national self and local geography as oriental objects for the exotic pleasure of the European gaze and Western consumption. Hence the paradoxical position of cinematography in the culture, from the very beginning, as a positive and negative medium at the same time, articulating the beauty of the country and showing its glorious achievements while also denigrating it and turning it into an object for use by others. The ambivalence of such cinematic messages increased the opposition of the traditionalists and even sparked resistance to its inception in some Arab countries, lasting to today in Saudi Arabia, adding cinema to the list of new narrative genres that allegedly corrupted social mores and fostered moral looseness.

Cinema, however, was not alone in this position, particularly at this crucial moment in the development of Arab culture and history. The turn of the twentieth century was a time of major change and cultural transition and which brought radical shifts in the allocation of symbolic power and exertion of symbolic violence. This was a time of embracing modernity, with its rational and liberal ideals, and at the same time of being acutely antagonistic to some aspects of its European sources, e.g. colonialism. The newly educated class and its intelligentsia fought a dual battle, on the one hand, against the traditional and mostly regressive intellectual elite, and, on the other hand, against European colonial domination. The former battle involved the acquisition of the symbolic capital that previously had been monopolised by the traditional intellectuals; the latter conflict led the new intelligentsia to wage a battle of representation and counter-presentation against the hackneyed clichés of orientalism. Some of these clichés were marked by equivocation and ambivalence, but they acquired an unsettling power, since they were part of the colonial state apparatus and thus enmeshed in the dynamics of social-political power, even after independence. Hence the battle that the new intelligentsia waged was double-edged: to separate these clichés and patterns of representation from the negative traces and residue of their colonial usage, and to give them a new role in the national consciousness. This, as Frantz Fanon asserted, 'is not nationalism' (Fanon 1967: 199). From the start, when Arab intellectuals embarked on film-making, they were concerned with the shaping of a truly *inter*national consciousness.

Dual-track Theorising

Approaching cinema as a product of the socio-cultural development in the Arab world, and dealing with it through the concept of 'cognitive mapping' requires abandoning rigid theoretical paradigms for a more flexible approach that takes into account the uneven development and different histories of Arab countries. The common denominator in the Arab world, despite these uneven developments, is the emergence of the concept of *watan* (nation or homeland) by the turn of the twentieth century in most Arab countries. Without the concept of *watan* supplanting that of *millah* (people of a certain religion), it would have been impossible to perceive the Turks, who share with the Arab the same religion, as being as inimical to their progress and independence as the British or the French, and, more importantly, to forge stronger bonds between the members of the same *watan* despite their religious differences. This radical change in the perception of allies and enemies implies a radical transformation of the world order and the traditional scale of values. The wide interest in the archaeological excavations at the time strengthened the rising sense of nationalism, and rooted the new concept of homogeneous calendrical time into the individual as well as the national consciousness.   **229**

The emergence of the new concept of the nation posed the thorny problem of its representation. This created, from the beginning of the twentieth century, a tension between the traditional political establishment, which used to monopolise power unchecked, and the new intelligentsia, with their claims for representation and democracy. The least one can say is that the tension between the two created a deep-seated distrust on both sides. This difficult situation was exacerbated by the long tradition of unrepresentative and despotic governments in the Arab world. To protect its interests, the political establishment used severe censorship laws to shackle cultural and literary production in general, and theatre and cinema in particular, since these reached a wider audience than the printed word. Harsh censorship laws started in Egypt with the British occupation in 1882, but those were primarily directed against theatre and the printed word. When cinema appeared on the scene, the laws applied to theatre were used against it, but soon (in 1904) they were supplemented by further ones especially tailored for cinema. The most notorious of them was the 1947 law of film censorship in Egypt, where the five major areas of prohibition (loose morality, politics, religion, seditious ideologies and violence) of the 1904 and 1911 laws were detailed and augmented to seventy-one. Ironically, the 1947 law admitted in its preamble that it was based on its American counterpart, but it is also deeply rooted in a long Arab tradition of undemocratic legislation repressing the freedom of individuals and shackling artistic and literary expression. This law remains virtually in force until now. Its rules were relaxed in 1955, but then viciously reinforced again by the universally detested law of 1976 which went back to the 1947 law and, in addition, gave the clergy censoring powers, thus providing fundamentalism with the final say in film censorship. The 1976 law remains in force until today despite many attempts to revoke it or even to suspend its rule.

This legislative framework in Egypt illustrates the conditions under which the most prolific Arab cinema, responsible for more than 80 per cent of its total output, operates. Such laws have been replicated in most other Arab countries. This legal censorship, with its panoply of taboos and prohibitions, 'protects' or rather removes large areas of experience from cinematic treatment. It not only prevents film-makers from addressing religion, morality, sex and politics, it tries to erase also many other experiences and even characters: historical topics and/or personalities, representations of political figures, speeches, political propaganda, labour revolts, demonstrations, criticism of public officers and foreigners, as well as of life in friendly countries, and so on. The list is long, but any attempt to theorise the national in Arabic cinema must take into account the severe impact of the lack of freedom and democracy in the Arab world on the elaboration of literary and artistic works. One consequence was, for instance, the production of a flood of escapist cinema, aiming to entertain, rather that to address more directly, the serious issues animating society. A second consequence is the prevalence of a metaphoric and allegorical treatment of issues of national or social concern in Arabic cinema, which in turn helps to explain why literary idioms are so central to Arabic cinema's way of dealing with ideas current in the culture. This pressure is further strengthened by the need for film-makers to overcome the lower intellectual status of cinema in the cultural field, in Pierre Bourdieu's sense of the term (1993) and to be recognised as serious artists. This is clearly a case where, in Bakhtin's phraseology (1986: 1–9), 'unequal power relations between discourses' create their own dynamics.

Although there is a certain unity that binds Arabic cinemas together as a unitary cultural product, there are equally many differences that account for its richness, scope and vitality. The cultural unity of Arabic cinema depends largely on an imagined identity, which, like most imagined constructs, is ambivalent and problematic, largely informed by a structure of feeling, a sense of shared lineage, cultural heritage and common experience. Yet the regional differences are clearly articulated, even celebrated, and they lead, in the field of cinema in particular, to different trajectories. Any theorisation of the national in Arabic cinema needs to strike a delicate balance between generalisation and specificity, between the abstract and the concrete. In this respect, I would like to suggest a kind of dual-track theorising: one that takes account of the different national cases and identifies their diverse trajectories, and one that registers the double nature of cinema itself as both an artform and a commercial industry.

Adorno credited Siegfried Kracauer with the 'discovery of film as a social fact', and its 'decoding as ideology'. He went on to demonstrate the importance of these discoveries and cinema's role in shaping the needs of its audience as well as its impact on the development of a 'new spirit': 'When a medium desired and consumed by the masses transmits an ideology that is internally consistent and cohesive, this ideology is presumably adapting to the needs of the consumers as much as, conversely, it is progressively shaping them. For Kracauer, 'plucking the leaves of the ideology of film amounted to describing the phenomenology of a new stage of objective spirit in the process of formation' (Adorno 1992: 66). It is this interactive role of film that takes it beyond the mimetic and enables it to play an active role in reflecting and shaping the national that led Jameson to associate fantasy with cognitive mapping: 'If fantasy is epistemological, as Deleuze has argued in the *Anti-Oedipus*, indeed if narrative is itself a form of cognition, then an obvious next step lies in the systematic harnessing of the energies of those hitherto irrational activities for cognitive purposes. The conception of cognitive mapping [w]as intended to include that possibility as well, and to be prescriptive as well as descriptive' (Jameson 1992: 188). If one extends the epistemological nature of fantasy and narrative to cinema, one finds that most of its activities, far from being irrational, harnessed (or contributed to the inscription of) an audience's sense of national identity and firmly established its emblems on their cognitive map. Although most Arab countries have suffered from colonialism, their experience of it differed radically. Some, like Egypt and the Levant, experienced it as impeding their own independent project of modernity, which had been taking root since the beginning of the nineteenth century. Others, such as Algeria and the countries of the Maghrib, were dragged into modernity by colonialism. This led to two radically different approaches in dealing with the national in Arabic cinema. One approach engaged with the national question in a comprehensive and largely cultural manner, constructing a cognitive map of the nation through an elaborate and varied cartography, setting its own agenda of representation, articulating the national imaginary, reducing the colonial experience to a mere episode in its history and, confident of its national consciousness and identity, posited its own vision of a different future. This tendency is exemplified in the cinema of Egypt, Lebanon, Syria and, to a certain extent, of Iraq, 231 with the Palestinian cinema as the noted exception in this region, for obvious reasons. Egyptian cinema is the most productive, continuous and well established of these and has therefore been selected as the focus for this study.

The approach adopted by the cinema of the Maghrib is radically different. Whereas in the first group, cinema started as an indigenous project, cinema in the Maghrib was started mostly by Europeans, predominantly French, but also Italians, Dutch and Greek. In these countries, cinema was from the outset absorbed into the colonial legacy: it was consumed by it, totally preoccupied by its legacy and wounds, constantly reacting to its ever-increasing burden on the national psyche. In those countries, the cognitive mapping of the national and social totality is crippled by the legacy of colonialism, as can be seen in the most cinematically accomplished of the Maghrib countries, Algeria, where it generates a post-colonial cinema par excellence. The Maghrib's is a cinema still suffering a lasting colonial legacy, manifested not only in its topics and themes, but also in its linguistic and geographical dichotomies. Here one encounters the problems of filmic identities, for the diasporic cinema made by the North-African-born or first generation French and Belgium film-makers poses serious questions of identity and classification. It is a diasporic cinema of marginal or marginalised identities.[4] Unlike the cinema of Egypt and the Levant, in which one finds many different film genres, from comedy to musical, thriller, film noir, light entertainment, romance, social exposes and art films, the post-colonial cinema of the Maghrib did not generate such a generic variety. Nevertheless, despite the clear difference between the two approaches to the national, the cinemas of the Maghrib and those of the Levant are in a way complementary to each other, together delineating the dual-track development of Arabic cinema.

Cinema and Nation

In his seminal book, *Imagined Communities*, Anderson demonstrates the paradoxical nature of the nation: 'If nation states are widely conceded to be *new* and *historical*, the nation states to which they give political expression always loom out of an immemorial past, and, still more important, glide into limitless future. It is the magic of nationalism to turn chance into destiny' (Anderson 1983: 12). Although Anderson credited the novel with the task of elaborating this paradoxical nature of the nation, cinema, particularly in the Arabic case, seems to be an artistic medium even more conducive to turning chance into destiny because of the high rate of illiteracy in the Arab world. Cinema seized the early novels of national elaboration and turned them into films. The first Egyptian films, mostly shorts and documentaries, illustrate this link between cinema and the nation very clearly,[5] not only because their maker, Muhammad Bayyumi, was a nationalist officer, but also because his first film recorded the return of Sa'd Zaghlul, the nationalist leader, from exile in 1923. Bayyumi was dismissed from the army for his role in the 1919 revolution against the British occupation and went to Austria to study cinema, returning two years later with the basic equipment to establish the Bayyumi Studio in 1923. These are key years in the history of Arabic cinema, marked further by the screening of Bayyumi's *al-Bashkatib* (*The Clerk*) (1923), an adaptation of a popular play, and Victor Rosito and Bayyumi's first full-length film, *Fi Bilad Tutankhamen* (*In the Country of Tutankhamen*) (1921). The latter is an eighty-minute feature set in the context of the discovery of Tutankhamen's tomb. Bayyumi's use of Pharaonic themes in the first Egyptian feature film can be interpreted as the other side of his patriotic concerns, emphasising the Egyptianness of his country and visualising the interaction between its people and their nationalist leader. The film's rudimentary narrative focuses on the discovery of the tomb, using this momentous event to tour the sites of splendid Pharaonic monuments and to demonstrate the good-natured generosity of the Egyptians. But it can also be seen as the first step in the battle to recapturing the sceptre of 'representation', the use of the ancient past and its visual splendour beginning to move away from the exotic and being deployed instead in the service of the national. In fact many of the other films of this insightful pioneer are steeped in nationalistic verve, recording not only the return of the leader of the 1919 revolution from exile and the rapturous mass welcome that he received, but also the release of another nationalist leader, 'Abd al-Rahman Fahmi, and the opening of the first nationalist parliament in 1924 following the first Egyptian constitution of 1923. A year later, Bayyumi convinced Tal'at Harb, the organiser of independent Egypt's economy and the founder of the Misr Bank, to include a film production company in the series of enterprises that he established to vitalise and, more importantly, Egyptianise the economy. Although political struggle for independence had dominated national politics since 1919 with only modest success, the Egyptinisation of the economy and its liberation from foreign domination was the main achievement of the national movement, giving national cinema a major boost. In 1925, the Sharikat Misr li-l-Tamthil wa-'l-Sinima (Egypt Company for Acting and Cinema, ECAC) was founded with Bayyumi as its first director. Although Harb was a shrewd economist and a nationalist who believed that political independence could not be achieved without economic independence, it is a mark of his nationalist insight and cultural vision that he established a company devoted to acting and cinema. Its charter stipulated that it was a 'not-for-profit company, aiming to serve the public without incurring great losses'. In addition to cinema, the company also promoted theatre,[6] forging a strong link between cinema and theatre from the start, as well as between cinema and the rest of the literary and cultural movements. Two years later, in 1927, Harb sent four Egyptians at his bank's expense to study cinema in France and Germany,[7] while film production continued in Egypt with a steadily increasing number of shorts and documentaries as well as feature films: one feature was produced in 1927, six in 1928, five in 1929 and six in 1930. The late 1920s also saw the first films in Syria, with *Al-Muttaham a-Bari'* (*The Innocent Accused*) (1928), and in Lebanon, with *Mughamarat Ilyas Mabruk* (*The Adventures of Ilyas Mabruk*) (1929). Although it is not clear whether the first Syrian film, a rudimentary adventure story, had any nationalistic overtones, its Lebanese counterpart was motivated by the national Lebanese experience of migration and return. It tells of the return of Ilyas to his home village after several years in the United States to improve the lot of his family and of Lebanon itself.

In the 1930s, two significant events for the interaction between cinema and the shaping of an imagined community marked the interaction between cinema and the novel in Arabic culture. The first was Muhammad Karim's silent film *Zaynab* (1930)[8] adapted from Muhammad Husain Haykal's novel *Zaynab* (1912), widely considered to be the first mature Arabic novel. It is an emblematic text that laid the cornerstone of the elaboration of the imagined community of the Egyptian nation. Its heroine, Zaynab, a beautiful peasant girl, has often been interpreted as a metaphor for Egypt itself, and her suffering as a presentation of the malaise that afflicted the national 'self'. Karim was aware of this iconic significance of the novel and he asked to include shots of the Egyptian army: 'In every nation, the army is the emblem of its renaissance, the symbol of its strength, and the embodiment of its pride and glory, and it is imperative that cinema implant these meanings in the mind of the audience' (Karim 1972: 47). Ironically, his demand was refused. However, the adaptation of *Zaynab* consolidated a bond between Arabic cinema and the Arabic novel that continues to the present day.

A few years later, in 1935, an earlier historical novel, Jurji Zaydan's *Shajarat al-Durr* (1908), was made into a film by Ahmad Jalal. Being released after the movement for the emancipation of women had taken root, this film proved even more significant. It inaugurated in Arabic cinema the use of the historical film genre for national political purposes. Shajarat al-Durr was the first woman to rule Egypt in its Islamic phase and her ascent to power resonated with the reality of Egypt's struggle for independence when the film was made. She was a beautiful, cultured and highly polished *jariyah*, slave girl, who rose to fame and became the wife of the Sultan and the mother of the heir at the time of the seventh Crusade (1249–54). When the Sultan died, she managed to hide the news of his death and ran the affairs of state so smoothly that the news would not hinder the army's fight against

234 *Al-Nasir salah al-Din* (Yusuf Shahin, 1963)

the Crusaders, contributing to its victory and the arrest of Louis IX. When in the film a harbinger comes from the front declaring the victory of Egypt over the Crusaders, the audience applauded (Ramzi 1986: 26).

This success motivated the making of another historical film with similar message, *Salah al-Din* (*Saladin*) (Ibrahim Lama, 1941), also dealing with an episode of the war against the Crusaders. Both films nourished the audience's confidence in the ability of Arabs to wage a defensive war, defeat its enemy and achieve victory by regaining the occupied land. This message clearly suited the patriotic battle against colonialism waged throughout the Arab world since the 1919 uprisings in Egypt and Palestine, and the 1920s revolt in Iraq and Jerusalem. Independence was the leitmotiv of the Arab patriotic struggle since the time of Muhammad Ali (1805–48) in Egypt and the Lebanese autonomy of 1860, and cinema seized this theme from its early stages to help integrate the new medium into the major concerns of the nation. The same topics were mobilised again to convey a nationalist message some twenty years later, underlining the need for a pan-Arab unity and to warn against the perils of factionalism. In the early 1960s, at the zenith of Nasser's policies, *Wa-Islamah* (*Oh My Islam*) (Yusuf Shahin, 1961) and *Al-Nasir salah al-Din* (*Saladin the Victorious*) (Yusuf Shahin, 1963) retold the stories of Sajarat al-Durr and Saladin. Although the former was not successful and its message was confused despite its reliance on a well-known novel by 'Ali Ahmad Bakathir, *Saladin the Victorious*, with a script that benefited from the vision and expertise of a large number of leading writers such as Naguib Mahfouz, 'Abd al-Rahman al-Sharqawi and Yusuf al-Siba'I, achieved great acclaim and popularity. It harmonised with Nasser's pan-Arab politics and his call to win the battle against an old enemy who had returned in a different guise to occupy Palestine, inflicting a new wound on the national consciousness.

The Politics of Modernity

By 1935, the infrastructure for Egypt's film industry was in place and the Studio Misr was inaugurated, not only as a production company, but also as a training facility for the development of new talent and expertise.[9] All the key names in the development of Arab cinema – directors, editors, cinematographers – over the following forty years or so were trained there.[10] The fact that these talents were trained within an Egyptian institution gave them a sense of national pride, and the move of many writers, playwrights and theatre actors to work in the new medium further enhanced the nationalist fervour while consolidating the interaction between cinema and the cultural and literary movements. The full significance of ECAC and Studio Misr cannot be grasped without placing them in the context of the nationalist upsurge following the 1919 revolution and the call for the creation of *Adab Qawmi*, a national literature, definitely Egyptian in character. The first two decades of the twentieth century saw the birth of new Arabic narrative genres and their maturation in the crucible of patriotic struggle. Not only the novel and the short story were developed as literary genres, but also drama, modern painting, sculpture and modern music, all of them inaugurating new forms with highly nationalist themes, evidenced in the writings, painting, plays and songs of Muhammad Husain Haykal (1888–1956), Muhammad (1892–1921) and

Mahmud Taymur (1894–1973), 'Isa 'Ubaid (1894–1922), Tawfiq al-Hakim (1898–1987), Najib al-Rihani (1891–1949), Sayyid Darwish, Mahmud Mukhtar (1891–1938) and Mahmud Sa'id. It is only natural that the early Egyptian films did the same. As soon as a base for a film industry had been established, together with a network of cinemas and distribution, not only in Egypt but also in other countries of the Levant, particularly Syria and Lebanon, film production grew and gained new ground in many Arab countries. The Egyptian film pioneer Ahmad Badrakhan noted in his important book, *Cinema* (1936), that 'the Egyptian film will not be worthy of serious consideration unless it reflects the Egyptian spirit, which is different from its American, French or German counterparts', reflecting the call for national art and literature debated in the cultural scene a few years earlier. But he also called for a light cinema of glamour, romance and entertainment: 'cinema is the art of the visual, and the lower-middle class, which makes up the bulk of the cinemagoers, does not want to see its sordid life reflected on the screen, but the glamorous life that it does not know and reads about in fiction' (Badrakhan 1936: 14). He advised writers that 'some of the most suitable locales for a film treatment are: theatres, music halls, newspaper buildings, large hotels, the stock exchange, beaches, horse racing, department stores, sport clubs, casinos and other similar places' (Badrakhan 1936: 22). His model was clearly Hollywood, which had established its dominance in the world market from 1919 onwards. But he also paid attention to the cultural call for a national art and literature prevalent in Arabic culture at the time. All the places that he listed are emblematic sites of modernity, particularly that of the rich and upper strata of society. This meant that the cinema of Badrakhan, and of many others who followed in his footsteps, was a cinema clearly influenced by the 1930s and 1940s American cinema of light romance, entertainment and glamour. In fact, the bulk of the films of the 1940s and 1950s were of this type, creating a decidedly modern cinematic social geography with characters well versed in the idioms of modern living, romance and extravagant behaviour. These films inscribed the sites of the modern in the visual memory of the ever-growing number of cinemagoers, putting them firmly on their cognitive map, and gave them an iconic place in the consciousness of an audience clearly willing to embrace modernity.

The geography outlined in the public's cognitive map also included two major spectacular vistas that played a significant role in the elaboration of the national: the desert and the mountains of Lebanon. Since the natural market for Egyptian cinema is the Arab world,[11] it was only natural to include these emblematic sites. Apart from its breathtaking beauty, the desert offered the modern spectator a chance to visualise his/her distant past as Bedouin. This trend is as old as Egyptian cinema itself: three of the first nine films produced in Egypt, between 1927 and 1930,[12] are desert films, and when they became successful also in the rest of the Arab world, opening new markets, many more films repeated the setting throughout the 1930s and 1940s. By the late 1940s, the desert ceased to be sufficient as a site of the past, simple life and innocence; the need was felt to endow the desert locale with a historical or cultural dimension. This engendered two different types of film: one drew on the cultural reservoir of traditional Arabic narrative from *The Arabian Nights* to the great tradition of folk epics,[13] while the other extended the historical tradition emphasising the early

Arabic phase, thus motivating the use of the desert as a locale. The former provided the cinema with a large number of love stories, inscribing platonic love in the psyche of the audience and legitimising a modern mode of interaction between the sexes by giving it a historical dimension. Many of the early films, particularly those of the famous singer Umm Kalthum, *Widad* (Fritz Kramp, 1936),[14] *Dananir* (Ahmed Badrakhan, 1940) and *Sallamah* (Togo Mizrahi, 1943), are of this Bedouin type, opening the floodgates for the musical films that followed.[15] The musical, with its constant demand for more singers and new voices, mobilised the largest number of Arab culture's talents, integrating them into an Egypt-ian/Arab setting, enabling them to inscribe themselves in these films as part of a composite Arab self. The combination of the musical and the desert opened the door to another important thread in the tapestry of the Arab nation: the depiction of early Islam and its major characters. Many films[16] were made registering Islam as a common thread in an Arab ident-ity and a popular theme with the wider Arab audience, making a common Arab identity both possible and visible until, nearly four decades later, the censorship law of 1976 made it impossible to approach such religious issues in film.[17]

The desert setting in all of these films did not rival, let alone replace, the modern settings on the audience's 'cognitive map'. On the contrary, it served in a curious way to reinforce and confirm them as the norm, with the desert as their bygone antecedent. The bulk of the films produced since the 1940s have modern settings, many of them glamorous, conforming to Badrakhan's list. No doubt, this trend was largely driven by commercial factors. By 1940 all of the elements for a thriving film industry (an industrial infrastructure, an urban mass audience with disposable income, distribution and exhibition networks, speculative capital) were available in abundance in Egypt, and since Lebanon provided the Egyptian film industry with many actors, singers and producers,[18] and, more importantly, with audiences and a distribution network, the inclusion of Lebanese settings became inevitable. The intro-duction of Lebanese settings, soon to be followed by other locales, had two dramatic effects. The first was the introduction, in a film's plot, of a visit to Lebanon, allowing the Lebanese audience an opportunity to identify while exploiting the spectacular Lebanese landscapes – its lush green hills and beautiful mountains. The second was more crucial with regard to a sense of the national: it enabled the imagining of a general Arab national identity, rather than a more narrowly defined Egyptian or Lebanese one. Titles demonstrating the wide interest of Egyptian films in other Arab locales include Husain Fawzi's *Bahbah fi Baghdad* (*Bahbah in Baghdad*) (1942) and *Lubnani fi al-Jami'ah* (*A Lebanese in the University*) (1947), Badrakhan's *Qublah fi Lubnan* (*A Kiss in Lebanon*) (1945) and *Al-Qahirah-Baghdad* (*Cairo Baghdad*) (1947), Muhammad's *Abd al-Jawwad's Misri fi Lubnan* (*An Egyptian in Lebanon*) (1952), Yusuf Shahin's *Jamilah* (1958) and 'Atif Salim's *Thawrat al-Yaman* (*The Revolution of Yemen*) (1966). Other Arab actors and singers followed the Lebanese influx of talent into Egyptian cinema: Durayd Lahham, Su'ad Muhammad, Raghdah and Fahd Ballan from Syria; Warda from Algeria; Latifa and Hind Sabri from Tunisia; Habiba from the Maghrib. The presence of so many Arab actors and singers made cinema a truly Arab space inhabited by characters from most Arab coun-tries where Egyptian films were widely shown, mapping the landscape of a wider, fraternal national imaginary.

The Political and the Social

Nothing, however, enhanced the national imaginary like the patriotic films depicting the nation's trials and tribulations in its quest for freedom and independence. Egyptian cinema started with the depiction of the return from exile of the Egyptian leader of the 1919 revolution, and nationalist motifs continued to dominate throughout its development. Although censorship made sure that controversial political issues were out of a films' reach, film-makers found many ways to demonstrate their patriotic feelings through metaphors and allusions. In his use of the classical love story of 'Antar and 'Ablah in the pre-Islamic era, Abu-Saif's *Mughamarat 'Antar wa- 'Ablah* (*The Adventures of 'Antar and 'Ablah*) (1948) turned this classic romance into a metaphor for the Arab defeat in Palestine and a call for unity. The Palestinian *nakbah* (catastrophe) triggered a more direct treatment of the national and the political in Arabic cinema. Politics had been addressed in cinema before: one of the early films of Studio Misr, Fritz Kramp's *Lashin* (1938) had been censored for advocating mass revolt against the corrupt ruling elite. The following year, Kamal Salim's *Al-'Azimah* (*Determination*) (1939), inaugurated a new genre of critical realism in Arabic cinema, attacking injustice and corruption. The depiction of the harshness of life in Egyptian alleys, a microcosm for the world of the poor and a metaphor for the whole country, inaugurated a new aesthetic, countering Badrakhan's insistence on glamour and enabling cinema to voice criticisms of local and British authorities in a notable departure from the allegorisation of Egypt as a beautiful peasant girl striving for freedom and romance, shackled only by outdated mores and conventions. Salim, responding to the 1930s world recession and World War II that followed, demonstrated the acute social polarisation fermenting under the surface. The major achievement of his film was the articulation of a distinct chronotope,[19] a unique time-space dialectic that captured the audience's imagination and took Egyptian cinema away from the Hollywood-inspired fantasy world. Although the alley's world is closed and static, almost frozen in a cyclical-ritualistic time (what Benjamin calls 'messianic time, a simultaneity of past and future in an instantaneous present'[1973: 265]), it is at the same time a part of a wider world in which socio-economic temporality engendered the imagining of the nation, making it a space particularly propitious for allegorical narratives. Salim's film was followed by another Studio Misr production, Kamil al-Tilmisani's *Al-Suq al-Sawda'* (*Black Market*) (1945), a powerful feature using the alley to outline the dire condition Egypt found itself in during World War II. Like *Lashin*, this film also suffered at the hands of the censor for its criticism of black-market profiteers, a corrupt and weak government, the British, and for its advocacy of a popular revolt as the solution to save the alley.

The genre of critical realism and the chronotope of the alley proved to be one of the most enduring elements in Egyptian cinema. It continued to address the trials and tribulations of culture and society over the succeeding decades. Salah Abu-Saif, the assistant director of *Determination*, followed in Salim's footsteps and produced many powerful films in this genre, most of them focusing on the alley.[20] This was also the genre in which Yusuf Shahin directed some of his best films,[21] but the genre reached its pinnacle of complexity in the work of one of Arabic cinema's most talented directors, Tawfiq Salih.[22] Shahin, Salim and Salih's inspiring work played an important role in the development of a national cinema with

its own character, visual vocabulary and narrative world. Their impact on the following generation of film-makers throughout the Arab world was decisive in creating a national Arab
cinema, as evidenced, for instance, in the work of the group who, in 1968, formed Jama'at
al-Sinima al-Jadidah (The Association of New Cinema/ANC) and whose work is responsible for the most interesting films in Arabic cinema over the last three decades: Muhammad
Khan, Mamduh Shukri, Muhammad Radi, Khayri Bisharah, 'Ali 'Abd al-Khaliq, 'Ali
Badrakhan, 'Atif al-Tayyib, Dawud 'Abd al-Sayyid and Radwan al-Kashif made some of the
most memorable films with lasting metaphors distilling the complexity of the national and
political issues of the period into visual masterpieces.

However, to confine the representation of the national to the genre of social exposé and
critical realism would not do justice to other genres, such as the musical and comedy. In
many of the musicals, from Umm Kalthum to the present time of 'Amr Diyab, one often
finds treatments of national and political issues in a light-hearted manner, particularly in the
construction of the visual setting and the selection of tunes and lyrics. Even in comedies, the
national remained one of the major preoccupations. Isma'il Yasin's series can be seen as per-
ceptive and shrewd deconstructions of once-prestigious institutions, particularly before the
1967 defeat. His *Isma'il Yasin fi al-Jaysh (Isma'il Yasin in the Army)* (1955), *Fi al-Bulis (In the
Police)* (1956), *Fi al-Ustul (In the Navy)* (1957), *Bulis Harbi (In the Military Police)* (1958), *Fi al-
Tayaran (In the Air Force)* (1959) and *Bulis Sirri (In the Secret Police)* (1959), all directed by the
ex-army officer Fatin 'Abd al-Wahhab, can be seen as an insider's satirical take on venerable
institutions in a harsh political climate. In the 1950s, it was impossible to be critical of these
military institutions, not only because they produced the Free Officers' Movement that liberated Egypt from the British, but also because the regime succeeded in selling the military
defeat of 1956 as a victory because the aggressors had to leave and end the Suez crisis in
ignominy. In addition, the 1950s were the years of Nasser's rise, pan-Arab nationalism and
anti-colonial policies, in the wake of which cinema gained more leeway to address the
national. In the euphoric years of the 1952 revolution and the negotiation with the British
to evacuate the country, Husain Sidqi made a film straightforwardly called *Yasqut al-Isti'mar
(Down with Colonialism)* (1952).[23] Even Badrakhan directed his most patriotic film, *Mustafa
Kamil* (1952), a biography of a patriotic leader struggling against the British in 1906.[24] But
this euphoria receded and as the undemocratic policies of Nasser and his oligarchy increased,
only comedy remained as a way of puncturing the empty pomposity of the military institutions. Alas, the warning of these films was not heeded until another catastrophe afflicted the
nation in 1967, stripping them of their sanctity and opening the way for a more critical
treatment of political and national issues.

As for the Palestinian *nakbah*, its impact was so devastating that it led to a relative suspen-
sion of the rigid censorship rules, enabling a more direct treatment of political issues. The first
film on the tragic loss of Palestine, Mahmud Zulfaqqar's *Fatah min Falastin (A Woman from
Palestine)* (1948), came only a few months after the 1948 defeat. It told of two related families, one in Egypt the other in Palestine, demonstrating the vital link between the two countries and the impact of what happened in Palestine on the neighbouring Arab countries. The
film featured actors from three Arab countries and many patriotic songs performed by the   **239**

Syrian singer-actress Su'ad Muhammad, appealing for Arab unity and adherence to the Palestinian cause. Some of the songs became emblematic and were still in popular use during the Iraqi wars. The film's heroine and producer, the pioneering actress 'Azizh Amir, followed up this success the next year with *Nadiyah* (1949), directed by the ex-army officer Fatin 'Abd al-Wahhab. The heroine of the film is a strong woman who devoted her life to the upbringing of her brothers and sister after the death of their father, a thinly veiled allegory for an Egypt ready to sacrifice all for her children while emphasising the *nakbah*'s destructive impact on a family deprived of a man who was expected to provide it with a better future.

Palestine remained one of the few themes that inspired films in almost every Arab country, particularly Egypt, Lebanon, Syria and Iraq.[25] The sheer number and decades-long flow of films with a Palestinian theme is in itself a strong indication that the Palestinian cause constitutes a common thread in Arab national consciousness, generating a cinematic genre on national issues while exploring the social and psychological impact of a string of successive defeats. The nature of these films changed after the 1967 defeat with the loss of the rest of Palestine and territories of four more Arab countries (Egypt, Syria, Jordan and Lebanon). Some of the most mature treatments of the Palestinian question and its place in the Arab national consciousness came after 1967, often linking the loss of Palestine to the successive wars that devastated the region from the Suez war onwards. Though the Suez invasion itself produced few films,[26] the next war, in June 1967, was even more devastating and triggered an intense questioning of the Arab project and its future. This national shock seeped slowly into the national consciousness and produced many significant films,[27] all of which pose pointed questions of the Arab establishment as they sought to identify the causes of the 1967 disaster. The following war, in 1973, also produced its fair share of films,[28] but most of them avoided confronting its problematic outcome in a stalemate, at the end of which Egypt lost more land that it had gained by occupying the Sinai. Apart from Ashraf Fahmi's *Hatta Akhir al-'Umr* (*Until the End of One's Life*) (1975), with its potent symbolism of the crippled and impotent pilot whose war-plane was shot down at the beginning of the war and through whose consciousness the film is narrated, most of these films simply blamed the corrupt *ancien régime* for the 1967 defeat, congratulating the present one for its 'victory'. They failed to raise the difficult questions about the conduct of the war, its outcome, or the political vision inherent in its political management, and sought to give credence to the dubious official version of its 'victorious' result, perhaps because by then people were fed up with successive defeats. The deceptive presentation of a defeat as a victory in order to facilitate the radical social changes introduced by Sadat's *infitah* (open-door) economic policy did not last. It was soon reversed when the bread riots of the 1977 showed that the *ancien régime* could not be blamed for all the present ills. The power of critical cinema returned with the advent of the younger generation of the ANC. Their films targeted the corruption of the new regime, its illegitimacy and its lack of any national project.[29] In this closed horizon, violence and counter-violence developed, and after the assassination of Sadat in 1981, many Arab films started to warn against the dangers of terrorism and of the Islamic fundamentalism fuelled by the US-backed Mujahidin's war in Afghanistan. These films often showed the sources of the violence as well as the counter-violence of the state and its impact on national and cultural identity.[30]

The Maghrib Model

The cinema of the Maghrib countries (Algeria, Tunisia, Morocco and, to a lesser extent, Mauritania) is more concerned with form and aesthetics, not so much for its awareness of European cinema, but mainly because of its quest for narrative codes capable of expressing a constantly shifting reality, an elusive, complex identity caught between pre-modernity, colonial and post-colonial modernities, and an anticipated emergence of subjectivities unmarked by any form of coloniality. The filmic language elaborated over the years in the mainstream Egyptian cinema, with its commercial bent, star system, structural platitudes, character prototypes and clichés, was inadequate and incongruous in the context of the new realities emerging after independence in the Maghrib countries. Many outstanding directors did succeed in elaborating a new vocabulary and a different narrative grammar that were capable of addressing the specificity of their situation. Frantz Fanon, one of the founders of post-colonial theory and an activist in the Algerian war of independence, published his acute insights into the damaged, fragmentary and image-based history of the colonised, crucially informing the thinking of many Maghrib film-makers.[31] They understood the image in ways best phrased by Walter Benjamin: 'An image is that in which the past and the now flash into a constellation. In other words: an image is the dialectic at a standstill. For while the relation of the present to the past is a purely temporal, continuous one, that of the past to the now is dialectical – it is not development but image, capable of leaping out' (1973: 262–3). In an attempt to explain the *malédictions du cinéma arabe* in the Maghrib, Boughedir suggested that 'it addresses itself to the mother, France, because its father, the Third World, does not understand it' (Boughedir 1987: 15). In spite of the unfortunate Oedipal language, Boughedir put his finger on one of the major features of this cinema: its double tradition, both Arabic and French. Unlike the cinema of Egypt and the Levant, which assimilated Western cinematic influences and inscribed them into its own cultural dynamics, the Maghrib cinema had to work in a dual milieu and cultural tradition, resulting in a two-toned cinema. It simultaneously interacted with the Arabic cultural heritage – including its modern culture and filmic tradition – and with the European one, especially its French version. Without denying the importance of the financial and cultural links between the Maghrib cinema and France, this is not a parent-child relation, but an ambivalent and highly equivocal cultural dialogue.

The film-makers espoused Fanon's dictum that a national culture

is not a folklore, nor an abstract populism that believes it can discover the people's true nature. It is not made up of the inert dregs of gratuitous actions, that is to say, actions that are less and less attached to the ever present reality of the people. A national culture is the whole body of the efforts made by a people in the sphere of thought to describe, justify, and praise the action through which that people has created itself and keeps itself in existence. (Fanon 1963: 233)

The other main reference in this context is to Amilcar Cabral's characterisation of the dialectics of culture and history:

History allows us to know the nature and extent of the imbalances and conflicts (economic, political and social) which characterize the evolution of a society; culture allows us to know the dynamic syntheses which have been developed and established by social conscience to resolve these conflicts at each stage of its evolution, in the search for survival and progress. (Cabral 1993: 55)

Consequently, Maghrib cinema emphasised the role of national popular culture and the relationship of cultural processes to the forces and relations inherent in the prevailing mode of production, paying considerable attention to the structures of the social totality in which a culture functions. This has given the quest for independence and national identity in the films a distinct flavour, probing the shifting nature of identity, both national and individual, yielding films as varied as Ahmad Rashidi's (Rachedi) *Fajr al-Mu'adhdhabin (The Dawn of the Wretched)* (1965) and *al-Afyun wa 'l-'Asa (Opium and the Club)* (1969), and Muhammad al-Akhdar Hamina's (Lakhdar-Hamina) *Rih al-Uras (The Wind of Aurès)* (1967) and *Waqa'i' Sanawat al-Jamr (Chronicles of the Ember Years)* (1974); in Algeria, Mirzaq 'Ulwash's (Allouache) *Bab al-Wad al-Humah (Bab al-Ouad City)* (1994); while Tunisia contributed 'Abd al-Latif Bin 'Ammar's *Sijnan (Two Prisons)* (1974), Rida Bahi's *Shams al-Diba (The Sun of the Hyena)* (1976) and *'Ubur (Crossing)* (1982) by Mahmud Bin Mahmud. Other films combine the issues of the national with explorations of gender and the position of women in society. Algeria generated Allouache's *Omar Gettlato (Omar: Lethal Macho* aka *Omar Gatlato)* (1976) and Sayyid 'Ali Mazif's *Layla wa Akhawatuha (Layla and Her Sisters)* (1978); Tunisia 'Ammar Khalifi's *Surakh (Cries)* (1972), Salma Bakkar's *Fatimah 75 (Fatima 75)* (1978), Bin 'Ammar's *'Azizah (Aziza)* (1980), Najiyyah bin Mabruk's *al-Sammah (The Trace)* (1988)[32] and Mufidah Talatli *Samt al-Qusur (Silence of the Palaces)* (1994); Morocco Mu'min al-Sumayhi's (Smihi) *al-Sharqi (The Oriental)* (1976), Jilali Farhati's *'Ara'is min Qasab (Reed Dolls)* (1981) and 'Abd al-Rahman al-Tazi's *al-Bahth 'an Zawj Mirati (Looking for a Husband for My Wife)* (1992).[33]

One of the recurring themes in the Maghrib is the conflict between modernity and tradition, often treated in terms of its relevance to notions of identity, to rural-urban migration and, especially in Algeria, to land reform and its problematic impact on the peasants. This is evident in 'Abd al-'Aziz Tulbi's film derived from the outstanding Algerian writer al-Tahir Wattar's story, *Nuwwah (Noua)* (1972), demonstrating the interaction between cinema and the Algerian novel as well as the processes of social liberation and the construction of a national identity. Other films demonstrate how the national is often subsumed in the tension between self and (usually colonial) 'other', including the 'others' who continued colonial practices in the post-independence era. Films include, in Algeria, Sayyid 'Ali Mazif's *Masirat al-Ru'ah* or *al-Ruhhal (The Nomads)* (1975) and *al-Fahham (The Charcoal Maker)* (1972) and Muhammad Bu- 'Ammari's (Bouamari) *al-Mirath (The Inheritance)* (1974); in Tunisia, Ibrahim Babay's *Wa-Ghada (Tomorrow)* (1972) and al-Tayyib al-Wuhayshi's (Taïeb Louhichi) *Zill al-Ard (Shadow of the Earth)* (1982); in Morocco, Ahmad al-Bu'nani's *al-Ayyam al-Ayyam (Days, Days)* (1978), Muhammad al-Tazi's *'Abbas (Abbas)* (1986) and 'Abd al-Rahman al-Tazi's *Ibn al-Sabil (The Long Journey)* (1981). In a number of them, the national dimension is posed in terms of a conflict between self and other in the context of a migration to France and its impact on both the migrant and the traditional 'self' embodied by those left behind. Migration to France is seen in most of these films as the beguiling mirage that entices the youth of the country but which only offers them disappointment and destruction. For historical and economic reasons, Tunisia seems most concerned with this theme. Its scarce natural resources and dependence on tourism make its youth more vulnerable to the mirage. Nasir Qattari's (Ktari) *Al-Sufara'* (*Ambassadors*) (1975/6) and Louhichi's *Zill al-Ard* are clear examples of how the problems of modernity constantly interact with those of 'self' and 'other'.

A different, highly symbolic treatment of the modernity-tradition motif can be found in *al-Sarab* (*Mirage*) (1980), directed by the Moroccan poet and writer Ahmad al-Bu'nani. The film is set in a nightmarish atmosphere between fantasy and reality, past illusions and present hardship. Ahmad Rashidi's *'Ali fi Bilad al-Sarab* (*Ali in Mirage Country*) (1979) again identifies the destructive illusion of a desirable 'elsewhere', associating it with a devastating loss of self-respect. The fragmentation and near obliteration of national memory, particularly in the case of Algeria, which remained under French colonial rule for over 130 years during which the systematic Gallicisation of its culture was overwhelming, resulted in a recurring interest in the fabric of both historical and personal memory. Muhammad Bu-'Ammari's (Bouamari) *al-Mirath (The Inheritance)* adds a significant dimension to this motif by identifying the heritage of the colonial period as that of scorched earth, obliterated memory and linguistic amnesia. The hero forgets his own language except for one word: colonialists. He regains his linguistic memory and identity through liberation and by reclaiming the scorched land. In fact, a preoccupation with the fabric of personal and historical memory pervades virtually every film in the Maghrib cinema and may well account for the relative absence of a varied menu of cinematic entertainment genres, for which the Maghrib audiences turn to Egyptian cinema.[34] However, it must be remembered that the common features of the Maghrib cinema are matched by diversity and difference in the history and traditions of each country. The concern for history, politics and the mythic aspects of traditional culture is prevalent in all these cinemas, but each one expresses it in different forms, as demonstrated in the Algerian case, the richest and most representative cinema of these countries.

The Algerian Case

Arabic cinema in Algeria only started seriously after independence. It appeared to have all the prerequisites for success. The French assumption that Algeria was a *département de la France* had a positive impact on the infrastructure necessary for film production and distribution, which independent Algerian cinema inherited. This was a colonial structure, elements of which persisted after independence, some even to the present day. However, this infrastructure did not engender an indigenous Algerian cinema: 'In Algeria – which in 1933 already had 150 theatres, more than Egypt in the same period – not a single feature film was shot by a native director before independence in 1962' (Shafik 1998: 15). The embryonic forms of Algerian cinema were conceived, so to speak, on the battlefield, and born in the *maquis*, the   **243** underground movement of the Front de Libération Nationale (FLN). In 1957 in Tebessa, Constantine, the first Algerian cinema group was formed, the Groupe Farid, its six members being committed to involving the cinema in the armed struggle,[35] documenting it to inform *inter*national as much as local opinion. Most reels have been lost, but surviving ones, some of them written by Frantz Fanon, are important as the first purely Algerian films linking the inception of cinema to the national cause. After independence the state assumed the administration of the film industry without significantly changing its structures. Despite the theoretical rejection of commercial cinema, codified in the National Charter and other political pronouncements, the industry was run on a primarily commercial, rather than educative and cultural basis. Yet, constant state intervention in cinema was maintained to regulate and control its ideological function. Although the close relationship between cinema and politics in Algeria is one of the major causes of its decline, particularly after 1980, the key factor in its demise, censorship, was inherited from its colonial predecessor. From 1964 onwards, every film shown required official authorisation. A literary and artistic commission was established to examine each project and supervise each script. In 1968 the Ministry of Information took responsibility for censorship, removed large sections from and banned complete films which allegedly 'threatened public order or good morals' (Maherzi 1982: 208).[36] No clear guidelines were laid down, although the industry asked for them.

From the start, Algerian cinema considered itself a major player in the cinema of the Third World and in its liberation movement. Ahmad Rashidi's (Rachedi) *Fajr al-Mu'adhdhabin* (*The Dawn of the Wretched*), regarded as the first truly Algerian film, shows a strong concern for the Third World dimension of the national identity, including archive footage of the struggles in Vietnam, South Africa, Angola and so on, and a commentary by the eminent francophone Algerian writer Mouloud Mammeri. In Salim Riyad's *Sana'ud* (*We Will Return*) (1972), the Palestinian *fedayeen* include an Algerian fighter to demonstrate the importance of the Arab dimension of the Algerian identity and the concern for the Palestinian question. This is also the main theme of Faruq Billufah's *Nahlah* (1988), depicting the Lebanese civil war as a microcosm of the Arab world in quest of a unifying national symbol.

Nationalisation of the film industry in Algeria was a mixed blessing. It freed film-makers from constraints of the market but subjected them to rigid state control, political guidelines and official censorship. This not only led to bad organisation and an insidious self-censorship, it also perpetuated the propagandistic attitudes inherited from the colonial regime. On the artistic plane, this generated anodyne themes, stereotypical characters – particularly the idealised *mujahid* in the liberation struggle – and the propagation of simplistic oppositions between town/country, hero/anti-hero, good/evil, which became fundamental identity construction strategies. The study of the rise and decline of Algerian cinema is, at one level, a study of the transformation of both the national and individual notions of identity. In the words of Edward Said:

The closeness of the world's body to the text's body forces readers to take both into consideration. Worldliness, circumstantially, the text's status as an event having sensuous particularity as well as historical contingency, are considered as being incorporated in the text, an infrangible part of its capacity for conveying and producing meaning. (Said 1983: 39)

Algerian cinema's germination on the battlefield left a lasting mark on its structure and vision for many years, continuing beyond independence. It became a militant cinema with an educative mission, brimming with metaphors of change, rebirth and the forces of nature, equating change with the sweeping winds that cleanse and refresh or the glowing fire that purifies and forges new realities.

The early Algerian films of the 1960s and early 1970s were energised by revolutionary verve, but also by a desire to exorcise the ghosts of the 'epistemic violence' involved in the production of colonial subjects (Spivak 1990: 77). Fanon's brilliant analysis of the subaltern mentality produced by a 130-year history of colonial violence spurred the pioneer film-makers in Algeria, formed in the *maquis* of the liberation war, to rewrite the history of the victims and to construct a new sense of identity assuming the desire to control one's own political destiny. To this end, they mobilised stark, often simplistic oppositions between, on the one hand, a positive hero, the *mujahid* (revolutionary or freedom fighter), the peasant and/or the intellectual, and, on the other, his counterpart, the anti-hero, either a French sol-dier or an Algerian collaborator. The *mujahid* is always noble, generous, proud and ready to sacrifice everything for the revolution. In 'Ammar al-'Askari's (Laskari) *Dawriyyah nahwa la-Sharq* (*Eastern Patrol*) (1972) and Muhammad al-Akhdar Haminah's (Lakhdar-Hamina) *Waqa'i' Sanawat al-Jamr* (*Chronicles of the Ember Years*) (1974) even the hero's name becomes emblematic: Larbi (the Arab). In the former film, Larbi has a lively eye, an attentive ear and a firm, lithe step. One soldier continues shaving under bombardment while another whis-tles a revolutionary tune! In the latter film, Si Larbi, the intellectual nationalist, is the very incarnation of reason, kindness and awareness. In Ahmad al-'Allam's (Lallem) *Mantiqah Muharramah* (*Forbidden Zone*) (1972), girls comment admiringly about the fighters' size and white teeth. Lakhdar Hamina's *Hasan Tiru* (*Hasan the Terror*) (1967) shows, through a comic reversal, how any true Algerian cannot but be a *mujahid*: the more the simpleton Hasan tries to avoid politics, the deeper he finds himself embroiled in its stratagems. The discovery of identity is synonymous with the unveiling of the *mujahid* inside everyone.

In the *mise en scène*, the *mujahid* is associated with the heart of the country, its mountains and countryside, partly, no doubt, because cities such as Algiers and Oran were dominated by the French. *Forbidden Zone* and *Eastern Patrol*, as well as Hamina's *Rih al-Uras* (*The Wind of Aurès*), emphasise the solidarity between peasants and guerrillas. Rachedi's *Opium and the Club* stresses the harshness of a fighter's life as its hero, a medical doctor, leaves his clinic and comforts in the capital to joins the *maquis* in the mountains. In *Chronicles of the Ember Years*, a wholesome moral and intellectual power structure is portrayed, with honest leaders acting as a positive unifying force. The *mujahid* is also the staunch fighter in Hamina's *December* (1972) whose steadfast resistance and endurance lead his French torturer to denounce his own brutality.

The French soldier in these films presents the ugly face of colonialism. Tulbi's *Noua* nar-rates a vast panorama spanning the history of modern Algeria over two centuries, effectively **245** exposing the French armed forces. In *Hasan the Terror*, the brutality of the French is only matched by their stupidity, while Mustafa Badi''s *Hurub Hasan Tiru* (*The Escape of Hasan*) (1974) denounces French brutality in an attack on the *qasabah*, the popular quarter of Algiers. In Muhammad Zinat's *Tahya ya Didu* (*Long Live Didu!*) (1971), a French soldier's brutality outlives his involvement in the war when, on a nostalgic trip to Algeria, he meets the man he had tortured. This typology was so deeply ingrained that, when Hamina portrayed Col. Saint-Meran as showing remorse over the torture of an Algerian revolutionary in *December*, the film was subjected to virulent critical attacks. However, some sympathetic portrayals of individual soldiers can be found: in *Opium and the Club*, Rashidi pays tribute to French deserters. The binary opposition between the Algerian 'self' and the French 'other' extends to the depiction of the degradation and exploitation of the rural poor by settlers (*colons*), often colluding with local feudal potentates, as in *Noua* and in Salim Riyad's *Rih al-Janub* (*South Wind*) (1975), based on a well-known Algerian novel by 'Abd al-Hamid Bin Hadduqah, who also wrote the script.

The national intellectual is also a positive hero. In his comprehensive study of Algerian cinema, Maherzi defines the intellectual in a Gramscian sense, including schoolteachers, students, revolutionary politicians and doctors. In *Chronicles of the Ember Years*, Si Larbi is the intellectual: he wears round spectacles and European clothes, reads newspapers avidly, subscribes to the unifying power of Islam, but is distrusted by the peasants until he proves himself as a fighter. The schoolteacher, in Muhammad Bu-'Ammari's (Bouamari) *al-Fahham* (*The Charcoal Maker*) (1972), raises the hero's consciousness, and in *South Wind*, another schoolteacher, Tahir (literally: the pure one) is the incarnation of reason and wisdom as well as the embodiment of a pan-Arab identity; he was educated at the al-Zaytunah Mosque in Tunisia and reads the major Egyptian writers, including Taha Husain and Naguib Mahfouz. In their different ways, such figures represent an 'antagonistic sense of national identity by seeking to reconnect with traditions that got lost or were displaced or distorted by colonial rule' (Pines and Willemen 1989: 18). Whereas the simple binary structure of the narrative opposed the *mujahid* and the French soldier, the intellectual hero's antagonist is the Algerian feudalist, the *marabout* or the bureaucrat. With each of these adversaries, sub-plots are developed to mirror the main conflict, mostly referring to an 'enemy within', suggesting that many film-makers assumed that Algerians were effectively colonised by other Algerians.[37]

This opposition between the national protagonist and his several corrupt antagonists is analogous to the spatial opposition between city and country. Most of the French and other Europeans lived in cities, while the bulk of Algerians lived in the country and the mountains. If they lived in cities, it was either in the old *qasabah, madina* or in *bidonvilles*. In 1954, when the struggle for independence started, Algeria had 9 million Muslim Algerians while the European population was almost 1 million. In *South Wind*, the city is portrayed as representing knowledge, power and equality, and the 'lure of the city occupies central place in a number of Algerian films' (Maherzi 1982: 238). But 'the greater part of the Muslim population was crowded into the less productive part of the land, without the capital to develop it and with limited facilities for credit, in spite of small and late attempts by the government to provide them. As a result, living standards were low and the rate of rural unemployment high' (Hourani 1991: 369). The reclaimed 'European' city may at first be seen as a paradise of wealth, sex and technology, but the city itself is divided into two distinct parts: the European city of the *colon*, graced with the school, the church, the *mairie*, the barracks and the police station, and the Arab city with slums, half-naked children, people suffering from eye disease, in other words, the 'village *nègre*' of *Opium and the Club* or of *Chronicles of the Ember Years*.

The narrative polarisation between heroes and anti-heroes, country and city, self and other, with a manichaean but nonetheless effective sense of identity, is the natural product of the FLN's eight years of painful and bloody struggle for liberation culminating in independence, with its concomitant sense of self-confidence and euphoria. By the mid-1970s, the euphoria had ebbed away under the pressure of rapid demographic change, economic stagnation, political failure, nepotism and rampant corruption. It was replaced by a sense of frustration and despair. The years of embers, as Hamina called them, ceased to glow or inspire confidence. By the end of 1970s they had turned into ashes, the bitter taste and suffocating effect of which were widely experienced by the young. The revolutionary values and ideals had become the official narrative of the ruling establishment, legitimating its oppressive power. Free discussion of the official version of history was forbidden. By the 1980s, 70 per cent of Algerians had been born after independence and did not know anything about the glorious years of FLN except what they had learned in history books and heard in the discredited official discourse. For most of them, the reality of the new Algeria, with its economic crisis, wide social disparities, unemployment, housing shortage, sexual frustration, rampant corruption and dwindling educational system, was depressing. The new realities started to speak louder than the narrative of heroism and the cult of positive heroes, reaching its climax in the riots of October 1988. The familiar linear and narrowly syllogistic narratives could not convey the complexities of these new conditions, as became clear from the success of films such as Mirzaq 'Ulwash's (Allouache) *Omar Gatlato* and Sayyid 'Ali Mazif's *Layla wa-Akhawatuha* (*Layla and Her Sisters*) (1978). In Allouache's *Omar Gatlato*, the old patriotic *mujahids* of the 1950s and early 1960s have become the nouveaux riches and all-powerful bureaucrats of the late 1970s and 1980s. The menacing march of Omar and his friends through the squalid streets of the poverty-ridden quarter of Bab al-Wad in Algiers at the beginning is contrasted to Omar's powerlessness throughout the rest of the film. The realisation of a dream turns it into a nightmare, and the more possessive the dream, the more claustrophobic the nightmare. Omar's inaction, almost impotence, made him the new hero, or rather the anti-hero, of the post-independence era. The film heralded a new Algerian cinema with narratives that disrupt any form of identification.

Four years earlier, Bouamari's *The Charcoal Maker* had initiated such changes to the narrative conventions with his Eisensteinian rhythmic montage and quasi-static narrative mode. Bouamari then went on to further experimentation, culminating in his *al-Khutwah al-Ula* (*First Step*) (1981) and *al-Rafd* (*Refusal*) (1985). The use of rhythmic montage allowed Bouamari to create sequences in which the sound track is unsynchronised with the beat of the cutting to convey the asynchrony at the heart of the nation. The narration of the disintegration of the charcoal maker's old world under the onslaught of 'progress' undermines the linear logic of the narrative structure, an effect underlined by the graphic tonalities produced by charcoal marks on his face and limbs, and by the degrees of illumination and light vibration, conveying the director's critical vision in a way that enabled him to avoid the censor's scissors. With *Omar Gatlato*, unequivocally one of the masterpieces of the new Algerian cinema, this technique was developed into a full-scale cinematic alienation-effect. Omar's piece-to-camera at the beginning of the film initiates an interesting conflict between the character and its double: the audience, replicated inside the film in the many scenes of ordinary Algerians watching Indian films and recording their songs off the screen. This creates a different kind of identification in which the actual audience does not identify with the events of the narrated film or with its hero, Omar, but with the audience within the film, mirroring its most objectionable traits. This inversion of cinema's recreational space into a space for incrimination and indictment distinguishes the new cinema from its ancestor. Here one witnesses the deconstruction of national myth, its clash with the changing reality and an emerging sense of a different identity. Such devices are used again effectively in Allouache's recent film, *Bab al-Ouad City* (1994).

Costa Gavras, who had worked with Algerians on his co-production *Z* or *Anatomy of Political Assassination* (1968), appears to have inspired *al-Kharif: October fi al-Jaza'ir* (*Autumn: October in Algiers*) (1992) by Malik Lakhdar-Hamina, the son of the famous film director.[38] *Autumn* probes both the fermenting discontent that exploded in the riots of October 1988, deploying the autumn metaphor to talk about the creeping decay of a whole nation that found itself in an impasse between Islamic fanatics and a corrupt establishment. Ahmad Rashidi's *Al-Tahunah* (*The Mill*) (1983) also shows how this plague has burrowed deep inside the political establishment. This film is remarkable in its use of satire to investigate the major Algerian problems through the simple, realistic device of a small village mill and its nationalisation. Its daring criticism of the leader of the political establishment at the beginning of independence adds to its credibility.[39] The 'leader', conveniently referred to as *al-za'im* to avoid close identification with the past, is to visit a small village. The bureaucrats of the local committee rush to nationalise everything in sight while a journalist provides a suitably 'spun' narrative of events. His counter-factual account is highly appreciated by the authorities. Rashidi went back to his own village, Tebessa, in the district of Constantine, which also happens to be the birth-place of the Algerian cinema itself: that was where the Groupe Farid was formed in 1957. Going back thirty years later demonstrates that Algerian cinema is rejuvenating its vision and renewing its agenda.

The trajectory of Algerian cinema can be seen as itself allegorising the nation, torn between various binary oppositions that confined its sense of nationalism and froze it into a claustrophobic, static frame. This, of course, is in marked contrast to the story of the Egyptian cinema, which sees the national as open, flexible and fluid, inscribed into all aspects of human experience, including its precarious, impossible paradoxes.

Notes

1. All Arabic names and titles of books and films will be transliterated according to a simplified version, i.e. without diacritical marks, of the standard system. When a director is known in the

West by a different spelling, this has been added in parentheses, unless the difference is deemed not to impede recognition. The only exception concerns the names of some film-makers from the Maghrib who are well known by the often peculiar spelling of their names in Latin script.

2. For a detailed account of the history of this period see Ahmad al-Hadari (1987).

3. The first proclamation of the French expedition to Egypt in July 1798 praised the glory of ancient Egypt and emphasised the Egyptians' difference from their neighbours.

4. One is speaking here of a large group of film-makers and a sizeable output of films, amounting to some forty features over the last three decades and narrating, since 1970, the vicissitudes of immigrant life in the margins of contemporary European societies. Such output does include the work of Yasmina Benguigui and Fatima Jebli, but refers mainly to that of the film-makers who constitute *beur* cinema, a term formed by the inversion of the two consonants in the word 'Arabe' (RB); examples are Mohamed Benayat, Mehdi Charef, Abdelkrim Bahloul, Rachid Bouchareb, Okacha Touita, Amor Hakkar, Malik Chibane, Karim Dridi and Farida Belghoul.

5. Viola Shafik suggests that the first Egyptian film documented the funeral of the patriotic leader Mustafa Kamil in 1909, claiming that she got the information from Hadari. However, Hadari states clearly that he is not sure who filmed this funeral because many of the newsreels at the time were filmed by foreigners (Shafik 1998: 11) and (Hadari 1987: 96).

6. Egypt had a vibrant theatre movement since the 1860s. The proliferation of theatre houses contributed dramatically to the spread of cinema in Egypt.

7. Ahmad Badrakhan and Muris Kassab studied film-directing in France; Muhammad 'Abd al-'Azim and Hasan Murad studied cinematography in Germany. After their return, these four film-makers played a crucial role in the development of Egypt's film industry.

8. Karim remade the film in 1952, a sign of the text's iconic importance in the culture.

9. By the beginning of Word War II there were nine more studios in Egypt.

10. Such as Kamal Salim, Ahmad Kamil Mursi, Kamil al-Tilmisani, Salah Abu-Saif, Muhammad Karim, Ahmad Badrakhan, 'Abd al-'Aziz Fahmi, 'Imad Hamdi, Kamal al-Shaikh, Hasan Murad and Sa'id al-Shaikh.

11. For decades the distribution of Egyptian films in other Arab countries was responsible for 50 per cent of the Egyptian film industry's revenues, a factor no producer could ignore.

12. See Ibrahim Lama's *Qublat fi al-Sahra'* (*Kiss in the Desert*) (1928) and *Faji'ah Fawq al-Haram* (*A Disaster on the Pyramid*) (1929) and Widad 'Urfi's *Ghadat al-Sahra'* (*The The Belle of Desert*) (1929).

13. Films sourced in *The Arabian Nights* and other traditional narratives include Niyazi Mustafa's *Antar and 'Ablah* (1945), *Layla al-'Amiriyyah* (*Layla of the 'Amir Tribe*) (1948), *'Antar Ibn Shaddad* (1961) and *al-Badawiyyah a;-'Ashiqah* (*The Loving Bedouin*) (1963), Fu'ad Jazayirli's *Shehrazad* (1946) and *Juha wa-l-Saba' Banat* (*Juha and the Seven Girls*) (1947), Salah Abu-Saif's *Mughamarat 'Antar wa-'Ablah* (*The Adventures of 'Antar and 'Ablah*) (1948) and Husain Fawzi's *Hallaq Baghdad* (*The Barber of Baghdad*) (1954).

14. According to Galal El Charkawi, contributing to G. Sadoul (1966: 81), Badrakhan was the assistant of the German director of this massively popular musical, the first of Studio Misr's productions.

15. Subsequently, the musical thrived as a genre deploying all the major singers – e.g. Muhammad **249**

'Abd al-Wahab, Asmahan, Layla Murad, Frid al-Atrash, Sabah and 'Abd al-Halim Hafiz, all the way to the contemporary singers 'Amr Diyab and Latifah. Many of the musicals had an important nationalist dimension.

16. These films started with Fu'ad Jazayirli's *Fath Misr* (*The Conquest of Egypt*) (1948) and continued with, among others, Ibrahin 'Izziddin's *Zuhur al-Islam* (*The Rise of Islam*) (1951), Ahmad Tukhi's *Intisar al-Islam* (*Victory of Islam*) (1952), *Bilal Mu'azzin al-Rasul* (*Bilal the Muezzin of the Prophet*) (1953) and *Bayt Allah al-Haram* (*The Sanctified Ka'bah*) (1957), Husain Sidqi's *Khalid Ibn al-Walid* (*Khalid Ibn Walid*) (1958), Ibrahim 'Imarah's *Higrat al-Rasul* (*The Higra of the Prophet*) (1964), Salah Abu-Saif's *Fajr al-Islam* (*The Dawn of Islam*) (1971), and Husam al-Din Mustafa's *Al-Shayma' Ukht al-Rasul* (*Shayma' the Sister of the Prophet*) (1972).

17. For a full list, see Hashim al-Nahhas (1986: 185–7).

18. This is evidenced in the work of, for instance, Bishara Wakim, Ilyas Mu'addib, 'Abd al-Salam al-Nabulsi, Farid al-Atrash, Asmahan, Sabah, Nur al-Huda, Najah Sallam, Nilly, Mary Qwini, Asia Daghir.

19. For a detailed discussion of the chronotope see Bakhtin (1981: 84–257), Todorov (1984: 78-93) and Morson and Emerson (1990: 366–432).

20. Examples include *Al-Usta Hasan* (*Master Hasan*) (1951), *Al-Wahsh* (*The Gangster*) (1954), *Shabab Imra'ah* (*Youth of a Woman*) (1956), *Al-Futuwwah* (*The Bully*) (1957), *Al-Qahira 30* (*Cairo 1930*) (1966), *Hammam al-Malatili* (*Malatili Hamam*) (1973), *Al-Saqqa Mat* (*Death of a Water Carrier*) (1977) and *Al-Muwatin Misri* (*An Egyptian Citizen*) (1991).

21. For instance *Sira' fi al-Wadi* (*A Struggle in the Valley*) (1953), *Bab al-Hadid* (*Cairo Central Station*) (1958), *Fajr Yawm Jadid* (*A Dawn of a New Day*) (1965), *Al-Ard* (*The Egyptian Earth*) (1969) and *Al-'Usfur* (*The Sparrow*) (1974).

22. Salih only made six features during his long career: *Darb al-Mahabil* (*Fools Alley*) (1955), *Sira' al-Abtal* (*Heroes Struggle*) (1962), *Al-Mutamarridun* (*The Rebels*) (1968), *Yawmiyyat Na'ib fi al-Aryaf* (*Diaries of a Country Magistrate*) (1969), *Zuqaq al-Sayyid al-Bulti* (*The Alley of Mr Bulti*) (1969) and *Al-Makhdu'un* (*The Duped*) (1972).

23. Similar films were made in other Arab countries, such as Subhi Saifuddin's *al-Rajul al-Samad* (*The Formidable Resister*) (1976), about Abu-'Ali Milham Qasim's struggle against the occupying Ottoman in 1910, and Nabil al-Malih's *Al-Fahd* (*The Leopard*) (1972), from a novel by the well-known Syrian writer Haydar Hayder, showing the heroic struggle of a simple peasant against the army in Syria. Muhammad Shukri Jamil's *al-Mas'ala al-Kubra* (*The Crucial Question*) (1983) shows the struggle of the Iraqis against British colonialism during Rashid Ali al-Kilani's revolt of 1920 and the heroic deeds of the famous tribal leader Dari Mahmud, told from the perspective of the colonised. Seeing it some twenty years later one is struck by its relevance to the present Iraqi situation, with America repeating in 2004 the mistakes made by the British in 1920.

24. Films on leading national figures became a genre in itself, with Yusuf Shahin's *Jamilah* (1958), featuring the struggle of the Algerian Jamila BuHraid against the French, and, more recently, Samir Zikra's *Turab al-Ghurba* (The *Strangers' Dust*) (2002), celebrating the Syrian dissident intellectual al-Kawakibi's fight against tyranny and his call for a pan–Arab nationalism.

25. In Egypt, there were *Arad al-Abtal (The Land of Heroes)* (Nizi Mustafa, 1953), *Wada' fi al-Fajr* (*Farewell at Dawn*) (Hasan al-Imam, 1956), *Allah Ma'ana* (*God with Us*) (Badrakhan, 1955), *Ard al-*

Salam (*Land of Peace*) (Kamal al-Shaikh, 1957), *Rudd Qalbi* (*Return My Heart*) ('Izziddin Zulfaqqar, 1957). In Lebanon *Al-Filistini al-Tha'ir* (*The Rebellious Palestinian*) (Rida Miyassar, 1969), *Fidak Ya Filastin* (*For You Palestine*) (Rida Miyassar, 1969), *Ajras al-'Awdah* (*Bells of Return*) (Taysir 'Abbud, 1969), *Kuluna Fada'iyyun* (*We Are All Freedom Fighters*) (Muna Salim, 1969), *Kafr Qasim* (Burhan 'Ulwiyyah, 1974). In Syria *Iklil al-Shawk* (*Crown of Thorns*) (Nibil al-Malih, 1969), *'Amilyyat al-Sa'a al-Sadisa* (*Six O'clock Operation*) (Sayfuddin Shawkat, 1970), *Al-Sikkin* (*The Knife*) (Khalid Hamadah, 1970) and *Rijal That al-Shams* (*Men Under the Sun*) (Muhammad Shahin, Marwan Mu'azzin and Nabil al-Malih, 1971), *Al-Maghdu'un* (*The Duped*) (Tawfiq Salih, 1972), *Al-Abtal Yuladun Marratayn* (*Heroes Are Born Twice*) (Salah Duhni, 1977) and Amin Al-Bunni's trilogy *Firdaws al-Hadarah* (*Paradise of Civilization*) (1974), *Al-Yawm al-Tawil* (*Long Day*) (1976) and *Filistin hiy al-Asl* (*Palestine is the Source*) (1978). In Iraq *Risalah Ilayk* (*A Letter for You*) ('Ali Siyam, 1968) and *Al-Tariq Ila al-'Awdah* (*The Way to Return*) ('Abd al-Wahhab al-Hindi, 1969). In Jordan *Al-Bayt* (*Home*) (Kazim al-'Itri, 1976), *Al-Haql* (*The Field*) (Subaih 'Abd al-Karim, 1977) and *Al-Aswar* (*Walls*) (Muhammad Shukri Jamil, 1979).

26. For instance, 'Izziddin Zulfaqqar's *Bur-Sa'id* (*Port Said*) (1957) and *Nahr al-Hubb* (*River of Love*) (1960), Nizi Mustafa's *Shayatin al-Jaww* (*Devils of the Air*) (1956), *Sajin Abu-Za'bal* (*The Prisoner of Abu-Za'bal*) (1957) and *Samra' Sina'* (*The Dark Beauty of Sinai*) (1959), Hasan al-Imam's *Hubb min Nar* (*Love Flames*) (1958), Rimon Mansur's *Nur al-Layl* (*Night Light*) (1959), Sayyid Budair's *'Amaliqat al-Bihar* (*The Lords of the Sea*) (1960), Salah Abu-Saif's *La Tutfi' al-Shams* (*Don't Put Out the Sun*) (1961), Majidah's *Man Uhibb* (*Whom Should I Love*) (1965) and Husam al-Din Mustafa's *Jarimah fi al-Hayy al-Hadi'* (*A Crime in a Calm Quarter*) (1966).

27. For instance, Husain Kamal's *Thartharah Fawq al-Nil* (*Drifters on the Nile*) (1971) and *Ihna Butu' al-Utubis* (*We Were Caught in the Bus*) (1978), Sa'id Marzuq's *Al-Khawf* (*Fear*) (1972), 'Ali 'Abd al-Khaliq's *Ughniyyah 'ala al-Mamarr* (*A Song in the Passes*) (1973), Muhammad Radi's *Abna' al-Samt* (*Children of Silence*) (1974) and *Wa Da' Hibbi Hunak* (*And There My Love Was Lost*) (1982), Ghalib Sha'ath's *Al-Zilal fi al-Janib al-Akhar* (*Shadows on the Other Side*) (1973), Yusuf Shahin's *Al-'Usfur* (*The Sparrow*) (1974), an Egyptian–Algerian co-production, and Nadir Jalal's *48 Sa'ah fi Isra'il* (*48 Hours in Israel*) (1998).

28. For instance, Hilmi Raflah's *Al-Wafa' al-'Azim* (*Great Loyalty*) (1974), Nadir Jalal's *Budur* (1974), Husam al-Din Mustafa *Al-Rasasah La-Tazal fi Jaybi* (*The Bullet is Still in My Pocket*) (1974), Ali Badrakhan's *Al-Karnak* (*Karnak*) (1975), Ashraf Fahmi's *Hatta Akhir al-'Umr* (*Until the End of One's Life*) (1975), Muhammad Radi's *Al-'Umr Lahzah* (*Life is a Moment*) (1978) and Ihab Radi's *Fatah min Isra'il* (*A Girl from Israel*) (1999).

29. Films such as Muhammad Khan's *Zawjat Rajul Muhimm* (*A Wife of an Important Man*) (1988), *Ahlam Hind wa-Kamilya* (*Dreams of Hind and Kamilya*) (1988) and *Faris al-Madinah* (*The Knight of the City*) (1992), 'Atif al-Tayyib's *Sawwaq al-Utubis* (*Bus Driver*) (1983), *Katibat al-I'dam* (*Execution Brigade*) (1989), *Naji al-'Ali* (1992) and *Didd al-Hukumah* (*Against the Government*) (1993), Muhammad al-Najjar's *Zaman Hatim Zahran* (*The Time of Hatim Zahran*) (1988) and *Al-Hajjamah* (*The Fighters*) (1992), and Dawud 'Abd al-Sayyid's *Ard al-Khawf* (*Land of Fear*) (2000).

30. There are many films on this theme, such as Nadir Jalal's *Al-Irhab* (*Terror*) (1989), Sharif 'Arafah's *Al-Irhab wa-l-Kabab* (*Terror and Kebab*) (1992) and *Tuyur al-Zalam* (*Birds of Darkness*) (1995), Nadir Jalal's *Al-Irhabi* (*The Terrorist*) (1994) and Sa'd 'Arafah's *Al-Mala'ikah La Taskun al-Ard*

(*Angels Don't Dwell on Earth*) (1995). These films explored the roots of terror and foreshadowed its proliferation.

31. For a detailed account of Fanon's concept of national culture, see Fanon (1963: 208–48).

32. Najiyyah bin Mabruk's *al-Sammah* literally translates as 'The Poisoned' or 'The Contaminated', but it was screened by Channel Four in Britain as *The Trace*.

33. The relatively large number of films dealing with gender issues in Tunisia is due to the special position of women there. In Tunisia, the only country in the Arab world with a particularly strong women's movement, personal laws are not based on the strict Islamic *shari'ah* (religious jurisprudence).

34. This argument was put forward by Muhammad Barradah at a round-table reported in the *Al-Quds Newspaper*, London, 19 April, 1995, p. 7.

35. The group consisted of Ali Jannawi (Djanaoui), Muhammad Junaiz (Guenez), Jamal Shandarli, Ahmad Rashidi and René Vautier, a French film-maker committed to the Algerian cause who went underground with others, cameras in hand, to film the resistance fighters. Three of the members of this group died on the battlefield during the liberation war. This model was later adopted by the Palestinian cinema after the rise of Palestinian resistance.

36. In his detailed study of the role of the censor in Algeria, Lotfi Maherzi (1982) demonstrates the arbitrary wielding of power and the haphazard nature of Algerian censorship.

37. See Al-Amin Mirbah's (Lamine Merbah) *Bani Hindil* or *The Uprooted* (1976), or Laskari Hadj Buqarmudah's *al-Mufid* (*The Benevolent*) (1979).

38. Although it is an important film in its own right, *Autumn* raises the old accusations of nepotism and mismanagement often levelled against Muhammad Lakhdar-Hamina. The film is directed by one of his sons, Malik, and produced by another, Tariq Lakhdar-Hamina. Malik also acts in the film with his uncle, Marwan Hamina.

39. Criticism of a previous political leader is, by and large, permissible in most Arab countries, but not of the present one. Artists use this as an alibi to avoid the censor, but they generally aim at the present, using the past as a mirror.

References

Abu-Shadi, 'Ali (1998), *al-Sinima wa-l-Siyasah* (*Cinema and Politics*), Cairo: Dar Sharqiyyat.

Adorno, Theodor W. (1992), *Notes to Literature* 2, edited by Rolf Tiedemann, translated by Shierry Webber Nicholsen, New York: Columbia University Press.

Badrakhan, Ahmad (1936), *Sinima* (*Cinema*), Cairo.

Bakhtin, M. M. (1981), *The Dialogic Imagination,* translated by Caryl Emerson and Michael Holquist, Austin: University of Texas Press.

Bakhtin, M. M. (1986), *Speech Genres and Other Late Essays*, translated by Vern W. McGee, Austin: University of Texas Press.

Benjamin, Walter (1973), *Illuminations*, edited by Hannah Arendt, translated by Harry Zohn, London: Fontana.

Bhabha, Homi (ed.) (1990), *Nation and Narration*, London: Routledge.

Boughedir, Ferid (1987), 'Malédictions des cinémas arabes', *CinémAction: Les Cinémas Arabes*, Paris.

Bourdieu, Pierre (1993), *The Field of Cultural Production: Essays on Art and Literature*, Cambridge: Polity Press.

Cabral, Amilcar (1993), 'National Liberation and Culture', in Williams, Patrick and Chrisman, Laura, (eds), *Colonial Discourse and Post-Colonial Theory*, Hemel Hempstead: Harvester Wheatsheaf: 53–65.

Eisenstein, Sergei (1977), *Film Form: Essays in Film Theory,* edited and translated by Jay Leyda, New York: Harvest Books.

Fanon, Frantz (1963), *The Wretched of the Earth*, translated by Constance Farrington, New York: Grove Press.

Fanon, Frantz (1967), *Black Skin White Masks*, translated by C. Lam Markmann, New York: Grove Press.

Hadari, Ahmad al- (1987), *Tarikh al-Sinima fi Misr*, Part I, 1896–1930, Cairo: Nadi al-Sinima.

Hafez, Sabry (1993), *The Genesis of Arabic Narrative Discourse: A Study in the Sociology of Modern Arabic Literature*, London: Saqi Books.

Hourani, Albert (1991), *A History of the Arab Peoples*, London: Faber and Faber.

Jameson, Fredric (1991), *Postmodernism or the Cultural Logic of Late Capitalism*, London: Verso.

Karim, Muhammad (1972), *Memoirs*, edited by Mahmud 'Ali, Cairo:

Kennedy-Day, Kiki (2002), *Books of Definition in Islamic Philosophy: The Limits of Words*, Richmond: Curzon.

Lynch, Kevin (1972), *The Image of the City*, Cambridge, MA: MIT Press.

MacCabe, Colin (1992), 'Preface', in Jameson (1992).

Maherzi, Lotfi (1982), *Le Cinéma algerien: institutions, imaginaire, idéologie*, Algiers: Sociéte Nationale d'Edition et de Diffusion.

Morson, Gary and Emerson, Caryl (1990), *Mikhail Bakhtin: Creation of a Prosaics*, Stanford: Stanford University Press.

Nahhas, Hashim al- (1986), 'al-Huwiyyah al-Qawmiyyah fi al-Sinima al-'Arabiyyah', in 'Abd al-Mun'im Tillimah (ed.), *Al-Huwiyyah al-Qawmiyyah fi al-Sinima al-'Arabiyyah* (*Arabic Identity in Arabic Cinema*), Beirut: Markaz Dirasat al-Wihdah al-'Arabiyyah.

Ramzi, Kamal (1986), 'Irtibat Nushu' al-Sinima al-'Arabiyyah bi-Harkat al-Taharir al-'Arabi' ('The Correspondence between the Rise of Arabic Cinema and Arab Liberation Movement', in 'Abd al- Mun'im Tillimah (1986).

Said, Edward (1983), *The World, the Text and the Critic*, Cambridge, MA: Harvard University Press.

Spivak, Gayatri Chakravorty (1990), *The Post Colonial Critic: Interviews, Strategies, Dialogues,* London: Routledge.

Todorov, Tzvetan (1984), *Mikhail Bakhtin: The Dialogic Principle*, translated by Wald Godzich, Minneapolis: University of Minnesota Press.

18 National/International/ Transnational

The Concept of Trans-Asian Cinema and the Cultural Politics of Film Criticism

Mitsuhiro Yoshimoto

Films from Hong Kong, Japan, Korea, the People's Republic of China and Taiwan have been in the international spotlight since the 1980s. In production, distribution and reception of films, there exist complex flows and networks of financial, human and cultural capital criss-crossing the East Asia region. It is increasingly becoming difficult to determine the nationality of many Asian films produced in these and other countries and areas. Nor are the sites of reception and consumption neatly contained by national boundaries either. Do all these facets of the cinematic conditions allow us to talk about a transnational Asian cinema? Before immediately embracing transnational Asian cinema as a possible object of film history and criticism, let us first note that the notion of Asian cinema itself is not a self-evident idea. It is a product both of specific institutional demands and of the geopolitics and economics of cinema as an industry. Asian cinema is a construct that needs to be scrutinised from a range of critical perspectives. What has contributed to the emergence of the idea of Asian cinema? What purpose does it serve in film scholarship and criticism? What position does it occupy in the study of national cinemas? These are separate yet related factors that need to be discussed if we want to elucidate what underpins the formation of Asian cinema as a critical concept that, today, has become widely accepted.

Firstly, we must re-examine the idea of Asian cinema in relation to the changing economic reality of a world transformed into a global market. The emergence of Asian cinema is inseparable from the globalisation of the American economy and the rise of East Asia as an important region for it. Some have even argued that it is not the emergence but the re-emergence of Asia as a central player in world economics that has characterised the last twenty years or so.[1] From this perspective, there is nothing particularly surprising about the general acceptance of the notion of Asian cinema in recent years.

Secondly, the widespread use of the term Asian cinema appears to be simultaneous with the increasingly problematic status of national cinema in film criticism. Historians of national cinemas have tended to presuppose the unity of the nation-state and national culture, and to interpret the cinema of a particular nation as a reflection of national character, sensibility or spirit. But as we have become more aware of the constructed-ness of the nation-state and
the crucial role modern technology and cultural production such as the cinema play in the

formation of national identity, studies of national cinemas have grown more reflexive of the theoretical assumptions that underpin them. The idea of Asian cinema has partly been embraced in the search for an alternative to the form of essentialism that has informed the historiography of national cinemas. One effect of such essentialism has been a polarisation, within film studies departments, between, on the one hand, the centre – Hollywood and one's own national cinema – and, on the other, the cinemas of the rest of the world.

Thirdly, we must take into account the central role played by international film festivals and a new global-ecumenical film culture in the construction of Asian cinema. In a market increasingly controlled by multinational conglomerates, so-called local film production is extremely difficult to sustain. Films are bifurcated into two categories: Hollywood and 'international productions'. The location of cinematic production and reception can no longer easily be discussed in terms of 'inside' and 'outside' the national boundaries. Independent and national cinemas try to survive either by producing films for the international film festival circuits or by targeting Hollywood producers. Furthermore, these two circuits are increasingly difficult to differentiate. The concept of Asian cinema must be scrutinised as a product of global circulation where, rather than functioning as the opposite of each other, the cultural and the economic thoroughly interpenetrate.

All these factors have contributed to the emergence of Asian cinema as a widely accepted notion. Although they are closely related to each other, these factors do not constitute a unified discursive field. As a result, Asian cinema cannot be reduced to a single definition or meaning. What makes Asian cinema an interesting notion is precisely that its definition is in flux – its meaning constantly renegotiated. The purpose of this essay is not to trace transnational flows of films and culture in East Asia. Others have done so and provided detailed information on the production, distribution and exhibition of contemporary Asian films. As a film historian based in North America, I am more interested in re-examining the disciplinary history and the institutional politics that have contributed to the construction of Asian cinema as a critical category.

In North American film studies departments the concept of Asian cinema is a relatively recent invention. 'Asian cinema' did not exist as part of the standard vocabulary of film scholarship until the late 1980s. Before that, there were Japanese, Indian and Chinese cinemas, but not Asian cinema. How can we explain the creation of this new category in film criticism and in academic film studies? What exactly is meant by Asian cinema? Is it a convenient blanket term to refer to the sum of the various national cinemas in the continent or does it have its own coherence, specificity and identity? There is of course no single factor that can be taken to be solely responsible for the emergence of Asian cinema as an object of scholarship, but a brief look at the institutional history of film studies can illuminate why, over the last decade, such a thing as 'Asian cinema' has become a widely accepted category.

Many traditional disciplines, despite their universalist orientation, privilege the West as the locus of meaning, value and agency. We can see the same tendency operating even in relatively new disciplines such as film studies, the exponential expansion of which, from the 1970s, was facilitated by the introduction of poststructuralist (Lacanian and Althusserian) film **255** theory exemplified by the British film journal *Screen*. In spite, or perhaps precisely because, of its enormous influence, *Screen* theory and the paradigms it helped to promote soon came under attack from a variety of fronts. For our purpose, it is enough to say that the success and demise of *Screen* theory came from its inability to critique the cultural assumptions that underpinned a certain fetishisation of cinematic specificity. The group of cultural historians and practitioners who worked around *Screen* was undoubtedly varied, and great differences obtained between their approaches to films. However, the version of *Screen* theory that was finally institutionalised *as* the academic discipline of 'film studies', in Britain and in the USA, was unreflectively presented and used as a universal theory of cinema and its functioning, while in effect its applicability was quite limited. With the academic field of film studies organised in and around European and North American films, the notion of Asian cinema did not gain critical currency.

This is not to say that Asian cinemas as concrete objects of study were not on the agenda. During this period, Japanese cinema was eagerly studied as part of the canon because of its status as the 'other' of Hollywood cinema. Selected Japanese directors and their works were scrutinised in search for an alternative mode of representation – alternative, that is, to a cinema – Hollywood – that was vaguely perceived as a problem. This search for alternative modes of address and concomitant subject formations miserably failed because the terms of comparison remained the ones dictated by Hollywood films. Hollywood cinema's modes of narration silently continued to function as the classical or institutional mode of narration and representation. In this context, the study of Japanese cinema simply reinforced Hollywood cinema's canonic centrality. Constituted as the polar opposite or negative image of Hollywood as the 'norm', Japanese cinema was essentially a phantom entity.

The rapid wane of vanguard politics in the late 1980s brought an end to the perceived need to study Japanese cinema. The attention to the cultural and political specificity of films was replaced by the historical study of film as texts. That is to say, the political radicalism of vanguard theory (Eurocentric universalism) gave way to the academic formalism of historicism (multicultural particularism). In this process, it was the culturalist discourse that gained currency in the field of Japanese cinema studies. Situated at the margins of the discipline, Japanese cinema became once again an exotic object for a few connoisseurs of cultural particularities.[2]

This is when Asian cinema began to appear as a category of film studies. Simultaneously, films from mainland China and other Asian countries began to win awards at large international film festivals, resulting in a growing interest in new Asian auteurs and Asian national cinemas other than Japanese cinema. However, these developments did not constitute an expansion of critical horizons, nor did they result in the formulation of a new canon of Asian films. The general orientation of new scholarship about Asian cinemas at this time was decidedly different from that of the Japanese cinema studies of the 1970s and early 1980s. Gone was any attempt to search for an alternative to Hollywood cinema. Whereas the otherness of Japanese cinema had been constructed relationally as 'different from' the Hollywood norm, 'Asian cinema' was now celebrated as a positive difference in itself. Asian cinema was believed to be worth studying because of its unique difference, not because of a simple dyadic hierarchy within which Asian cinema would be nothing more than a negative mirror reflection of a dominant Hollywood.

Underlying the invention of Asian cinema as a scholarly object was a belief in the pluralistic coexistence of diverse national cinemas and film practices. Does this mean that we should see a positive development in the widespread acceptance of Asian cinema as a category of film studies? There is no doubt that since the 1990s the number of scholars and students working on Asian cinema or on various national cinemas in Asia has increased exponentially. Yet, it is also true that film studies has become a distinctly mono-cultural discipline in which Hollywood cinema dominates more than ever. To the extent that, in the 1970s and early 1980s, scholarship on so-called classical Hollywood cinema presented itself as a set of objective descriptions and analyses, it also functioned as an active agent in the positioning and consolidation of Hollywood cinema as the universal cinematic norm. In this context, formalism and stylistic analysis did not lead to a radical critical break. Similarly, the shift in focus away from humanist notions of auteurs as individuals, with distinct world views and unique signatures, towards structuralist conceptualisations of the film auteur as a theoretical category caught in, and symptomatic of, specific industrial dynamics, generic conventions, modes of narration, etc., did not fundamentally challenge the centrality of Hollywood in or *as* the canon. Hollywood cinema increasingly became equated with 'the cinema'. On the whole, the formalist and structuralist strands within *Screen* theory, with their attention to a monolithically conceived cinematic apparatus, its ideology and its subject, contributed to sustain and reinforce the hegemony of Hollywood cinema because it claimed an objectivist outlook without making overt the evaluative and interpretative terms that underpinned their object of study.

The overwhelming centrality of Hollywood in film studies and the emergence of Asian cinema as a new category of film scholarship are related phenomena. The key term in this connection is globalisation. Globalisation is, of course, a hotly contested term and what it means varies depending on who is using it and in what context. At one level, notions of globalisation certainly evoke an image of Hollywood films as conquering every corner of the global film market and, in the process, homogenising (film) culture the world over. At the same time, globalisation can also be understood as a process whereby heterogeneities and differences multiply. In this second sense, globalisation leads to a diversity of multicultural particularities and to a polycentric imagining of the world, where no single centre monopolises the production and circulation of audiovisual images, nor does such a centre dictate the terms by which particular meanings and values attach to them.

Globalisation has become a key term in film studies because it can refer to both of these seemingly contradictory phenomena simultaneously. Uses of globalisation as a contradictory synthesis of two opposite movements allow film studies to consolidate its disciplinary power and to prioritise the study of Hollywood cinema as 'the' cinema while, at the same time, celebrating the diversity of global film culture through a set of fixed (national, regional, cultural, gender, ethnic and so forth) differences. As a result, what is often expected of scholars in film studies is no longer detailed knowledge of any particular national cinema, but expertise in 'the' cinema – read Hollywood cinema – and, as an optional skill, a general familiarity with **257** 'world cinema', including Asian cinema as a type of cinematic genre. Film studies has embraced the concept of globalisation in order to present itself as cosmopolitan and multicultural while simultaneously disinvesting its institutional capital from the study of that which falls outside Hollywood cinema. In this sense, Hasumi Shigehiko's rather severe critique of film studies in the United States as a parochial academic exercise is probably too hasty, yet not completely off the mark (Hasumi Shigehiko et al. 2000).[3]

These observations suggest that Asian cinema as a disciplinary object cannot but be a site of institutional struggle and critical contention and that a politically neutral study of Asian cinema is never possible. The concept of Asian cinema can easily become, and to a great extent has already become, an instrument for ghettoisation. Token acknowledgment of 'the rest' of the world is used to exclude 'the rest' from a discipline that maintains its Euro-American focus and bias under the guise of cosmopolitanism. The problem is not simply the discipline's fundamental indifference to Asian cinemas. Scholarship on Asian cinema itself often contributes to the marginalisation of Asian cinemas by accepting the ethnocentric terms of film studies and, in the process, accepting low-quality standards of research. But if today Asian cinema has become widely accepted for the purpose of preserving the centrality of European and American films in the curriculum, all the more reason to rearticulate this category in such a way that it can challenge what constitutes legitimate knowledge in the study of film.

Can the dominant role of Hollywood in academic film courses be counteracted simply by increasing the number of Asian cinema specialists, books and articles on Asian cinema? Is it possible to create a more progressive identity for Asian cinema capable of defying film studies' multiculturalism or its lip service to cosmopolitanism? What does it mean to promote actively the idea of Asian cinema in film criticism and scholarship? These are difficult questions to answer – questions it is necessary to wrestle with continuously as we engage in critical activities focusing on Asian cinema.

In order to transform Asian cinema into a viable critical concept, it is first necessary to resist ascribing too hastily to that category any unproblematic positive identity. Larger regional categories are no less problematic than national ones, and the idea of Asian cinema must not bypass the issues that have been raised in the context of debates on national cinema. A new category of cinema based on a geopolitical region as the term for the films' unity and coherence can never be politically neutral. In the case of Asian cinema, the greatest danger is still that what appears to be its positive attribute can easily turn out to be nothing more than a product of the pervasive dichotomy of Hollywood and 'the rest'.

To be critically and historically viable, the idea of Asian cinema should not be a derivative of a Hollywood-centred paradigm. And yet, it is not easy to re-conceptualise Asian cinema completely outside this dichotomy. Transnational flows of money, people and films are an important aspect of the transnationalisation of Asian cinema, and there is clearly the need for a study of the multiple ways in which Asian cinema is globally circulated and watched by heterogeneous audiences. But exactly what this type of study can tell us about the transnationality of Asian cinema remains to be seen. Scholarship about the transnational reception of Asian films should not be confined to ethnographic studies of how Chinese, Korean or Japanese films circulate as videocassettes, VCDs, laserdiscs or DVDs in Asia, in metropolitan areas in the United States, or in Asian diasporic communities throughout the world. This type of ethnographic research becomes especially problematic when it merely affirms the hybridity of reception and spectatorship. Notions of hybridity as celebrated within discourses of the post-colonial have been criticised by many for erasing history, substantialising the autonomy and purity of original cultures, and for obfuscating the concrete relationships of political domination and economic exploitation. Moreover, the hybrid identities of consumers and commodities are not some new discovery by scholars of postcolonialism, postmodernism or cultural globalisation. Rather, it is what CEOs and executives of multinational corporations are not only very familiar with, but have actively promoted and capitalised on for some time now. The mere assertion that transnational cultural flows are fundamentally changing human experience does not give rise to a radically different type of critical discourse on cinema.

The focus on cultural hybridity and transnational flows also tends to reinforce as unproblematic the centrality of geographical locations and physical boundaries in the construction of the national, the international and the transnational. What makes a national cinema a 'national' cinema is not some pre-existing national identity which a particular cinema embraces as its own. On the contrary, a national cinema emerges precisely when it intensely scrutinises the idea of the national and refuses any facile equation of the national with a particular group of people, a geographical location or cultural traditions, for the purpose of creating an imaginary sense of national homogeneity (Willemen 1994). The identity of national cinema is now problematised not because films are routinely produced and completed at multiple geographical locations in several national territories by a heterogeneous group of film-makers of different nationalities. Nor is it because films are watched by heterogeneous groups of audiences located both within and outside particular national boundaries. What has become problematic is the unreflective use of identity as the one determining factor in discussions of national cinema, regardless of whether such identity is conceptualised as homogeneous (as an embodiment of national character or essence) or heterogeneous (hybrid or straddling transnational cultural flows). The important dimension of current re-examinations of national cinema is therefore not the fact of films and other image commodities' global circulation per se. Rather, the questions that should be asked are: what happens to the positionality of address when films are routinely produced, circulated and consumed across national boundaries? Is it still possible to examine critically the specificity of the national in/of films against the overwhelming force of transnational capital without falling back on nostalgic, and decidedly fraudulent, notions of nationalism?

I resist the idea of a transnational Asian cinema because it carries with it the danger of merely reaffirming the agenda of transnational capital. Asian cinema must be refashioned in such a way that, as a critical concept, it is not available to be equated with an imaginary alternative to Hollywood, a mere local inflection of Hollywood, or a manifestation of essentialised cultural patterns or civilisational features. Transnational Asian cinema can be reabsorbed into the discourse of transnationalism and cultural globalisation (read **259**

Americanisation) all too easily. Within this framework it can still function as a supplement to a Hollywood industry that is more powerful and dominant than ever.

As an alternative to both Asian cinema and transnational Asian cinema, I therefore would like to propose the notion of a trans-Asian cinema. As a critical category, trans-Asian cinema refuses any unproblematic assertion of the uniqueness of Asian cinema as such, and of the various national cinemas in Asia. It also resists the logic of transnational capital, which de-historicises and de-politicises difference and very real boundaries in the name of multiculturalism. Transnational capital transforms Chineseness, Japaneseness and Koreanness into empty signifiers the value of which is determined purely relationally rather than by any substantive features or essence. Yet, precisely because of this emptying out of positive meanings and characteristics, categories such as Chineseness, Japaneseness and Koreanness become reified as 'things' in themselves. By contrast, trans-Asian cinema is a transformative, reflexive practice, in which the production of films and critical discourses are firmly intertwined. It produces a multiplicity of cinematic practices and critical frameworks, which are not reducible either to the false universality of Hollywood as a transnational standard or to its mirror image, the particularity of identity embraced by multiculturalism and transnational capitalism.

Trans-Asian cinema studies can help to highlight the urgent necessity for introducing a genuine comparative perspective into film studies. Comparative studies does not necessarily mean that two or more different national cinemas or types of cinema are compared to each other. Nor is it a mere replication of what comparative literature scholars do with various national literatures and literary schools. Rather, comparative studies can introduce in film scholarship a historically defensible understanding of any national cinema in its unique cultural specificity, that is to say, not as the 'other' of some other national cinema which, for its commercially dominant or aesthetically influential position on a global scale, is equated to 'the cinema' as a whole.

If film studies has become a rather ossified discipline in the last decade or so, this is largely due to its false universalism. The object of research in film studies has been the cinema as a medium that exists beyond any particular national and cultural differences. In reality, however, this universal idea of cinema has been taken to be interchangeable with Hollywood and a select canon of European films. In this academic context, once a film scholar manages to master what are assumed to be the fundamental principles of 'the cinema', s/he is free to study any particular instantiations of cinema, including Asian cinema, without being required to have any specialised knowledge, except, that is, for his or her expertise in 'the cinema'. As long as this disciplinary structure is maintained, the acquisition of linguistic, historical, socio-economic or any other cultural expertise will not fundamentally challenge the false universalism that underpins film studies. As it is happening in the field of comparative literature, the uncritical assertion of Asian cinema as an area of expertise will only end up reproducing, within film studies, the model of area studies. It is this coloniality of film studies (and of Asian studies) which is responsible for the discipline's utter failure to deal with Asian cinema as a legitimate object of film history and theory. And it is this that a notion of trans-

Asian cinema – a comparative approach to the cinemas of Asia in relation to each other as constitutive players in the global circulation of films – can, at last, begin to oppose, to the benefit of the study of any cinema, including that produced in Hollywood.

Notes

1. For example, Andre Gunder Frank has demonstrated that the hegemony of Europe as an economic power lasted only briefly, and that the recent shifts are not some new phenomenon but a return to the long-term dominance of Asia as the world's economic centre (Frank 1998).
2. For a more detailed examination of the institutional history of film studies and the role of Japanese cinema in the formation of film studies as an academic discipline see Yoshimoto (2000: 8–49.)
3. I would like to thank Markus Ab Nornes for alerting me to the publication of this article.

References

Frank, Andre Gunder (1998), *ReOrient: Global Economy in the Asian Age*, Berkeley: University of California Press.

Hasumi Shigehiko, Kobayashi Yasumo and Matsuura Hisaki (2000), 'Hyosho bunka ron no genzai to mirai' *UP* 29 (1): 1–23.

Yoshimoto, Mitsuhiro (2000), *Kurosawa: Film Studies and Japanese Cinema*, Durham: Duke University Press.

19 Not a Biography of the 'Indian Cinema'

Historiography and the Question of National Cinema in India

Valentina Vitali

In India, the first three decades of the twentieth century – from the beginning of cinema worldwide to the consolidation of a domestic film industry – coincided with the initial formulations of a project that encompassed a variety of horizons, and with the sedimentation of some of those prospects into the coalition ready to forge a state out of the British Raj. That this dialectic between the film industry and the Indian nation-state is indeed constitutive of Indian cinemas as 'national cinema' is not to say that the relation of the industry to the state can be conceptualised unproblematically as a synchronic relation, where films 'reflect' what is supposed to be happening in the nation-state. How then, to speak of the cinemas of India as 'national cinema'?

One of the most influential models of nationalism available to the Congress in the run up to independence was the USA. India was not unique in this respect. Whether as a constitutional model or as an economic power, by the 1930s the USA were emulated and aspired to by many national formations. First published in 1939, Lewis Jacobs' *The Rise of the American Film: A Critical History* was not only one of the first biographies of a national cinema, but also an account of the apotheosis of all other cinemas' most powerful competitor. Unsurprisingly, most historiographies of national cinemas are still narrated on the template of Jacobs' book, and India is no exception. *The Rise of the American Film* used a linear model of history that Jacobs derived from nationalist history: the founders, the coming of sound, the studios and, within them, the great auteurs, carefully selected so as to give Americans a cultural lineage worthy of their future as the largest exporter of cultural goods. Within this evolutionist frame, the set of conventions dominant in nineteenth- and early twentieth-century European and American literature and the 'fine arts', namely, the conventions of realism, were adopted as the preferred criteria for 'good' or 'mature' cinema. *Indian Film* (Barnouw and Krishnaswamy), a book that has marked the study of Indian cinemas since its publication in 1963, closely followed the path laid out by Lewis Jacobs: the beginnings of cinema in 'India' with the Lumière brothers' screening in Bombay in 1896; the founder, Dadasaheb Phalke, a photographer born into an upper-caste family and a committed nationalist; the coming of sound, which helped to consolidate a domestic film industry producing and exhibiting films in the national languages; the rise of a studio system around New Theatres in Calcutta (producing Bengali films), the Prabhat Film Company in Pune (making films in Marathi, Hindi and some in Tamil), and Bombay Talkies in Bombay; finally, around 1947, the emergence of an indigenous form of realism and concomitant auteurs out of New Theatres.

There are several problems with this account of the cinema in India. There is, to begin with, an issue of terminology: whereas the first films recorded to have been made by South Asians date back to 1897, India did not come into being as a nation-state until 1947. As the editors of the *Encyclopaedia of Indian Cinema* observe,

> to restrict an account of Indian cinema to the geo-temporal frame constituted by the Indian nation-state since Independence, or more accurately, since Partition, would require us to ignore some of the most admirable cinematic achievements realised in Colonial India. More damagingly, it would also rule out any engagement with the longer-term dynamics which have shaped post-Partition Indian cinema. (Rajadhyaksha and Willemen 1999: 9)

It is not simply a matter of what individual accounts of national cinemas leave out – in the case of India, figures such as Paul Zils, a UFA director born in Wuppertal (Germany) who was to become an influential figure in Indian documentary cinema – but, more importantly, of the obstacles posed by 'theory' to an understanding of ourselves as cultural subjects. In *Indian Film* the adoption of the American blueprint produced not only exclusions which accumulate into a historically incorrect account of what the cinema was in India before and after 1947, but also a view of Indian cinemas as 'still developing', less refined versions of European and US cinemas. In reality, and in spite of the historians' reverence for the kind of realist films made by New Theatres in Calcutta and its Bengali auteurs, by 1935 New Theatres' realism had become a minor trend within an industry thriving on mythological, historical and stunt films, along with other genres. Bombay Talkies, one of the biggest studios of the pre-war period and the only one to be a fully fledged corporate venture, was responsible for many of these 'non-realist' films, as well as for the work of some of the most influential auteurs of Hindi cinema, such as Bimal Roy and Nitin Bose. More often than not, the 'style' of these auteurs derived precisely from a tangible discomfort with the rules of realist narration in cinema. Yet, to this day, the narrative strategies of Indian cinemas continue to be discussed through the lenses of realisms of various persuasions.

Language adds a further set of problems. In 1947 Hindi was adopted as the one official language of independent India. However, by 1960 Jawaharlal Nehru's government had conceded the creation of linguistic states, as well as the upgrading of their regional languages to the status of national languages. There are today three large film production centres in India. Although until the early 1960s films in Hindi were produced in Bombay, by the end of the decade Madras, the capital of Tamil Nadu, had become India's largest production centre, making films to be dubbed in most of the sixteen national languages of India, including Hindi. Throughout the 1950s and 1960s Hindi melodramas were the only kind of films to receive a margin of national exposure. They constituted the mainstream and continue to do 263 so to a large extent today. However, as the movement of directors, actors and other 'talent', as well as of technology, indicates, the circulation of cinematic forms and practices across the Hindi and other Indian cinemas has always been anything but a one-way traffic. In this context, Hindi films are but nominally dominant. Production figures reveal that films in Hindi did increase steadily in the run-up to independence, stabilising in the ten to fifteen years after 1947. From the mid-1960s productions of so-called 'regional cinemas', which include films in Tamil, Telegu and Malayalam, began to outnumber Hindi films (Rajadhyaksha and Willemen 1999: 31). Encouraged by the creation of linguistic states, the rise of 'regional cinemas' was soon to be followed by and, as in Tamil Nadu, often became an adjunct of, the rise of devolutionist, secessionist nationalist movements in the South and other parts of India.

Within any one society different temporalities coexist that are associated with interest groups struggling to gain control over the institutions of social reproduction and wealth accumulation. Texts produced within the context of those tensions necessarily bear the marks of the co-presence of these contending interest groups and the cultural-historical temporalities associated with them. In order to speak of the cinemas of India as 'national cinemas' it is necessary to think of 'India' (as of any national formation)

> not as a fixed entity, but a socio-cultural process, a changing contested set of overlapping frameworks (always temporarily) stabilised by governmental institutions, be they the Colonial administration, the Indian government or the various institutions seeking to regulate [. . .] the interface between culture and economy within, at any given time, specific territorial limits. (Rajadhyaksha and Willemen 1999: 9).

It is at the level of such dialectics between the cultural and the economic that the adoption of a historiographic model based on the functioning of Hollywood, like Jacobs', has created the greatest obstacles to the visibility, the documenting and the understanding of Indian cinema as a social practice with material functions and effects. For instance, research priorities have tended to stress film production at the expense of all other sectors of the film industry, because, at least until the 1970s, Hollywood was a production-oriented enterprise. The discourse of technology as dictated by the Hollywood mode of production has been projected onto all national cinemas, including India's, even if – perhaps even 'because' – to this day, the Indian film industry relies on technology that is primarily imported. Distribution and exhibition, on the other hand, remain largely unexplored areas, even if there are good indications that, if properly researched, they alone would offer a far more accurate picture of the functioning of Indian cinemas than existing accounts have been so far able to do. The fundamental differences between the concrete processes of cultural industrialisation and, more generally, of economic modernisation in India and in the USA have not prevented film historians from looking at Indian cinemas through the lenses of Hollywood cinema, but they have done so with all the difficulties, contradictions and erasures mentioned above. A better understanding of (a) where the diverse cinemas of India must have come from, (b) how they function within a global process of industrialisation as encountered by Indian society, and (c) the nexus between that and the reshaping of Indian people's habits and lives through, precisely, the narrative strategies of films, requires that these cinemas be reconsidered and examined as adjuncts of the long- and medium-term economic dynamics that have shaped modern India.

During the Raj, India was turned into a provider of cheap primary material and labour, as well as a market for British-made industrial goods. The transformation of the, by then fragmented, structures of a collapsing Mughal empire into an agricultural economy subservient to the industrialisation of Britain not only inhibited the development of indigenous trade and industry. It also required that, in parts of India at least, such as Bengal, the economic and social remnants of the Mughal empire, many hierarchical in nature, be further entrenched and redefined along the lines of English landlordism.

Francesca Orsini's research has shown that, at the level of cultural production, this resulted in a seemingly contradictory movement. On the one hand, in the late nineteenth and early twentieth centuries, Indian cultural life was marked by the spread of the printing press and the proliferation of cheap magazines, some carrying the message of nationalism and others purely commercial in nature. On the other, cultural industrialisation, of which these magazines were a product, did not always go hand in hand with the secularisation of narratives and ideologies. For instance, detective stories were a regular feature of entertainment magazines. The lineage of this genre, in India, goes back to European literature, as well as to Persian mystery stories and indigenous 'revelation' narratives. Whereas nineteenth-century Bengali stories reveal a clear move towards notions of secular truth – that is, a move towards causal explanation of an event originally presented as a 'mystery' – within the Hindi belt similar stories, often inspired by the Bengali versions, took the opposite direction: causal narratives turn out to be 'mysteries' revealed (Orsini 2004). This narrative priority can be plausibly linked to the fact that in the Hindi-speaking region, that is, a region less exposed to the discourses of modernisation incarnated by British officials and, on the whole, less metropolitan and trade-oriented than colonial Calcutta, printing presses were often sponsored by local potentates who, until then, had acted as patrons of pre-industrial cultural practices. The pre-capitalist nature of the interests circulating as printed 'entertainment' left its mark on the narratives.

After Independence and Partition, for the Congress the question was no longer whether India would industrialise or not, but how it would do so. Having inherited from the Raj a situation of uneven development, where merchant capital had emerged and been allowed to develop in the coastal cities of Bombay, Calcutta and Madras to the exclusion of other parts of the country, throughout the 1950s the Congress pursued a domestic policy aimed at advancing the regional bourgeoisie of the different states. Meghnad Desai has argued that, as a result, the two players in the Indian economy have been an industrial 'big bourgeoisie' – which operates on a national market and is internationalist in intent, but which is at the same time not sufficiently strong to dictate the Congress' policies nor to compete on the global markets, thus effectively depending on government programmes for industrial expansion and on economic protectionism; and, secondly, a politically far more influential 'small bourgeoisie' – which mobilises regional, often landed, capital and relies for its labour and market on the **265** local population. Until the Emergency, Congress rule depended on this 'small bourgeoisie': Nehruvian socialism was a compromise designed to orchestrate the complex cohabitation between industrial and landed interests with the latter as the dominant force. In the 1950s and 1960s this produced violent struggles for the creation of linguistic states, but, in the longer term, the government-promoted growth of regional capital in no way hindered the complementary expansion of national capital, nor did these struggles exclude an underlying harmony between the two (Desai 1975).

> After the defeat in the border war with China and the indecisive clash with Pakistan, in the mid-1960s the Indian Government greatly stepped up its military spending. Famines in both 1965–6 and 1966–7 also forced the government to import large quantities of wheat from the United States. Inflation accelerated and the balance of payment soared. Under international pressure the rupee was devalued in 1966. (Desai 1975: 11)

In a gigantic effort at political and economic centralisation that responded to the rise of finance capital in the United States by sheltering India from its pressures, in 1969 Indira Gandhi nationalised the fourteen largest private banks. Centralisation of credit had huge repercussions on the shape of the Indian industry and finance that grew under the state's protectionist umbrella. Government-controlled financial institutions played a key role in inter-corporate wars by helping one monopoly or another to benefit at the expense of the rest, through mergers and acquisitions as well as through government red-tape. Combined with inherited disparities between local and national capital, credit centralisation promoted the country's industrialisation under the aegis of large, government-run companies providing public services and agricultural goods, of a few large private corporations, such as the Tata and Birla groups, and of small-scale industrial units, which constitute by far the vast majority to date. Profitability is higher in this sector than in the corporate sector: small units tend to substitute capital with labour and to use the latter more intensely. Unpaid family labour is often used and paid labour exploited more ruthlessly: wages, job security and unionisation are much lower in small-scale industrial units. Responsible for one quarter of India's exports in the late 1980s, the small-scale industrial sector has since grown, for the tendency among big corporate companies has been to decentralise production through subcontracting while centralising marketing and purchasing operations (Vanaik 1990: 32–3).

Finally, the sector to grow the most as a direct and immediate result of credit centralisation was the so-called 'black' economy (Vanaik 1990: 36). Although a black economy first developed in South Asia during World War II, the large body of work written on this particular feature of the Indian economy has tended to agree on two points: that the 'black' economy has since grown and keeps growing, and that the 'black' and the 'white' economies are closely integrated, if only because of the array of government regulation and red-tape. 'Black savings flow into the capital market and into bank deposits (with few questions asked), thus providing resources for investment' (Vanaik 1990: 36). With the 1969 nationalisation of the banks, a spiralling share of primarily regional Indian capital found a parallel and, on the whole, cheaper channel of circulation in the film industry. This fact and the type of small-scale, labour-intensive production that Indian capital works with are responsible for the forms and contents of Indian cinemas to date.

In 1953 Eric Johnston, then the president of the Motion Picture Association of America, explained to a Senate Committee that 'Pictures give an idea of America which it is difficult to portray in any other way, and the reason, the main reason [. . .] is because our pictures are not obvious propaganda.' Johnston proceeded to remind Senator J. William Fulbright, that 'we [Hollywood] are a commercial enterprise' (Guback 1986: 252). Johnston's declarations notwithstanding, the US film industry has always profited from enormous state support, especially as it set out to further penetrate foreign markets after World War II. In India, however, the US majors' operation has been marginal since the coming of sound. In the 1970s, US film distributors were further displaced by Indira Gandhi's protectionist policies.[1] Yet, like Hollywood, the Indian film industry was never nationalised. After 1947, when the Congress launched a programme of economic modernisation which made possible the industrialisation of agriculture and the setting in place of a national grid of public services under direct state administration, the film industry was explicitly excluded from the programme. Even so, Indian cinemas, like Hollywood, are a commercial enterprise at the crossroads of a global process of industrialisation and of the nation-state, the agency regulating the movement of capital within the nation. Unlike Hollywood, these cinemas flourished as adjuncts of an economic fabric that is sustained and regulated by the Indian nation-state.

A domestic film industry was at work in India by the 1920s. Its growth from the mid-1930s has been narrated as a struggle between two coexisting tendencies: concentration of production around three main studios on the one hand; 'regional' or 'independent' decentralisation on the other. In reality, the focus on production is misleading and the term 'independent' ahistorical. Arguing that

> there is evidence of an ongoing struggle between two broadly defined tendencies within the [Indian film] industry – one committed to the ideological mission in keeping with the goals of the postcolonial state's controlled capitalist development and aspiring to the achievement of a homogenized national culture, the other moored in a precapitalist culture, employing a patchwork of consumerist and pre-capitalist ideologies and determined to maintain its hold over the production process from the outside (Prasad 1994: 47),

Madhava Prasad has emphasised that, in practice, the 1930s saw the formation of what became by far the most common mode of film finance and production in the decades to follow, also known as the 'minimum guarantee policy' system: a financier-distributor advances the money for production under an agreement that assures the producer a minimum return on each film, after which the revenues are shared between producer, distributor and exhibitor. The amount that is fixed as the minimum guarantee is usually the amount advanced to the producer during the making of the film. In Hollywood, too, producers, distributors and exhibitors share what remains after production, distribution and exhibition costs and fees are met, either as part of an externally (agent) stipulated agreement, or because production, distribution and exhibition **267** are integrated departments within the same studio. However, in India, the balance of power between these three sectors is not the same as in the US.[2]

Since its beginning, cinema in South Asia was marked by a scarcity of equipment and by the predominance of exhibition, in the 1910s the one activity most immediately accessible to South Asians. At the time, licences would be issued by the Raj for mobile projectors, not to the exhibition site, which was often already in use for other types of public activities. Films could be seen in town halls and fairground shows, at religious festivals or in conjunction with wrestling matches (Bhaumik 2001: 22–7). Consistent production of Indian features did not kick off until after World War I, when the population of undivided India, and especially the urban population, began to increase at a very high rate (Desai 2004: 22–3). Unlike imported films, which could be acquired cheaply and circulated rapidly, generating faster turnovers, locally produced films were expensive to make and, to recover the costs, screened for weeks at a time. However, by the end of the 1920s, in Bombay at least, exhibition had not only become stratified, with films released first in the up-market theatres of Grant and Lamington Roads, and then traded off to suburban and mill-area halls (Bhaumik 2001: 36), but had also emerged as a means to raise land prices. At that point, exhibition of Indian films became more lucrative than that of imported ones.

Distributors of Indian films hardly existed in the 1910s, when producers dealt directly with exhibitors. Due to the misleading research emphasis on production, it is unclear as to whether, with the coming of sound, distribution grew in importance. Sound was introduced in the 1930s gradually. Initially, due to the cost of equipment and its concentration in a few centres (Bombay, Calcutta and Madras), films would be made in one language and dubbed in the desired regional language(s) after production. Combined with a tripling of the Indian population in the years between the two world wars (Desai 2004: 22–3), the possibility to show films in the regional languages led to the expansion of the distribution sector. By 1948 there were no less than 887 distributors across India (Barnouw and Krishnaswamy 1980: 145). As these figures suggest, they are certainly not comparable to Hollywood distributors, which have traditionally operated as a cohesive force fully integrated into a monopolistic studio system. After 1947, India was divided into five distribution territories or circuits and external markets regularly reached by Indian films, such as East and South Africa, were sometimes treated as a sixth territory. Today these have further fragmented into a total of twelve domestic territories.

Whereas by the 1950s Hollywood cinema was the product of a fully corporate venture the economic priority and operational emphases of which were on production, this has never been the case for the cinema in India, where production is a highly fragmented sector of small-scale units that rely on very localised sources of finance. Funding for film production is often raised by distributors, who operate at regional level. Rarely do exhibitors fund production, but this is not to say that distributors determine the modalities of film production. India has one of the world's lowest number of cinemas. By controlling the few exhibitions outlets, exhibitors can impose whatever fees they wish, in the process not only determining the amount available to the distributor for film production, buy also indirectly presiding over the modalities by which films are made.

A breakdown of the capital composition of the Indian film industry in 1968 reveals that, out of a total investment of RS 4.1 million, RS 2.6 million (or 60 per cent) were invested by exhibitors alone, while producers and studios' input was no more than RS 0.6 million (*Screen* 5 July 1968: 13). Whereas production and distribution remained highly fragmented sectors, by the 1960s exhibition had grown into a cohesive force that tended, however, to mobilise local regional capital. That the Indian film industry's locomotive was then and remains today the exhibition sector, is crucial for an understanding of the socio-economic fabric that buttresses Indian films both as commodities and as discursive fields of the Indian national configuration.

From the late 1940s to the early 1970s, the feudal family romance (or melodrama) dominated the Hindi mainstream market. Madhava Prasad has convincingly argued that the consolidation of the feudal family romance in the 1950s was an effect of the fact that films were conceived as single units put together by an *impromptu* combination of financier-producer-director-stars, a rented studio and a large number of underpaid, ad hoc extras and technical staff. Characterised by a loose, all-encompassing plot, and often referred to as 'masala film', the feudal family romance owes its dominance to its narrative frame's capacity to subordinate other genres internally – by incorporating from them disparate ingredients, and externally – 'by reducing the number of films with a distinctly different generic identity and/or by relegating them to the more provincial or subcultural exhibition outlets' (Prasad 1994: 88). The feudal family romance's generic conventions were symptomatic of the films' function as means to circulate capital which was generated within a 'passive revolution', that is, in a context where a modernising centre ruled on the basis of a compromise with a reluctant and powerful landed bourgeoisie still very much entrenched in localised, regional financial networks. Feudal family romances were expensive and glossy productions, at times with extremely long turnover times, so that producers, depending on local distribution and exhibition networks, remained more or less confined within the allocated linguistic, district belt.

The consolidation of this mode of operation in the 1950s relied both on language and on a calculation of the role of the star in the success of a film. Star exploitation owes much of its function in the Indian film industry not simply to the fact that, as in Hollywood, a star can guarantee box-office revenues, but also to the possibilities it has historically offered for links with a 'black' economy. In the 1930s, with the open support of the nationalist Congress, film stars were offered a sizeable share of their salary in the form of unaccounted money. Part of it would be '(colonial) tax free', and its reception considered a nationalist act (Barnouw and Krishnaswamy 1980: 57). Then, and to a much greater degree after World War II, the Indian film industry has functioned as an ancillary circulation belt for undeclared money. The star has played a crucial role in this respect, not only because part of a star's salary is undeclared, that is, paid with free-floating, unaccounted-for money, but also because casting a star requires the producer to borrow a greater amount of money from the distributor-financier, which in turn allows the latter to circulate a greater amount of money. In addition, a share of the total sum advanced to the producer during the making of the film can and often is constituted by last-minute loans conceded at extortionary rates of interests and **269** necessitated by unanticipated shooting delays. Often, a major reason for such delays is the star's involvement in several productions simultaneously.

With credit centralisation in 1969, as more investors turned to the cinema as an alternative means to put capital to work, it became evident that a better way had to be found to circulate money faster and in larger quantities than melodramas, confined to the upper end of the market, had ever been able to do. Fuelled by the greater amount of money available that sought to flee state control, in 1970 Hindi productions reached an all-time high, yet the production sector did not expand in a cohesive manner; ad hoc productions proliferated instead. Distributors did invest larger amounts of money into the one film, but, initially at least, a large share of the budget was reserved to secure exhibition at any cost. As a result, within a year of credit centralisation, 400 new cinemas opened, mainly in suburban areas, bringing the total number of venues in the country to 6,900. Gradually, as exhibition priorities began to feed back on production, larger amounts of money came to be invested into those production ingredients that were deemed to guarantee high box-office returns. The recovery of the Hindi cinema in the domestic and Hindi markets in the mid-1970s – primarily through Amitabh Bachchan's action 'vehicles' – and the rise of Hindi exports in the same period, coincided with a massive rise in production costs. Whereas in 1970 the average Hindi film was produced for under RS 1 million, a star-studded films for about RS 5 million and a low-budget film for RS 150,000, by the late 1980s, the average Hindi film required about RS 7.5 million, a star-studded film between RS 20 and RS 30 million and a low-budget film close to RS 2.5 million (Pendakur 1990: 32).

Today, within the Indian film industry, the rate of failure is very high. 'It is widely believed in the industry that more films [were] not recovering their investment [in 1989] than was the case ten years [earlier]' (Pendakur 1989: 70). The fact is that, in spite of the apparent unprofitability of film-making, the number of Indian films produced has increased significantly. It would appear that the expansion of the Hindi film industry has taken place not 'in spite', but because, of the phenomenal increase in declared 'production losses'. For the exhibition sector, which constitutes the industry's locomotive, these are not, strictly speaking, 'losses'. Rather, they offer good indications that the industry's links with, or rather its function *as*, a 'black' economy is a growing formation, in which 'production losses' constitute a different type of capital gain. In addition, since Rajiv Gandhi's liberalisation of the Indian economy and its opening to international finance and industrial capital, strong links have developed between both film exhibition and production, and real-estate speculation. This is not a new development, since connections between Bombay's urban development and the opening of cinemas can be traced back to the late 1910s (Bhaumik 2001). Half a century later, when the cotton mills in Bombay's city centre began to close down to make room for new apartment blocks, the empty premises would be rented out to film companies as production sites and locations (D'Monte 2002). From the 1980s, with the gradual collapse of Bombay's industrial sector, the relentless transformation of industrial sites into free land plots and, in the 1990s, the rise of real estate as the city's driving economic force, the opening of film production cities has served also as a means to invest in, and raise the price of, land, irres-

pective of whether the production sites in question or the films produced there generate profits.

Given that the functioning of cinema in India takes these forms, how to speak of the cinemas of India as 'national cinema'? Ernest Gellner claimed that it is the homogenising effect
of industrial capitalism – a system that led to the breaking down of pre-industrial, hierarchical, self-contained social categories – that leads to the 'invention' of nationalism. The
organism that held together the different temporalities and forces at work within the one
territory under the direct political control of the state is, Gellner argued, culture, but culture
understood as 'education' (Gellner 1983). In India, however, and elsewhere, cinema, unlike
education, is not, and has never been, under the direct control of the state. Writing in the
mid-nineteenth century, Otto Bauer contested the idea, then held by many on the left, that
modern society would result in a sort of flat, uniform cosmopolitanism. He stated that all
modern nations experienced industrial capitalism in similar ways, but they did not experience it in common. Commonality, cutting across class lines, linked specific groups by what
he called 'community of destiny', read not quasi-metaphysically as ancient doom, but as
shared will towards the future. This will, which is subject to constant change also within the
one nation in the struggle for life of its citizens, is precipitated through shared language,
habits of everyday life, shared culture and, eventually, shared political institutions (Bauer
1996). Both as an industry and as a series of filmic texts addressing the nation, cinema in
South Asia (as elsewhere) has never offered 'reflections' of a pre-existing, linear process of
nation-building. It is rather the other way around: cinema has always been the adjunct of a
process of industrialisation, of which both nationalism and films are products. And just as
films can differ one from the other, so can diverse, even contrasting 'nationalisms' – intended
as shared wills for the future – manifest themselves within the one nation.

In spite of this, the notions of history and of culture that underpin much film historiography today hardly help understand exactly how cinema interconnects South Asians into
what Bauer called 'a community of destiny', that is to say, into a discursive field over which
the trajectory of independent India in its encounter with capitalism was, and continues to
be, negotiated, distinctly from the institutions of the state, by interest groups which may and
may not be the dominant ones at any given time. As the circulation of undeclared capital via
cinema in India shows, a synchronic model of text-context connections is inadequate to
account for the ways in which Indian cinemas meet that function. Indian cinemas grew
under the protection of a nation-state, but, as the independent state became increasingly consolidated (centralising political power and protectionist of the national economy), the same
cinemas grew even further as a capital circulation network parallel to the state. This suggests
that it is possible to establish connections between specific cultural formations and the socio-
historical dynamics underpinning them only on condition that both formations and dynamics are reconceptualised, not as linear trajectories, but as unstable terrains where multiple and
concurring, often contending temporalities and social vectors are at work simultaneously.
One implication of this is that a better way of conceptualising what film, or any other industrial cultural practice, does, is to think of it not as 'reflecting' the dynamics of a constellation,
but as 'staging' desired trajectories that, irrespective of whether in line or not with the state 271

of affairs dominant at a particular time, are inevitably partial ('incomplete' and 'partisan') rearrangements of simultaneous but differently codified narrativisations of 'the nation' as the real and variegated sphere the films address. Since from the point of view of the cinema as a money-making business, this sphere is as much an economic as a cultural horizon, the material contingencies presiding over cinematic mediation should also serve as the ground whence questions can begin to be formulated as to how films imagine, and in the process construct, a 'nation'.

Notes

1. Like all other foreign companies operating in India at the time, US majors were allowed to repatriate only 40 per cent of their profits. As the remaining 'blocked funds' were to be administered by the Indian state and made available to government-controlled bodies as interest-free loans for five years (after which time they could be returned to the majors and repatriated), US majors took to rechanneling a large share of these funds into their operation in India, partly for the production of US films, and partly in higher-than-average fees to Indian exhibitors. In the late 1960s, this practice secured the exhibition of a growing number of US imports in prime city centre cinemas, at the expense of Indian films. However, in 1970, following a squabble between the Indian and American governments about reciprocal film import and export quotas, US majors launched an embargo that lasted for five years. In 1975 an agreement was reached that reduced the number of foreign films allowed into India to a yearly maximum of a hundred.

2. Observing that 'As a result, the producer often gets no revenue from a film after production because the minimum return has already been given in the form of loans' (Prasad 1994: 68), Prasad concludes that, unlike Hollywood, which operated as a vertically integrated business, the Bombay film industry's mode of production is 'heterogeneous', and the industry not fully integrated. Historically, Hollywood films have been financed through combinations of bank loans and box-office revenues. That in the Bombay system the producer should get no additional revenue on top of the minimum return is no fault of the 'minimum guarantee policy' itself, but of a different equilibrium between production, distribution and exhibition than was at work in Hollywood. The question, in other words, is not whether one industry is integrated or not, but of the different nature of the integration.

References

Anderson, Benedict (1996), 'Introduction', in Gopal Balakrishnan (ed.), *Mapping the Nation*, London and New York: Verso.

Barnouw, Erik and Krishnaswamy, S. (1963), *Indian Film*, New York and London: Columbia University

Bauer, Otto (1996), 'The Nation', in Balakrishan 1996: 39–77.

Bhaumik, Kaushik (2001), *The Emergence of the Bombay Film Industry 1913–1936*, Oxford: PhD dissertation for Oxford University. Press. Second Edition (1980) New York, Oxford and New Delhi: Oxford University Press.

Desai, Meghnad (1975), 'India: Emerging Contradictions of Slow Capitalist Development', in Robin Blackburn (ed.) *Explosion in a Subcontinent*, Harmondsworth: Penguin and *New Left Review*.

Desai, Meghnad (2004), *Nehru's Hero: Dilip Kumar in the Life of India*, New Delhi: Roli Books.

D'Monte, Darryl (2002), *Ripping the Fabric: The Decline of Mumbai and its Mills*, New Delhi: Oxford University Press.

Gellner, Ernest (1983), *Nations and Nationalism*, Oxford: Blackwell.

Guback, Thomas (1986), 'Shaping the Film Business in Postwar Germany: The Role of the US Film Industry and the US State', in Paul Kerr (ed.), *The Hollywood Film Industry*, London and New York: Routledge and Kegan Paul. First published in Guback, Thomas (1969), *The International Film Industries*, Bloomington: Indiana University Press.

Jacobs, Lewis (1939), *The Rise of the American Film: A Critical History*, New York: Teachers College Press Columbia University.

Orsini, Francesca (2004), 'Detective Novels: A Commercial Genre in Nineteenth-Century North India', in Vasudha Dalmia and Stuart Blackburn (eds), *India's Literary History: Essays in the Nineteenth Century*, Delhi: Permanent Black.

Pendakur, Manjunath (1989), 'New Cultural Technologies and the Fading Glitter of Indian Cinema', *Quarterly Review of Film and Video* 11.

Pendakur, Manjunath (1990), 'India', in John Lent (ed.), *The Asian Film Industry*, London: Christopher Helm.

Prasad, Madhava M. (1994), *The State and Culture: Hindi Cinema in the Passive Revolution*, Pittsburgh: PhD dissertation University of Pittsburgh. Published as (1998), *Ideology of the Hindi Film: A Historical Construction*, New Delhi: Oxford University Press.

Rajadhyaksha, Ashish and Willemen, Paul (eds) (1999), *Encyclopaedia of Indian Cinema*, London and New Delhi: BFI and Oxford University Press.

Vanaik, Achin (1990), *The Painful Transition: Bourgeois Democracy in India*, London and New York: Verso.

Vasudevan, Ravi S. (1991), *Errant Males and the Divided Woman: Melodrama and Sexual Difference in the Hindi Social Film of the 1950s*, Norwich: PhD dissertation University of East Anglia.

Vasudevan, Ravi S. (1993), 'Shifting Codes, Dissolving Identities: The Hindi Social Film of the 1950s as Popular Culture', *Journal of Arts and Ideas* 23–4.

20 On the National in African Cinema/s

A Conversation[1]

John Akomfrah

VV/PW: Do you have any thoughts on the problem of the national in the context of African cinema?
JA: I think certain distinctions have to be made before you can even begin to talk about this. The first being that one should talk of African cinemas, in the plural, rather than about African cinema as a kind of genre. But these are distinctions one makes with some qualifications. For instance, it seems to me that the generation of the great 1960s pioneers, like Hampate Ba, Sembène Ousmane and Lionel Ngakane, were clearly very consciously working with, and for, an idea of African cinema but without ever forgetting that they were each working in quite specific locations. So, on one level, their work yields its most profound insight when we take into account that what they were trying to create was a Senegalese or an Ivorian cinema, or whatever. At the same time, there is in their work a collective project, a collective influence: a continental drift towards a very specific notion of 'africanity', which begins to take hold of a number of individuals across the continent sometime in the early 1950s, early 1960s. This idea takes hold in a way that is too general to be a mere coincidence or an accident of history. When it started to go sour Manthia Diawara called it 'afro-pessimism', but at its birth it was a utopian project, laced with optimism.

I am not talking about some post-colonial moment, or the moment of independence. It is something more local. You could smell its presence, for instance, at the all-African conference in Accra in 1960–1. You can also see it in Nkrumah's writings on the setting up of the film and television industry in Ghana. There was, if you like, a definite move towards trying to construct something that one might call an African national aesthetic, and, crucially, the people involved knew they were not talking about something that already existed. They knew that they were moving towards something that needed to be constructed on the back of recent political developments. So, FEPACI (Féderation Panafricaine des Cinéastes) or FESPACO (Festival Panafricain du Cinéma in Ouagadougou) or the Film Festival in Burkina Faso were all attempts to pull together and move towards a set of shared but constructed commonalities and interests. The idea was to create something that could be called an African cinema. For that generation, there was something called an African cinema, but it was something that you had to work towards. You knew it was something that was allied to the independence movements, something that took its cue from the renewed interest in national cultures, or from the idea of the cultural that came out of the late 1940s and early 1960s once it became clear that the idea of colonial rule was a bankrupt moral and intellectual norm.

VV/PW: Would you draw a connection between this desire for an African cinema and the négritude[2] *movement in literature of the previous decades?*

JA: I think the Césairean moment, which marked the 1940s and 1950s, clearly fed into the development of an African cinema because it raised, reified and championed the, if you like, aesthetic detour as a necessary route to a new African subjectivity. But the relation between that cinema and the *négritude* movement is quite a complicated one. As complicated as the relationship with Jean Rouch. In some ways the figure whose influence is most palpable on that particular generation of film-makers is Frantz Fanon. And Fanon's relationship to the africanity of Senghor or Césaire was quite complex. He realised that the idealised vision of Africa that emerged from the writings of Césaire or Senghor may well have been necessary, but felt that by the time you got to the late 1950s and early 1960s, it could and should be transcended. The fight for independence had to come first, determining, rather than following, forms of cultural reassertion which he deemed moribund and reactionary. And so Fanon's impact on those film-makers was greater, I suspect, than Césaire or Senghor's. Sembène's relationship to *négritude*, for instance, is extremely ambivalent, and he is the key figure here. From the very beginning, even in his writings, Sembène always took a much more sceptical and agnostic attitude to the Africa that emerges from the writings of Senghor, maybe also of Césaire.

My feeling is that what begins to happen after 1960–1, when the Organisation for African Unity gets going, is more important than the earlier, pre-independence cultural renaissance, although residues of what Senghor and Césaire were talking about clearly seep into the discourse on African cinema that emerges after 1962. The period between 1959 and 1962 is a crucial one. Fanon was really central for that generation, not so much for his writing, but for his political interventions at African cultural meetings in 1960–1. Senghor and Césaire are of the generation of Nkrumah. By 1952–3, Nkrumah is already in power, although in a limited way. So, to some extent, the political and cultural project that Nkrumah, Senghor and Césaire wanted was about to reach fruition. But the project for an African cinema does not really get going until later, and here people like Amilcar Cabral,[3] talking about the national popular, will have a major impact. Now, in saying all this I don't want to understate the seismic significance of Césaire or Senghor. *The Discourse of Colonialism* appeared in 1952–3, I think, and its claims for africanity were extremely valuable. Don't forget that when it was published, the colonial film units still supplied most of what passed for film entertainment throughout Africa. The cultural project of these film units was very much tied to the political and pedagogic project of colonial rule. *Négritude* posed the first cultural challenge to that hegemony.

VV/PW: Would you agree that Senghor and Césaire's project may be called a nation/al-building project?

JA: Yes, absolutely.

VV/PW: So, the situation confronting Sembène and other film-makers coming on stream as African film-makers at the end of the 1950s and in the early 1960s is a patchwork of African states in the process of developing and articulating a nation-building discourse. In order to formulate a cultural discourse in the context of the struggle for independence, this generation of film-makers had to involve themselves in a project that implies a whole set of negotiations and strategic accommodation, that is to say, they had to engage in the political negotiations that play out also in the cultural domain. As soon as you have nationally based power blocs, the film-makers who come on stream at that stage have to confront the newly formed state; at the same time, these film-makers are part of the industrial and cultural structures of those states. They don't have the money or the technological and industrial infrastructure to build a film industry; the exhibition and distribution sectors are still colonised at that time. In that context, their options are limited: without a national market, they cannot really align themselves with their newly formed nation-states. In order to engage in nation-building work, the economic and industrial resources have to be drawn in from elsewhere. The pan-African market is still not in place either, so the only alternative is to address Europe for funding, but that, in turn, opens up for them a space from where to be more critical of the state than had been available to the generation before them. All that revolves around, on the one hand, the notion of nation-building, and, on the other, the positions that are available once there is a kind of national structure in place. This, I think, pushes the film-makers away from the national projects, but it also has positive consequence, in that it may open up a space of relative independence from the state.

JA: There is an implied hostility in your question to the notion of the national which I don't think was ever so clearly enunciated for African film-making. There is also an idea of the nationalist project as a state to be 'transcended' that I also don't think was ever fully realised, if indeed that was the aim in the first place. The continent's short century had multiple political genealogies, but somewhere at the centre of it, at least initially, was the Padmore/Nkrumah/Kenyatta political project of 1945. That project's latent pan-Africanism and Garveyism basically claimed that no individual country could consider itself free until, and only if, the whole continent was free. That remained a dominant, consistent and necessary cultural logic from 1945 until about 1961–2. By 1962 the idea that continental freedom is desirable *above* national freedom was accepted more or less by everybody, the odd exceptions being a Mobutu or a Houphet Biongy in politics. But they were politicians; I don't know of a comparable figure in the film-making of that period. So, to that extent, the post-colonial moment/movement absolutely announced the cultural moment/movement, and film-making was part of that. But you are right to stress that there were film-makers, Sembène in particular, who, from the mid-60s, realised that buying wholeheartedly into the national project placed peculiar burdens on artists and cultural activists, even with as enlightened a patron as Senghor (who was then prime minister). The problem, simply put, is that, translated in state terms, a pan-African project began to mean the creation of national industries: film companies and TV stations that serviced the state. Many film-makers literally did just that. I suspect that the reason why, on the whole, in Ghana you don't find the secessionist tendencies that can be seen in Francophone Africa – as when Sembène claimed to be *simply* an African film-maker – is that many took this idea of service to its logical conclusion and bought wholeheartedly into the idea that what you do as a film-maker is to film the president or the prime minister getting on and off the plane, or that you work for the national documentary unit where you continued trying to educate people about the perils of the tse tse fly. Sembène's, Paulin Soumanou Vieyra's and the project of Oumarou Ganda, who played Edward G. Robinson in Jean Rouch's *Moi, un noir* (1957), is absolutely crucial here, because it was about something else. It was about an agnostic attitude towards the claims of the newly emerging African states, many of which were mutating into neo-colonial entities. Sembène's *Xala (The Curse)* (1974) was about precisely this but, to follow the religious analogy, it is important to stress that this scepticism never developed into a full-blown agnosticism. To take *Xala* as an example, the film was a critique of neo-colonialism but with impeccable pan-African credentials.

So the question is: where does that pan-African cultural agenda come from? It is clearly there from the start, otherwise they would not have called themselves 'African film-makers'. The likes of Lionel Ngakane, Sembène or Paulin Soumanou Vieyra clearly felt that, in addition to the political claims pan-Africanism made on you as a subject, there was also something called a film culture that had to be built on the basis of a completely internationalist credo that simply says: 'I'm just a film-maker; I'm going to live in Paris and make films.' In contrast to the colonial film unit, with their manic emphasis on the local, this new approach, too, could be called African film-making, and it had to be worked for. To be an African film-maker meant making a bid for freedom from the constraints actually implied in and by the pan-African project, but this new freedom necessarily plunged you into uncertainties as to where you would get the money, support and resources to make films. It is this resignation to the fact that you were *both* free and absolutely alone that forced a number of these film-makers to start looking abroad to see how they could patch together enough money to sustain some sort of independence.

The lives of early FEPACI film-makers always mirrored the tensions and ambiguities of saying 'there is something called African film-making'. Because, of course, African cinema was, and continues to be, an impossible cinema. To begin with, there is not enough money on the ground to sustain it. The debate as to whether you put money into cinema or, say, healthcare, or literacy, is always there. As long as the individual governments continue to see cinema as part of the general pan-African project – and for most of them that means a sub-ordinated cinema – the question of where it fits in the hierarchy of priorities will not go away. African cinema was always an impossible project, and film-makers recognised that – they recognised that if they relied only on their nation-states, it was going to be a problem. Which means that there was and is a very real tension between calling yourself a Senegalese film-maker and an African film-maker. Whichever position you choose, your options are severely circumscribed.

VV/PW: That is the political argument. What about the economic argument? There are issues of linguistic diversity, including the problem of subtitling for an audience that is still largely illiterate. There are questions of distribution and exhibition, both of which would require major investments to develop. The independent states inherited the colonial borders, which, by and large, were not coherent, linguistically or in any other way, making it so that there is not a national market for films. Individual states **277**

Xala (Sembène Ousmane, 1974)

were prepared to sacrifice the industrial aspect of cinema in favour of other nation-building programmes. If you align that with the linguistic problem – that is, the fact that for a cinema to become industrially feasible a kind of monoglot terrain is required – then I would have that, in addition to the political argument, there are economic factors that militate against the possibility of a national cinema. Added to problems of infrastructure, insuperable market problems pushed people towards collaboration with Europe. Initially this becomes an address to the European market.

JA: Like everywhere else where the primacy of the economic appears to be a millstone, people look to other cultural forms which appear to have found answers. In Africa music provided some clues – highlife music in particular. In that music's regional success they saw possibilities; they knew that highlife musicians from Nigeria, like Rex Lawson or Victor Olaiya, or Ghanaians, like E. T. Mensah and Jerry Hansen, made music, sometimes in local languages, that was both extremely popular and commercially successful across large parts of Africa. They knew that you could buy a popular South African magazine like *Drum* in just about every small town in Africa. The economic barriers were not insurmountable, but there were, and continue to be, massive regional variations at stake. Immediately after 1961–2, several sections of the continent began putting in place structures that might lead to something called a film industry so as to create national TV stations and to produce feature films and documentaries. So, if you were Ghanaian film-maker in 1960 and you were seen as talented you got a huge budget from the Ghana film unit to make a big-budget 35mm feature documentary on Ghana's new republic status. For many this was absolutely exhilarating. In some instances though, all that happened was that the local film unit – people primarily making ethnographic films or educational films about, say, how to deal with malaria – was moved to making slightly more agitational films. In some cases, there are remarkable continuities – film-makers trying to see through, in pan-Africanist terms, the Griersonian project started by the colonial film units. One of the interesting things is that, back then, no one really thought that the language question was going to be a problem. The so-called master languages were English and French, and many of the early films seem to have been made in those languages. As in other areas, Sembène is, of course, the exception here too, but for most – and this included official film units – there was really no attempt to use local languages. Ngugi Wa Thiong'o's arguments came much later. It was not a matter of simple obedience to European values. There was an audience for films; that audience understood, and had already seen films in, those languages. The first film I saw as a kid was a Hammer film called *The Eye of the Cat* (David Lowell Rich, 1969) in English. I don't remember anyone ever saying that that was a problem. It really becomes a problem slightly later on.

The notion of an 'impossible' pan-African cinema works so well also, I think, because when one tries to understand its origins one has to address that cinema's almost Heideggerian will to overcome the economic. At the beginning, even the poorest among the African countries thought 'this is the chance for us to do something new, and the way we are going to do it is not to turn our backs on anything. We are free, and free people have a cinema.' There was also a pride in sustaining the multiplicity of cinemas and film from the colonial period. No one really tried to nationalise any film industry overnight, as they did instead with many other things. There were nationalised film industries, but they coexisted with the **279**

Indian- or the Lebanese-run cinemas, and with the one or two British and American cinemas that were still around at the time. It was a patchwork of cinema, and the newly emerging African cinema was supposed to survive in that. But slowly, almost inexorably, the economic began to raise its hydra head. The state-sponsored films had the state-sponsored cinemas. There were not many, but they were there. You could go and see Steve Reeves' films, peplums made in Italy, or Indian melodramas, in the other cinemas. But if you made *Borom Sarret* (Sembène, 1964), where could you show it? So, suddenly, this cinema came about where you made films with a patchwork of funds and no solid foundations.

I also think that in talking about cinema in an African setting the ideological, the cultural and the historical raise sometimes more important questions than the economic. After all, no colonial film unit was opened in Africa to make money. So, at the beginning, the key question for African cinema to demystify was the assumption that the infrastructure that made *Men of Two Worlds* (Thorold Dickinson, 1946) should be kept because it was the best film-making model and that all you had to do was to replace the key heads of departments and you would be fine. Part of the reason why it had to be demystified, and replaced with the idea that Africans could come up with their own models, is that I am not sure that in 1960–1 anybody actually thought that Africans could make films. That was African cinema's first real problem. Even before money became an issue, the problem was one of legitimacy. Self-government was a recognised capacity, and therefore you could have someone like Nkrumah, who had been 'trained' by the British government from 1952–7. You could even have young doctors or businessmen. But no one really thought that you could do the same thing with cinema. To allow yourself to think so, you would have had to value African culture in a way that it just was not, even after the UNESCO document of 1948. Secondly, a film-making facility would, of course, prove that the African could actually make the transition from being simply consumers to being also producers, active cultural agents. I have not come across a British colonial film document that even remotely contemplated this idea. Basically, the idea that Africans should be encouraged to make films was totally absent in the colonial film documents from the 1930s onwards. Most of the time, the worry was that 'they' might watch the 'wrong' films. Colonial film documents were really quite specific in this respect; the colonial governments feared that some films might inflame passions – and I don't mean political passions, I mean 'lustful' passions.

From the minute the colonial film policies were put into motion, two markets came into operation. There was the formal cinema market, where you paid your money and you could see what you wanted, be it Steve Reeves or Audie Murphy; and then there was the state-run market, with vans that took films across the country. This second market had a huge audience, and the films that circulated in it were primarily educational films. Occasionally there would be some old Hollywood films (Charlie Chaplin's, for example). African film culture has kept these two features: you had, and continue to have, a diet of 'edifying' films, and slightly more illicit pleasures on the side. If you had the money, you would go for the slightly more dangerous and illicit pleasures, which were always premised on violence, heroic encounters and so on. If you couldn't afford to, then you waited for the more wholesome or more innocent mobile cinema fare. These two cinemas were the dominant traditions. From the beginning, the key decision for African cinema was whether to follow one of the two, or whether to create a third stream, to try to fight these two strands. In countries like Ghana you had mobile cinemas as well as state-built and state-run cinemas. When a third stream was introduced, it was really only to cater for officially made films. But that still failed to leave room for African cinema, or what little there was of it. Questions of distribution became absolutely critical around 1965–6. African-made films had to decide which of these three distribution avenues was available to them. I suspect that if they found any room at all, it was usually in the state-run cinemas.

VV/PW: There are complex reasons why, after independence, the notion of a national cinema did not loom large beyond the creation of certain institutional infrastructures – that is, why the context within which the newly trained generation of film-makers had to work necessarily had to have a pan-African dimension. These film-makers could not address a viable set of national institutions for commercial purposes. Would you say that there came a point when the FESPACO and the pan-African cinema project fragmented or retreated into a sense of national cultural formations? A moment, that is, when the Senegalese, the Nigerian or the possible Ghanaian cinemas became absorbed into, or attracted by, the magnetic pole of a national industrial context? And if you think that this ever happened, when and for what reasons?

JA: Yes. Two things happened, and I suspect that both have something to do with the absolutely modernist nature of the so-called African cinema project. The notion of an African cinema was always premised on the resolutely modernist assumption that the films were going to be inventive in some way; that they were going to tackle all kinds of cultural and political questions – in short, that they would necessarily be, by nature, avant-garde films. They just *had* to be. This meant that in order to be considered an African film certain precepts had to be put in motion. But not all films made in Africa made that grade. That is how, by default, the national begins to emerge. There were certain national traditions that never bought into the kind of Senegalese definition of what constituted the African cinema project. You can almost see a line that goes from the Senegalese cinema of the 1960s and 1970s to the Burkinabe cinema of the 1980s and 1990s. African cinema was a very specific project, and not all continental film-makers bought into that. Some simply bought the old colonial film unit idea that films have to be edifying, to educate and to provide useful or necessary information about diseases and so on. That continues to be a viable approach today: NGO-funded films of this kind still thrive across Africa. The difference is that now AIDS has replaced malaria. There were always other film-makers, in Ghana and the Ivory Coast, for instance, who, looking to the commercial model, made comedies and melodramas. That alone would cause tension within the African film-making camp.

The return to the national, understood as an ambition, was partly a move away from the modernist assumptions that underscored the African film-making agenda of the 1960s. The minute film-makers started getting audiences for what they were doing locally, the national came on the agenda. This is true to the point that certain kinds of film-making, for instance Nigerian cinema, was never, never seduced by the idea of an African cinema (with the exception of Ola Balogun). On the whole, Nigeria simply ignored it, nor did it go 281 anywhere near FESPACO. Nigeria had a very, very different agenda, which said: 'We use these films to make some money and address essentially local concerns.' The fact is that a quarter of all Africans *are* Nigerians. This is a potentially huge market and an enormous economic advantage that is not available to anyone else in Africa.

VV/PW: *The Nigerian cinema – with its commercial agenda and its refusal to take the pan-African route, going instead for a domestic market – seems to illustrate the problem facing the pan-African cinema project, namely that, precisely as a project, it was deeply rooted in the absence of a national market in any given area (outside of Nigeria).*

JA: Yes. On the other hand, I don't want to be too economically determinist about this. The fact that Nigeria had this huge potential market did not, in and of itself, necessarily generate a film culture. It is safe to say that, as far as film-making was concerned, until the 1990s at least, Nigeria was a cultural desert. In other words, the paradox is that something called an African cinema had to emerge first, as a precondition for the development of the diverse activities that one could call film-making in Africa. I suspect that, without it, Nigerian cinema would never have emerged either. Because, of course, many of the pioneers of 'Nollywood' were in the African film-making camp. For example, Tunde Kielani, whose work was showcased at Rotterdam recently, came from the London International Film School.

VV/PW: *By the same token, one could argue that the cultural dimension of the pan-African cinema discourse could not get off the ground until specific national markets – such as the Yoruba cinema in Nigeria – did not get off the ground. Other cinemas were condemned to keep struggling on a film-by-film basis, often relying on European co-production funds.*

JA: I resist that argument because we must try to resist playing the numbers game. Two caveats are in order here. If you happen to be a Burkinabe film-maker, the distinction we are trying to make – between the cultural dimension of the pan-African discourse and the national market as a pre-requisite for such a discourse – does not make sense. Burkinabe film-makers are both African and national film-makers at the same time. Their cinema definitely has a hold in Burkina Faso. Similarly, Senegalese film-makers, such as Sembène or Djibril Diop Mambéty, are huge figures nationally. They are like national folk icons. This is to say that there are cases for which the two things are not mutually exclusive at all: you can be an African film-maker who holds to the precepts of the modernist project *and* a local figure at the same time. It is also possible to be a halfway house, as I suspect Ghanaian films continue to be. Kwaw Ansah's *Love Brewed in the African Pot* (1981) completely subscribes to the modernist project. The film was made between 1963 and 1983 and Kwaw Ansah was part of a generation of film-makers who made films that continued to go to FESPACO, even though they never expected to win the main prize. FESPACO very quickly became a broad church that never fully subscribed to the modernist point of view. Halfway houses were viable too, if by 'viable' you mean that they had an audience.

    Many of the halfway films where also made by film-makers whose problems were not uniquely African – problems which they shared with film-makers from Eastern Europe.

If you worked for the Ghana Film Corporation before it was privatised, many questions that we are raising simply didn't apply: you were like a Soviet film-maker, you had a salary, and if you came up with a feasible project, it was rubber-stamped and you went and made it. None of the classic capitalist questions need raising: you are a state-funded film-maker and that is that. There are no crises: you simply make your films. Or, rather, your crisis was the collective one of dwindling state coffers, scarcity, censorship and so on. Of course, if you happen to be in a country like Burundi, where you do not have a nationalised film industry, you face the classic problem: you have to find the projects, the money and the space to show the film. This kind of patchwork situation continues even now. What has happened is that, following technological developments that were inevitable, the Nigerian scene, which is in no way a new thing, has got bigger. In some respects, Nigerian cinema stands as the final confirmation of the Lebanese ideal, namely that it is possible to find African audiences who are prepared to pay (directly, as opposed to via the state) for their pleasures and to come to special places to watch those films. Although some people do want to see that phenomenon as more than that, in effect the key question for that cinema is: 'Do you have the money or not?' There is no other question to be asked.

The Nigerian way of making cinema – direct to video, bypassing classic distribution channels – has in fact become a West African way of making cinema. The countries on the west coast now have nascent local film-making on DVCD, DVD and VHS that goes straight to the local market. A lot of it also makes its way out of the country. Nigeria happens to be the biggest, but it is a kind of region-wide phenomenon which points to, among other things, the collapse of classical cinema across Africa. What is very rarely stressed is that while people are always talking of the failure of African cinema, African film-makers are not the only ones who failed in Africa. Hollywood has still not managed to make sense of Africa and its markets. With the exception of South Africa, existing models of distribution, exhibition and production do not seem to make sense or work in the African reality. In the absence of these options, the viable ones fill the vacuum, as by resorting to video. But that too is beginning to turn. I am told that now multiplexes are beginning to emergence in Africa too, as, for instance, in Ghana and even Nigeria. They are run by people who have made their money, and acquired the know-how, from the distribution of direct-to-video productions and from working with film-makers. This is an African exhibition sector which is emerging and which is not completely in the hands of Hollywood or other 'outsiders'. The Lebanese elite were just as comfortable running a UGC cinema or some such chain, in a way that did not require them to be culturally committed to their programmes. By contrast, now you are beginning to have people who are culturally committed to an entertainment industry in which film figures prominently.

The main traffic in films for countries with large diasporic populations follows specific migration routes: from Accra to London and Washington, and so on. Films follow the diasporic routes *and* spread on a pan-African dimension. These films do not seem to entertain a dependent relationship to an 'outside', as earlier models did. They seem capable of generating the monies from within their own market-spaces, if only largely because of the very low production costs. A genuine cinematic model of exhibition has come about that does not **283** need the pan-African market to survive. It is a cinema that survives pretty much on its own within West Africa and which looks to the diaspora as a way of raising extra money, rather than as a terrain they have to tap in order to survive. There are, of course, interconnections with other models that should not be underestimated. For instance, in Cameroon, people like Jean-Marie Teno or Bassek Ba Kobhio, or, in the Congo, Balofu Bakuba Kanida, were involved in what one could call the classic modernist project for African cinema, but now they have begun looking to the national market as a more viable option. What happened to three or four film-makers in the international frame – to Suleymane Cissé or to Idrissa Oue-draogo – was crucial in this development, in that it has forced a number of people to reassess what they thought was the apex of the modernist project. At some point along the way, this apex became equivalent to the problem of getting films abroad and selling them. As people began to learn about the vagaries of that international market, they also realised that it was sometimes as detrimental to their development as was the poverty of their local scene. Except that, with the local scene at least, where those film-makers did have some power, they retained the option of trying something. If they could distribute their own films in their countries or find ways of setting up units, they could begin to see something happening. Bassek's experience across the West African region started to impact on what video-makers saw as the way forward. Some started out by making films for Accra or some such place, and then realised that there were African films which managed to cross borders. Except that this time around, they crossed borders in order to make money, not just for cultural reasons. They used whatever language they thought was most appropriate (in Bassek's case, French). We are talking comedies or melodramas with a shared, francophone set of assumptions, themes that were capable of drawing in audiences across 'national boundaries' but with a distinctly national flavour.

VV/PW: What do you mean by a 'national flavour'?
JA: In the late 80s and early 90s, the modernist African cinema tried to do two things that are quite complicated: to be national – by resorting to local languages and dialects, as in *Yeelen* (S. Cissé, 1987), *Yaaba* (I. Ouedraogo, 1989) and *Tilai* (I. Ouedraogo, 1991) – and, sim-ultaneously, to carve out a genre that would be recognisable across the whole of West Africa. They proposed a return to a certain kind of village idyll, while, at the same time, resorting to markers of regional specificity that were so opaque that those evoked villages could have been anywhere. And that was achieved partly by de-accelerating the pace at which these films work. The scripts became unnecessary. Information was removed to the point that these films almost seemed like universal statements about what it is like to live in 'the rural'. Here I would include *Yeelen*. Any fragment of the *Sundiata* epic could have constituted *Yeelen*. Even though the film appeared to be about the potency of magic realism, underneath that magic realism, most of *Yeelen* attempts to forge a variant on universalist ruralism. What became known as 'village films' – largely Burkinabe- and some Mali-based – are extremely silent. The approach to drama is almost Bressonian, just enough to carry certain scenes, while the cadences and rhythms of how people spoke are as important as what they are saying. In a
284 strange way, the film-makers gave these films an African flavour without necessarily locating

them firmly in any one place. You don't know where these villages are nor in what year the stories take place. In that sense, these films were completely epic. One or two film-makers tried to follow that path, but not very well, like Sissoko.

After that relative failure, from the mid-1990s, films began to be made that impart more information through the narrative, with the result that they appear as films that could only have been made in those specific places. In these videos, the vernacular is not simply a decorative element, something to be subtitled; it is what people actually sound like in those places. That is what I mean by distinctly local flavours. In many of the post-village films, the time and place of the stories are very clear. They can be set in central Accra, central Lagos or some such place, and the location is absolutely critical to understanding and enjoying the films. The films do draw on things that were actually part of the modernist project, but in its margins. They are made by film-makers who never won a grand prize in Burkina Faso and who often make comedy films, like Désiré Ecaré, and other Ivoirians who were more into that kind of film-making, like Moïse Ngangura with his Congolese film *La vie est belle* (B. Lamy and M. Ngangura, 1987). It is impossible to understand these films without simultaneously realising that they are from these specific places: it is to do with the language, the location and other things that are more intangible, like tempos, gestures, intonations – the fabric of the place. By contrast, *Yaaba* minimises particularities and distractions, such as excessive gestures or language, and this austerity is carried through rigorously to every aspect of the *mise en scène*. It is an attempt to construct a classical archetype of African villages, with the dialect fixing the archetype, but for all intents and purposes, that dialect was meaningless to us, because we, in fact the vast majority of people, who watched it didn't understand it. I would argue that the dialogue in those films was conceived in such a way that it would work only with, or as, subtitles, and as rhythm, rather to impart verbal information. In fact, in *Yaaba*, the characters rarely speak, and if they say anything to each other it is perfunctory things, such as 'How are you?', 'I am fine', 'How is your village?', 'It's fine.' It is a kind of zero degree of language. That austerity was part of *Yaaba*'s appeal; you could see that an attempt was being made to construct *a cinema*. With film-makers like Idrissa Ouedraogo, it clearly had this double-sided address: the films worked in Burkina Faso as Burkinabe films, while at the same time a line pointed very firmly to the international market.

VV/PW: *But the changes in landscape in* Yeelen, *from swamp to desert to mountains, mark that film as a very Malian film, since elsewhere in Africa a different weight would be given to such landscapes and to the shifts from one to the other.*

JA: I think that Cissé was the second major African film-maker, after Sembène, to understand the value of *mise en scène*. But *Waati* (Cissé, 1995) failed precisely because it tried to push to its logical conclusion those questions of landscape and *mise en scène*. Cissé attempted a road movie that started off in South Africa and ended up in Mali. The idea was to commandeer a plethora of landscapes as a way of speaking about the 'African condition', and he did it in a way that, I think, most African film-makers at the time would not have really understood. Cissé was genuinely trying to update the modernist idiom but without Sembène's political flamboyance. *Waati* is a culmination of the project Cissé started with *Yeelen*: **285**

to offer distinct alternatives to the two versions of the modernist scenario that were available at the time. One was to follow in the footsteps, or in the shadow, of Sembène by seeing the cinema as endless political parables revolving around certain unchanging conditions (our powerlessness vis-à-vis Europe; what 'our' culture is and what it means). The other alternative, which emerged more visibly in the 1990s, says 'who cares about politics or culture; our mission is to provide a *mise en scène* that can translate the African sublime as a universal constant; and we can do that only if we forget all the others who concentrate on "side issues", with politics or political speech being one such issue. We have to turn to eternal verities because that is where we can locate the African sublime: go to the village, find an old woman who has a universal problem, put her with a young boy and let's see what happens.' *Yeelen* was very much an attempt to come up with something else. I think Cissé felt that what was missing was the mythic. If you could add the mythic to Sembène's search for the appropriate political parable, combine that with the village films' simplicity, and with a more heightened sense of what was achievable cinematographically, then you could come up with an alternative model.

VV/PW: *Why did that come out of Mali?*
JA: Mali does have some of the major African epics. There is no question about that. The *Sundiata* epic is a Malian epic. But my feeling is that to acknowledge certain pre-existing traces is not enough; one has to also focus on how people are playing with what they regard as pre-existing traces. Knowing that Mali has an abundance of epics, Cissé works to make that alignment actively and consciously, so that, to me and to you, that is a Malian film. There is a definite attempt to construct what one could call a Malian tradition even as that 'tradition' announces its newness. The alternative is to fall into a determinist mode of thinking that makes him and his films a product of Malian culture that is given. I want to resist that, but I also want to accept that there are pre-existing elements that one cannot wish away. At any time, there are traces of forms, some fossilised, some in the process of becoming, some dying, that one could call 'cultural traits'. As the grandson of a major *griot*, I am very aware of that. There is a sense of continuity in the premises that underpin 'traditional norms'. When my grandfather used to pour a libation, the kind of thing that would open every event, he would go through the names of his ancestors going back hundreds of years. There is in the culture this sense that people somehow embody things that pre-exist them. On the other hand, we are not just Ghanaians: we also happen to be members of a small, insignificant kind of clan that is struggling to be both alive and part of an entity called Ghana – an entity that is evolving and unfolding and which by no means is already achieved. Post-colonial people cannot afford most of the rhetorical excesses of nationalism, its absurdities, the luxury of nationalism, because the sense of having to create this 'national' is still within their living memory. I know that we have not been around forever and that what constitutes us is not eternal.

Mali is an unusual country in many ways. Most people in West Africa are secessionists from older African empires of one form or another. All these people migrated and their migrations are relatively recent, still in living memory. So when they evoke tradition, that evocation is always premised on the understanding that it is a relatively new tradition. Mali is a different story. The settlements there go back a very long time and the territory itself has been the space of empire after empire. Whereas in West Africa people are, or were, nomads and migratory, in Mali they are relatively sedentary. Which means that they can speak about embodying traditions in a way that someone like me cannot. It is not possible to generalise the Malian situation across the continent. Its national cultural character could have been accessed only via the routes that people want to counterpose to it, the alternative to it. Cissé, who absolutely works within the modernist African paradigm, is far from claiming to be the harbinger of something unconnected to the continental dimension. He does affirm his Malian formation, but he is clearly also saying: 'I have seen Dovzhenko, I know that I am from Mali because I have an understanding of the epic; but I am also an African film-maker who wants to speak to Africans in this shared language.' This is one thing that keeps me attached to African film-making in a way that I do not find elsewhere. On the whole, other film-makers are quite happy to accept these national designations unproblematically, in a way that most African film-makers do not. African film-makers are more uneasy with them, I think, than others.

The DuBoisian idea of double consciousness may help explaining this. A number of the major film-makers are very comfortable with being seen as, say, Burkina-based, or Senegalese. Even though *Touki-Bouki* (Djibril Diop Mambéty, 1973) continues to function as an emblematic, resolutely modernist statement of Africanity, in some of its obsessions and concerns, it is also resolutely Senegalese. Diop Mambéty would have been happy to regard it as a Senegalese film *and* as an African film. There is a way in which people do not, and never did, see those things as mutually exclusive. There are two sets of reasons for that. A film-maker's ability to function in an international frame rests also, if not largely, in the fact that festivals work with quotas. Everyone denies it, but it is true: to qualify as 'international', a festival has to have a certain number of African or Asian films. Even today, within this international frame, the selection criterion remains that of 'African film', rather than Nigerian or Senegalese film. African film-makers are as aware of this as anybody else. But the special burden that African film-makers have to carry is that they know that they cannot really afford to forget one frame at the expense of the other. The local and the international have to be in the frame at all times. You need to secure a certain degree of international recognition, but you cannot function without the local either, and therein lies a paradox. Francophone African film-makers who have lived in Paris for thirty years are still regarded as African film-makers, even as African film-makers from very specific countries. They are given funds *because* they are from those specific countries, which means that they cannot afford to forget, nor to not say, that they are from there.

It is not just a cynical calculation either. The film-makers genuinely feel that they are from those specific places, but they know that the language of nationality does not make sense if divorced from the all-embracing pan-African discourse. That is what actually helps the national dialogue to cohere. It is both a reality and a rhetoric. It is a reality because a number of West African countries share similar problems, be they cultural or economic. With, say, *Yaaba*, you can tell that the film-maker is deploying certain standard West African **287** tropes as to what the relationship between young and old people should be. Those tropes are recognised by any West African, and that is not just fiction, it is real. The rhetorical dimension lies in the fact that, in the film, those tropes are presented as a uniquely Burkinabe rural thing, something that is both human and African at the same time. I do not think that people are denying national identities, but they are not overstating their value either: the national does not stand above other things. That is my view.

When we edited our Nkrumah film, *Testament* (J. Akomfrah, 1988), it was clear to me that we were about to excavate a unique form of melancholia, or mourning, which only those who have experienced the Ghanaian post-independence euphoria would understand. This does not mean that it would not resonate in other West African countries. In fact, it did: I was invited to other countries to show the film and people talked about what Nkrumah meant to them. But the genesis of the project was to excavate that uniquely Ghanaian form of melancholia and energy. People knew that the songs we used in that film were specific to that period, when Ghanaians really wanted to be something. That project had a uniquely national orientation in the sense that it was about trying to excavate something that I knew resided within the borders of what one would call Ghana. That orientation was necessary, because the failure of the project was about the failure to safeguard the sovereignty of those borderlines.

If you made a similar film about Sekou Touré's reign in Guinea, or Sankara's in Burkina Faso, I expect that it would be possible to excavate broadly similar, distinct forms of melancholia. They are a sort of elegy for a lost time, a time which even then was an impossible time, and which is part of a dramaturgy of national belonging: we were going to try to be one more time a great nation while at the same time participating in the great drama of being Africans. Some of the factors underpinnings these are economic; they have to do with industrialisation policies and other measures that varied from place to place. But because in the act of remembering cultural artefacts are mobilised, you are necessarily also forced to go down those cultural byways and alleyways. This is not to downplay the uniqueness of certain socio-economic formations, but to stress other dimensions. For instance, there are certain forms of choral singing that emerge in Ghana in the nineteenth century only as a result of the encounter between European Presbyterianism, especially Scottish Presbyterianism, and African music. Those forms were an attempt to offer an alternative to the drumming, which was seen as too African to be part of the religion. The Ghanaian composer Ephraim Amu's work drew heavily on that in its construction of something that could be called a Ghanaian choral tradition. Its elements may not be 'native' in origin, but they are nevertheless of a flavour that is unique enough for people to know that you are evoking things that over-determined that particular place at a particular time.

So, there are national traces, institutions, practices which, especially in West Africa, cannot be limited to being national in character. There is also the assumption, among film-makers, that we share ideas about what place a film-maker occupies on the continent. That shared language does not constrict the way we talk in uniquely national terms. I recently participated in a Ghanaian discussion about the government's plans for the film industry. I argued that the time when it made sense to have hierarchies of priorities – between, say, education on the one hand, and film on the other, was over. The two, now, are connected, because if you put money into a film, you *are* actually taking care of starvation too. It is that simple.

A government in Ghana has a certain amount of confidence, some World Bank money, an industrial base and so on. These things are important because that is not the case in, say, the Ivory Coast, or in Burkina Faso, where lack of access to those resources does not allow that kind of discussion. So there are national inflections in the socio-economic sphere that make it possible to have quite specific discussions about a national film culture within specific national boundaries, but those national boundaries do not over-determine what the film-makers from that place see as their sole raison d' être. It just means that you cannot have that particular conversation.

VV/PW: There is a way in which those conversations about African cinema/s are conducted in the future tense, addressing specific nation-state policies and conditions with an aspiration to improve the film industry conditions. Is this dynamic away from the pan-African, towards a specification of the nation-state, of a national formation, discernible or even dominant?

JA: You have to remember that some of the things that I am saying are abhorrent to some African film-makers. For the pan-Africanists, there is simply no conversation about possible national formations and their specificity. They have a continental frame within which national specificities are simply variations on a universal African theme. There are also quite serious scholarly attempts to make this continental vision take precedence over everything. But those dialogues and discourses exist. They have things of value in them, which help to make sense of actual film-making-living conditions. At the same time I do not want completely to commit to them, because doing so over-determines things that are still to be worked out.

Across the continent, the drift is towards embracing the elements of globalisation that are present everywhere. There is, for instance, across the continent a booming and growing youth culture absolutely committed to hip hop and all manner of ghetto mythologies. The cultural critic Greg Tate recently made the point that for large parts of the world, the ghetto has become synonymous with the American Dream, the ghetto *is* the American Dream. Gestures that emerged from the inner cities of America have been embraced as emblematically American signs of success. No one buys this idea more than contemporary mainland African youth culture. Many, who see in it a complete erasure of the national, worry about this. But the West Coast itself is a product of one such mix. There were 134 forts across the West African coastline. In order to account for what one could call Ghanaian culture, you have to note that Scottish Presbyterianism and German Protestantism played a major structuring role in inaugurating and sustaining what passes for Ghanaian national identity. The idea that something is going to come from the outside which will destroy something that is in some way organic to the place is not true because there never was such a thing, at least not for the last four or five hundred years. It always already was a mixture of elements.

While people worry about hip hop, I find others things more alarming. Globalisation pushes the African national into the corner of national specification because Africans are held **289** accountable to, and by, that globalising dynamic, which is towards national specification. The World Bank says 'we want a certain kind of thing to happen across Africa', but that has very national implications because the World Bank effectively operates on a nation by nation basis. It does want certain things to happen trans-continentally – an example being the Trans-African highway – but at the same time it asks individual countries to denationalise their industries. Even in the World Bank's approach national boundaries are reified and simultaneously dissolved.

Nobody on the African West Coast, and certainly no film-maker, can afford the luxury of disavowing national identity. The first time I went to Telluride, in 1989, Isaac Julien and I were on a panel with the then gurus of British cinema – Peter Greenaway, Dennis Potter and a whole host of others. Every single one of them disavowed their national identity, which produced a somewhat paradoxical situation, since the only two film-makers on the panel who were speaking about British cinema were the two black film-makers. Greenaway, who got his funding from several countries, thought that all this talk about British cinema was vulgar, whereas Isaac and I were locked into British funding mechanisms and groups. Within most of the African national cinemas, funding patterns absolutely lock film-makers into national places. If you want to take distance from some national identity and apply to the European fund for African Caribbean Production, you would soon have to realise that those funds are not available unless you are from a very specific place, and have a passport to prove it, because the funds come from donations made to the specific countries. At the moment, the EU is a key funding source for African film-makers. No amount of rhetorical flamboyance about being a film-maker of the world is of any use in that context. Even if people felt that they are not Ghanaian, Nigerian or Senegalese, you are not going to hear them announcing that as a basis for their film-making – except, that is, in contexts like FES-PACO.

There are certain elective affinities to African 'place' that were put under enormous strain in the grim years from the late 1970s to the 1990s. These became a source of shame for most Africans and the basis for migration on the scale that characterised those three decades. For instance, my uncle went to Sweden and became a big cheese in Swedish television. He was very happy not to be thought of as a Ghanaian at all. Now he is slowly making his way back to Ghana. That is clearly a result of certain engines that were put into place by globalisation, its sweeping away of arcane institutions, some good and some bad, with the accompanying buzz of 'progress'. Globalisation reawakens those elective affinities were a source of shame for many years. At the same time, it also brings everything closer. You don't feel so far from anything any more.

During those years of hardship the key sense you got from film-makers in Ghana was that they just wanted to get out of the country, because somewhere else is where it's at, so to speak. Now, they still want to leave, but not because 'out there' is more 'with it' than Accra or Lagos. Recently I taught a group at the Ghana Film School and with them you really got a sense of this change. These were young people who seemed to want to do two things that were mutually exclusive before: to have the advantages of applying for money abroad and to work on national subjects. They are happy to be seen as Ghanaian film-makers. That is unusual.

When denationalisation took place and things started closing down, people just left the country. And while at the beginning of this process you would have thought that the key engine for manufacturing local talent had gone, now you go to the National Film School and find that it is still there. There are people who do want to finish and leave, but the majority actually wants to stay. They write to me, asking for sources where they can raise the funding to make films there. People connect far more practically to the diaspora, both of the American and the British varieties, the old and the new. The kids at the National Film School are clearly the product of two engines simultaneously. On the one hand, denational-isation, the opening of borders, a new government and so on are enabling access to all kinds of things that the generation before did not have access to. That animates them to want to do things both there and abroad. The flipside is that the immediacy of, for instance, the inter-net, also makes them feel that they do have to leave in order to have access to things. But the tension is not the same as for earlier generations. There is not the same sense of urgency to the notion that one has to relocate geographically in order to gain access to something. They are much more comfortable with being there. If they are not swallowed up by institu-tions like television or local radio, after film school they may be able to translate the auton-omy that they crave for into something meaningful and valuable. It is clear to me that what they told me that they want to do cannot be done in those institutions. If you take these kids as a group whose lives you can use to figure out where things are heading, then I would say that less of them will leave than has been the case before. More will make films in Ghana than they have done for a long time. They are likely to be able to do so because video and film cultures are now familiar to them, and they will improvise something out of that. The accoutrements of globalisation – internet, cybercafés – are also there, and they will make use of that to a degree that the previous generation could not.

Notes

1. After a long conversation between John Akomfrah, Valentina Vitali and Paul Willemen in London in the summer of 2003, John Akomfrah reworked the edited transcript and assumed authorship of this text. In order to convey something of the text's conditions of production, aspects of the conversational process have been preserved, including Vitali and Willemen's questions, which are designed to function here rather like chapter headings.

2. After the Harlem Renaissance associated with the names of Marcus Garvey and W. E. B. Dubois, a number of African and American intellectuals in Paris set up *La Revue du monde noir* in 1931–2. It became a platform for the formulation of a black people's consciousness rooted in what Fanon called 'the lived experience of black people'. This cultural ferment spawned more periodicals, including *L'Étudiant noir* (1935), which published the work of young writers like Léopold Sédar Senghor – who became Senegal's first president in 1980 – and Aimé Césaire – the Martiniquan poet who represented Martinique in French government circles who became the first president of the Martiniquan Regional Council in 1982. The term *négritude* was coined by Césaire to refer to the shared dimensions of black people's experiences the world over, but it was Senghor who gave it its political and cultural content, using *négritude* to designate 'the cultural heritage, the values and especially the spirit of negro-african civilization'. Franz Fanon **291**

was one of the movement's severest critics, arguing that no cultural renaissance was possible without first having struggled for, and won, political independence.

3. Amilcar Cabral was the founder (1956) and secretary-general of the Partido Africano da Independência da Guiné e Cabo Verde (PAIGC; African Party for the Independence of Guinea and Cape Verde). With Agostinho Neto he was co-founder (1956) of a liberation movement in Angola. Educated in Lisbon, Cabral there helped to found (1948) the Centro de Estudos Africanos. From 1962 he took his party into an open struggle for the independence of Portuguese Guinea. In the late 1960s he was the de facto ruler of the parts of Portuguese Guinea not occupied by Portuguese army units. In 1972 he established a Guinean People's National Assembly as a step towards independence. He was assassinated outside his home in Conakry in 1973.

21   Spaces of Identity

Communications Technologies and the Reconfiguration of Europe[1]

David Morley and Kevin Robins

Within the terms of the '1992' debate it has been argued that television has a particular role to play in 'promoting the cultural identity of Europe'; it is said to be able to 'help to develop a people's Europe through reinforcing the sense of belonging to a Community composed of countries which are different yet partake of a deep solidarity' (Commission of the European Communities 1988: 4). Television, it is suggested, can actually be an instrument of integration. 'Television', the Commission maintains, 'will play an important part in developing and nurturing awareness of the rich variety of Europe's common cultural and historical heritage. The dissemination of information across national borders can do much to help the people of Europe to recognise the common destiny they share in many areas' (Commission of the European Communities 1984: 28).

 Thus the European Commission stresses the 'essential' nature of our 'Common European identity':

> European culture is marked by its diversity of climate, countryside, architecture, language, beliefs, taste and artistic style. Such diversity must be protected, not diluted. It represents one of the chief sources of the wealth of our continent. But underlying this variety there is an affinity, a family likeness, a common European identity. Down the ages, the tension between the continent's cultural diversity and unity has helped to fuse ancient and modern, traditional and progressive. It is undoubtedly a source of the greatness of the best elements of our civilisation. (Commission of the European Communities 1983: 1)

The Construction of Cultural Identities

Up to the present, many of the debates surrounding the questions of cultural identity and cultural imperialism have functioned with a largely uninterrogated model of what cultural identities are. On the whole, the question has been posed (with varying degrees of technological determinism) as one of the impact or potential impact of a new technology (for example, satellite broadcasting) on a set of pre-given objects (national or cultural identities). We want to suggest that that is a badly posed question, and that rather than searching for a 293 better answer to that question, we might be better advised to try, in the first instance, to formulate a better question.

One way of beginning to reformulate the questions at issue into more productive terms is offered by Philip Schlesinger, who has recently argued that in communications research, collective identity has functioned as a residual category. He argues that we now need to turn around the terms of the conventional assessment: '*not* to start with communications and its supposed effects on national identity and culture, but rather to begin by posing the problem of national identity itself, to ask how it might be analysed and what importance communications practices might have in its *constitution*' (Schlesinger 1987: 234).

Similarly, James Donald has argued that we might usefully focus on the apparatuses of discourse, technologies and institutions which produce what is generally recognised as 'national culture'. The nation, he suggests, 'is an effect of these cultural technologies, not their origin. A nation does not express itself through its culture: it is cultural apparatuses that produce "the nation" ' (Donald 1988: 32). Thus Donald argues for reconceptualising the production of the national culture in terms of the effects of cultural technologies. This is no abstract process: '"Literature", "nation", "people" [a]re never [p]urely conceptual. They exist only as they are instituted through education, publishing, the press, the media, the Arts Council and other such institutions' (Donald 1988: 35).

Rather than analysing cultural identities one by one and then, subsequently (as an optional move), thinking about how they are related to each other (through relations of alliance or opposition, domination or subordination), we must grasp how these identities, in Saussure's terms, are originally constructed in and through their relations to each other. Thus, to make the argument more concrete, it is inappropriate to start by trying to define 'European culture', for example, and then subsequently analysing its relations to other cultural identities. Rather, from this perspective, 'European culture' is seen to be constituted precisely through its distinctions/oppositions to American culture, Asian culture, Islamic culture and so on. Thus, difference is constitutive of identity. Again Schlesinger offers a useful formulation. He argues that identity is as much about exclusion as about inclusion and that the 'critical factor for defining the ethnic group therefore becomes the social *boundary* which defines the group with respect to other groups . . . not the cultural reality within those borders' (Schlesinger 1987: 235).

Schlesinger's argument is that, viewed in this way, collective identity is based on the (selective) processes of memory, so that a given group recognises itself through its recollection of a common past. Thus, he argues, we can develop a dynamic view of identity – focusing on the ability of social and ethnic groups to continually recompose and redefine their boundaries.

From this perspective, then, national identity is a specific form of collective identity:

All identities are constituted within a system of social relations and require the reciprocal recognition of others. Identity [i]s not to be considered a 'thing' but rather a 'system of relations and representations'. [T]he maintenance of an agent's identity is [a] continual process of recomposition rather than a given one, in which the two constitutive dimensions of self identification and affirmation of difference are continually locked. [I]dentity is seen as a dynamic *emergent* aspect of collective action. (Schlesinger 1987: 236–7)

In a similar vein John Hartley has argued that nations cannot be understood in terms simply of their own, supposedly intrinsic and essential features, but only in relational terms, each nation being defined by its relations to other nations (Hartley 1987). Difference is thus at the heart of the issue, a point well made by Donald in his analysis of popular fictions. Donald's point is that these popular fictions speak to fundamental psychic processes, and attention to them can help us to make sense of what he calls the 'paranoid strand in popular culture, the clinging to familiar polarities and the horror of difference': 'Manifest in racism, its violent misogyny, and its phobias about alien culture, alien ideologies and "enemies within" is the terror that without the known boundaries, everything will collapse into undifferentiated, miasmic chaos; that identity will disintegrate; that "I" will be suffocated or swamped' (Donald 1988: 44).

This is the fear at the heart of the question of identity – whether posed at the level of the individual or of the nation. Driven by such fears, as the Mattelarts have noted, the defence of a given 'cultural identity' easily slips into the most hackneyed nationalism, or even racism, and the nationalist affirmation of the superiority of one group over another (Mattelart et al. 1984). The question is not abstract: it is a matter of the relative power of different groups to define their own identities, and of the ability to mobilise these definitions through their control of cultural institutions. Here we enter the terrain of what is referred to as the invention of tradition. Tradition is not a matter of a fixed and given set of beliefs or practices which are handed down or accepted passively. Rather, as Patrick Wright has argued, tradition is very much a matter of present-day politics and of the way in which powerful institutions function to select particular values from the past and to mobilise them in contemporary practices (Wright 1985; Hobsbawm and Ranger 1983). Through such mechanisms of cultural reproduction, a particular version of collective memory and thus a particular sense of national and cultural identity, is produced.

The fundamental principle for political attachment in capitalist societies has been through national and nationalist identities, through citizenship of the nation-state. This allegiance is now being increasingly undermined – the resurgence of national-populist ideologies in the 1980s may well be a rearguard response to this tendency – and we are seeing the emergence of both enlarged (continental European) and restricted (local, regional, provincial) conceptions of citizenship. New forms of bonding, belonging and involvement are being forged out of the global–local nexus. The most apparent tendency is, perhaps, towards a new or renewed localism. The key issue is whether such affiliations will necessarily be conservative, parochial and introspective, or whether it is possible to reimagine local communities in more cosmopolitan terms. Sarah Benton has pointed to some of the possibilities and potential emerging from alliances between regionalist and Green politics in Europe (Benton 1989).

While they should not be seen as the determinant and causal factor, it is undoubtedly the case that the new information and communications technologies are playing a powerful role in the emergence of new spatial structures, relations and orientations. Corporate communications networks have produced a global space of electronic information flows. The new media conglomerates are creating a global image space, a 'space of transmission [that] cuts across – as a new geographic entity, which has its own sovereignty, its own guarantors – the geographies of power, of social life, and of knowledge, which define the space of nationality and of culture' (Rath 1985: 203). What the new technologies make possible is a new kind of relationship between place and space: through their capacity to transgress frontiers and subvert territories, they are implicated in a complex interplay of deterritorialisation and reterritorialisation.

In discussing the question of European geographies it is as well to remember that it has never been entirely clear what that entity called 'Europe' is: the very definition of the term itself is a matter of history and politics. Once we depart the terrain of physical geography, the questions, naturally, become even more complex. As Banks and Collins argue:

> European economic, political and cultural realms are not congruent. [T]he single market of the EEC is not congruent with the cultural unities of Europe: three of Europe's four German-speaking states are outside the EEC (though the largest is in it). The EEC's two Anglophone states have the experience – unique among European states – of being subordinate members of their world language [and cultural] community and have, therefore, a 'culture' that finds Paris more foreign than Boston, Hamburg further away than Melbourne. (Banks and Collins 1989: 10)

Again, basic cultural issues are already at stake in these definitions. As Collins asks: 'what will become of European culture should Turkey, an Islamic (albeit a modernised and secularised) state, join the community?' (Banks and Collins 1989: 17).

As we argued earlier, the debate around European culture has largely been stimulated by a fear that heavy viewing of television programmes from other (principally American) cultures would, over time, erode the culture, values and traditions of the nations or Europe. Operating in response to this fear, current European Community (EC) initiatives can thus be seen as an attempt to intervene so as to (re)create a distinctive European culture – an enterprise which Collins describes as culminating in the 'absurd spectacle of a retreat to the Middle Ages for a coherent vision of European identity' (Banks and Collins 1989: 22); a retreat perhaps to the (distinctly pre-electronic) moment in which, as Donald argues, 'the literary forms of the European languages provided the medium for the definition and diffusion of national vernaculars, in opposition to the transnational jargon of Latin and subnational regional dialects' (Donald 1988: 33). The cultural politics at stake are of a quite contradictory character.

It may be that what is most apparent and remarkable in the present context is the accelerating formation of global communications empires, such as those of Murdoch, Maxwell, Berlusconi, Bertelsmann, Sony, Disney, Paramount and so on. Internationalisation is not, of

course, a new phenomenon; it has always been a constitutive aspect of capitalist development. But it is now entering a new stage, and the maintenance of national sovereignty and identity are becoming increasingly difficult as the unities of economic and cultural production and consumption become increasingly transnational.

As broadcasting nations, the countries of Europe are, of course, not only different, but also, in various senses, at odds with each other. We might emphasise the advantageous position of the anglophone states within the European Community (given the position of English as the *lingua franca* of the region). Thus, Britain is a significant exporter of television material to the rest of Europe, and is in a quite different relation to American programming than is the rest of Europe, by simple virtue of the shared and hegemonic language. Philip Schlesinger notes both how the 'Big Four' (Britain, France, West Germany and Italy) dominate all television exchanges within the European Broadcasting Union (EBU), and how the EBU itself exports three times as much to the East European International Radio and TV organisations (OIRT) as it imports (Schlesinger 1986). There are, of course, historical issues at stake as well. As Walker noted in his analysis of the significance of the inauguration of the Single European Market in 1992, there are those within Europe who might well see 1992 as 'the last campaign, the third battle of the Ardennes, at which the Anglo-Saxons are finally defeated [a]nd Britain takes its (humble) place within the Fourth (Deutschmark) Reich' (Walker 1988a). There are certainly those who foresee that 'a dynamic Europe should be built around the Franco-German duo'.[2] As with the definition of national cultural identities, so too is the shaping of a European culture and identity centred around the relative power of different parties.

Degrees of Exportability

Within this broader context, let us now consider the central issue of the transnationalisation of culture – as a fundamental process in which the 'vertical' organisation of people within national communities is (to varying extents, and in varying contexts) being supplanted by their organisation into 'horizontal' communities – people are connected electronically rather than by geographical proximity. In his analysis of the increasing significance of cross-border transmissions in creating electronic communities, Rath argues that 'frontiers of a national, regional or cultural kind no longer count: what counts much more is the boundary of the territory of any given nation state' (Rath 1985: 202).

   If we wish to avoid a form of technological determinism we should not, of course, presume that any of these technological developments will be uniform in their effects. In our view, the key questions concern the ways in which a range of social and cultural divisions (matters of generation and education, for example) inflect both the take-up and the cultural impact of the new communications technologies. Commercial broadcasters and their market research agencies are in a position, given their necessary sensitivity to questions of audience research, penetration rates and the like, to throw some light on these questions from an empirical point of view.

   There is, for example, already evidence that, within Northern Europe, it is young people who are the heaviest viewers of satellite channels. Thus, in her summary of the empirical material available on the development of an international audience within Europe, Pam Mills notes 'the heightened appeal of imported programmes to young people. Older viewers are more likely to avoid imported programmes, for language and cultural reasons. Younger viewers are, however, increasingly familiar with foreign-language material' (Mills 1985: 493). Similarly, in 1987, John Clemens reported AGB Television International's work as indicating that 'the high entertainment output (of Sky and Super Channel) is attracting the young Dutch audience and may well predict the pattern of the future', and that in Belgium, 'amongst children once again . . . (consumption patterns) are biased away from the national broadcasters' (Clemens 1987: 306–7). Again, Collins notes a tendency, specifically in the sphere of musical culture, towards 'the rupturing of national cultural communities along a fault-line of age' (Collins 1989: 11).

It is, of course, not only a matter of age. In the survey quoted above, Mills summarises the overall position in Britain: 'Acceptance of foreign-language material is predictably highest among the better educated, those in the higher social groups and those living nearer the capital' (Mills 1985: 4). Rather than concern ourselves with the 'Europeanisation' or 'transnationalisation' of culture in the abstract, we need to ask more concrete questions. For which particular groups, in which types of places is this prospect becoming a reality? And what can this tell us about the future?

Martin Walker worries about the emergence of a standardised 'Euro-business' class clutching their inevitable filofaxes and sporting the standard 'business Euro-uniform worn from Glasgow down to Naples' (Walker 1988b). These, presumably, are precisely the people for whom 'Europe' is becoming a tangible reality. They are also people to whom Collins refers in his comments on the current development of the European newspaper market – those on the upper side of the fault-line of social class, across Europe – who, given their competence in English, are particularly likely to 'become differentiated from their co-linguists and integrated into a new cosmopolitan culture where the growth of "horizontal" links to similar strata elsewhere will supplant the longer established "vertical" links with [their own] national language community' (Collins 1989: 11).

This, of course, gets us back to the question of the terms in which European culture is, even if only for some particular groups within our societies, being transnationalised. And those terms are, of course, literally, English – or anglophone. Our analysis of the cultural impact of any form of domination must always be differentiated, concerned to establish which groups, in which places, are receptive (or not) to it. Similarly, we now want to argue, we must pay close attention to the *relative* popularity or exportability of different parts of the cultural repertoire, of the (in this case, anglophone) cultural products in question. It is the anglophone (and principally American) audiovisual media that are cutting horizontally across the world audience, engaging the attention and mobilising the enthusiasm of popular audiences, and often binding them into cultural unities that are transnational. They are 'restratifying national communities and separating elite from mass or popular taste, and thus threatening the cultural hegemony enjoyed by the national cultural elites' (Collins 1989: 10).

However, not all anglophone cultural products are equally exportable. We must ask a **298** more specific question about which types and varieties of anglophone product are exportable to whom, under what conditions. Colin Hoskins and Rolf Mirus offer the concept of 'cultural discount' to account for the fundamental process through which 'a particular programme, rooted in the culture, and thus attractive in that environment, will have a diminished appeal elsewhere, as viewers find it difficult to identify with the style, values, beliefs, institutions and behavioural patterns of the material in question' (Hoskins and Mirus 1988: 500). The point, however, is that cultural discount can be argued to apply differentially to various types of information products as they are exported. In an attempt to offer a more differentiated analysis Collins argues that 'cultural discount is likely to be lower for audiovisual products than for written works, and within the audiovisual category, lower for works with little linguistic content than for works in which speech is an important element' (Collins 1988: 1).

For this reason, the argument runs, programming with a high speech content, because it is so much subject to misunderstanding, is unpopular with 'foreign' viewers. Conversely, a channel such as MTV builds its international appeal precisely on the fact that there is little problem with language, in so far as, according to MTV's European Chief Executive Officer, 'for the bulk of our music programming, the words are practically irrelevant' (Collins 1988: 30). The point is supported by Mills, who argues that 'programming that is not dependent on understanding the language – for example, an opera or ballet channel or a pop channel – will attract widely dispersed and sometimes potentially large audiences, but informational programming [w]ill meet language barriers' (Mills 1985: 501).

Attempts to attract a European audience with English-language programming, not unlike the attempt to create European advertising markets, do seem to have largely foundered in the face of the linguistic and cultural divisions in play between the different sectors of the audience. Witness the difficulties experienced by Super Channel in its attempt to develop pan-European programming. We seem now to be experiencing a form of revisionism among the advertisers and the major satellite channels, in their retrenchment to strategies more closely adapted to the linguistic divisions across the continent (Mulgan 1989).

While everyone seems to agree (by and large) about the difficulties, different commentators offer contradictory scenarios for the future. Thus Collins suggests that cultural discount will be higher for entertainment than for informational programming, while Clemens argues that, conversely, a more likely scenario is one in which we see a combination of privately owned pan-European channels specialising in entertainment programming with multi-lingual soundtracks, alongside national state channels specialising in news and current affairs programming (Collins 1989; Clemens 1987).

However, despite these uncertainties as to the most likely course of future development, some things are clear. There is a growing realisation that the success of American-style commercial programming in Europe is context-dependent in a very specific sense. US imports only do well when domestic television is not producing comparable entertainment programming – and whenever viewers have the alternative of comparable entertainment programming in their own language, the American programmes tend to come off second best (Mills 1985; Clemens 1987; Silj et al. 1988).

There is some evidence to suggest that, in the larger European countries at least, the 'most popular domestic programmes consistently outperform the leading US ones' (Waterman 1988). Michael Tracey suggests that the international communications system is more complex than is usually allowed for, and that there has been a gross underestimation of 'the strengths of national cultures, the power of language and tradition, the force that flows, still, within national boundaries.' Audiences are also more discriminating than is generally acknowledged: 'US television was never as popular, or even widespread as was assumed . . . national populations basically prefer national programming' (Tracey 1988: 22–4). Recent research has pointed to the quite varied ways in which audiences from different cultural backgrounds use, perceive and interpret programmes in the light of the cultural resources and 'filters' at their disposal (Breton and Proulx 1989).

So, to return again to the issue of which question we should be asking about these developments, we can perhaps now reformulate it as a question about the potential cultural impact of some types of American (or pan-European) programming on some specific audience categories, in some particular types of context (as defined by national programming policies). And even then, within that more highly specified context, we need to be quite cautious in attributing effects (on audiences) to programmes. That is not simply because programmes do not have simple or straightforward effects on their viewers which can be easily predicted from an analysis of their content (or their production history). It is also because, precisely in order to be exportable, programmes such as *Dallas* have to operate at a very high level of abstraction, and the price of this approach to a universality of appeal is a higher level of polysemy or multi-accentuality. The research of Ang and of Katz and Liebes (Ang 1984; Katz and Liebes 1989) reminds us just how open these types of programmes are to reinterpretation by audiences outside their country of origin. Which brings us, finally, to the question of the audience.

Domestic Viewing as National Ritual: Family, Television, Nation

We have spent some time engaging with the debates about cultural identity, new technologies and the transnationalisation of culture in the terms in which they are customarily posed – that is, from the point of view of production economics, the changing technologies of distribution and their potential cultural effects on the media audience. We now want to reverse the terms of the argument, and look at the question from the point of view of the domestic users and audiences of these new technologies, as they function in the context of household and family cultures. The question to be asked is how the new patterns of supply of programming will be filtered and mediated by the processes of domestic consumption. The key issues, we suggest, concern the role of these technologies in disrupting established boundaries (at the national and domestic levels, simultaneously) and in rearticulating the private and public spheres in new ways. Our argument is that analysis of the processes of creation of new image spaces and cultural identities needs to be grounded in the analysis of the everyday practices and domestic rituals through which contemporary electronic communities are constituted and reconstituted (at both micro and macro levels) on a daily basis.

As Anderson puts it: 'An American will never meet, or even know the names of more than a handful of his fellow Americans. He has no idea of what they are up to at any one time. But he has complete confidence in their steady, anonymous, simultaneous activity' (Anderson 1983: 31). Wherein lies this simultaneity? Among other sources we can perhaps look to the regulation of simultaneous experience through broadcast schedules. Where does this confidence come from? Among other sources, Anderson points to the newspaper as a mechanism for providing imaginary links between the members of a national community. As Hartley puts it, newspapers are 'at one and the same time the ultimate fiction, since they construct the imagined community, and the basis of a mass ritual or ceremony that millions engage in every day' (Hartley 1987: 124).

Herman Bausinger develops the point about the newspaper as a linking mechanism between the rituals of the domestic, the organisation of the schedules of everyday life and the construction of the 'imagined community' of a nation. Bausinger comments on the nature of the disruption caused when a morning edition of a newspaper fails to appear. His point concerns that which is missed. As he puts it: 'Is it a question [o]f the missing content of the paper? Or isn't it rather that one misses the newspaper itself? Because the newspaper is part of it (a constitutive part of the ritual of breakfast for many people), reading it proves that the breakfast time world is still in order' (Bausinger 1984: 344). And, of course, vice versa.

A similar point, and indeed, a stronger one, given the necessary simultaneity of broadcast television viewing, could be made in relation to the watching of evening news broadcast for many viewers – where the fact of watching, and engaging in a joint ritual with millions of others, can be argued to be at least as important as any informational content gained from the broadcast. For our purposes, the point we would stress here is the potential usefulness of the model offered in Bausinger's analysis for focusing our analysis on the role of communications media in articulating our private and public worlds.

The further point, inevitably, involves the significance of these arguments in the context of current and prospective changes in the structure of broadcasting. The proliferation of broadcast channels through cable and satellite television is likely to move us towards a more fragmented social world than that of traditional national broadcast television. These new forms of communication may in fact play a significant part in deconstructing national cultures, and the interactive and 'rescheduling' potentialities of video and other new communications technologies may disrupt our assumptions of any 'necessary simultaneity' of social experience.

There is a substantial body of evidence that broadcast television constitutes a significant cultural resource on which large numbers of people depend, to a greater or lesser extent, for supplying their needs, both for information and for entertainment. There is further evidence that broadcast television plays a significant role (both at a calendrical and at a quotidian level) in organising and scheduling our participation in public life, in the realms of politics and leisure activities. The arrival of satellite television is bringing about significant changes both in the extent and the nature of the supply of programming (directly, through its own programme strategies, and indirectly, through the responses which existing broadcast institutions are making in order to compete with their new rivals). Given these premises, the need is clear for the cultural impact of these changes in programme supply to be closely monitored during this key period of broadcasting history, in which, in Europe and North **301**

America, established patterns of consumption may be expected to fragment in a number of directions. The key issue concerns the role of the new technologies in offering a changed (and varying) menu of cultural resources, from and by means of which we will all be constructing our senses of self-identity. In analysing those processes, we must attend closely to how cultural identities are produced, both at the macro and micro levels, and ask what role these various media play in the construction of our sense of ourselves – as individuals and as members of communities at various levels – whether families, regions, nations or supranational communities. But, above all, we must not address these issues as a set of political abstractions, for they are, finally, matters of our (mediated) everyday lives.

To return to the global questions with which we began, concerning new communications technologies, changing cultural identities and the various modes of cultural imperialism, it may be that we have much to learn from those for whom the question of cultural imperialism has long been unavoidable. Confronted now by fears of domination by American and multinational corporations in the new communications industries, there is an understandable tendency to tall back into a 'Fortress Europe' posture, designed to fend off 'America', and a concern to defend indigenous national cultures against the threat of 'Brussels'. However, as Martin-Barbero puts it, this is to define our indigenous culture as a 'natural fact', a kind of pre-reality, static and without development, the 'motionless point' of departure from which modernity is measured. From this perspective 'transformed into the touchstone of identity, the indigenous would seem to be the only thing which remains for us of the "authentic", that secret place in which the purity of our cultural roots remains and is preserved. All the rest is contamination and loss of identity' (Martin-Barbero 1988: 459). The rejection of such calls for 'authenticity' or 'purity' in defence of national culture is the precondition of our effective engagement with the current processes of cultural reconfiguration in Europe.

Notes

1. Extract from an article that originally appeared in *Screen* 30 (4) (Autumn 1989): 10–34.
2. French Finance Minister Pierre Beregovoy (quoted in Walker 1988c).

References:

Ang, Ien (1984), *Watching Dallas*, London: Methuen.

Banks, Marian and Collins, Richard (1989), 'Tradeable Information and the Transnational Market', unpublished paper CCIS Polytechnic of Central London.

Bausinger, Herman (1984), 'Media, Technology and Everyday Life', *Media, Culture and Society* 6 (4).

Benton, Sarah (1989), 'Greys and Greens', *New Statesman and Society* 2 June.

Breton, Philippe and Proulx, Serges (1989), *L' Explosion de la communication*, Paris: La Découverte.

Clemens, John (1987), 'What Will Europe Watch?', *Journal of the Royal Television Society* 24 (6).

Collins, Richard (1988), 'National Culture: A Contradiction in Terms?', paper presented at the International Television Studies Conference, London.

Collins, Richard (1989), 'The Peculiarities of English Satellite Television in Western Europe', paper presented at the Programme on Information and Communications Technologies Conference, Brunel University, May.

Commission of the European Communities (1983), 'The Community of Culture', *European File* 5/83.

Commission of the European Communities (1984), *Television without Frontiers* COM (84) 300 Final, Brussels: Commission of the European Communities.

Commission of the European Communities (1988), 'Towards a Large European Audio-Visual Market', *European File* 4/88.

Donald, James (1988), 'How English is it? Popular Literature and National Culture', *New Formations* 6: 31–47.

Hartley, John (1987), 'Invisible Fictions', *Textual Practice* 1 (2): 121–38.

Hobsbawm, Eric and Ranger, Terence (1983), *The Invention of Tradition*, Cambridge: Cambridge University Press.

Hoskins, Colin and Mirus, Rolf (1988), 'Reasons for the US Dominance of the International Trade in Television Programmes', *Media, Culture and Society* 10 (4).

Katz, Elihu and Liebes, Tamar (1989), 'On the Critical Ability of Television Viewers', in Seiter, Ellen, Borchers, Hans, Keutzner, Gabrille and Warth, Eva-Maria (eds), *Remote Control*, London: Routledge.

Martin-Barbero, Jesus (1988), 'Communication from Culture: The Crisis of the National and the Emergence of the Popular', *Media, Culture and Society* 10: 447–65.

Mattelart, Armand, Delcourt, Xavier and Mattelart, Michelle (1984), *International Image Markets*, London: Comedia.

Mills, Pam (1985), 'An International Audience?', *Media, Culture and Society* 7.

Mulgan, Geoff (1989), 'A Thousand Beams of Light', *Marxism Today*, April.

Rath, Claus-Dieter (1985), 'The Invisible Network: Television as an Institution of Everyday Life', in Drummond, Philip and Paterson, Richard (eds), *Television in Transition*, London: BFI.

Schlesinger, Philip (1986), 'Any Chance of Fabricating Eurofiction?', in *Media, Culture and Society* 8 (1).

Schlesinger, Philip (1987), 'On National Identity: Some Conceptions and Misconceptions Criticised', *Social Science Information* 26 (2): 219–64.

Silj, Alessandro et al. (1988), *East of Dallas: The European Challenge to American Television*, London: BFI.

Tracey, Michael (1988), 'Popular Culture and the Economics of Global Television', *Intermedia* 16 (2).

Walker, Martin (1988a), 'Fortress Vision of a Market Future', *The Guardian*. 14 November.

Walker, Martin (1988b), 'A Pigsty without Frontiers', *The Guardian*, 15 November.

Walker, Martin (1988c), 'The Boom across Borders', *The Guardian*, 17 November.

Waterman, David (1988), 'World Television Trade: The Economic Effects of Privatisation and New Technology', *Telecommunications Policy* 12 (2).

Wright, Patrick (1985), *On Living in an Old Country*, London: Verso.

Bibliography

A comprehensive bibliography for the study of 'the national' as an issue would constitute a book all by itself, and a further volume would be required to provide an exhaustive listing of books and essays on national cinemas. Here, we have chosen to limit the bibliography according to three main criteria. Firstly, we have provided references to the main works that have inspired and oriented our thinking on the question of the national. These works we consider to be essential sources for anyone wishing to address the complex arguments and analyses that must inform the study of an aesthetic practice such as cinema in relation to the formation and histories of nations, states and nation-states. Secondly, we have endeavoured to provide a bibliographic resource for the study of particular national cinemas. These references include materials that, at times, do not directly discuss cinema, but indicate the kinds of analysis that should more directly inform its study. Such sources have not been provided for every national cinema. They appear mainly in sections devoted to cinemas that are of special interest to the editors of this collection and function as pointers towards the national contexts that must inform any study of twentieth- and twenty-first-century industrially based artforms. Thirdly, we have limited ourselves to languages familiar to the editors.

1 General

Adelman, Jeremy (2002), 'Andean Impasses', *New Left Review* (II) 18: 41–72.

Adorno, Theodor W. (1991), *The Culture Industry: Selected Essays on Mass Culture*, London: Routledge.

Adorno, Theodor W. (1998), *Critical Models: Interventions and Catchwords*, translated by Henry W. Pickford, New York: Columbia University Press.

Anderson, Benedict (1983), *Imagined Communities: Reflections on the Origin and Spread of Nationalism*, London: Verso.

Anderson, Benedict (1988), *The Spectre of Comparisons: Nationalism, Southeast Asia and the World*, London: Verso.

Anderson, Perry (1992), *English Questions*, London: Verso.

Anderson, Perry (2002), 'Internationalism: A Breviary', *New Left Review* (II) 14: 5–25.

Appadurai, Arjun (1996), *Modernity at Large: Cultural Dimensions of Globalization*, Minneapolis: University of Minnesota Press.

Arrighi, Giovanni (1994), *The Long Twentieth Century: Money, Power, and the Origins of Our Times*, London: Verso.

Bibliography

Augé, Marc (1995), *Non-Places: Introduction to an Anthropology of Supermodernity*, London: Verso.

Balakrishnan, Gopal (ed.) (1996), *Mapping the Nation*, London: Verso.

Barbéris, Pierre (1978), *Aux sources du réalisme: aristocrates et bourgeois*, Paris: UGC.

Barlow, Tani E. (ed.) (1997), *Formations of Colonial Modernity in East Asia*, Durham, NC: Duke University Press.

Barthes, Roland (1975), *S/Z*, translated by Richard Miller, London: Jonathan Cape.

Bourdieu, Pierre (1987), *Distinction: A Social Critique of the Judgement of Taste*, translated by Richard Nice, Cambridge, MA: Harvard University Press.

Bourdieu, Pierre (1996), *The Rules of Art: Genesis and Structure of the Literary Field*, translated by Susan Emanuel, London: Polity Press.

Buck-Morss, Susan (2000), *Dreamworld and Catastrophe: The Passing of Mass Utopia in the East and West*, Cambridge, MA: MIT Press.

Bürger, Peter (1984), *Theory of the Avant-Garde*, translated by Michael Shaw, Minneapolis: University of Minnesota Press.

Bürger, Peter (1992), 'Some Reflections upon the Historico-Sociological Explaination of the Aesthetics of Genius in the Eighteenth-Century', in *The Decline of Modernism*, Cambridge: Polity Press, 57–69.

Chatterjee, Partha (1993), *The Nation and its Fragments: Colonial and Postcolonial Histories*, Princeton, NJ: Princeton University Press.

Crane, Diane (ed.) (1994), *The Sociology of Culture*, Oxford: Blackwell.

Crary, Jonathan (1990), *Techniques of the Observer: On Vision and Modernity in the Nineteenth Century*, Cambridge, MA: MIT Press.

Debray, Régis (1996), *Media Manifestos: On the Technological Transmission of Cultural Forms*, translated by Eric Rauth, London: Verso.

Debray, Régis (2002), *Des machines et des âmes*, Paris: Descartes & Cie.

Donald, James (1999), *Imagining the Modern City*, London: Athlone Press.

Douglas, Mary (1975), *Implicit Meaning: Essays in Anthropology*, London: Routledge and Kegan Paul.

Douglas, Mary and Ney, Steven (1998), *Missing Persons: A Critique of the Social Sciences*, Berkeley: University of California Press.

Dussel, Enrique (1998), 'Beyond Eurocentrism: The World-System and the Limits of Modernity', in Jameson, Fredric and Miyoshi, Masao (eds), *The Cultures of Globalization*, Durham: Duke University Press, 3–31.

Eagleton, Terry (1984), *The Function of Criticism: From The Spectator to Post-Structuralism*, London: Verso.

Eagleton, Terry (2002), 'Capitalism and Form', *New Left Review* (II) 14: 19–31.

Frankovits, Andre, Sidoti, Chris et al. (1995), *The Rights Way to Development: A Human Rights Approach to Development Assistance*, Marrickville, NSW: The Human Rights Council of Australia Inc.

Gebauer, Gunter and Wulf, Christoph (1992), *Mimesis: Culture – Art – Society*, translated by Don Reneau, Berkeley: University of California Press.

Gilroy, Paul (2003), 'Where Ignorant Armies Clash by Night: Homogeneous Community and the Planetary Aspect', *International Journal of Cultural Studies*, 6 (3): 261–76.

Godzich, Wlad (1994), *The Culture of Literacy*, Cambridge, MA: Harvard University Press.

Godzich, Wlad and Kittay, Jeffrey (1987), *The Emergence of Prose: An Essay in Prosaics*, Minneapolis: University of Minnesota Press.

Gumperz, John (1982), *Discourse Strategies*, Cambridge, MA: Cambridge University Press.

Habermas, Jürgen (1962), *The Structural Transformation of the Public Sphere: An Inquiry into a Category of Bourgeois Society*, translated by Thomas Bürger, Cambridge, MA: MIT Press 1989.

Habermas, Jürgen (2001), *The Postnational Constellation: Political Essays*, translated and edited by Max Pensky, Cambridge: Polity Press.

Hall, Stuart (ed.) (1997), *Representation: Cultural Representations and Signifying Practices*, London: Sage/Open University.

Harvey, David (1999), *The Limits to Capital*, London: Verso.

Harvey, David (2001), *Spaces of Capital: Towards a Critical Geography*, Edinburgh: Edinburgh University Press.

Hobsbawm, Eric (1993), *Nations and Nationalism Since 1780: Programme, Myth, Reality*, Cambridge: Cambridge University Press.

Hobsbawm, Eric (1996), 'The Cult of Identity Politics', *New Left Review* 217: 38–47.

Hobsbawm, Eric and Ranger, Terence (eds) (1983), *The Invention of Tradition*, Cambridge: Cambridge University Press.

Huyssen, Andreas (1986), *After the Great Divide: Modernism, Mass Culture, Postmodernism*, Bloomington: Indiana University Press.

Jakobson, Roman (1978 [1921]), 'On Realism in Art', in Matejka, Ladislav and Pomorska, Krystyna (eds), *Readings in Russian Poetics: Formalist and Structuralist Views*, Ann Arbor: University of Michigan, Michigan Slavic Contributions, 8.

Jameson, Frederic (1986), 'Third-World Literature in the Era of Multinational Capitalism', *Social Text* 15: 65–88.

Jameson, Frederic (1992), *The Geopolitical Aesthetic: Cinema and Space in the World System*, London: BFI.

Jameson, Fredric (2000), 'Taking on Globalization', *New Left Review* (II), 4: 49–68.

Jameson, Fredric and Miyoshi, Masao (eds) (1998), *The Cultures of Globalisation*, Durham, NC: Duke University Press.

Jay, Martin (1993), 'Scopic Regimes of Modernity', in *Forcefields: Between Intellectual History and Cultural Critique*, London: Routledge.

Jay, Martin and Brennan, Teresa (eds) (1996), *Vision In Context: Historical and Contemporary Perspectives on Sight*, New York: Routledge.

Lotman, Iurii (1977), *The Structure of the Artistic Text*, translated by Gail Lenhoff and Ronald Vroon, Ann Arbor: Michigan Slavic Contributions 7, University of Michigan.

Lotman, Iurii (1990), *Universe of the Mind: A Semiotic Theory of Culture*, translated by Ann Shukman, London: I. B. Tauris.

Marcus, George E. (ed.) (2000), *Rereading Cultural Anthropology*, Durham: Duke University Press.

McKeon, Michael (1987), *The Origins of the English Novel 1600–1740*, Baltimore: Johns Hopkins University Press.

Nairn, Tom (1997), *Faces of Nationalism: Janus Revisited*, London: Verso.

Ohmann, Richard (1996), *Selling Culture: Magazines, Markets and Class at the Turn of the Century*, London: Verso.

Prasad, Madhava M. (1992), 'On the Question of a Theory of (Third World) Literature', *Social Text* 31/32.

Prendergast, Christopher (ed.) (2004), *Debating World Literature*, London: Verso.

Taylor, Lucien (ed.) (1994), *Visualizing Theory: Selected Essays from V.A.R. 1990–1994*, London: Routledge.

Todorov, Tzvetan (1993), *On Human Diversity: Nationalism, Racism and Exoticism in French Thought*, translated by Catherine Porter, Cambridge, MA: Harvard University Press.

Todorov, Tzvetan (2000), *Éloge de l'individu: Essai sur la peinture flamande de la Renaissance*, Paris: Adam Biro.

Willemen, Paul (1995), 'Regimes of Subjectivity and Looking', *UTS Review* 2: 101–29.

Williams, Raymond (1981), *Culture*, London: Fontana.

Žižek, Slavoj (1997), *The Plague of Fantasies*, London: Verso Books.

2 Cinema and the National

Altman, Rick (1999), *Film/Genre*, London: BFI.

Barbasch, Ilsa amd Taylor, Lucien (1997), *Cross-Cultural Filmmaking: A Handbook for Making Documentary and Ethnographic Films and Videos*, Berkeley, CA: University of California Press.

Brunetta, Gian Piero (ed.) (1999–2001), *Storia del cinema mondiale, Vol. 4: Americhe, Africa, Asia, Oceania: Le cinematografie nazionali*, Turin: Einaudi.

Charney, Leo and Schwartz, Vanessa R. (1995), *Cinema and the Invention of Modern Life*, Berkeley: University of California Press.

Clarke, David B. (ed.) (1997), *The Cinematic City*, London: Routledge.

Bibliography

Devereaux, Leslie and Hillman, Roger (eds) (1995),
    *Fields of Vision: Essays in Film Studies, Visual
    Anthropology and Photography*, Berkeley, CA:
    University of California Press.

Downing, John D. H. (1987), *Film and Politics in the
    Third World*, New York: Autonomedia.

Elsaesser, Thomas (ed.) (1990), *Early Cinema: Space
    Frame Narrative*, London: BFI.

Ferro, Marc (1976), *Analyse de film, analyse de société*,
    Paris: Hachette.

Ferro, Marc (1993), *Cinéma et histoire*, revised
    edition, Paris: Gallimard.

Gabriel, Teshome (1982), *Third Cinema in the Third
    World*, Ann Arbor: University of Michigan Press.

Garçon, François (ed.) 1992), *Cinéma et histoire
    autour de Marc Ferro*, Paris: CinémAction 65.

Grieveson, Lee and Krämer, Peter (eds) (2004),
    The Silent Cinema Reader, London: Routledge.

Hall, Stuart (1989), 'Cultural Identity and Cinematic
    Representation', *Framework* 36: 68–81.

Heath, Stephen (1981), *Questions of Cinema*,
    London: Macmillan.

Hennebelle, Guy and Guy, Agnès (eds) (1993),
    Les revues de cinéma dans le monde, Paris:
    CinémAction 69.

Hill, John and Church Gibson, Pamela (eds)
    (1998), *The Oxford Guide to Film Studies*,
    Oxford: Oxford University Press.

Hjort, Mette and MacKenzie, Scott (eds) (2000),
    Cinema and Nation, London: Routledge.

Jameson, Fredric (1992), *The Geopolitical Aesthetic:
    Cinema and Space in the World System*, London:
    BFI.

Lavrijsen, Ria (ed.) (1998), *Global Encounters in the
    World of Art: Collisions of Tradition and Modernity*,
    Amsterdam: Royal Tropical Institute.

MacDougall, David (1998), *Transcultural Cinema*,
    Princeton, NJ: Princeton University
    Press.

Mattelart, Armand (1983), *Transnationals and the
    Third World: The Struggle for Culture*, S. Hadley,
    MA: Bergin & Garvey.

Mattelart, Armand (2002), 'An Archaeology of the
    Global Era: Constructing a Belief', *Media,
    Culture & Society* 24: 591–612.

Morley, David and Robins, Kevin (1995), *Spaces of
    Identity: Global Media, Electronic Landscapes and
    Cultural Boundaries*, London: Routledge.

Naficy, Hamid and Gabriel, Teshome H. (1993),
    *Otherness and the Media: The Ethnography of the
    Imagined and the Imaged*, Chur: Harwood.

Nowell-Smith, Geoffrey (ed.) (1996), *The Oxford
    History of World Cinema*, Oxford: Oxford
    University Press.

Pines, Jim and Willemen, Paul (eds) (1989),
    Questions of Third Cinema, London: BFI.

Prokop, Dieter (1970), *Soziologie des Films*, Berlin:
    Hermann Luchterhand Verlag.

Rosen, Philip (2001), *Change Mummified: Cinema,
    Historicity, Theory*, Minneapolis: University of
    Minnesota Press.

Shohat, Ella and Stam, Robert (1994), *Unthinking
    Eurocentrism: Multiculturalism and the Media*,
    London: Routledge.

Sorlin, Pierre (1980), *The Film in History: Restaging
    the Past*, Oxford: Blackwell.

Thompson, Kristin (1985), *Exporting Entertainment:
    America in the World Film Market 1907–1934*,
    London: BFI.

Thompson, Kristin (1996), 'National or
    International Films? The European Debate
    during the 1920s', *Film History* 8 (3): 281–96.

Trinh, Minh-ha T. (1989), *Woman Native Other*,
    Bloomington: Indiana University Press.

Trinh, Minh-ha T. (1991), *When the Moon Waxes
    Red: Representation Gender and Cultural Politics*,
    London: Routledge.

Walsh, Michael (1996), 'National Cinema, National
    Imaginary', *Film History* 8 (1): 5–17.

Willemen, Paul (1994), *Looks and Frictions: Essays in
    Cultural Studies and Film Theory*, Bloomington:
    Indiana University Press.

Williams, Alan (ed.) (2002), *Film and Nationalism*,
    New Brunswick, NJ: Rutgers University Press.

Williams, Linda (ed.) (1997), *Viewing Positions: Ways
    of Seeing Films*, New Brunswick, NJ: Rutgers
    University Press.

Wollen, Peter (2002), *Paris Hollywood: Writings on
    Film*, London: Verso.

Yoshimoto, Mitsuhiro (2003), 'Hollywood,
    Americanism and the Imperial Screen:

Geopolitics of Image and Discourse after the End of the Cold War', *Inter-Asia Cultural Studies* 4 (3): 451–9.

Yúdice, George (2003), *The Expediency of Culture: Uses of Culture in the Global Era*, Durham, NC: Duke University Press.

3 National Cinemas

CONTINENTS

Africa

Armes, Roy and Malkmus, Lizbeth (1991), *Arab and African Filmmaking*, London: Zed.

Bakari, Imruh and M'Baye, Cham (eds) (1996), *African Experiences of Cinema*, London: BFI.

Barlet, Olivier (2000), *African Cinemas: Decolonising the Gaze*, London: Zed.

Berrah, Mouny, Bachy, Victor and Boughedir, Férid (eds) (1981), *Cinémas du Maghreb*, Paris: CinémAction 14/L'Afrique littéraire 59–60.

Berrah, Mouny, Lévy, Jacques and Cluny, Claude Michel (eds) (1987), *Les cinémas arabes*, Paris: Le Cerf and Institut du Monde Arabe/ CinémAction 43.

Boughedir, Férid (1987), *Le cinéma africain de A à Z*, Brussels: OCIC.

Cham, Mbye (ed.) (1992), *Ex-Iles: Essays on Caribbean Cinema*, Trenton, NJ: Africa World Press.

Cinema dei paesi arabi (1976), Pesaro: Mostra internazionale del nuovo cinema, Quaderno informativo 68.

Cluny, Claude Michel (1978), *Dictionnaire des nouveaux cinémas arabes*, Paris: Sindbad.

Diawara, Manthia (1992), *African Cinema: Politics and Culture*, Bloomington: Indiana University Press.

Givanni, June (ed.) (2000), *Symbolic Narratives/African Cinema: Audiences, Theory and the Moving Image*, London: BFI.

Gugler, Josef (2003), *African Film: Re-Imagining a Continent*, Bloomington: Indiana University Press.

Hafez, Sabry (ed.) (1995), 'Arab Cinematics: Toward the New Alternative', *Journal of Comparative Poetics* 15.

Hafez, Sabry (2000), 'The Novel, Politics and Islam', *New Left Review* (II) 5: 117–41.

Hennebelle, Guy (ed.) (1972), *Les cinémas africains en 1972*, Dakar: Société Africaine d'Édition.

Hennebelle, Guy and Ruelle, Catherine (eds) (1978), *Cinéastes d'Afrique noire*, Paris: CinémAction 3.

Martin, Angela (ed.) (1982), *African Films: The Context of Production*, London: BFI.

Ngugi wa Thiong'o (1986), *Decolonising the Mind: The Politics of Language in African Literature*, London: James Currey and Heinemann.

Otten, Rik (1984), *Le cinéma au Zaïre, au Rwanda et au Burundi*, Brussels: OCIC/L'Harmattan.

Pfaff, Françoise (ed.) (2004), *Focus on African Films*, Bloomington: Indiana University Press.

Russell, Sharon A. (1998), *Guide to African Cinema*, Westport, CT: Greenwood Press.

Sadoul, Georges (1966), *Les cinémas des pays arabes*, Beirut: Centre Interarabe de Cinéma et de la Télévision.

Shafik, Viola (1998), *Arab Cinema: History and Cultural Identity*, Cairo: The American University in Cairo Press.

Shaka, Femi Okiremuete (2004), *Modernity and the African Cinema: A Study in Colonialist Discourse, Postcoloniality and Modern African Identities*, Trenton, NJ: Africa World Press.

Thome, Christine and Abu Rayyan, Mona (eds) (2002), *Homeworks: A Forum on Cultural Practices in the Region – Egypt, Iran, Iraq, Lebanon, Palestine and Syria*, Beirut: Ashkal Alwan.

Ukadike, Nwachuku Frank (1994), *Black African Cinema*, Berkeley: University of California Press.

Vieyra, Paulin Soumanou (1975), *Le cinéma africain des origines à 1973*, Paris: Présence Africaine.

Asia

Chua Beng-huat (2004), 'Conceptualising an East Asian Popular Culture', *Inter-Asia Cultural Studies* 5 (2): 200–21.

Coppola, Antoine (2004), *Le cinéma asiatique*, Paris: L'Harmattan.

Dissanayake, Wimal (ed.) (1988), *Cinema and Cultural Identity: Reflections on Films from Japan, India, China*, Lanham: University Press of America.

Dissanayake, Wimal (ed.) (1993), *Melodrama and Asian Cinema*, Cambridge: Cambridge University Press.

Dissanayake, Wimal (ed.) (1994), *Colonialism and Nationalism in Asian Cinema*, Bloomington: Indiana University Press.

Ehrlich, Linda C. and Desser, David (eds) (1994), *Cinematic Landscapes: Observations on the Visual Arts and Cinema of China and Japan*, Austin: University of Texas Press.

Feng, Peter X. (2002), *Identities in Motion: Asian American Film and Video*, Durham: Duke University Press.

Lent, John A. (1990), *The Asian Film Industry*, London: Christopher Helm.

Tang, Xiaobing and Snyder, Stephen (eds) (1996), *In Pursuit of Contemporary East Asian Culture*, Boulder: Westview Press.

Tesson, Charles, Paquot, Claudine and Garcia, Roger (2001), *L'Asie à Hollywood*, Locarno: Edizioni Olivares/Paris: Cahiers du cinéma.

Europe

Cowie, Peter (ed.) (1990), *Le cinéma des pays nordiques*, Paris: Centre Georges Pompidou.

Eleftheriotis, Dimitris (2001), *Popular Cinemas of Europe*, New York: Continuum.

Elsaesser, Thomas (1992), 'Comparative Style Analysis for European Films, 1910–1918', *Deuxième Colloque International de Domitor, Lausanne*, 1 July, Lausanne: Domitor.

Everett, Wendy (ed.) (1996), *European Identity in Cinema*, Exeter: Intellect Books.

Forbes, Jill and Street, Sarah (eds) (2000), *European Cinema: An Introduction*, Basingstoke: Palgrave.

Fowler, Catherine (ed.) (2002), *The European Cinema Reader*, London: Routledge.

Konstantarakos, Myrto (ed.) (2000), *Spaces in European Cinema*, Exeter: Intellect.

Nowell-Smith, Geoffrey and Ricci, Steve (eds) (1998), *Hollywood and Europe: Economics, Culture, National Identity 1945–1995*, London: BFI.

Petrie, Duncan (ed.) (1992), *Screening Europe: Image and Identity in Contemporary European Cinema*, London: BFI.

Sieglohr, Ulrike (ed.) (2000), *Heroines Without Heroes: Reconstructing Female and National Identities in European Cinema 1945–51*, London: Cassell.

Soila, Tytti, Soderbergh-Widding, Astrid and Iversen, Gunnar (1998), *Nordic National Cinemas*, London: Routledge.

Sorlin, Pierre (1991), *European Cinemas, European Societies*, London: Routledge.

Vincendeau, Ginette (ed.) (1995), *The Encyclopaedia of European Cinema*, London: BFI.

Wayne, Mike (2002), *The Politics of Contemporary European Cinema*, Bristol: Intellekt.

Latin America

Burton, Julianne (ed.) (1990), *The Social Documentary in Latin America*, Pittsburgh: University of Pittsburgh Press.

King, John (1990), *Magical Reels: A History of Cinema in Latin America*, London: Verso.

King, John, Lopez, Ana M. and Alvarado, Manuel (eds) (1993), *Mediating Two World: Cinematic Encounters in the Americas*, London: BFI.

Martin, Michael T. (1997), *New Latin American Cinema*, 2 vols, Detroit: Wayne State University Press.

Schelling, Vivian (ed.) (2000), *Through the Kaleidoscope: The Experience of Modernity in Latin America*, London: Verso.

COUNTRIES
Argentina

España, Claudio (ed.) (1994), *Cine Argentino en democracia 1983–1993*, Buenos Aires: Fondo Nacional de las Artes.

Caneto, Guillermo et al. (1996), *Historia de los primeros años del cine en Argentina, 1895–1910*, Buenos Aires: Fundación Cinemateca de Argentina.

Australia

Dermody, Susan and Jacka, Elizabeth (1988), *The Screening of Australia*, Sydney: Currency Press.

Frow, John and Morris, Meaghan (eds) (1993), *Australian Cultural Studies: A Reader*, St Leonards, NSW: Allen & Unwin.

Langton, Marcia (1993), *'Well, I heard it on the radio and I see it on the television. . .': An Essay for the Australian Film Commission on the Politics and Aesthetics of Filmmaking by and about Aboriginal People and Things*, Sydney: Australian Film Commission.

Moran, Albert and O'Regan, Tom (eds) (1985), *An Australian Film Reader*, Sydney: Currency Press.

O'Regan, Tom (1996), *Australian National Cinema*, London: Routledge.

Austria

Fritz, Walter (1981), *Kino in Österreich: Der Stummfilm 1896–1930*, Vienna: Österreichischer Bundesverlag.

Fritz, Walter (1984), *Kino in Österreich: Film zwischen Kommerz und Avantgarde 1945–1983*, Vienna: Österreichischer Bundesverlag.

Belgium

Jungblut, Guy, Leboutte, Patrick and Païni, Dominique (eds) (1990), *Une encyclopédie des cinémas de Belgique*, Paris: Yellow Now.

Mathijs, Ernest (ed.) (2003), *The Cinema of the Low Countries*, London: Wallflower.

Moseley, Philip (2001), *Split Screen: Belgian Cinema and Cultural Identity*, Albany: State University of New York Press.

Brazil

Denison, Stephanie and Shaw, Lisa (2004), *Popular Cinema in Brazil 1930–2001*, Manchester: Manchester University Press.

Foster, David William (1999), *Gender and Society in Contemporary Brazilian Cinema*, Austin: University of Texas Press.

Johnson, Randal (1997), *The Film Industry in Brazil: Culture and the State*, Pittsburgh: University of Pittsburgh Press.

Johnson, Randal and Stam, Robert (eds) (1982), *Brazilian Cinema*, Austin: University of Texas Press.

Nagib, Lúcia (ed.) (2003), *The New Brazilian Cinema*, London: I. B. Tauris.

Paranaguá, Paulo Antonio (ed.) (1987), *Le cinéma Brésilien*, Paris: Centre Georges Pompidou.

Schwarz, Roberto (1992), *Misplaced Ideas: Essays on Brazilian Culture*, translated by John Gledson, London: Verso.

Willemen, Paul (ed.) (1985), Special Issue *Brazil – Post Cinema Novo*, Framework 28.

Xavier, Ismail (1997) *Allegories of Underdevelopment: Aesthetics and Politics in Modern Brazilian Cinema*, Minneapolis: University of Minnesota Press.

Bulgaria

Holloway, Ronald (1986), *The Bulgarian Cinema*, Cranbury, NJ: Associated University Presses.

Cameroon

Si Bita, Arthur (1993), *Le cinéma au Cameroun*, Brussels: OCIC/L'Harmattan.

Canada

Carel, Sylvain and Pâquet, André (eds) (1992), *Les cinémas du Canada*, Paris: Centre Georges Pompidou.

Gittings, Christopher E. (2002), *Canadian National Cinema*, London: Routledge.

Posner, Michael (1993), *Canadian Dreams: The Making and Marketing of Independent Films*, Vancouver: Douglas and McIntyre.

Wilden, Anthony (1980), *The Imaginary Canadian*, Vancouver: Pulp Press

China

Bergeron, Régis (1977), *Le cinéma chinois: 1905–1949*, Lausanne: Alfred Eibel.

Bergeron, Régis (1984), *Le cinéma chinois: 1943–1983*, 3 vols, Paris: L'Harmattan.

Berry, Chris (ed.) (1991), *Perspectives on Chinese Cinema*, London: BFI.

Berry, Chris (ed.) (2003), *Chinese Films in Focus: 25 Takes*, London: BFI.

Bibliography

Berry, Chris and Farquhar, Mary (2001), 'From National Cinemas to Cinema and the National: Rethinking the National in Transnational Chinese Cinemas', *Journal of Modern Literature in Chinese* 4 (2): 109–22.

Bordwell, David (2000), *Planet Hong Kong: Popular Cinema amd the Art of Entertainment*, Cambridge, MA: Harvard University Press.

Browne, Nick, Pickowicz, Paul G., Sobchack, Vivian and Yau, Esther (eds) (1994), *New Chinese Cinemas: Forms, Identities, Politics*, Cambridge: University of Cambridge Press.

Chen Kuan-Hsing (2003), 'Civil Society and Min-Jian: On Political Society and Popular Democracy', *Cultural Studies* 17 (6): 876–96.

Chow, Rey (1993), *Writing Diaspora: Tactics of Intervention in Contemporary Cultural Studies*, Bloomington: Indiana University Press.

Chow, Rey (1995), *Primitive Passions: Visuality, Sexuality, Ethnography and Contemporary Chinese Cinema*, New York: Columbia University Press.

Chun, Allen (1996), 'Fuck Chineseness: On the Ambiguities of Ethnicity as Culture as Identity', *Boundary 2* 23 (2): 111–38.

Clark, Paul (1987), *Chinese Cinema: Culture and Politics Since 1949*, Cambridge: University of Cambridge Press.

Dai Jinhua (2002), *Cinema and Desire: Feminist Marxism and Cultural Politics in the Work of Dai Jinhua*, edited by Jing Wang and Tani E. Barlow, London: Verso.

Fu, Poshek (2003), *Between Shanghai and Hong Kong: The Politics of Chinese Cinemas*, Stanford, CA: Stanford University Press.

Fu, Poshek and Desser, David (eds) (2000), *The Cinema of Hong Kong: History, Arts, Identity*, Cambridge: Cambridge University Press.

Garcia, Roger (ed.) (1978), *Cantonese Cinema Retrospective (1950–1959)*, Hong Kong International Film Festival.

Garcia, Roger and Rayns, Tony (eds) (1979), *Hong Kong Cinema Survey (1946–1968)*, Hong Kong International Film Festival.

Hou Hsiao-hsien, Chu Tien-Hsin, Tang Nuo and Hsia Chi-Joe (2004), 'Alliance for Ethnic Equality: Tensions in Taiwan', *New Left Review* (II), 28: 19–42.

Jarvie, I. C. (1977), *Window on Hong Kong: A Sociological Study of the Hong Kong Film Industry and its Audience*, Hong Kong: University of Hong Kong.

Kuoshu, Harry H. (2002), *Celluloid China: Cinematic Encounters with Culture and Society*, Carbondale, IL: Southern Illinois University Press.

Lau Shing-hon (ed.) (1980), *A Study of the Hong Kong Martial Arts Film*, Hong Kong International Film Festival.

Lau Shing-hon (ed.) (1981), *A Study of the Hong Kong Swordplay Film (1945–1980)*, Hong Kong International Film Festival.

Law Kar (ed.) (1992), *Overseas Chinese Figures in Cinema*, Hong Kong International Film Festival.

Law Kar (ed.) (1993), *Mandarin Films and Popular Songs: 40s–60s*, Hong Kong International Film Festival.

Law Kar (ed.) (1994), *Cinema of Two Cities: Hong Kong – Shanghai*, Hong Kong International Film Festival.

Law Kar (ed.) (1995), *Early Images of Hong Kong and China*, Hong Kong International Film Festival.

Law Kar (ed.) (1999), *Hong Kong New Wave: Twenty Seven Years After*, Hong Kong International Film Festival.

Law Kar and Bren, Frank (2004), *Hong Kong Cinema: A Cross-Cultural View*, Lanham, MD: Scarecrow Press.

Leyda, Jay (1972), *Dianying: Electric Shadow: An Account of Films and the Film Audience in China*, Cambridge, MA: MIT Press.

Li Cheuk-to (ed.) (1984), *A Study of Hong Kong Cinema in the Seventies*, Hong Kong International Film Festival.

Li Cheuk-to (ed.) (1985), *The Traditions of Hong Kong Comedy*, Hong Kong International Film Festival.

Li Cheuk-to (ed.) (1986), *Cantonese Melodrama 1950–1969*, Hong Kong International Film Festival.

Li Cheuk-to (ed.) (1987), *Cantonese Opera Film Retrospective*, Hong Kong International Film Festival.

Li Cheuk-to (ed.) (1988), *Changes in Hong Kong Society Through Cinema*, Hong Kong International Film Festival.

Li Cheuk-to (ed.) (1989), *Phantoms of the Hong Kong Cinema*, Hong Kong International Film Festival.

Li Cheuk-to (ed.) (1990), *The China Factor in Hong Kong Cinema*, Hong Kong International Film Festival.

Lu, Sheldon Hsiao-peng (ed.) (1997), *Transnational Chinese Cinemas: Identity, Nationhood, Gender*, Honolulu: University of Hawaii Press.

Lu Tonglin (2001), *Confronting Modernity in the Cinemas of Taiwan and Mainland China*, Cambridge: Cambridge University Press.

Ma Ning (2003), 'Signs of Angst and Hope: History and Melodrama in Chinese Fifth-Generation Cinema', *Screen* 44 (2): 183–99.

Morris, Meaghan (2004), 'Transnational Imagination in Action Cinema: Hong Kong and the Making of a Global Popular Culture', *Inter-Asia Cultural Studies* 5 (2): 181–99.

Morris, Meaghan, Chan, Stephen C. K. and Li, S. L. (eds) (2005), *Hong Kong Connections: Transnational Imagination in Action Cinema*, Hong Kong: Hong Kong University Press.

Müller, Marco (1985), *Taiwan: Nuove Ombre Elettriche*, Venice: Marsilio/Pesaro.

Ni Zhen (2002), *Memoirs From the Beijing Film Academy: The Genesis of China's Fifth Generation*, translated by Chris Berry, Durham, NC: Duke University Press.

Quiquemelle, Marie-Claire and Passek, Jean-Loup (eds) (1985), *Le cinéma chinois*, Paris: Centre Georges Pompidou.

Rayns, Tony and Meek, Scott (eds) (1980), *Electric Shadows: Chinese Cinema*, London: BFI.

Reynaud, Bérénice (1999), *Nouvelles chines nouveaux cinémas*, Paris: Eds. Cahiers du cinéma.

Shu Kei (ed.) (1982), *Cantonese Cinema Retrospective (1960–69)*, Hong Kong International Film Festival.

Shu Kei (ed.) (1983), *A Comparative Study of Post-War Mandarin and Cantonese Cinema: The Films of Zhu Shilin, Qin Jian and Other Directors*, Hong Kong International Film Festival.

Stokes, Odham and Hoover, Michael (1999), *City on Fire: Hong Kong Cinema*, London: Verso.

Teo, Stephen (1997), *Hong Kong Cinema: The Extra Dimension*, London: BFI.

Widmer, Ellen and Wang, David Der-wei (eds) (1993), *From May Fourth to June Fourth: Fiction and Film in Twentieth-Century China*, Cambridge, MA: Harvard University Press.

Yang, Edward (2002), 'Taiwan Stories', *New Left Review* (II), 11: 129–36.

Yau, Esther C. M. (ed.) (2001), *At Full Speed: Hong Kong Cinema in a Borderless World*, Minneapolis: University of Minnesota Press.

Zhang Xudong (1997), *Chinese Modernism in the Era of Reforms*, Durham, NC: Duke University Press.

Zhang Yingjin (ed.) (1999), *Cinema and Urban Culture in Shanghai 1922–1943*, Stanford: Stanford University Press.

Zhang Yingjin (2004), *Chinese National Cinema*, London: Routledge.

Zhang Yingjin and Xiao Zhiwei (1998), *Encyclopedia of Chinese Film*, London: Routledge.

Zhao, Henry Y. H. (1995), *The Uneasy Narrator: Chinese Fiction from the Traditional to the Modern*, Oxford: Oxford University Press.

Zhu Ying (2001), 'Cinematic Modernization and Chinese Cinema's First Art Wave', *Quarterly Review of Film and Video* 18 (4): 451–71.

Cuba

Chanan, Michael (1985), *The Cuban Image*, London: BFI.

Paranaguá, Paulo Antonio (ed.) (1990), *Le cinéma Cubain*, Paris: Centre Georges Pompidou.

Czechoslovakia / Czech and Slovak Republics

Passek, Jean-Loup (ed.) (1996), *Le cinéma Tcheque et Slovaque*, Paris: Centre Georges Pompidou.

Denmark

Mottram, Ron (1988), *The Danish Cinema Before Dreyer*, Metuchen, NJ: Scarecrow Press.

Passek, Lean-Loup (ed.) (1979), *Le cinéma Danois*, Paris: Centre Georges Pompidou.

Egypt

Gordon, Joel (2001), 'Class-Crossed Lovers: Popular Film and Social Change in Nasser's New Egypt', *Quarterly Review of Film and Video* 18 (4): 385–96.

France

Abel, Richard (1984), *French Cinema: The First Wave, 1915–1929*, Princeton: Princeton University Press.

Abel, Richard (1988), *French Film Theory and Criticism: A History / Anthology, 1907–1939*, 2 vols, Princeton: Princeton University Press.

Abel, Richard (1994), *The Ciné Goes to Town: French Cinema 1896–1914*, Berkeley: University of California Press.

Andrew, Dudley (1995), *Mists of Regret: Culture and Sensibility in Classic French Film*, Princeton: Princeton University Press.

Debray, Régis (1981), *Teachers, Writers, Celebrities: The Intellectuals of Modern France*, translated by David Macey, London: Verso.

Ezra, Elizabeth and Harris, Sue (eds) (2000), *France in Focus: Film and National Identity*, Oxford: Berg.

Green, Naomi (1999), *Landscape of Loss: The National Past in Postwar French Cinema*, Princeton: Princeton University Press.

Hayward, Susan (1993), *French National Cinema*, London: Routledge.

Hayward, Susan and Vincendeau, Ginette (eds) (2000), *French Film: Texts and Contexts*, London: Routledge (2nd edn).

Kermabon, Jacques (ed.) (1994), *Pathé: Premier empire du cinéma*, Paris: Centre Georges Pompidou.

Silou, Osange (1991), *Le cinéma dans les Antilles françaises*, Brussels: OCIC/L'Harmattan.

Temple, Michael and Witt, Michael (eds) (2004), *The French Cinema Book*, London: BFI.

Williams, Alan (1992), *Republic of Images: A History of French Filmmaking*, Cambridge, MA: Harvard University Press.

Gabon

Bachy, Victor (1986), *Le cinéma au Gabon*, Brussels: OCIC/L'Harmattan.

Germany

Bathrick, David and Hansen, Miriam (eds) (1981–2), *New German Critique* 24–5, special issue on New German Cinema.

Behn, Manfred and Bock, Hans-Michael (eds) (1988–9), *Film und Gesellschaft in der DDR: Material Sammlung*, 2 vols, Hamburg: Cinegraph.

Bergfelder, T., Carter, E. and Göktürk, D. (eds) (2002), *The German Cinema Book*, London: BFI.

Bock, Hans-Michael and Töteberg, Michael (eds) (1992), *Das Ufa Buch*, Frankfurt: Verlag 2001.

Elsaesser, Thomas (1989), *New German Cinema: A History*, London: Macmillan.

Elsaesser, Thomas (ed.) (1996), *A Second Life: German Cinema's First Decades*, Amsterdam: Amsterdam University Press.

Elsaesser, Thomas (2000), *Weimar Cinema and After: Germany's Historical Imaginary*, London: Routledge.

Hake, Sabine (2002), *German National Cinema*, London: Routledge.

Kaes, Anton (1989), *From Hitler to Heimat: The Return of History as Film*, Cambridge, MA: Harvard University Press.

Knight, Julia (2004), *New German Cinema: Images of a Generation*, London: Wallflower.

Kracauer, Siegfried (1947), *From Caligari to Hitler: A Psychological History of the German Film*, Princeton: Princeton University Press.

Petro, Patrice (1989), *Joyless Streets: Women and Melodramatic Representation in Weimar Germany*, Princeton: Princeton University Press.

Rentschler, Eric (1984), *New German Cinema in the Course of Time*, Bedford Hills, NY: Redgrave.

Rentschler, Eric (ed.) (1986), *German Film and Literature: Adaptations and Transformations*, London: Methuen.

Rentschler, Eric (1996), *The Ministry of Illusion: Nazi Cinema and its Afterlife*, Cambridge, MA: Harvard University Press.

Greece

Demopoulos, Michel (ed.) (1995), *Le cinéma Grec*, Paris: Centre Georges Pompidou.

Schuster, Mel (1979), *Contemporary Greek Film*, Metuchen, NJ: Scarecrow Press.

Hungary

Cunningham, John (2004), *Hungarian Cinema: From Coffee House to Multiplex*, London: Wallflower.

Nemeskürty, Istvan (1974), *Word and Image: History of the Hungarian Cinema*, Budapest: Corvina.

Passek, Jean-Loup (ed.) (1979), *Le cinéma Hongrois*, Paris: Centre Georges Pompidou.

Petrie, Graham (1981), *History Must Answer to Man: The Contemporary Hungarian Cinema*, Budapest: Corvina.

India

Barnouw, Erik and Krishnaswamy, S. (1980), *Indian Film*, revised edition, New York: Columbia University Press.

Baskaran, Theodore, S. (1981), *The Message Bearers: The Nationalist Politics and the Entertainment Media in South India 1880–1945*, Madras: Cre-A.

Bhaumik, Kaushik (2001), *The Emergence of the Bombay Film Industry 1913–1936*, Oxford: PhD dissertation.

Chandra, Bipan (1979), *Nationalism and Colonialism in Modern India*, Hyderabad: Orient Longman.

Chandra, Bipan (2003), *In the Name of Democracy: JP Movement and the Emergency,* New Delhi: Penguin Books India.

Chandrasekhar, Indira and Seel, Peter C. (eds) (2003), *Body City: Siting Contemporary Culture in India*, New Delhi: Tulika Press.

Chatterjee, Sudipto (1999), 'The Nation Staged: Nationalist Discourse in Late Nineteenth-Century Bengali Theatre', in Gilbert, Helen (ed.), *(Post)Colonial Stages. Critical & Creative Views on Drama, Theatre & Performance*, Hebden Bridge: Dangaroo Press, 10–25.

Das, Veena (1995), *Critical Events: An Anthropological Perspective on Contemporary India*, Delhi: Oxford University Press.

Desai, Meghnad (1975), 'India: Emerging Contradictions of Slow Capitalist Development', in Blackburn, Robin (ed.), *Explosion in a Subcontinent*, Harmondsworth: Penguin, 11–50.

Dissanayake, Wimal and Gokulsing, Moti K. (1998), *Indian Popular Cinema – A Narrative of Cultural Change*, London: Trentham Books.

Dwyer, Rachel and Pinney, Christopher (eds) (2001), *Pleasure and the Nation: The History, Politics and Consumption of Popular Culture in India*, Delhi and Oxford: Oxford University Press.

Eck, Diana (1981), *Darsan: Seeing the Divine Image in India*, Chambersburg: Anima Books.

Hughes, Steve P. (1996), *'Is There Anyone Out There?' Exhibition and the Formation of Silent Film Audiences in South India*, PhD dissertation, University of Chicago.

Hughes, Steve P. (2002), 'The "Music Boom" in Tamil South India: Gramophone, Radio and the Making of Mass Culture', *Historical Journal of Film, Radio and Television* 22 (4): 445–73.

Hughes, Steve P. (2003), 'Pride of Place: Rethinking Exhibition in the History of Cinema in India', *Seminar (India), Unsettling Cinema: a symposium on the place of cinema in India* 525: 28–32.

Kapur, Geeta (2000), *When Was Modernism? Essays on Contemporary Cultural Practice in India*, New Delhi: Tulika Press.

Mukherjee, Meenakshi (1994 [1984]), *Realism and Reality: The Novel and Society in India*, Delhi: Oxford University Press.

Niranjana, Tejaswini, Sudhir, P. and Dhareshwar, Vivek (eds) (1993), *Interrogating Modernity: Culture and Colonialism in India*, Calcutta: Seagull Books.

Orsini, Francesca (2002), *The Hindi Public Sphere, 1920–1940: Language and Literature in the Age of Nationalism*, New Delhi and Oxford: Oxford University Press.

Pandian, S. S. (1992), *The Image Trap: M. G. Ramachandran in Film and Politics*, New Delhi: Sage.

Pinney, Christopher (1997) *Camera Indica: The Social Life of Indian Photographs*, Chicago: University of Chicago Press.

Prasad, Madhava M. (1998a), 'Back to the Present', *Cultural Dynamics*, 10 (2): 123–32.

Prasad, Madhava M. (1998b), *Ideology of the Hindi Film: A Historical Construction*, Delhi: Oxford University Press.

Prasad, Madhava M. (1998c), 'The State in/of Cinema' in Chatterjee, Partha (ed.), *Wages of Freedom: Fifty Years of the Indian Nation State*, Delhi: Oxford University Press, 123–46.

Prasad, Madhava M. (1993), 'Cinema and the Desire for Modernity', *Journal of Arts and Ideas*, 25–6: 71–86.

Prasad, Madhava M. (1999a), 'Cine-Politics: On the Political Significance of Cinema in South India', *Journal of the Moving Image*, 1: 37–52.

Prasad, Madhava M. (1999b), 'Television and the National Culture', *Journal of Arts and Ideas* 32–3: 119–29.

Rai, Alok (2001), *Hindi Nationalism*, New Delhi: Orient Longman.

Rajadhyaksha, Ashish (1987), 'The Phalke Era: Conflict of Traditional Form and Modern Technology', *Journal of Arts and Ideas* 14–15: 47–78.

Rajadhyaksha, Ashish (1993), 'The Epic Melodrama', *Journal of Arts and Ideas*, 25-6: 55-70.

Rajadhyaksha, Ashish and Willemen, Paul (1999), *Encyclopaedia of Indian Cinema*, revised edition, Delhi: Oxford University Press.

Srinivas, S. V. (2000), 'Is There a Public in the Cinema Hall?', *Framework* 42.

Thapar, Romila (2000), *History and Beyond*, New Delhi: Oxford University Press.

Thomas, Rosie (1989), 'Sanctity and Scandal: The Mythologization of Mother India', *Quarterly Review of Film and Video* 11.

Vanaik, Achin (1990), *The Painful Transition: Bourgeois Democracy in India*, London: Verso.

Vanaik, Achin (2004), 'Myths of the Permit Raj', *New Left Review* (II) 29: 153–60.

Vasudevan, Ravi (ed.) (2000), *Making Meaning in Indian Cinema*. New Delhi: Oxford University Press.

Vasudevan, Ravi S. (1989), 'The Melodramatic Mode and the Commercial Hindi Cinema: Notes on Film History, Narrative and Performance in the 1950s', *Screen* 30 (3): 29–50.

Vasudevan, Ravi S. (2000), 'Addressing the Spectator of a "Third World" National Cinema: The Bombay "Social" Film of the 1940s and 1950s', in Stam, Robert and Miller, Toby (eds), *Film Theory: An Anthology*, Oxford: Blackwell, 381–402.

Vitali, Valentina (2000), 'The Families of Hindi Cinema: A Historical Approach to Film Studies', *Framework* 42.

Vitali, Valentina (2002), 'The Politics of Film Historiography', *Southern Review: Communication, Politics & Culture* l.35 (2): 131–5.

Vitali, Valentina (2004), 'Nationalist Hindi Cinema: Questions of Film Analysis and Historiography', *Kinema* 22 (Autumn): 63–82.

Willemen, Paul (1991), 'Negotiating the Transition to Capitalism: The Case of *Andaz*', *East-West Film Journal* 5 (1): 56–66.

Willemen, Paul and Gandhy, Behroze (eds) (1982), *Indian Cinema*, London: BFI.

Workshop on Telugu Cinema: History, Culture, Theory (1999), Anveshi Research Centre for Women's Studies, Hyderaba CSCS, Bangalore.

Indonesia

Heider, Karl G. (1991), *Indonesian Cinema: National Culture on Screen*, Honolulu: University of Hawaii Press.

Sen, Krishna (ed.) (1988), *Histories and Stories: Cinema in New Order Indonesia*, Melbourne/Clayton: Centre for Southeast Asian Studies, Monash University.

Sen, Krishna (1994), *Indonesian Cinema: Framing the New Order*, London: Zed Books.

Iran

Dabashi, Hamid (2001), *Close Up: Iranian Cinema, Past, Present, and Future*, London: Verso.

Devictor, Agnès (2004), *Politique du cinema iranien*, Paris: CNRS Eds.

Issari, Mohammad Ali (1989) *Cinema in Iran, 1900 to 1979*, Metuchen, NJ: Scarecrow Press.

Ireland

Gibbons, Luke (1996), *Transformations in Irish Culture*, Cork: Cork University Press.

McLoone, Martin (2000), *Irish Film: The Emergence of a Contemporary Cinema*, London: BFI.

Rockett, Kevin (1996), *The Irish Filmography: Fiction Films 1896–1996*, Dublin: Red Mountain Press.

Rockett, Kevin (2004), *Irish Film Censorship: A Cultural Journey from Silent Cinema to Internet Pornography*, Dublin: Four Courts Press.

Rockett, Kevin, Gibbons, Luke and Hill, John (1987), *Cinema and Ireland*, London: Croom Helm.

Israel

Loshitzky, Yosefa (2001), *Identity, Politics on the Israeli Screen*, Austin: University of Texas Press.

Italy

Allen, Beverly and Russo, Mary (1997), *Revisioning Italy: National Identity and Global Culture*, Minneapolis: University of Minnesota Press.

Aprà, Adriano and Pistagnesi, Patrizia (eds) (1979), *The Fabulous Thirties*, Milan: Electa.

Bernardini, Aldo and Gili, Jean A. (eds) (1986), *Le cinéma Italien de La prise de Rome à Rome ville ouverte*, Paris: Centre Georges Pompidou.

Bondanella, Peter (1990), *Italian Cinema: From Neorealism to the Present*, New York: Continuum.

Brunetta, Gian Piero (1980), *Storia del cinema italiano 1905–1945*, Rome: Editori Riuniti.

Brunetta, Gian Piero (1982), *Storia del cinema italiano: Dal 1945 agli anni ottanta*, Rome: Editori Riuniti.

Bruschini, Antonio and Tentori, Antonio (1993), *Malizie Perverse: Il Cinema Erotico Italiano*, Bologna: Granata Press.

Chiti, Roberto, Lancia, Enrico, Poppi, Roberto and Pecorani, Mario (eds) (1991–2001), *Dizionario del Cinema Italiano* (6 vols), Rome: Gremese.

Dall'Asta, Monica (1992), *Un cinéma musclé: Le surhomme dans le cinéma muet italien 1913–1926*, Brussels: Eds. Yellow Now.

Dalle Vacche, Angela (1992), *The Body in the Mirror: Shapes of History in Italian Cinema*, Princeton: Princeton University Press.

Frayling, Christopher (1981), *Spaghetti Westerns: Cowboys and Europeans From Karl May to Sergio Leone*, London: Routledge and Kegan Paul.

Landy, Marcia (2000), *Italian Film*, Cambridge: Cambridge University Press.

Nowell-Smith, Geoffrey, Hay, James and Volpi, Gianni (eds) (1996), *The BFI Companion to Italian Cinema*, London: BFI.

Sorlin, Pierre (1996), *Italian National Cinema 1896–1996*, London: Routledge.

Wyke, Maria (1997), *Projecting the Past: Ancient Rome, Cinema and History*, London and New York: Routledge.

Ivory Coast

Bachy, Victor (1983), *Le cinéma en Côte d'Ivoire*, Brussels: OCIC/L'Harmattan.

Japan

Anderson, Joseph L. and Richie, Donald (1982), *The Japanese Film: Art and Industry*, Princeton: Princeton University Press.

Barrett, Gregory (1989), *Archetypes in Japanese Film: The Sociopolitical and Religious Significance of the Principal Heroes and Heroines*, Selingsgrove: Sesquehanna University Press.

Bernardi, Joanne (2001), *Writing in Light: The Silent Scenario and the Japanese Pure Film Movement*, Detroit: Wayne State University Press.

Bordwell, David (1995), 'Visual Styles in Japanese Cinema', *Film History* 7 (1): 5–30.

Burch, Noël (1979), *To The Distant Observer: Form and Meaning in the Japanese Cinema*, London: Scolar Press.

Cazdyn, Eric (2002), *The Flash of Capital: Film and Geopolitics in Japan*, Durham, NC: Duke University Press.

Davis, Darrell William (1996), *Picturing Japaneseness: Monumental Style, National Identity, Japanese Film*, New York: Columbia University Press.

Fujii, James (1993), *Complicit Fictions: The Subject in the Modern Japanese Prose Narrative*, Berkeley: University of California Press.

Geist, Kathe (1991), 'English in Non-English Language Films', *World Englishes* 10 (3): 263–74.

Gluck, Carol (1985), *Japan's Modern Myths: Ideology in the Late Meiji Period*, Princeton: Princeton University Press.

Harootunian, Harry and Sakai, Naoki (1999) 'Japan Studies and Cultural Studies', *Positions – East Asia Cultures Critique* 7 (2): 593–647.

Hirano, Kyoko (1992), *Mr Smith Goes to Tokyo: Japanese Cinema under the American Occupation 1945–1952*, Washington, DC: Smithsonian Institute Press.

Karatani, Kojin (1980), *Origins of Modern Japanese Literature*, Durham, NC: Duke University Press 1993.

McCormack, Gavan (1991), 'The Price of Affluence: The Political Economy of Japanese Leisure', *New Left Review* 188: 121–34.

McCormack, Gavan (2002), 'Japan's Iron Triangle', *New Left Review* (II), 13: 5–23.

Miyoshi, Masao (1991), *Off Center: Power and Culture Relations Between Japan and the United States*, Cambridge, MA: Harvard University Press.

Miyoshi, Masao and Harootunian, Harry (eds) (1989), *Postmodernism and Japan*, Durham, NC: Duke University Press.

Morris-Suzuki, Tessa (1995), 'The Invention and Reinvention of "Japanese Culture"', *The Journal of Asian Studies* 54 (3): 759–80.

Napier, Susan J. (1996), *The Fantastic in Modern Japanese Literature: The Subversion of Modernity*, London: Routledge.

Nolletti, Arthur and Desser, David (eds) (1992), *Reframing Japanese Cinema: Authorship, Genre, History*, Bloomington: Indiana University Press.

Ollman, Bertell (2001), 'The Emperor and the Yakuza', *New Left Review* (II) 8: 73–98.

Sato, Tadao (1982), *Currents in Japanese Cinema*, translated by Gregory Barrett, Tokyo: Kodansha.

Silverberg, Miriam (1992), 'Constructing the Japanese Ethnography of Modernity', *The Journal of Asian Studies* 51 (1): 30–54.

Standish, Isolde (2000), *Myth and Masculinity in the Japanese Cinema: Towards a Political Reading of the 'Tragic Hero'*, Richmond: Curzon.

Washburn, Dennis and Cavanaugh, Carole (eds) (2001), *Word and Image in Japanese Cinema*, Cambridge: Cambridge University Press.

Korea

Amsden, Alice H. (1990), 'Third World Industrialization: Global Fordism or a New Model?', *New Left Review* 182: 5–31.

Aprà, Adriano (ed.) (1993), *Le cinéma Coréen*, Paris: Centre Georges Pompidou.

Cho Han, Hae-joang (2000), ' "You are Entrapped in an Imaginary Well": the Formation of Subjectivity within Compressed Development – A Feminist Critique of Modernity and Korean Culture', *Inter-Asian Cutlural Studies* 1 (1): 49–69.

Choi, Chungmoo (1995), 'Transnational Capitalism, National Imaginary and the Protest Theatre in South Korea', *Boundary 2* 22 (1): 235–61.

Cummings, Bruce (1998), 'The Korean Crisis and the End of "Late" Development', *New Left Review* 231: 43–71.

Kim Jongil (1987), *The Theory of Cinematic Art*, Pyongyang: Korean Workers' Party Publishing House.

Kim Soyoung (2001), 'Modernity in Suspense: The Logic of Fetishism in Korean Cinema', *Traces* 1.

Lee, Hyangjin (2000), *Contemporary Korean Cinema: Identity, Culture, Politics*, Manchester: Manchester University Press.

Lee Yong Kwan (ed.) (1997), *Kim Ki-Yong: Cinema of Diabolical Desire and Death*, Pusan: Pusan International Film Festival.

McHugh, Kathleen (2001), 'South Korean Film Melodrama and the Question of National Cinema', *Quarterly Review of Film and Video* 18 (1): 1–14.

Malaysia

Ahmad, Mahyuddin (2002), *Reading P. Ramlee: Cinema, Ideology and Modernity in Malaysia*, doctoral dissertation, Coventry University.

Gray, Gordon T. (2002), *Malaysian Cinema and Negotiations with Modernity*, doctoral dissertation, Edinburgh: Napier University.

Sulong, Jamil (1973), 'Aperçu sur l'histoire du cinéma malais', *Archipel* 5: 231–41.

Van der Heide, William (2002), *Malaysian Cinema, Asian Film: Border Crossings and National Cultures*, Amsterdam: Amsterdam University Press.

Mali

Bachy, Victor (1983), *Le cinéma au Mali*, Brussels: OCIC/L'Harmattan.

Mexico

García Riera, Emilio (1993–5), *Historia Documental del Cine Mexicano*, 17 vols, Guadalajara: Universidad de Guadalajara.

Gilbert, Joseph, Rubenstein Anne and Zolov, Eric (eds) (2001), *Fragments of a Golden Age: The Politics and Culture of Mexico Since 1940*, Durham, NC: Duke University Press.

Monsiváis, Carlos (1997), *Mexican Postcards*, translated and edited by John Kraniauskas, London: Verso.

Paranaguá, Paulo Antonio (ed.) (1995), *Mexican Cinema*, London: BFI.

Rashkin, Elissa J. (2001), *Women Film-makers in Mexico*, Austin: University of Texas Press.

New Zealand

Blyth, Martin (1994), *Naming the Other: Images of the Maori in New Zealand Film and Television*, Metuchen, NJ: Scarecrow Press.

Niger

Ilbo, Ousmane (1993), *Le cinéma au Niger*, Brussels: OCIC/L'Harmattan.

Nigeria

Balogun, Françoise (1984), *Le cinéma au Nigeria*, Brussels: OCIC/L'Harmattan.

Okome, Onookome and Haynes, Jonathan (eds) (1997), *Cinema and Social Change in West Africa*, Jos: Nigerian Film Corporation.

Poland

Falkowski, Janina and Haltof, Marek (eds) (2003), *The New Polish Cinema*, Trowbridge: Flick Books.

Fusiewicz, Jacek (1989), *Le cinéma polonais*, Paris: Le Cerf.

Haltof, Marek (2002), *Polish National Cinema*, New York: Berghahn Books.

Michalek, Boleslaw (ed.) (1992), *Le cinéma Polonais*, Paris: Centre Georges Pompidou.

Portugal

Passek, Jean-Loup (ed.) (1982), *Le cinéma Portugais*, Paris: Centre Georges Pompidou.

Russia/Soviet Union/(ex) Soviet Republics

Albera, François (1995), *Albatros: Des Russes à Paris 1919–1929*, Paris: Cinématheque française and Milan: Mazzotta.

Beumers, Birgit (ed.) (1999), *Russia on Reels: The Russian Idea in Post-Soviet Cinema*, London: I. B. Tauris.

Condee, Nancy (ed.) (1995), *Soviet Hieroglyphics: Visual Culture in Late Twentieth-Century Russia*, London: BFI.

Eisenschitz, Bernard (ed.) (2000), *Lignes d'ombre: Une autre histoire di cinéma soviétique (1926–1968)*, Milan: Mazzotta.

Kenez, Peter (2001), *Cinema and Soviet Society: From the Revolution to the Death of Stalin*, London: I. B. Tauris.

Leyda, Jay (1960), *Kino: A History of the Russian and Soviet Film*, London: Allen & Unwin.

Passek, Jean-Loup (ed.) (1981), *Le cinéma Russe et soviétique*, Paris: Centre Georges Pompidou.

Radvanyi, Jean (ed.) (1988), *Le cinéma Georgien*, Paris: Centre Georges Pompidou.

Radvanyi, Jean (ed.) (1991), *Le cinéma d'Asie centrale soviétique*, Paris: Centre Georges Pompidou.

Radvanyi, Jean (ed.) (1993), *Le cinéma Armenien*, Paris: Centre Georges Pompidou.

Taylor, Richard and Christie, Ian (eds) (1988), *The Film Factory: Russian and Soviet Cinema in Documents 1896–1939*, Cambridge, MA: Harvard University Press.

Taylor, Richard and Christie, Ian (eds) (1991), *Inside the Film Factory*: London: Routledge.

Taylor, Richard, Wood, Nancy, Graffy, Julian and Iordanova, Dina (eds) (2000), *The BFI Companion to Eastern European and Russian Cinema*, London: BFI.

Tsivian, Yuri (ed.) (1989), *Silent Witness: Russian Films 1908–1919*, London: BFI.

Tsivian, Yuri (1994), *Early Cinema in Russia and its Cultural Reception*, London: Routledge.

Senegal

Vieyra, Paulin Soumanou (1983), *Le cinéma au Senegal*, Brussels: OCIC/L'Harmattan.

Singapore

Millet, Raphaël (2003), *Le cinema de Singapour: Paradis perdu, doute existenciel, crise identitaire et mélancolie contemporaine*, Paris: L'Harmattan.

South Africa

Tomaselli, Keyan (ed.) (1986), *Le cinéma sud-africain est-il tombé sur la tête*, Paris: CinémAction 39.

Tomaselli, Keyan (1989), *The Cinema of Apartheid: Race and Class in South African Film*, London: Routledge.

Spain

Caparrós Lera, José María (1999), *Historia crítica del cine Español: Desde 1897 hasta hoy*, Barcelona: Ariel.

Herdero, Carlos (1993), *Las huellas del tiempo: Cine Español 1951–1961*, Madrid: Filmoteca Española.

Kinder, Marsha (1993), *Blood Cinema: The Reconstruction of National Identity in Spain*, Berkeley: University of California Press.

Reboll, Antonio Lázaro and Willis, Andrew (eds) (2004), *Spanish Popular Cinema*, Manchester: Manchester University Press.

Talens, Jenaro and Zunzunegui, Santos (1998), *Modes of Representation in Spanish Cinema*, Hispanic Issues 16, Minneapolis: University of Minnesota Press.

Triana-Toribio, Nuria (2003), *Spanish National Cinema*, London: Routledge.

Sri Lanka

Crusz, Robert (ed.) (1989), Special issue, *Framework* 37.

Jayamanne, Laleen (2001), *Toward Cinema and Its Double: Cross-Cultural Mimesis*, Bloomington: Indiana University Press.

Thailand

Anderson, Benedict (1990), 'Murder in Progress in Modern Siam', *New Left Review* 181: 33–48.

Turkey

Basutçu, Mehmet (ed.) (1996), *Le cinéma Turc*, Paris: Centre Georges Pompidou.

Renda, G. and Korpeter, C. M. (eds) (1986), *The Transformation of Turkish Culture: The Atatürk Legacy*, Princeton: Princeton University Press.

Robins, Kevin and Aksoy, Asu (1997), 'Peripheral Vision: Cultural Industries and Cultural Identities in Turkey', *Paragraph* 20 (1): 75–99.

United Kingdom

Allon, Yoram, Cullen, Del and Patterson, Hannah (eds) (2001), *Contemporary British and Irish Film Directors: A Wallflower Critical Guide*, London: Wallflower.

Aspinall, Sue and Murphy, Robert (eds) (1983), *Gainsborough Melodrama*, London: BFI.

Barr, Charles (ed.) (1986), *All Our Yesterdays: 90 Years of British Cinema*, London: BFI.

Barr, Charles (1993), *Ealing Studios*, London: Studio Vista (revised edn).

Berry, David (1994), *Wales and the Cinema*, London: BFI.

Chanan, Michael (1980), *The Dream that Kicks: The Prehistory and Early Years of Cinema in Britain*, London: Routledge and Kegan Paul.

319

Dickinson, Margaret (ed.) (1999), *Rogue Reels: Oppositional Film in Britain, 1945–90*, London: BFI.

Dickinson, Margaret and Street, Sarah (1985), *Cinema and the State: The Film Industry and the British Government 1927–84*, London: BFI.

Gledhill, Christine, *Reframing British Cinema 1918–1929: Between Restraint and Passion*, London: BFI.

Higson, Andrew (1989), 'The concept of National Cinema', *Screen* 30 (4): 36–46.

Higson, Andrew (1995), *Waving the Flag: Constructing a National Cinema in Britain*, Oxford: Oxford University Press.

Hill, John (1986), *Sex, Class and Realism: British Cinema 1956–1963*, London: BFI.

Hill, John (1999a), 'Allegorising the Nation: British Gangster Films of the 1980s', in Chibnall, Steve and Murphy, Robert (eds), *British Crime Cinema*, London: Routledge.

Hill, John (1999b), *British Cinema in the 1980s: Issues and Themes*, London: BFI.

Hill, John, McLoone, Martin and Hainsworth, Paul (eds) (1994), *Border Crossing: Film in Ireland, Britain and Europe*, London: BFI.

Macpherson, Don (ed.) (1980), *British Cinema: Traditions of Independence*, London: BFI.

McArthur, Colin (ed.) (1982), *Scotch Reels: Scotland in Cinema and Television*, London: BFI.

Murphy, Robert (1992), *Sixties British Cinema*, London: BFI.

Murphy, Robert (ed.) (1997), *The British Cinema Book*, London: BFI.

Murphy, Robert (ed.) (2000), *British Cinema of the 90s*, London: BFI.

Richards, Jeffrey (ed.) (1998), *The Unknown 1930s: An Alternative History of the British Cinema, 1929–1939*, London: I. B. Tauris.

Upper Volta

Bachy, Victor (1983), *La Haute-Volta et le cinéma*, Brussels: OCIC/L'Harmattan.

USA

Balio, Tino (ed.) (1976), *The American Film Industry*, Madison: University of Wisconsin Press.

Bordwell, David, Staiger, Janet and Thompson, Kristin (1985), *The Classical Hollywood Cinema: Film Style and Mode of Production to 1960*, London: Routledge and Kegan Paul.

Burgoyne, Robert (1997), *Film Nation: Hollywood Looks at U.S. History*, Minneapolis: University of Minnesota Press.

Davis, Mike (1990), *City of Quartz: Excavating the Future in Los Angeles*, London: Verso.

Davis, Mike (2002), *Dead Cities and Other Tales*, London: Verso.

Guback, Thomas (1986), 'Shaping the Film Business in Postwar Germany: The Role of the US Film Industry and the US State', in Kerr, Paul (ed.), *The Hollywood Film Industry: A Reader*, London: BFI, 245–75.

Gunning, Tom (1991), *D. W. Griffith and the Origins of American Narrative Film*, Urbana: University of Illinois Press.

Harpole, Charles (ed.) (2000 sqq), *History of the American Cinema*, 10 vols, Berkeley: University of California Press.

James, Nick (ed.) (2002), *The Wallflower Critical Guide to Contemporary North American Directors*, London: Wallflower.

Lears, Jackson (1981), *No Place of Grace: Antimodernism and the Transformation of American Culture 1880–1920*, New York: Pantheon Books.

Vietnam

Willemen, Paul (ed.) (1984), Special Issue, *Framework 25.*

Yugoslavia/(ex) Yugoslav Republics

Tasic, Zoran and Passek, Jean-Loup (eds) (1986), *Le cinéma Yougoslave*, Paris: Centre Georges Pompidou.

Zimbabwe

Burns, James McDonald (2002), *Flickering Shadows: Cinema and Identity in Colonial Zimbabwe*, Research in International Studies – Africa Series 77, Athens: Ohio University Press.

4 Journals

Boundary 2 (Durham, NC: Duke University Press)

Critical Inquiry (Chicago: University of Chicago Press)

Deep Focus (Bangalore)

East-West Film Journal (Honolulu; defunct)

Framework (New York: Wayne State University Press)

Inter-Asia Cultural Studies (London: Routledge)

Iris (Paris: Eds Analeph)

Journal of Arts and Ideas (New Delhi: Tulika Press)

Journal of the Moving Image (Calcutta)

New Cinemas: Journal of Contemporary Film (London: Intellect)

New German Critique (Milwaukee: University of Wisconsin Press)

New Left Review (London: Verso)

Positions (Durham, NC: Duke University Press)

Public Culture (Chicago: University of Chicago Press)

Quarterly Review of Film and Video (New York: Harwood Academic Publishers)

Rouge (rouge.com.au)

Senses of Cinema (www.sensesofcinems.com)

Social Text (Durham, NC: Duke University Press)

Traces (Hong Kong: Hong Kong University Press)

List of Illustrations

Whilst considerable effort has been made to correctly identify the copyright holders, this has not been possible in all cases. We apologise for any apparent negligence and any omissions or corrections brought to our attention will be remedied in any future editions.

M, Nero Film; *Iris*, © Fox Iris Productions/Intermedia Film Equities/BBC Films; *Ju Dou*, Tokuma Shoten Publishing/Tokuma Communications/China Film Co-production Corporation/China Film Export and Import Corporation; *Cabiria*, Itala Film; *Chapayev*, Lenfilm; *The Secret of Roan Inish*, Skerry Movies Corporation/Jones Entertainment Group/Peter Newman Productions; *Chariots of Fire*, Enigma Productions/Twentieth Century Fox Film Corporation/Allied Stars; *Banshun*, Shochiku Co. Ltd; *A City of Sadness*, 3-H Films; *Spider-Man 2*, Columbia Pictures Industries, Inc.; *Être et avoir*, Maïa Films/Arte France Cinéma/Films d'Ici/Centre National de Documentation Pédagogique; *Por primera vez*, El Instituto Cubano/Lombarda Industria Cinematografia; *Al Nasir Salah al-Din*, Lotus Films/Egyptian Cinema Organisation/ASSIA Productions; *Xala*, Filmi Doomireew/Société National de Cinématographie.

Index